York St John
Library and Information Services
Normal Loan

Please see self service receipt for return date.
If recalled the loan is reduced to 10 days

Fines are payable for late return

D1350848

Spanish Town, Jamaica: Emancipation, 1 August 1834.

CONTRARY
VOICES

*Representations of West Indian
Slavery, 1657–1834*

Edited by

Karina Williamson

University of the West Indies Press
Jamaica • Barbados • Trinidad and Tobago

University of the West Indies Press
7A Gibraltar Hall Road   Mona
Kingston 7   Jamaica
www.uwipress.com

12 11 10 09 08   5 4 3 2 1

Contrary voices : representations of West Indian slavery, 1657–1834 /
edited by Karina Williamson.

p. cm.

Includes bibliographical references.

ISBN: 978-976-640-208-2

1. Slavery in literature. 2. Plantation life in literature. 3. West Indies in
literature. 4. Slavery – Social aspects – West Indies. I. Williamson,
Karina.

PR1195.S44 C67 2008   821.008

Book and cover design by Robert Harris.
Set in Dante MT Regular 11/15 x 24
Printed in the United States of America.

Contents

Part 3 • Resistance and Rebellion

Part 4 • On the Haitian Revolution

Part 5 • Songs

ACKNOWLEDGEMENTS

In preparing this collection, I have received encouragement, support and advice from a great number of people, far more than I can hope to name individually. But for particular acts of kindness or patience in answering questions, I remember with gratitude friends, colleagues or correspondents in Britain, including Trevor Burnard, Paula Burnett, Mark Duffill, John Gilmore, Gad Heuman, David Howard, David Lambert, Michael Moss, Diana Paton, Gemma Robinson, and Iain Whyte. My thanks equally to Bridget Brereton and Barbara Lalla in Trindad; to Verene Shepherd in Jamaica; and to Lise Winer and David Geggus in Canada and the United States respectively. I acknowledge, with special gratitude, textual material as well as moral support from Gertrud Aub-Buscher, and from James Basker whose own anthology of poems about transatlantic slavery, *Amazing Grace*, is a model of its kind. And I gladly acknowledge as both a source and an inspiration the ground-breaking collection of Jamaican texts edited by Jean D'Costa and Barbara Lalla, *Voices in Exile*.

Without the helpfulness beyond the call of duty of curators and staff of numerous libraries this work would have been impossible. I am grateful especially to Edinburgh University Library (Special Collections), the National Library of Jamaica, and the National Library of Scotland; and to the Abbotsford Collection, the Bodleian Library, Liverpool University

Library, the Mitchell Library, Glasgow, Newcastle University Library, and to Major (Retd) J.R. Chapman, former curator of the Regimental Museum of the Green Howards. I am grateful also for the watchful editorial eye of Shivaun Hearne at the University of West Indies Press. Finally, my work was made immeasurably easier by having as a base for research the Institute for Advanced Studies in the Humanities at the University of Edinburgh: most cordial thanks to the director, Professor Susan Manning, and to Anthea Taylor and Donald Ferguson.

INTRODUCTION

The purpose of this anthology, as the title indicates, is to highlight contrarieties in representations of slavery in the West Indies. Although it draws on poetry as well as prose, it is not in the narrow sense a literary anthology, nor is it intended primarily as a source of factual knowledge or authoritative interpretation, even though it draws on documentary evidence as well as narrative and descriptive representations.[1] By presenting a wide repertoire of voices and genres, it is designed partly to illustrate differences between the reports of pro- and anti-slavery writers but also, and more important, to contrast the voices of free, usually white, male observers with those of the enslaved Africans and creoles themselves. Similarities between published accounts by observers of slavery are also significant: they show how a dominant rhetoric developed in abolitionist and anti-abolitionist discourse alike, regardless of social and political differences between individual writers.

Study of the history of transatlantic slavery and the slave trade in the long eighteenth century has already been enriched by the publication within the past twenty years of several other collections of contemporary printed texts and images relating directly or indirectly to transatlantic slavery and drawn from British and American sources.[2] These collections show the powerful impact of the dissemination of knowledge about slavery in the Americas on the perception, conscience and literary imagination of white writers on either side of the Atlantic. The present work concentrates on writings relating to slavery in the West Indies alone, for in the minds of British writers and readers, especially after the American Declaration of Independence in 1776, slavery and the slave trade were, above all, West Indian problems. Indeed, from the 1820s onwards, during the long-running debate about slavery in Parliament and the press, the issue was referred to simply as "the West India question".

Between the 1770s and the Emancipation Act of 1833, the majority of works dealing with slavery which were published in Britain were designed to promote one side or the other of the "West India question" and were frequently written by authors who had no direct acquaintance with conditions in the West Indian colonies themselves. Since, however, the present collection is concerned more with the sociology of West Indian slavery than with the political, economic and ethical arguments advanced for and against it, texts are drawn predominantly from writings based on first-hand experience or observation of slave societies in the West Indies. The exceptions are writings which became exemplary in some way, such as Richard Steele's retelling of the "Inkle and Yarico" episode. Steele's narrative was the prime source of a story from Barbados which attained quasi-mythological status in eighteenth-century writing as an emblem of the nobility of the black or "Indian" enslaved subject, contrasted with the base materialism of white colonizers.[3] William Cowper's hugely popular poem "The Negro's Complaint" similarly acquired iconic value as a representation of the sufferings of the enslaved blacks of the West Indies.

The very success of Cowper's poem as abolitionist rhetoric obviously compromises its validity as "representation" – in the sense of supposedly impartial description – of slave experience. But up to three overlapping senses of *representation* are at play in most texts here: mimesis (imitation of an external "reality"); normative description (the re-presentation, displacement or encoding of reality, as in colonialist discourse); and metonymy (where particular aspects of slavery stand in for the total reality of enslavement). While authors of historical and descriptive texts normally claim or attempt to offer true accounts of reality as they perceive it, such texts are always and inevitably distorted to some degree by the limited perspective and consciousness of the perceiver. On the one hand, then, this collection challenges the illusion that the "real" experience of slavery – in the West

Indies or anywhere – can be truly known through its textual representations. On the other hand, by providing varied and conflicting testimonies it offers the possibility of closer understanding of that experience through critical reading and comparison.

Cogent ethical questions have been raised in recent years about the replication of representations of black enslavement, and especially of images, both visual and verbal, of black suffering and torture.[4] It is nevertheless my belief that the reading of texts chosen from a wide variety of sources, perspectives and modes of discourse can foster a critical awareness of the very problems which, collectively and individually, they pose. Further related to these is an epistemological problem in attempting to contribute to the sociology of slavery by means of written reports by residents in or travellers to the West Indies. Such reports were written from one or more – usually a mixture – of different motives: to entertain, instruct, inform, persuade, make money or prove a case. Leaving aside the fact that all texts are ideologically positioned, and viewing these accounts simply as reflections of authorial intention, it is seldom easy to determine the point at which descriptive representation shades off into propaganda or special pleading. This is especially true of the long period from the 1770s onward, when abolition and emancipation were live issues in the public sphere, dividing opinion at all levels of society, and when the popular demand for books about the West Indies became correspondingly strong. To counter this problem, I have excluded texts whose sole object is to argue a case, whether about slavery in general or about the West Indian slave system in particular. For example, Alexander Barclay's *Practical View of the Present State of Slavery in the West Indies* (1826) provides lively and detailed descriptions of plantation life based on many years' first-hand experience, but I have omitted excerpts from this work because its declared primary purpose was to defend the practices of West Indian slave-masters against attacks by James Stephen, Thomas Cooper and others. On the other hand, I have included substantial excerpts from Edward Long's *History of Jamaica* (1774) in spite of Long's pro-slavery bias and notorious ethnographic prejudices, because these are not the motives which guide the selection of material for his comprehensive representation of people, customs and events. Moreover, by beginning chronologically with texts dating from the period before "the problem of slavery" became a political issue in Britain, I have tried to illustrate the variety of images of slavery in the West Indies which prevailed in the period before the political battle lines were drawn.

An unplanned consequence of the policy of concentrating on texts based on direct experience of West Indian slavery is the near exclusion of British women as authors. In spite of the prolific contribution of women to the discourse of slavery, and especially their zeal in anti-slavery campaigning in Britain, the fact is that very few of the women who wrote about slavery had witnessed it for themselves. As Moira Ferguson points out, with the notable exception of Aphra Behn in the late seventeenth century and of three pioneering Quaker women in the same period, "in the eighteenth and early nineteenth centuries, most white women's writings about slavery had no basis in personal experience".[5] Thus, for example, when in 1726 Lady Hertford versified the tale of Inkle and Yarico as told by Steele, she represented the Guianese and Barbadian landscapes by means of standard images of tropical scenery, replete with palms and tigers, while emphasizing those elements in the story which made it a paradigm of female servitude and white patriarchy in English society.[6]

So far I have been discussing representations of West Indian slavery by authors whose experiences or observations were written and published in the pre-emancipation era. These include a handful of people, such as Olaudah Equiano and Mary Prince, who had themselves been enslaved, but the vast majority of published testimonies come from people who were white and free, a substantial proportion of them slave owners, plantation managers or overseers. With a few notable exceptions, previous collections have concentrated on written material, largely excluding the oral utterances of the enslaved.[7] The omission is partly understandable; as Mimi Sheller points out, "seldom are there 'direct' sources of writing from a largely illiterate population; much of what we know is based on records kept by others, second or third-hand stories or oral histories and transcribed narratives".[8] The voices of the enslaved nevertheless survive through a range of channels, including published transcriptions of songs, folk-tales, proverbs, funeral orations, reported conversations and witness statements. The value and importance of this body of oral discourse, mediated and fragmentary though it is, has increasingly been acknowledged in recent years.

The "contrary voices" in this collection thus reflect a very broad spectrum of viewpoints. At the furthest extreme from the daily actualities of slave life are descriptions, anecdotes or impersonations (by writers such as Steele, Addison and Cowper) based on little or no direct knowledge of the West Indies. At the opposite extreme are the informal dialogues and snatches of conversation with field-hands and house slaves recorded by West Indian residents or visitors. Richard Madden's rueful account of a humiliating exchange with a former slave on his uncle's estate (page 300) is a vivid specimen of these. The songs sung by slaves at work, on the streets, at dances and funerals or simply extempore provide usually indirect but equally revealing insights. They are often eloquent by implication or understatement rather than by what is actually said. "If me want for go in a Ebo" (page 432), for example, tersely conveys a sense of dispossession and entrapment: exiled from their native or ancestral homeland, the enslaved Africans are not even allowed to go off the plantation to visit a neighbouring town. Slave narratives, represented here by excerpts from Equiano, Wedderburn, Warner and Prince, come somewhere between the two extremes; although these narratives are manifestly written or spoken out of personal experience of enslavement in the West Indies (their own or, in Wedder-burn's case, his mother's), their voices are mediated to varying degrees by British publishers, editors or transcribers, and more generally by the pressures of the book market or from their sponsors. Mary Prince's remarkable narrative, for example, was dictated in London to Susanna Strickland while Prince was in the service of Thomas Pringle, secretary to the Anti-Slavery Society. Sympathetic though both Strickland and Pringle were towards her personally, their primary interest in her story was for its propaganda value. As Moira Ferguson points out, it is hard to determine whether or how much her narrative was reshaped after dictation, but its conformity in many ways to conventional propagandist slave narratives means that it has to be read with a certain caution. That does not, however, diminish its value as the autobiography of "an indomitable self-made heroine"[9] or its authenticity as a representation of one woman's bitter experience of enslavement.

Parts 1 and 2 are intended to illustrate both change and continuity in representations of West Indian slavery. The texts are arranged chronologically, normally by date of first publication, with no distinction between prose and verse, because verse as much as prose remained during this period a vehicle for description, instruction, argument and propaganda. In part 3, Resistance and Rebellion, and part 4, On the Haitian Revolution, however, poems are printed separately at the end of each section. This section needs further explanation: although the focus of the collection generally is on slavery in the British colonies, texts relating to the insurrection of 1791 in the French colony of St Domingue (as Haiti was then called)[10] are included because of the great impact of the event in Britain and the British West Indian colonies. There were immediate economic repercussions in London, where "the price of sugar shot sky high and stocks fell immediately by 1 per cent".[11] But as David Geggus has shown, the Haitian rebellion also had powerful and enduring effects on public opinion in Britain, among British planters and residents in the West Indies[12] and not least among slaves on British plantations.[13] News of the rebellion quickly reached Jamaica; on 18 September 1791 Governor Williamson wrote:

> Many slaves here are very inquisitive and intelligent, and are immediately informed of every kind of news that arrives. I do not hear of their having shewn any signs of revolt, though they have composed songs of the negroes having made a rebellion at Hispaniola with their usual chorus to it.[14]

The songs the governor referred to have unfortunately not survived. Coming at a time when the campaign in Britain to abolish the slave trade was approaching a climax, the St Domingue uprising "sharpened the debate over slavery and gave it a new immediacy for the British public", providing cannon-fodder for both sides: the abolitionists argued that the insurrection demonstrated the inflammatory effect of the slave system itself, while the pro-slavery lobby claimed that the slaves were incited to revolt by hearing reports of British and French proposals for reform.[15] Public interest in the slaves of St Domingue waned in Britain after the defeat of the abolition campaign in 1792, but during the Napoleonic Wars the black leader Toussaint L'Ouverture seized the imagination of radical writers as an emblem of heroic resistance to tyranny and oppression. In the period leading up to the Emancipation Act (1823–34), the Haitian rebellion was again cited frequently as an object lesson by campaigners on either side of the "West India question".

Part 5 juxtaposes the songs sung by the enslaved themselves (Section A) with songs composed by white writers assuming the persona of a slave (Sections B–C). The contrast between the two groups is salutary. The songs of the enslaved display a sophisticated, adult, robust subjectivity, where white impersonators, whatever their political motives, project simplified images of enslaved Africans as, on the one hand, victims of oppression, whether suffering and despairing or (ineffectually) fierce and vindictive; on the other hand they are seen as childlike, carefree and joyful. Regrettably, reductive notions of black subjectivity stubbornly persist,[16] but, as Carolyn Cooper acidly comments, "written histories of enslavement, voicelessness and erasure that seem to have absolute authority in neo-colonial societies such as Jamaica are continually contested by alternate oral discourses that reclaim the self and empower the speaker".[17]

In reproducing texts from early editions, unless otherwise indicated, I have standardized the typography (capitals are retained, however, when nouns are treated as proper names, as often occurs with *Negro*); spelling and punctuation of the original have normally been preserved.

Notes

1. For the key role of representation in ethnographic studies and the capacity of poetry to be as "historical", "precise" and "objective" in representation as prose, see James Clifford's introduction to *Writing Culture: The Poetics and Politics of Ethnography*, ed. James Clifford and George E. Marcus (Berkeley and Los Angeles: University of California Press, 1986), 1–26.

2. See especially Peter J. Kitson and Debbie Lee, eds., *Slavery, Abolition and Emancipation: Writings in the British Romantic Period* (London: Pickering and Chatto, 1999); Thomas W. Krise, ed., *Caribbeana: An Anthology of English Literature of the West Indies 1657–1777* (Chicago: Chicago University Press, 1999); Marcus Wood, *Blind Memory: Visual Representations of Slavery in England and America 1780–1865* (Manchester: Manchester University Press, 2000); James G. Basker, ed., *Amazing Grace: An Anthology of Poems about Slavery, 1660–1810* (New Haven: Yale University Press, 2002); Marcus Wood, ed., *The Poetry of*

Slavery: An Anglo-American Anthology 1764–1865 (Oxford: Oxford University Press, 2003).

3. See introduction to Frank Felsenstein, ed., *English Trader, Indian Maid: Representing Gender, Race, and Slavery in the New World* (Baltimore: Johns Hopkins University Press, 1999).

4. For a recent review of these issues, see David Lambert, "Deadening, Voyeuristic and Reiterative? Problems of Representation in Caribbean Research", in *Beyond the Blood, the Beach and the Banana: New Perspectives in Caribbean Studies*, ed. Sandra Courtman (Kingston, Jamaica: Ian Randle, 2004), 3–14.

5. Moira Ferguson, *Subject to Others: British Women Writers and Colonial Slavery, 1670–1834* (New York: Routledge, Chapman and Hall, 1992), 69.

6. Lady Hertford's text can be found in Felsenstein, *English Trader*, 89–94, and Basker, *Amazing Grace*, 52–55.

7. Three important collections drawing on oral material are Roger D. Abrahams and John F. Szwed, eds., *After Africa: Extracts from British Travel Accounts and Journals of the Seventeenth, Eighteenth and Nineteenth Centuries Concerning the Slaves, Their Manners, and Customs in the British West Indies* (New Haven: Yale University Press, 1983); Paula Burnett, ed., *The Penguin Book of Caribbean Verse in English* (London: Penguin, 1986; reprinted 2006); and Jean D'Costa and Barbara Lalla, eds., *Voices in Exile: Jamaican Texts of the Eighteenth and Nineteenth Centuries* (Tuscaloosa: University of Alabama Press, 1989).

8. Mimi Sheller, *Democracy after Slavery: Black Publics and Peasant Radicalism in Haiti and Jamaica* (Basingstoke: Macmillan Education, 2000), 199.

9. Ferguson, *Subject to Others*, 26.

10. Saint-Domingue (the French colony at the western end of the island of Hispaniola) was renamed Haiti by Dessalines when independence was declared in 1804. Before that date, confusingly for modern readers, it was referred to in Britain as St Domingo, Santo Domingo being the alternative name for the whole of Hispaniola.

11. David Geggus, "Haiti and the Abolitionists: Opinion, Propaganda and International Politics in Britain and France, 1804–1838", in *Abolition and Its Aftermath: The Historical Context, 1790–1916*, ed. David Richardson (London: F. Cass, 1982), 123.

12. See, for example, the reference in John Augustine Waller's *A Voyage in the West Indies* (1820), on page 232.

13. See the statement of the slave Cuffee Ned after the rebellion in Barbados, page 338 below.

14. Quoted in David Geggus, *Slavery, War and Revolution: The British Occupation of Saint Domingue 1793–1798* (Oxford: Oxford University Press, 1982), 90.
15. Geggus, "Haiti and the Abolitionists", 125–26.
16. It was "the struggle to have blacks perceived as agents, as people with cognitive capacities and even with an intellectual history" that primarily impelled Paul Gilroy to write *The Black Atlantic: modernity and double consciousness* (London: Verso, 1993), 6.
17. Carolyn Cooper, *Noises in the Blood: Orality, Gender and the "Vulgar" Body of Jamaican Popular Culture* (London: Macmillan Education, 1993), 22.

Part 1.

1657–1807

"Jamaica negroes cutting cane in their working dresses", frontispiece to H.T. De La Beche, *Notes on the Present Condition of the Negroes in Jamaica* (London: Cadell, 1825). Courtesy of the Trustees of the National Library of Scotland.

RICHARD LIGON (CA. 1585–1662)

A True and Exact History of the Island of Barbados (1657)[1]

Ligon accompanied Thomas Modyford (afterwards governor of Barbados) on his voyage out to the West Indies in 1647 and lived for nearly three years, perhaps as manager or overseer, on the large sugar plantation acquired by Modyford in Barbados. His account of the island was written after his return in 1650, mostly while he was in prison in London for debt. The text here is from the first edition, but with minor spelling alterations incorporated from the second edition (1673). The following extract is from the section titled "Negroes" in Ligon's account of the inhabitants of Barbados. He begins by explaining that the enslaved Africans came to Barbados from many different parts of West Africa.

When they are brought to us, the planters buy them out of the ship, where they find them stark naked, and therefore cannot be deceived in any outward infirmity. They choose them as they do horses in a market; the strongest, youthfullest, and most beautiful, yield the greatest prices. Thirty pound sterling is a price for the best man *Negro*; and twenty five, twenty six, or twenty seven pound for a woman; the children are at easier rates. And we buy them so, as the sexes may be equal; for if they have more men than women, the men who are unmarried will come to their masters, and complain, that they cannot live without wives, and desire him, they may have wives. And he tells them, that the next ship that comes, he will buy them wives, which satisfies them for the present; and so they expect the good time: which the master performing with them, the bravest fellow is to choose first, and so in order, as they are in place; and every one of them knows his better, and gives him the precedence, as cows do one another, in passing through a narrow gate; for, the most of them are as near beasts as may be, setting their souls aside. Religion they know none; yet most of them acknowledge a God, as appears by their motions and gestures: For, if one of them do another wrong, and he cannot revenge himself, he looks up to heaven for vengeance, and holds up both his hands, as if the power must come from thence, that must do him right. Chast they are as any people under the sun, for when the men and women are together naked, they never cast their eyes towards the parts that ought to be covered; and those amongst us, that have breeches and petticoats, I never saw so much as a kiss, or embrace, or a wanton glance with their eyes between them. Jealous they are of their wives, and hold it for a great injury and scorn, if another man make the least courtship to his wife. And if any of their wives have two children at a birth, they conclude her false to his bed, and so no more adoe but hang her. We had an excellent *Negro* in the plantation, whose name was Macow, and was our chief musician; a very valiant man, and was keeper of our plantine-grove. This *Negro's* wife was brought to bed of two children, and her husband, as their manner is, had provided a cord to hang her. But the overseer finding what he was about to do, informed the master of it, who sent for Macow, to disswade him from this cruel act, of murdering his wife, and used all perswasions that possibly he could, to let him see, that such double births are in nature, and that diverse presidents [precedents] were to be found amongst us of the like; so that we rather praised our wives, for their fertility, than blamed them for their falseness. But this prevailed little with him, upon whom custom had taken so deep an impression; but resolved, the next thing he did, should be to hang her. Which when the master perceived, and that the ignorance of the man, should take away the life of the woman, who was innocent of the crime her husband condemned her for, told him plainly, that if he hang'd her, he himself should be hang'd by her, upon the same bough; and therefore wish'd him to consider what he did. This threatning wrought more with him than all the reasons of philosophy that could be given him; and so let her alone; but never car'd much for her afterward, but chose another which he lik'd better. For the planters there deny not a slave, that is a brave fellow, and one that has extraordinary qualities, two or three wives, and above that number they seldom go: But no woman is allowed above one husband.

At the time the wife is to be brought a bed, her husband removes his board, (which is his bed) to another room (for many several divisions they have, in their little houses, and none above six foot square). And leaves his wife to God, and her good fortune, in the room, and upon the board alone, and calls a neighbour to come to her, who gives little help to her delivery, but when the child is born, (which she calls her pickaninny) she helps to make a little fire near her feet, and that serves instead of possets, broaths, and caudles. In a fortnight this woman is at work, with her pickaninny at her back, as merry a soul as any is there: If the overseer be discreet, she is suffer'd to rest her self a little more than ordinary; but if not, she is compelled to do as others do. Times they have of suckling their children in the fields, and refreshing themselves; and good reason, for they carry burthens on their backs; and yet work too. Some women, whose pickaninnies are three years old, will, as they work at weeding, which is a stooping work, suffer the hee pickaninny, to sit a stride upon their backs, like St. George a horse-back; and there spur his mother with his heels, and sings and crows on her back, clapping his hands, as if he meant to flye; which the mother is so pleas'd with, as she continues her painful stooping posture, longer than she would do, rather than discompose her jovial pickaninny of his pleasure, so glad she is to see him merry. The work which the women do, is most of it weeding, a stooping and painful work; at noon and night they are call'd home by the ring of a bell, where they have two hours time for their repast at noon; and at night, they rest from six, till six a clock next morning.

On Sunday they rest, and have the whole day at their pleasure; and the most of them use it as a day of rest and pleasure; but some of them who will make benefit of that dayes liberty, go where the mangrave trees grow, and gather the bark, of which they make ropes, which they truck away[2] for other commodities, as shirts and drawers.

In the afternoons on Sundayes, they have their musick, which is of kettle drums, and those of several sizes; upon the smallest the best musitian playes, and the other come in as chorasses: the drum, all men know, has but one tone; and therefore variety of tunes have little to do in this musick; and yet so strangely they varie their time, as 'tis a pleasure to the most curious ears, and it was to me one of the strangest noises that ever I heard made of one tone; and if they had the variety of tune, which gives the greater scope in musick, as they have of time, they would do wonders in that art . . . .

I found Macow very apt for it of himself, and one day coming into the house (which none of the *Negroes* used to do, unless an officer, as he was,) he found me playing on a theorbo, and singing to it, which he hearkened very attentively to; and when I had done, he took the theorbo in his hand, and strook one string, stopping it by degrees upon every fret, and finding the notes to varie, till it came to the body of the instrument; and that the nearer the body of the instrument he stopt, the smaller or higher the sound was, which he found was by the shortning of the string, considered with himself, how he might make some tryal of this experiment upon such an instrument as he could come by; having no hope ever to have any instrument of this kind to practice on. In a day or two after, walking in the plantine grove, to refresh me in that cool shade, . . . I found this *Negro* (whose office it was to attend there) being the keeper of that grove, sitting on the ground, and before him a piece of large timber, upon which he had laid cross, six billets, and having a handsaw and a hatchet by him, would cut the billets by little and little, till he had brought them to the tunes, he would fit them to; for the shorter they were, the higher the notes, which he tryed by knocking upon the ends of them with a stick, which he had in his hand. When I found him at it, I took the stick out of his hand, and tryed the sound, finding the six billets to have six distinct notes, one above another, which put me in a wonder, how he of himself, should without teaching do so much. I then shewed him the difference between flats and sharps, which he presently apprehended, as between *fa* and *mi:* and he would have cut two more billets to those tunes, but I had then no time to see it done, and so left him to his own enquiries. I say thus much to let you see that some of these people are capable of learning arts . . . .

When any of them die, they dig a grave, and at evening they bury him, clapping and wringing their hands, and making a doleful sound with their

voices. They are a people of a timerous and fearful disposition, and consequently bloody, when they find advantages. If any of them commit a fault,
give him present punishment, but do not threaten him; for if you do, it is an
even lay, he will go and hang himself, to avoid the punishment.

What their other opinions are in matter of religion, I know not; but certainly, they are not altogether of the sect of the Sadduces: For they believe a
resurrection, and that they shall go into their own countrey again, and have
their youth renewed. And lodging this opinion in their hearts, they make it
an ordinary practice, upon any great fright, or threatning of their masters,
to hang themselves.

But Collonel Walrond having lost three or four of his best *Negroes* this
way, and in a very little time, caused one of their heads to be cut off, and set
upon a pole a dozen foot high; and having done that, caused all his *Negroes*
to come forth, and march round about this head, and bid them look on it,
whether this were not the head of such an one that hang'd himself. Which
they acknowledging, he then told them, That they were in a main errour in
thinking they went into their own countreys, after they were dead; for, this
man's head was here, as they all were witnesses of; and how was it possible,
the body could go without a head. Being convinc'd by this sad, yet lively
spectacle, they changed their opinions; and after that, no more hanged
themselves.

[After his account of the "Negroes", Ligon gives a short account of
"Indians", that is, indigenous peoples of the Caribbean region, on
Barbados. This passage is the source of the legend of Inkle and
Yarico.[3]]

As for the Indians, we have but few, and those fetcht from other countries;
some from the neighbouring islands, some from the [Spanish] Main, which
we make slaves . . . We had an Indian woman, a slave in the house, who was
of excellent shape and colour, for it was a pure bright bay; small breasts,
with the niples of a porphyrie colour, this woman would not be woo'd by
any means to wear cloaths. She chanc'd to be with child, by a Christian servant, and lodging in the Indian house, amongst other women of her own

country, where the Christian servants, both men and women came; and being very great, and that her time was come to be delivered, loath to fall in labour before the men, walk'd down to a wood, in which was a pond of water, and there by the side of the pond, brought her self a bed; and presently washing her child in some of the water of the pond, lap'd it up in such rags, as she had begg'd of the Christians; and in three hours time came home, with her child in her arms, a lusty boy, frolick and lively.

This Indian dwelling near the sea-coast, upon the Main, an English ship put in to a bay, and sent some of her men a shoar, to try what victuals or water they could find, for in some distress they were: But the Indians perceiving them to go up so far into the country, as they were sure they could not make a safe retreat, intercepted them in their return, and fell upon them, chasing them into a wood, and being dispersed there, some were taken, and some kill'd: but a young man amongst them stragling from the rest, was met by this Indian maid, who upon the first sight fell in love with him, and hid him close from her countrymen (the Indians) in a cave, and there fed him, till they could safely go down to the shoar, where the ship lay at anchor, expecting the return of their friends. But at last, seeing them upon the shoar, sent the long-boat for them, took them aboard, and brought them away. But the youth, when he came ashoar in the Barbadoes, forgot the kindness of the poor maid, that had ventured her life for his safety, and sold her for a slave, who was as free born as he: And so poor Yarico for her love, lost her liberty.

Notes

1. Richard Ligon, *A True and Exact History of the Island of Barbados* (London: P. Parker and T. Guy, 1657), 46–54.
2. *truck away*: barter.
3. See Richard Steele, "The History of Inkle and Yarico", *The Spectator*, no. 11 (1711), on page 35.

George Warren (FL. 1667)

An Impartial Description of Surinam (1667)[1]

"George Warren, Gent.", as the author is named on the title page, says he lived in Suriname for three years. His book probably provided source material for Aphra Behn's *Oroonoko*.

Chapter VIII
Of the Negroes or Slaves,

Who are most brought out of Guiny in Africa to those parts, where they are sold like *dogs*, and no better esteem'd but for the work sake, which they perform all the week with the severest usages for the slightest fault, till *Saturday* afternoon, when, they are allowed to dress their own gardens or plantations, having nothing but what they can produce from thence to live upon; unless perhaps once or twice a year, their masters vouchsafe them, as a great favour, a little rotten salt-fish: Or if a *cow* or *horse* die of itself, they get roast-meat: Their lodging is on hard board, and their black skins their covering. These wretched miseries not seldome drive them to desperate attempts for the recovery of their liberty, endeavouring to escape, and, if like to be re-taken, sometimes lay violent hands upon themselves; or if the hope of pardon bring them again alive into their masters power, they'l manifest their fortitude, or rather obstinacy in suffering the most exquisite tortures can be inflicted upon them, for a terrour and example to others without shrinking. They are there a mixture of several nations, which are always clashing with one another, so that no conspiracy can be hatching, but 'tis presently detected by some party amongst themselves disaffected to the plot, because their enemies have a share in't: They are naturally treasonous or bloody, and practice no religion there, though many of them are circumcis'd: But they believe the ancient Pythagorean errour of the soul's transmigration out of one body into another, that when they dye, they shall return into their own countries and be regenerated, so live in the world by a constant revolution; which conceit makes many of them overfondly wooe their deaths, not otherwise hoping to be freed from that indeed un-equall'd slavery.

Note

1. George Warren, *An Impartial Description of Surinam, upon the Continent of Guiana in America* (London: Nathaniel Brooke, 1667), 19–20.

Hans Sloane (1660–1753)

A Voyage to the Islands Madera, Barbados, Nieves, S. Christophers and Jamaica (1707)[1]

Sloane's observations date from his residence in Jamaica from December 1687 to March 1689. He travelled to the West Indies as personal physician to the governor of Jamaica, Christopher Monck, Duke of Albemarle, principally with the aim of studying the natural history of the tropics. His *Voyage* was widely known both as an important botanical work and as an authoritative source for the history and ethnology of Jamaica. Although Sloane was not himself opposed to the slave system, his description of the punishments of slaves in the West Indies became "the chief museum of horrors" for early anti-slavery campaigners.[2]

Introduction
Account of the inhabitants of Jamaica

The negros are of several sorts, from the several places of Guinea, which are reckoned the best slaves, those from the East-Indies or Madagascins, are reckoned good enough, but too choice in their diet, being accustomed in their own countries to flesh meat, &c. and do not well here, but very often die. Those who are Creolians, born in the island, or taken from the

Spaniards, are reckoned more worth than others in that they are season'd to the island . . . .

The negroes houses are likewise at a distance from their masters, and are small, oblong, thatch'd huts, in which they have all their moveables or goods, which are generally a mat to lie on, a pot of earth to boil their victuals in, either yams, plantains, or potatoes, with a little salt mackarel, and a calabash or two for cups and spoons . . . .

The negros from some countries think they return to their own country when they die in Jamaica, and therefore regard death but little, imagining they shall change their condition, by that means, from servile to free, and so for this reason often cut their own throats. Whether they die thus, or naturally, their country people make great lamentations, mournings, and howlings about them expiring, and at their funeral throw in rum and victuals into their graves, to serve them in the other world. Sometimes they bury it in gourds, at other times spill it on the graves.

They have every one his wife, and are very much concern'd if they prove adulterous, but in some measure satisfied if their master punish the man who does them the supposed injury, in any of his hogs, or other small wealth. The care of the masters and overseers about their wives, is what keeps their plantations chiefly in good order, whence they ever buy wives in proportion to their men, lest the men should wander to neighbouring plantations, and neglect to serve them. The negros are much given to venery,[3] and although hard wrought, will at night, or on feast days dance and sing; their songs are all bawdy and leading that way. They have several sorts of instruments in imitation of lutes, made of small gourds fitted with necks, strung with horse hairs, or the peeled stalks of climbing plants or withs. These instruments are sometimes made of hollow'd timber covered with parchment or other skin wetted, having a bow for its neck, the strings ty'd longer or shorter, as they would alter their sounds . . . . They have likewise in their dances rattles ty'd to their legs and wrists, and in their hands, with which they make a noise, keeping time with one who makes a sound answering it on the mouth of an empty gourd or jar with his hand. Their dances consist in great activity and strength of body, and keeping time, if it can be. They very often tie cows tails to their rumps, and add such other odd things to their bodies in several places, as gives them a very extraordinary appearance . . . .

They are fruitful, and go after the birth of their children to work in the field, with their little ones ty'd to their backs, in a cloth on purpose, one leg on one side, and the other on the other of their mother, whence their noses are a little flatted against their mothers back, which amongst them is a beauty. The same is the reason of the broadness of their and Indians faces. The mother when she suckles her young, having no cloths to keep her breasts from falling down, they hang very lank ever after, like those of goats.

Their unskilful cutting the navel-string, does occasion that swelling which usually appears in their navels, and makes their bellies prominent. Their children call'd *piganinnies* or rather *peguenos ninnos*, go naked till they are fit to be put to clean the paths, bring fire-wood to the kitchen, &c. when a boy overseer, with his wand or white rod, is set over them as their task-master.

They are rais'd to work so soon as the day is light, or sometimes two hours before by the sound of a *conche* shell, and their overseers noise, or in better plantations by a bell. They are suffered to go to dinner at twelve when they bring wood, &c. one burden lest they should come idle out of the field home, return to the field at one, and come home at night . . . .

They have Saturdays in the afternoon, and Sundays, with Christmas holidays, Easter call'd little or *piganinny*, Christmas, and some other great feasts allow'd them for the culture of their own plantations to feed themselves from potatos, yams, and plantanes, &c. which they plant in ground allow'd them by their masters, besides a small plantane-walk they have by themselves.

They formerly on their festivals were allowed the use of trumpets after their fashion, and drums made of a piece of hollow tree, covered on one end with any green skin, and stretched with thouls or pins. But making use of these in their wars at home in Africa, it was thought too much inciting them to rebellion, and so they were prohibited by the customs of the island . . . .

When a Guinea ship comes near Jamaica with blacks to sell, there is great care taken that the negros should be shav'd, trim'd, and their bodies and hair anointed all over with palm-oil, which adds a great beauty to them. The planters choose their negros by the country from whence they come, and their look. The blacks from the East-Indies are fed on flesh and fish at home, and therefore are not coveted, because troublesome to nourish, and those from Angola run away from their masters, and fancy on their deaths they are going home again, which is no lucriferous[4] experiment, for on hard usage they kill themselves . . . .

The Indians and negros have no manner of religion, by what I could observe of them. 'Tis true they have several ceremonies, as dances, playing,[5] &c. but these are so far from being acts of adoration of a God, that they are for the most part mixt with a great deal of bawdry and lewdness.

The negros are usually thought to be haters of their own children, and therefore 'tis believ'd that they sell and dispose of them to strangers for money, but this is not true, for the negros of Guinea being divided into several captainships, . . . have wars, and besides those slain in battles, many prisoners are taken, who are sold for slaves, and brought hither. But the parents here, altho their children are slaves for ever, yet have so great a love for them, that no master dare sell or give away one of their little ones, unless they care not whether their parents hang themselves or no.

Many of the negros, being slaves, and their posterity after them in Guinea, they are more easily treated by the English here, than by their own country-people, wherefore they would not willingly change masters.

The punishments for crimes of slaves, are usually for rebellions, burning them, by nailing them down on the ground with crooked sticks on every limb, and then applying the fire by degrees from the feet and hands, burning them gradually up to the head, whereby their pains are extravagant. For crimes of a lesser nature gelding, or chopping off half of the foot with an ax. These punishments are suffered by them with great constancy.

For running away they put iron rings of great weight on their ankles, or pottocks about their necks, which are iron rings with two long necks rivetted to them, or a spur in the mouth.

For negligence, they are usually whipt by the overseers with lance-wood switches, till they be bloody, and several of the switches broken, being first tied up by their hands in the mill-houses. Beating with Manati straps[6] is thought too cruel, and therefore prohibited by the customs of the country. The cicatrices[7] arre visible on their skins for ever after; and a slave, the more he have of those, is the less valu'd.

After they are whip'd till they are raw, some put on their skins pepper and salt to make them smart; at other times their masters will drop melted wax on their skins, and use several very exquisite torments. These punishments are sometimes merited by the blacks, who are a very perverse generation of people, and though they appear harsh, yet are scarce equal to some of their crimes, and inferior to what punishments other European nations inflict on their slaves.

Notes

1. Hans Sloane, *A Voyage to the Islands Madera, Barbados, Nieves, S. Christophers and Jamaica* (London: n.p., 1707), 1:xlvii–lvii.
2. Wylie Sypher, *Guinea's Captive Kings: British Anti-slavery Literature of the Eighteenth Century* (Chapel Hill: University of North Carolina Press, 1942), 39.
3. *venery*: sexual activity.
4. *lucriferous*: profitable.
5. *playing*: miming, masquerading, etc.
6. *Manati straps*: leather straps made from the hide of the Caribbean manatee.
7. *cicatrices*: scars.

"A Speech Made by a Black of Guardaloupe, at the Funeral of a Fellow-Negro"

From *A Letter from a Merchant at Jamaica* (1709)[1]

The letter which accompanies this speech is dated 10 October 1708. The author explains that it was prompted by a rumour that Parliament was about to debate the organization of the slave trade. He hopes that the speech, delivered at the funeral of a slave "kill'd by his master for taking a small loaf of bread as he pass'd thro the kitchen", together with the author's own testimony, will give a truer picture of the cruel treatment of the slaves "than either the planters or merchants, the company [the Royal African Company] or traders, will think it their business to shew, or for their credit or interest to have known." He stops short, however, of advocating the abolition of slavery itself, which he regards as economically important: "our plantations are of great consequence to both us and England. They are work'd and cultivated mostly by the hands of negroes, and it would be hard to do it by any others."

The pamphlet is described by Jack P. Greene as "a scathing indictment of Jamaican slave society", anticipating most of the arguments of anti-slavery writers later in the century. The speech itself is most unlikely to have been transcribed from an actual slave oration; not only does it show a command of grammar and rhetoric untouched by Caribbean linguistic habits, but, as Greene notes, the orator's familiarity with Christian doctrine and European social and political thought would have been exceptional for an enslaved

African of the period. He argues that it is more probably a carefully edited version of such a speech, or the author's own invention; nevertheless, it "reveals the author's awareness that funerals were important occasions for articulating and negotiating values in slave communities", with the clear implication that slaves had developed their own critique of the slave system, "drawing on some combination of African and European religious and legal traditions, . . . and their own sense of natural justice".[2] Both letter and speech are reprinted by Greene; the speech alone is reprinted in Krise.[3] The text here is abridged from the 1709 edition: a few redundancies have been omitted, inconsistencies in spelling ironed out and misprints silently corrected.

The great and beneficent *Creator*, the *best* of *beings*, as reason tells, and as our master's books assure us, when he had form'd this speck of earth, was pleased to crown the work, by making man, on whom he stamp'd the image of himself. All he expected in return, was but a just and grateful sense of the kind maker's bounty, and an honest care to copy after the divine original in doing good; that is, in other words, promoting his own and others *happiness*. The good and wise *Maker* had sufficiently furnish'd man with facultys necessary to so kind and glorious a design. He gave him the powers of perceiving, deliberating, judging: He implanted in him a strong desire of preserving his own being and happiness, and gave him unexpressible tenderness towards others. And as God made of the same *common mold all people*, so whilst he subjected the inferior animals to these little vice-roys, he left *them* all *free* to use and follow the *conduct* of that *divine* ray of *reason*, whereby they were shew'd and taught that reasonable service which he requir'd . . . . But, alas! how far is mankind fallen? How much degenerated from the pure and happy state in which God created them? Sin introduc'd sloth in some, wantonness and luxury in others. These were tempted to affect command over, and service from others, while those were again inclin'd to a base submission and dependence, rather than be at the pains of exerting those powers the wise author of Nature had given them, which were abundantly sufficient to all the purposes of life; and so they, like the profane *Esau*, whom we read of in our master's books, sold their birth-right and inheritance for a poor mess of pottage. Thus fond mankind forsook the divine light plac'd in their breasts, and by first becoming servants to their own lusts and appetites, became servants to each other . . . .

But still this extended no farther than their own consent had carry'd it; and the agreement being mutual, they were no longer bound by it than their masters perform'd their part, and treated them fairly. But the lust of domin-ion and the desire of possessing, seizing mens brains, they grew fierce and raging, broke thro the ties of nature and humanity; and upon slender, on only pretended causes, made war upon their weaker and more innocent neighbours. Hence is the source of all our woes and miserys; to these we owe our captivity and bondage; to these we must lay the innocent blood of our brother who lies murder'd, barbarously murder'd, before us. Good God! what have we done? What right have these cruel men thus to oppress, insult, and inhumanly butcher their fellow-creatures? Let us examine all their title, and see what it amounts to; and then we shall the better know, whether their usage of us, or our complaints, are the more just. They say, they bought us with their mony. – Confess'd; but who had power to sell? We were it may be condemn'd by colour of law, that is, the will of some great man, to be sold by way of banishment for some suppos'd crime. – But how did the buyer know there ever was a crime committed, or that the sentence was just? or if he did, what right can this confer? 'Tis plain, I think, it gives him only right to carry us whither he pleas'd, and make us work till we repaid him by our labour what we cost, with other charges.

It may be we were taken in war; what right then had the conqueror? or what did he transfer? Suppose the war against us was just, and that our buy-ers knew 'twas so; yet they likewise know, that 'tis barbarous and cruel to take a conquer'd enemy's life, when the injur'd can be safe without it; and that 'tis still more barbarous and inhumane for another to take it away, to whom he has sold and deliver'd his prisoner; since by the sale and price receiv'd he seems to have taken the mony for his security, and upon that consideration runs the hazard of the other's setting him at liberty if he thinks fit. So that 'tis plain, this gives them no such right over our lives, as any man that has the least tenderness or humanity (I might, I think, say justice) would make use of. And as for perpetual slavery – it must be cruel justice, that for so small a sum, so soon repaid, would purchase and exact what makes his fellow-creature, from whom he has nought to fear, so miserable for life. If they contend for this as a right which they are fond of, let them shew it, and let them take it and the sole glory of it. But who told our present lords the war was just? Do victory and right go always hand in hand? No, our masters by experience know they don't. This then at best can give but a dark doubtful right, which never can defeat that natural and undoubted one the God of Nature has bestow'd on men, to have, to own, no other lord but *him*.

It may have happen'd we were sold to pay our debts: What will this give them? In equity they have at most hereby a right to so much service as will pay the debt and charges of transporting us. The first was all the creditor could ask. But do they know what this debt was? No, they never so much as once enquir'd or ask'd to be inform'd. We were perhaps bought of some unkind unnatural father. Be it so. What have they got by this? Can a father transfer what he has not? or have they what he neither did or could possibly give them? surely no. A father has power indeed, and ought to help and feed his young and tender offspring, as all creatures do, but not to cast them out into the fields, or sell them wantonly to a base servitude. God gave him power to beget and become a father of men, not slaves. A father, as 'tis fit, has power too to guide and steer his childrens actions while reason's weak; and if by age, or otherwise, he's brought to want their help, they are oblig'd by nature, and by gratitude, to give their helping hand and best assistance. But still they are not his slaves or lasting property; for when wise Nature has fitted them to propagate and educate their kind, reason requires, and Nature loudly tells they are at liberty, they then are men. It's true, we seem oblig'd to our lords, that they were pleas'd to take us off the hands of cruel conquerors, or such wanton and unnatural parents as begot us only for their pleasure; either of which might likely have destroy'd, if they could not have sold us. But it would be remember'd, no benefit obliges further than the intention. Was it then for our sakes, or for their own, our masters built such mighty ships in which they plow the main? Was it for us they laid out so much wealth? Or was it to save our lives, they so much ventur'd and expos'd their own? Alas! the answer is too obvious: our hard labour, and harder fare, but most of all, our cruel punishments, and perpetual bondage, but too plainly shew for whose sake all this was done . . . . Further, many of us, it may be, are bought neither of the governor or conqueror, or creditor or parent; but of a treacherous friend, a perfidious husband, or an odious man-stealer. These are far from conferring any right, unless what can arise from the most unjust and inhuman acts in the world. What's now become of all their boasted right of absolute dominion? It is fled. Where all our obligations to perpetual servitude? They are vanish'd. However, we may perhaps owe them something; and it were but just, if so, they should be paid. Let us therefore, if from the account I have already given we can, make an estimate of the balance. – Supposing then one half of us were justly sold at first by those that had a right to all our services, if that may be suppos'd: Suppose likewise that our masters knew it too, and who the very persons were: They then would have at most a right to the labour of such persons during life; and of the rest, till they had earn'd and clear'd so much as was given to the captain who brought 'em hither. But since it is impossible for them to know on whom to place their several demands; and since they bought us all at random, without regard to right or wrong: let us for once suppose favourably for them, who never favour'd us; let us suppose our masters innocent of all the wrongs we first sustain'd. Suppose us men, women, and children come to their shoar from some far-off unknown land, under the power of a strange captain of a ship, who pretends he has a right to sell us. He offers to deliver us, great and small, into their hands at 20*l*. a-piece. They pay the mony. We are deliver'd up. What are we now in debt? 'Tis plain, I think, that since they neither know nor did regard his title, they can at best have one but till they're reimburs'd the cost and charge which they've been at. 'Tis sure we had a plain and natural right to life and liberty; which to take away upon a weak, presumptive, or a may-be title, were to make us of less value than beasts and things inanimate: a property in which, by reason's law, is never gain'd against a true and just owner upon slight presumptions, whatever may be done by laws of particular societys . . . .

Let any man but make the case his own, and he'll soon see the hardship. Would not any one think himself greatly injur'd, if another should make him his perpetual slave, only because he gave 20*l*. for him, to one who had him in his power? Methinks the very naming it is enough to shock a man; and he should need no further argument to convince him of the injustice of the thing. But men are hardly brought to see what makes against their interest. Taking the matter now to be as last stated. – Suppose twenty of us bought at once; the mony paid would be 400*l*. Suppose six of the twenty children; suppose also one of us to die each year; reckon the labour of each of those of sufficient age at 10*l*. a year, which is really less than it may be well accounted, seeing a great part of our poor sustenance is owing to our own hands and industry, which we are forc'd to employ in planting herbs and roots, whilst we should rest from our more toilsom labour. By this computation we should have paid all our joint debt in three years time. Yet would our lords but use us as men, we should not stick to a nice computation, but frankly serve them three or four years more, before we claim'd our freedom. Many of us here present have serv'd twice, some seven times the space our cruel lords can justly claim. Of our hard labour, let our weary'd limbs, their well-planted fields and full coffers all bear witness. Of their cruel and hard usage let our torn backs testify. Of their bloody inhumanity, let the corps of our dear countryman before us, weltring in its goar; let it, I say, for ever witness against the cruel authors of our woe: who not content to make us slaves for life, do use us worse than dogs, and deny us the compassion they would shew a horse. 'Tis true they willingly will teach and make us Christians; while they themselves want to be taught, both they and we are men. In this however we are somewhat better used than are our wretched friends in *English* isles;[4] where their hard masters forbear to do good, lest that oblige them to do more. Ridiculous superstition! that will not allow their servants to be Christians, lest they be forc'd to allow them to be men. This is to found dominion upon the gospel of that divine teacher Jesus, who told them plain as words could make it, his kingdom was not of this world. And as if none were intitled to the common privileges of Nature, except they please to allow them by washing or baptizing, they carefully forbid our brethren that. What I pray is this, but to make sport with the Creation, and to monopolize the blessings of our common mother Earth? Our hardy tutors know things better. They teach us what themselves seem hardly to believe; and by giving us hopes of a better world, endeavour to make us content that they alone should enjoy this: teach us to do good for evil; and when we have done no fault, to turn our cheeks to the smiter, and our backs to the scourger; to submit not only to froward and unjust, but even to merciless and cruel masters; remembring us that their gospel says, *Thro many sufferings and tribulations we must enter into the heavenly country*; that country where our dear, our patient, our murder'd brother's gone. But why should we complain of death, whose life's so miserable to us? To kill us, seems the greatest kindness that our bloody lords can do. We have lost our native country, our friends, our liberty; we are made slaves to haughty cruel men; we are fed and work'd hard; their will's our law; which when we do transgress, we suffer all the wanton cruelty they can devise: no prayers or tears can touch their harden'd hearts; relentless as rocks, they know no pity. What now remains in life to be desir'd? 'Tis better far to die, than, being men, be forc'd to live like beasts: beasts! and of those the most unhappy too. Still, tho our hardships are as great as the injustice of our oppressors; tho our sufferings are as many as the hated days we live; tho all their pleas of right are false or short: methinks I could forgive them all, did they not pretend necessity for their inhuman acts. They tell, it seems, the European world, we're of such base, such brutal natures, that nought will govern us, but downright force and fear; that like the horse we must be broke and rid with whip and spur, but with far closer reins. Abominable forgery! Hated imposture! What, are we not men? Have we not the common facultys and passions with others? Why else has Nature given us human shape and speech? Whence is't that some of these wise rational masters of ours give us sometimes charge, not only of their works and cash, but of their persons too; and make us judge when they're debauch'd enough in wine, and when it's time to lug them home upon our servile backs? Whence is it that some of us, without the help of books or letters, are found able to deliver a message, or do business better, even by their own confession, than they who intrust us with it? But were it a wonder, that while they use us so like beasts, we should not act as men? If they give us no motives to industry and obedience, but a base servile fear, is it at all strange, when that's remov'd, the hated service straight should cease? It would be strange indeed, should it be otherwise. Could they be brought to deal with us as men, they soon would see, we may be wrought upon by gentler methods far than blows and scourges. But while they use us thus, how can they e'er expect we should not hate them?

how can they hope our services should once proceed from hearts they never touch'd, unless with detestation? Let them make tryal of their own country-men, and see what will be the difference 'twixt them and us. As much slaves as they are already, this likely will be all the odds, they'll hate them more and bear their usage worse than we. To finish and compleat our miserys, these lords of ours, not content that we are slaves, slaves basely us'd for life, they make our innocent babes their property, as if they sprung from brutes. If their right to us be so uncertain or so small, as I have shew'd it is; with what pretence, with what face can they enslave our guiltless children? . . . Supposing we were justly theirs for life, which they can never shew; yet still, the most they can demand from innocents is some small time of labour, for the little sustenance which they receiv'd by means of these our lords. But not content with this, they carry on the wrong, and make them slaves for life as they made us; and claim our childrens children, and so on, to all posterity. Thus, our lords who call themselves white-men and Christians, led by their avarice and luxury, commit the blackest crimes without a blush, and wickedly subvert the laws of Nature, and the order of Creation. Let us, my dearest countrymen and fellow-sufferers! Let us in this our great distress and misery, look up to the great author of Nature, whose works and image are so basely us'd; and earnestly implore his mighty aid: Let us beseech him, for sure he hears the crys and groans of his oppress'd creatures, either to soften those adamantine hearts, which cut us in pieces; or to put it into the minds of some great, some God-like men, to come to our deliverance, that we may sing our maker's praise, and with assurance say, there is a God who governs the earth, and restrains the pride and cruelty of wicked men.

FINIS.

Notes

1. "A Speech Made by a Black of Guardaloupe, at the Funeral of a Fellow-Negro", from *A Letter from a Merchant at Jamaica to a Member of Parliament in London, Touching the African Trade* (London: A. Baldwin, 1709).

2. Jack P. Greene, " 'A Plain and Natural Right to Life and Liberty': An Early Natural Rights Attack on the Excesses of the Slave System in Colonial British America", *William and Mary Quarterly*, 3rd ser., 57 (2000): 793–808.

3. Krise, *Caribbeana*, 94–100.

4. Guadeloupe was at this date a French colony. The somewhat confusing passage which follows contrasts the attitudes of French planters (under the influence of the Church of Rome) towards the conversion of slaves to Christianity with those of planters in the English colonies, such as Jamaica, where plantation owners resisted attempts by missionaries to preach to and baptize slaves.

RICHARD STEELE (1672–1729)
"The History of Inkle and Yarico" (1711)[1]

This tale became hugely popular in the eighteenth century. Although its primary source was Ligon's history of Barbados (page 18 above), Steele's elaboration of Ligon's brief narrative provided the impetus for most later versions. As David Brion Davis comments, Steele's story may be read as "merely an early outburst of middle-class sentimentality", but it can also be viewed as "the first significant attempt to give imaginative expression to the meaning of slavery" in the Americas.[2] Steele's interest in slavery was not purely abstract; in 1706 he inherited a sugar plantation in Barbados with two hundred slaves, though the estate had been sold by 1711.[3] The motto attached to the essay is *Dat veniam corvis, vexat censura columbas* (Juvenal): "Censure pardons the crow but blames the dove." The conventional construct of blackness/guilt versus whiteness/innocence, implicit in the crow–dove opposition, is reversed in the story of Inkle and Yarico.

I was the other day amusing my self with Ligon's Account of Barbadoes; . . . I will give you (as it dwells upon my memory) out of that honest traveller, in his fifty fifth page, the history of Inkle and Yarico.

Mr. Thomas Inkle of London, aged 20 years, embarked in the Downs on the good ship called the *Achilles*, bound for the West-Indies, on the 16th of

June 1647, in order to improve his fortune by trade and merchandize. Our adventurer was the third son of an eminent citizen, who had taken particular care to instill into his mind an early love of gain, by making him a perfect master of numbers, and consequently giving him a quick view of loss and advantage, and preventing the natural impulses of his passions, by prepossession towards his interests. With a mind thus turned, young Inkle had a person every way agreeable, a ruddy vigour in his countenance, strength in his limbs, with ringlets of fair hair loosely flowing on his shoulders. It happened, in the course of the voyage, that the *Achilles*, in some distress, pulled into a creek on the main of America, in search of provisions: The youth, who is the hero of my story, among others, went ashore on this occasion. From their first landing they were observed by a party of Indians, who hid themselves in the woods for that purpose. The English unadvisedly marched a great distance from the shore into the country, and were intercepted by the natives, who slew the greatest number of them. Our adventurer escaped among others, by flying into a forest. Upon his coming into a remote and pathless part of the wood, he threw himself, tired and breathless, on a little hillock, when an Indian maid rushed from a thicket behind him: After the first surprize, they appeared mutually agreeable to each other. If the European was highly charmed with the limbs, features, and wild graces of the naked American, the American was no less taken with the dress, complexion, and shape of an European, covered from head to foot. The Indian grew immediately enamoured of him, and consequently sollicitous for his preservation: She therefore conveyed him to a cave, where she gave him a delicious repast of fruits, and led him to a stream to slake his thirst. In the midst of these good offices, she would sometimes play with his hair, and delight in the opposition of its colour, to that of her fingers: Then open his bosome, then laugh at him for covering it. She was, it seems, a person of distinction, for she every day came to him in a different dress, of the most beautiful shells, bugles and bredes. She likewise brought him a great many spoils, which her other lovers had presented to her; so that his cave was adorned with all the spotted skins of beasts, and most party-coloured feathers of fowls, which that world afforded. To make his confinement more tolerable, she would carry him in the dusk of the evening, or by the favour of moon-light, to unfrequented groves and solitudes, and show him where to lye down in safety, and sleep amidst the falls of waters, and melody of nightingales. Her part was to watch and hold him in her arms, for fear of her country-men, and wake him on occasions to consult his safety. In this manner did the lovers pass away their time, till they had learn'd a language of their own, in which the voyager communicated to his mistress, how happy he should be to have her in his country, where she should be cloathed in such silks as his wastecoat was made of, and be carried in houses drawn by horses, without being exposed to wind or weather. All this he promised her the enjoyment of, without such fears and alarms as they were there tormented with. In this tender correspondence these lovers lived for several months, when Yarico, instructed by her lover, discovered a vessel on the coast, to which she made signals, and in the night, with the utmost joy and satisfaction accompanied him to a ships-crew of his country-men, bound for Barbadoes. When a vessel from the main arrives in that island, it seems the planters come down to the shoar, where there is an immediate market of the Indians and other slaves, as with us of horses and oxen.

To be short, Mr. Thomas Inkle, now coming into English territories, began seriously to reflect upon his loss of time, and to weigh with himself how many days interest of his mony he had lost during his stay with Yarico. This thought made the young man very pensive, and careful what account he should be able to give his friends of his voyage. Upon which considerations, the prudent and frugal young man sold Yarico to a Barbadian merchant; notwithstanding that the poor girl, to incline him to commiserate her condition, told him that she was with child by him: But he only made use of that information, to rise in his demands upon the purchaser.

Notes

1. *The Spectator*, no. 11 (13 March 1711). The text here is from Donald F. Bond, *The Spectator* (Oxford: Clarendon Press, 1965), 2:49–51.
2. David Brion Davis, *The Problem of Slavery in Western Culture* (Ithaca: Cornell University Press, 1966), 11.
3. Felsenstein, *English Trader*, 13–14.

JOSEPH ADDISON (1672–1719)

"A Kind of Wild Tragedy" (1711)[1]

This is an early version of another story which, like that of Inkle and Yarico, became entrenched in anti-slavery legend in the eighteenth century.[2] Addison's essay is concerned with the importance of education for moral development. Vehemently rejecting the view that "savage nations" are deficient in moral capacity, Addison argues that first-hand reports show them to possess innate virtues which, for want of cultivation, manifest themselves as defects: "courage exerting it self in fierceness, resolution in obstinacy, wisdom in cunning, patience in sullenness and despair." His general argument is illustrated by examples of Africans enslaved in the British colonies. The source of the following story, said by Addison to have occurred in the Leeward Islands about 1699, has not been traced.

Mens passions operate variously, and appear in different kinds of actions, according as they are more or less rectified and swayed by reason. When one hears of negroes, who upon the death of their masters, or upon changing their service, hang themselves upon the next tree, as it frequently happens in our American plantations, who can forbear admiring their fidelity, though it expresses it self in so dreadful a manner? What might not that savage greatness of soul, which appears in these poor wretches on many occasions, be raised to, were it rightly cultivated? And what colour of excuse can there be for the contempt with which we treat this part of our species; That we should not put them upon the common foot of humanity, that we should only set an insignificant fine upon the man who murders them; nay that we should, as much as in us lies, cut them off from the prospects of happiness in another world as well as in this, and deny them that which we look upon as the proper means for attaining it?

Since I am engaged on this subject, I cannot forbear mentioning a story which I have lately heard, and which is so well attested, that I have no manner of reason to suspect the truth of it. I may call it a kind of wild tragedy that passed about twelve years ago at St. Christophers, one of our British Leeward Islands. The negroes who were concerned in it, were all of them the slaves of a gentleman who is now in England.

This gentleman among his negroes had a young woman, who was looked upon as a most extraordinary beauty by those of her own complexion. He had at the same time two young fellows who were likewise negroes and slaves, remarkable for the comeliness of their persons, and for the friendship which they bore to one another. It unfortunately happened that both of them fell in love with the female negro abovementioned, who would have been very glad to have taken either of them for her husband, provided they could agree between themselves which should be the man. But they were both so passionately in love with her, that neither of them could think of giving her up to his rival; and at the same time were so true to one another, that neither of them would think of gaining her without his friend's consent. The torments of these two lovers were the discourse of the family to which they belonged, who could not forbear observing the strange complication of passions which perplexed the hearts of the poor negroes, that often dropped expressions of the uneasiness they underwent, and how impossible it was for either of them ever to be happy.

After a long struggle between love and friendship, truth and jealousy, they one day took a walk together into a wood, carrying their mistress along with them: Where, after abundance of lamentations, they stabbed her to the heart, of which she immediately died. A slave who was at his work not far from the place where this astonishing piece of cruelty was committed, hearing the shrieks of the dying person, ran to see what was the occasion of them. He there discovered the woman lying dead upon the ground, with the two negroes on each side of her, kissing the dead corps, weeping over it, and beating their breasts in the utmost agonies of grief and despair. He immediately ran to the English family with the news of what he had seen; who upon coming to the place saw the woman dead, and the two negroes expiring by her with wounds they had given themselves.

We see, in this amazing instance of barbarity, what strange disorders are bred in the minds of those men whose passions are not regulated by vertue, and disciplined by reason. Though the action which I have recited is in it self full of guilt and horror, it proceeded from a temper of mind which might have produced very noble fruits, had it been informed and guided by a suitable education.

Notes

1. Joseph Addison, "A Kind of Wild Tragedy", *The Spectator*, no. 215 (6 November 1711). The text here is from Bond, *Spectator*, 2:339–40.
2. See Sypher, *Guinea's Captive Kings*, 143, and James Ramsay, *An Essay on the Treatment and Conversion of African Slaves* (1784), on pages 104–6 below.

"The Pleasures of Jamaica" (1738)[1]

This long "prospect poem", published in two parts in the
Gentleman's Magazine, paints an idyllic picture of the Jamaican land-
scape, agriculture and people. In the following passage from part
one, the author surveys the view from the heights above Kingston
and makes the only reference in the poem to the black labour by
which "our wealth" is produced.

Hither retiring, to avoid the heat,
We find refreshment in a cool retreat;
Each rural object gratifies the sight,
And yields the mind an innocent delight;
Greens of all shades the diff'rent plats adorn,   5
Here the young cane, and there the growing corn;
In verdant pastures, interspers'd between,
The lowing herds and bleating flocks are seen:
With joy his lord the faithful Negro sees,
And in his way endeavours how to please;   10
Greets his return with his best country song,
The lively dance and tuneful merry-wang.[2]
When nature by the cane has done her part,
Which ripen'd now demands the help of art,
How pleasant are the labours of the mill,   15

While the rich streams the boiling coppers fill,
With gladden'd hearts we see the precious juice
From tend'rest plants the useful sweet produce;
Oh! may the seasons never fail again,
Nor heav'n deny the kind refreshing rain,   20
To bless the soil, and fill the growing cane;
So shall our wealth with wonder still be told,
And sugar works preferr'd to mines of gold.

Notes

1. "The Pleasures of Jamaica. In an Epistle from a Gentleman to his Friend in London", *Gentleman's Magazine* 8 (March–April 1738): 158.
2. *merry-wang*: "a musical instrument imitating the guitar, made by negroes; prototype of the banjo". F.G. Cassidy and R.B. Le Page, eds., *Dictionary of Jamaican English*, 2nd ed. (Kingston: University of the West Indies Press, 2002), 299. Compare Edward Long, *The History of Jamaica* (1774), on page 80 below.
3. F.G. Cassidy and R.B. Le Page, eds., *Dictionary of Jamaican English*, 2nd ed. (Kingston: University of the West Indies Press, 2002), 299.

CHARLES LESLIE (FL. 1738–43)

A New History of Jamaica (1740)[1]

First published in Edinburgh as *A New and Exact Account of Jamaica* in 1739, this work was retitled and expanded by addition of a new letter describing events of 1739: the conclusion of the Maroon War and Vernon's victory at Porto-Bello. The main text remained unchanged apart from minor alterations in style. Little is known of the author apart from what may be inferred from his published works. He produced several volumes of verse, including political satires, essays and Masonic poems, all published in Edinburgh in 1738–42, some from the same press as *A New and Exact Account*. They show him to be a Scotsman and a Tory, but anti-Jacobite (unlike his namesake, the Nonjuror Charles Leslie). The other publications contain no references to the West Indies, but an entry in Thomas Thistlewood's journal sheds a glimmer of light on Leslie's residence in Jamaica. In 1757, while Thistlewood was reading Leslie's history, he was told by his friend William Wallace that the author had come over to Jamaica with him as his "fellow servant". Wallace said the book had been written "before he had been a year in the Island and not well informed", adding that "he has a good deal of impudence".[2] The comment was probably provoked by Leslie's criticisms of colonial society and his anti-slavery views. Leslie dedicated the 1739 version of his history to the Earl of Eglinton, with the declaration "You will see, in the following sheets, that slavery is the ruin of society, and that oppression is still attended with fatal inconveniences, even to the tyrant" (the dedication did not appear in *A New History*).

Letter XI

This Island contains three sorts of inhabitants, *Masters*, *Servants*, and *Slaves*. The *Gentlemen* are some of them extremely polite, and use their inferiors with a great deal of good-nature. However, all of them have something of a haughty disposition, and require submission: a stranger who knows how to apply to their humour, generally gets into good business; but they who are so unhappy as to mistake it, may look for business in another place.

The *Servants* who behave well, are respected and encouraged; if they be found honest, and worthy of their trust, they are handsomely used. I have known them dine on the same victuals with their master, and wear as good cloaths, be allowed a horse when they had occasion to go abroad, and a negro boy to attend them. Others, who are either stupid or roguish, are indeed hardly used; they are often put into the stocks, and beat very severely. Their salt provisions are weighed out, and they have nothing but what the law obliges the master to give. They have likewise another unhappiness; for, after the expiration of their four years, nobody is fond to employ them, and they generally remain in a low abject state, thro' the whole remainder of their lives. This ought to warn all who come over in such unhappy circumstances, to beware how they act, and endeavour to behave in such a manner as will most effectually recommend them to the good graces of their masters. The great thing which ruins most of these unfortunate fellows, is the combining with the negroes, who tell them many plausible stories, to engage them to betray their trust. The servants labour is not very hard, but is much less than that of the day-labourers in Britain. They who have no trades, are only imployed in looking after the negroes at work, or in overseeing the boiling of the sugars.

The condition of the *Blacks* is indeed worse, because their servitude is perpetual. I shall not now enter upon the question, whether the slavery of these unhappy creatures be agreeable to the laws of nature or not; tho' it seems extremely hard, they should be reduced to serve, and toil for the benefit of others, without the least advantage to themselves. Happy *Britannia!* where slavery is never known, where liberty and freedom chears every misfortune. Here we can boast of no such blessing; we have at least ten slaves to one freeman. I incline to touch the hardships, which these poor creatures suffer, in the tenderest manner, from a particular regard which I owe to many of their masters; but I can't conceal their sad circumstances intirely. The most trivial error is punished with a terrible whipping. I have seen some of them treated in that cruel manner, for no other reason, but to satisfy the brutish pleasure of an overseer, who has their punishment mostly at his direction. I have seen their bodies all in a gore of blood, the skin torn off their backs with the cruel whip; beaten pepper, and salt, rubbed in the wounds, and a large stick of sealing-wax dropped leisurely upon them. It is no wonder, if the horrid pain of such inhuman tortures incline them to rebel; at the same time, it must be confessed, they are generally very perverse, which is owing to the many disadvantages they lie under, and the bad example they daily see.

Their owners set aside for each a small parcel of ground, and allow them the Sundays to manure it: In it they generally plant maize, Guiney corn, plantains, yams, cocoas, potatoes, &c. This is the food which supports them, unless some of them, who are more industrious than others, happen to raise a stock of fowls, which they carry to markets on Sundays, (which is the only market-day in Jamaica) and sell for a little money, with which they purchase salt-beef, fish, or pork, to make their *oglios* or pepper-pot. 'Tis surprising to see the mean shifts to which these poor creatures are reduced: You'll see them daily about twelve o'clock, when they turn in from work, till two, scraping the dunghills at every gentleman's door for bones, which, if they are so happy as to find, they break extremely small, boil them, and eat the broth. Most of these slaves are brought from the coast of Guiney: When they first arrive, 'tis observed they are simple and very innocent creatures; but they soon turn to be roguish enough: and when they come to be whipt, urge the example of the whites for an excuse of their faults. Their notions of religion are very inconsistent, and vary according to the different countries they come from: But they have a kind of occasional conformity,[3] and join without distinction in their solemn sacrifices and gambols. They generally believe there are two Gods, a good and a bad one; the first they call *Naskew* in the Papaw language, and the other *Timnew*: The good God, they tell you, lives in the clouds; is very kind, and favours men; 'twas he that taught their fathers to till the ground, and to hunt for their subsistence. The evil God sends storms, earthquakes, and all kind of mischief. They love the one dearly, and fear the other as much. Their notions are extremely dark; they have no idea of Heaven, farther than the pleasures of returning to their native country, whither they believe every negro goes after death: This thought is so agreeable, that it chears the poor creatures, and makes the burden of life easy, which otherwise would be quite intolerable. They look on death as a blessing: 'Tis indeed surprising to see with what courage and intrepidity some of them will meet their fate, and be merry in their last moments; they are quite transported to think their slavery is near an end, and that they shall revisit their native shores, and see their old friends and acquaintance. When a negro is about to expire, his fellow-slaves kiss him, wish him a good journey, and send their hearty recommendations to their relations in Guiney. They make no lamentations, but with a great deal of joy interr his body, firmly believing he is gone home and happy.

When any thing about a plantation is missing, they have a solemn kind of oath, which the eldest negro always administers, and which by them is accounted so sacred, that except they have the express command of their master or overseer, they never set about it, and then they go very solemnly to work. They range themselves in that spot of ground which is appropriated for the negroes burying-place, and one of them opens a grave. He who acts the priest, takes a little of the earth, and puts into every one of their mouths; they say, that if any has been guilty, their belly swells, and occasions their death. I never saw any instance of this but one; and it was certainly fact that a boy did swell, and acknowledged the theft when he was dying: But I am far from thinking there was any connection betwixt the cause and effect; for a thousand accidents might have occasioned it, without accounting for it by that foolish ceremony.

I have discoursed them about the immortality of the soul, and some other important points; but I found their notions of these matters extremely obscure: Yet from the customs they use at their burials, I can gather some faint traces of their belief in that article. When one is carried to his grave, he is attended with a vast multitude, who conduct his corps in something of a ludicrous manner: They sing all the way, and they who bear it on their shoulders, make a feint of stopping at every door they pass, pretending, that if the deceased person had received any injury, the corps moves towards that house, and that they can't avoid letting it fall to the ground, when before the door. When they come to the grave, which is generally made in some savannah or plain, they lay down the coffin, or whatever the body happens to be wrapt up in; and if he be one whose circumstances would allow it, or if he be generally beloved, the negroes sacrifice a hog, in honour of him; which they contribute to the expences of, among themselves. The manner of the sacrifice is this: The nearest relation kills it, the intrails are buried, the four quarters are divided, and a kind of soup made, which is brought in a calabash, or gourd, and, after waving it three times, it is set down; then the body is put in the ground; all the while they are covering it with earth, the attendants scream out in a terrible manner, which is not the effect of grief, but of joy; they beat on their wooden drums, and the women with their rattles make a hideous noise: After the grave is filled up, they place the soup which they had prepared at the head, and a bottle of rum at the feet. In the mean time cool drink (which is made of the *Lignum Vitae* bark, or whatever else they can afford) is distributed among those who are present; one half of the hog is burnt while they are drinking, and the other is left to any person who pleases to take it; they return to town, or the plantation, singing after their manner, and so the ceremony ends.

They have a great many other remarkable customs, which you may see very curiously described in the Introduction to Sir Hans Sloane's *Natural History* of Jamaica. Sunday afternoon the generality of them dance or wrestle, men and women promiscuously together. They have two musical instruments, like kettle-drums, for each company of dancers, with which they make a very barbarous melody. They have other musical instruments, as a *Bangil*, not much unlike our lute in any thing but the musick; the *Rookaw*, which is two sticks jagged; and a *Jenkgoving*, which is a way of clapping their hands on the mouth of two jars: These are all played together, accompanied with voices, which make a very terrible kind of harmony.

They are so far superior in number to the whites, that one should think it would be unsafe, considering all circumstances, to live amongst them. The reasons of the planters security are these: The slaves are brought from several places in Guiney, which are different from one another in language, and consequently they can't converse freely; or, if they could, they hate one another so mortally, that some of them would rather die by the hands of the English, than join with other Africans in an attempt to shake off their yoke. None of them are allowed to touch any arms, unless by their master's command, or go out of the bounds of the plantation to which they belong, without a special permit signed by their owner or overseer. They are kept in such awe, that they are afraid even to make the least thought of liberty appear. And when they see the whites muster and exercise, there can be no terror in the world greater than what they lie under at that time. 'Tis true, the Creolian negroes are not of this number: They all speak English, and are so far from fearing a muster, that they are very familiar with it, and can exercise extremely well.

Notes

1. Charles Leslie, *A New History of Jamaica, from the Earliest Accounts, to the Taking of Porto Bello by Vice-Admiral Vernon. In Thirteen Letters from a Gentleman to His Friend* (Edinburgh: J. Hodges, 1740), 303–11.

2. Quoted by Trevor Burnard, *Mastery, Tyranny, and Desire: Thomas Thistlewood and His Slaves in the Anglo-Jamaican World* (Chapel Hill: University of North Carolina Press, 2004), 110.

3. *occasional conformity*: a legal term (used here facetiously) for the practice whereby dissenters could qualify for public position by receiving the sacrament according to the rites of the Church of England, but were permitted to worship in dissenting meeting-places during their period of office. The practice was disallowed in 1711.

JAMES GRAINGER (CA. 1727–66)

The Sugar-Cane: A Poem (1764)[1]

Grainger settled in St Kitts in 1759 as physician to several estates on the island and married into the plantocracy. He bought a number of slaves for hiring out for labour and had ambitions to purchase land of his own in the Leeward Islands. Apart from a visit to England in 1763–64 he remained in the West Indies until his early death. *The Sugar-Cane* was a literary success in the eighteenth century and recaptured attention in the twentieth century as "an important example of the literature of empire, and as a detailed exposition of plantation slavery and the attitudes which supported it".[2] The typology of Africans according to their supposed national or tribal identity (lines 1–65) became a standard feature of colonial discourse. But, as Gilmore points out,[3] captives arriving at African slave-trading ports had often travelled long distances, and many European traders unfamiliar with African languages simply assumed that all slaves from a given port were of the same national origin. The text here is from the first edition, with omission of Grainger's long botanical notes.

Book IV, lines 38–487

ARGUMENT. *Negroes when bought should be young, and strong. The Congo-negroes are fitter for the house and trades, than for the field. The Gold-Coast, but especially the Papaw-negroes, make the best field-negroes: but even these, if advanced in years, should not be purchased. The marks of a sound negroe at a negroe sale. Where the men do nothing but hunt, fish or fight, and all field drudgery is left to the women; these are to be preferred to their husbands. The Minnahs make good tradesmen, but addicted to suicide. . . . How salt-water, or new negroes should be seasoned. Some negroes eat dirt. Negroes should be habituated by gentle degrees to field labour. This labour, when compared to that in lead-mines, or of those who work in the gold and silver mines of South America, is not only less toilsome, but far more healthy. Negroes should always be treated with humanity. Praise of freedom. . . . Of the imaginary disorders of negroes, especially those caused by their conjurors or Obia-men. The composition and supposed virtues of a magic-phial. Field-negroes should not begin to work before six in the morning, and should leave off between eleven and twelve; and beginning again at two, should finish before sunset. Of the weekly allowance of negroes. The young, the old, the sickly, and even the lazy, must have their victuals prepared for them. Of negroe-ground, and its various productions.*

In mind, and aptitude for useful toil,
The negroes differ: muse that difference sing.
    Whether to wield the hoe, or guide the plane;
Or for domestic uses thou intend'st
The sunny Libyan: from what clime they spring,   5
It not imports; if strength and use be theirs.
    Yet those from Congo's wide extended plains,
Through which the long Zaire winds with chrystal stream,
Where lavish Nature sends indulgent forth
Fruits of high flavour, and spontaneous seeds   10
Of bland nutritious quality, ill bear
The toilsome fields; but boast a docile mind,
And happiness of features. These, with care,
Be taught each nice mechanic art: or train'd

To household offices: their ductile souls 15
Will all thy care, and all thy gold repay.
   But, if the labours of the field demand
Thy chief attention, and the ambrosial cane
Thou long'st to see, with spiry frequence, shade
Many an acre: planter, chuse the slave, 20
Who sails from barren climes; where want alone,
Offspring of rude necessity, compells
The sturdy native, or to plant the soil,
Or stem vast rivers for his daily food.
   Such are the children of the Golden Coast; 25
Such the Papaws,[4] of negroes far the best:
And such the numerous tribes, that skirt the shore,
From rapid Volta to the distant Rey.[5]
   But, planter, from what coast so'er they sail,
Buy not the old: they ever sullen prove; 30
With heart-felt anguish, they lament their home;
They will not, cannot work; they never learn
Thy native language; they are prone to ails;
And oft by suicide their being end. –
   Must thou from Africk reinforce thy gang? – 35
Let health and youth their every sinew firm;
Clear roll their ample eye; their tongue be red;
Broad swell their chest; their shoulders wide expand;
Not prominent their belly; clean and strong
Their thighs and legs, in just proportion rise. 40
Such soon will brave the fervours of the clime;
And free from ails, that kill thy negroe-train,
A useful servitude will long support.
   Yet, if thine own, thy childrens life be dear;
Buy not a Cormantee,[6] tho' healthy, young. 45
Of breed too generous for the servile field;
They, born to freedom in their native land,
Chuse death before dishonourable bonds:
Or, fir'd with vengeance, at the midnight hour,

Sudden they seize thine unsuspecting watch,   50
And thine own poinard bury in thy breast.
    At home, the men, in many a sylvan realm,
Their rank tobacco, charm of sauntering minds,
From clayey tubes inhale; or, vacant, beat
For prey the forest; or, in war's dread ranks,   55
Their country's foes affront: while, in the field,
Their wives plant rice, or yams, or lofty maize,
Fell hunger to repel. Be these thy choice:
They, hardy, with the labours of the Cane
Soon grow familiar; while unusual toil,   60
And new severities their husbands kill.
    The slaves from Minnah[7] are of stubborn breed:
But, when the bill, or hammer, they affect;
They soon perfection reach. But fly, with care,
The Moco-nation;[8] they themselves destroy   65
    There are, the muse hath oft abhorrent seen,
Who swallow dirt;[9] (so the chlorotic[10] fair
Oft chalk prefer to the most poignant cates:)
Such, dropsy bloats, and to sure death consigns;
Unless restrain'd from this unwholesome food,   70
By soothing words, by menaces, by blows:
Nor yet will threats, or blows, or soothing words,
Perfect their cure; unless thou, Paean,[11] deign'st
By medicine's power their cravings to subdue.
    To easy labour first inure thy slaves;   75
Extremes are dangerous. With industrious search,
Let them fit grassy provender collect
For thy keen-stomach'd herds. – But when the earth
Hath made her annual progress round the sun,
What time the conch[12] or bell resounds, they may   80
All to the Cane-ground, with thy gang, repair.
    Nor, Negroe, at thy destiny repine,
Tho' doom'd to toil from dawn to setting sun.
How far more pleasant is thy rural task,

Than theirs who sweat, sequester'd from the day,   85
In dark tartarean caves, sunk far beneath
The earth's dark surface; where sulphureous flames,
Oft from their vapoury prisons bursting wild,
To dire explosion give the cavern'd deep,
And in dread ruin all its inmates whelm? –   90
Nor fateful only is the bursting flame;
The exhalations of the deep-dug mine,
Tho' slow, shake from their wings as sure a death.
With what intense severity of pain
Hath the afflicted muse, in Scotia seen   95
The miners rack'd, who toil for fatal lead?[13]
What cramps, what palsies shake their feeble limbs,
Who on the margin of the rocky Drave,[14]
Trace silver's fluent ore? Yet white men these!
    How far more happy ye, than those poor slaves,   100
Who, whilom, under native, gracious, chiefs,
Incas and emperors, long time enjoy'd
Mild government, with every sweet of life,
In blissful climates? See them dragg'd in chains,
By proud insulting tyrants, to the mines   105
Which once they call'd their own, and then despis'd!
See, in the mineral bosom of their land,
How hard they toil! how soon their youthful limbs
Feel the decrepitude of age! how soon
Their teeth desert their sockets! and how soon   110
Shaking paralysis unstrings their frame!
Yet scarce, even then, are they allow'd to view
The glorious God of day, to whom they beg,
With earnest hourly supplications, death;
Yet death slow comes, to torture them the more!   115
    With these compar'd, ye sons of Afric, say,
How far more happy is your lot? Bland health,
Of ardent eye, and limb robust, attends
Your custom'd labour; and, should sickness seize,

With what solicitude are ye not nurs'd! –   120
Ye Negroes, then, your pleasing task pursue;
And, by your toil, deserve your master's care.
    When first your Blacks are novel to the hoe;
Study their humours: Some, soft-soothing words;
Some, presents; and some, menaces subdue;   125
And some I've known, so stubborn is their kind,
Whom blows, alas! could win alone to toil.
    Yet, planter, let humanity prevail. –
Perhaps thy Negroe, in his native land,
Possest large fertile plains, and slaves, and herds: 130
Perhaps, whene'er he deign'd to walk abroad,
The richest silks, from where the Indus rolls,
His limbs invested in their gorgeous pleats:
Perhaps he wails his wife, his children, left
To struggle with adversity: Perhaps   135
Fortune, in battle for his country fought,
Gave him a captive to his deadliest foe:
Perhaps, incautious in his native fields,
(On pleasurable scenes his mind intent)
All as he wandered; from the neighbouring grove,   140
Fell ambush dragg'd him to the hated main. –
Were they even sold for crimes; ye polish'd, say!
Ye, to whom Learning opes her amplest page!
Ye, whom the knowledge of a living God
Should lead to virtue! Are ye free from crimes?   145
Ah pity, then, these uninstructed swains;
And still let mercy soften the decrees
Of rigid justice, with her lenient hand.
    Oh, did the tender muse possess the power,
Which monarchs have, and monarchs oft abuse: 150
'Twould be the fond ambition of her soul,
To quell tyrannic sway; knock off the chains
Of heart-debasing slavery; give to man,
Of every colour, and of every clime,

Freedom, which stamps him image of his God.   155
Then laws, Oppression's scourge, fair Virtue's prop,
Offspring of Wisdom! should impartial reign,
To knit the whole in well-accorded strife:
Servants, not slaves; of choice, and not compell'd;
The Blacks should cultivate the Cane-land isles   160

[A long disquisition on diseases and their treatment follows.]

   Nor pine the Blacks, alone, with real ills,
That baffle oft the wisest rules of art:
They likewise feel imaginary woes;
Woes no less deadly. Luckless he who owns
The slave, who thinks himself bewitch'd; and whom,   165
In wrath, a conjuror's snake-mark'd staff[5] hath struck!
They mope, love silence, every friend avoid;
They inly pine; all aliment reject;
Or insufficient for nutrition take:
Their features droop; a sickly yellowish hue   170
Their skin deforms; their strength and beauty fly.
Then comes the feverish fiend, with firy eyes,
Whom drowth, convulsions, and whom death surround,
Fatal attendants! if some subtle slave
(Such, Obia-men are stil'd) do not engage,   175
To save the wretch by antidote or spell.
   In magic spells, in Obia, all the sons
Of sable Africk trust: – Ye, sacred nine!
(For ye each hidden preparation know)
Transpierce the gloom, which ignorance and fraud   180
Have render'd awful; tell the laughing world
Of what these wonder-working charms are made.
   Fern-root cut small, and tied with many a knot;
Old teeth extracted from a white man's skull;
A lizard's skeleton; a serpent's head;   185
These mix'd with salt, and water from the spring,

Are in a phial pour'd; o'er these the leach
Mutters strange jargon, and wild circles forms.
    Of this possest, each negroe deems himself
Secure from poison; for to poison they   190
Are infamously prone: and arm'd with this,
Their sable country daemons they defy,
Who fearful haunt them at the midnight hour,
To work them mischief. This, diseases fly;
Diseases follow: such its wondrous power!   195
This o'er the threshold of their cottage hung,
No thieves break in; or, if they dare to steal,
Their feet in blotches, which admit no cure,
Burst loathsome out: but should its owner filch,
As slaves were ever of the pilfering kind,   200
This from detection screens; – so conjurors swear.
    'Till morning dawn, and Lucifer withdraw
His beamy chariot; let not the loud bell
Call forth thy negroes from their rushy couch:
And ere the sun with mid-day fervour glow,   205
When every broom-bush opes her yellow flower;
Let thy black labourers from their toil desist:
Nor till the broom her every petal lock,
Let the loud bell recall them to the hoe.
But when the jalap her bright tint displays,   210
When the solanum fills her cup with dew,
And crickets, snakes and lizards 'gin their coil;
Let them find shelter in their cane-thatch'd huts:
Or, if constrain'd unusual hours to toil,
(For even the best must sometimes urge their gang)   215
With double nutriment reward their pains.
    Howe'er insensate some may deem their slaves,
Nor 'bove the bestial rank; far other thoughts
The muse, soft daughter of humanity!
Will ever entertain. – The Ethiop knows,   220
The Ethiop feels, when treated like a man;

Nor grudges, should necessity compell,
By day, by night, to labour for his lord.
  Not less inhuman, than unthrifty those;
Who, half the year's rotation round the sun,   225
Deny subsistence to their labouring slaves.
But would'st thou see thy negroe-train encrease,
Free from disorders; and thine acres clad
With groves of sugar: every week dispense
Or English beans, or Carolinian rice;   230
Iërne's[16] beef, or Pensilvanian flour;
Newfoundland cod, or herrings from the main
That howls tempestuous round the Scotian isles!
  Yet some there are so lazily inclin'd,
And so neglectful of their food, that thou,   235
Would'st thou preserve them from the jaws of death;
Daily, their wholesome viands must prepare:
With these let all the young, and childless old,
And all the morbid share; – so heaven will bless,
With manifold encrease, thy costly care.   240
  Suffice not this; to every slave assign
Some mountain-ground: or, if waste broken land
To thee belong, that broken land divide.
This let them cultivate, one day, each week;
And there raise yams, and there cassada's root: 245
From a good daemon's staff cassada sprang,
Tradition says, and Caribbees believe;
Which into three the white-rob'd genius broke,
And bade them plant, their hunger to repel.
There let angola's bloomy bush supply,   250
For many a year, with wholesome pulse their board.
There let the bonavist, his fringed pods
Throw liberal o'er the prop; while ochra bears
Aloft his slimy pulp, and help disdains.
There let potatos mantle o'er the ground;   255
Sweet as the cane-juice is the root they bear.

There too let eddas spring in order meet,
With Indian cale, and foodful calaloo:
While mint, thyme, balm, and Europe's coyer herbs,
Shoot gladsome forth, nor reprobate the clime.   260
    This tract secure, with hedges or of limes,
Or bushy citrons, or the shapely tree[17]
That glows at once with aromatic blooms,
And golden fruit mature. To these be join'd,
In comely neighbourhood, the cotton shrub;
In this delicious clime the cotton bursts   265
On rocky soils. – The coffee also plant;
White as the skin of Albion's lovely fair,
Are the thick snowy fragrant blooms it boasts:
Nor wilt thou, cocô, thy rich pods refuse;
Tho' years, and heat, and moisture they require,   270
Ere the stone grind them to the food of health . . . .
    But let some antient, faithful slave erect
His sheltered mansion near; and with his dog,
His loaded gun, his cutlass, guard the whole:
Else negro-fugitives, who skulk 'mid rocks   275
And shrubby wilds, in bands will soon destroy
Thy labourer's honest wealth; their loss and yours . . . .
    On festal days; or when their work is done;
Permit thy slaves to lead the choral dance,
To the wild banshaw's[18] melancholy sound.   280
Responsive to the sound, head, feet and frame
Move aukwardly harmonious; hand in hand
Now lock'd, the gay troop circularly wheels,
And frisks and capers with intemperate joy.
Halts the vast circle, all clap hands and sing;   285
While those distinguish'd for their heels and air,
Bound in the center, and fantastic twine.
Meanwhile some stripling, from the choral ring,
Trips forth; and, not ungallantly, bestows
On her who nimblest hath the greensward beat,   290

And whose flush'd beauties have inthrall'd his soul,
A silver token of his fond applause.
Anon they form in ranks; nor inexpert
A thousand tuneful intricacies weave,
Shaking their sable limbs; and oft a kiss   295
Steal from their partners; who, with neck reclin'd,
And semblant scorn, resent the ravish'd bliss.
But let not thou the drum their mirth inspire;
Nor vinous spirits: else, to madness fir'd,
(What will not bacchanalian frenzy dare?)   300
Fell acts of blood, and vengeance they pursue.

Notes

1. James Grainger, *The Sugar-Cane: A Poem in Four Books, With Notes* (London: R. and J. Dodsley, 1764).
2. John Gilmore, *The Poetics of Empire: A Study of James Grainger's* The Sugar-Cane (London: Athlone Press, 2000), 1. See also Sypher, *Guinea's Captive Kings*, 168–75; Kamau Brathwaite, *Roots* (Ann Arbor: University of Michigan Press, 1993), 137–42; Keith A. Sandiford, *The Cultural Politics of Sugar* (Cambridge: Cambridge University Press, 2000), 67–87.
3. Gilmore, *Poetics of Empire*, 248n.
4. Compare Bryan Edwards, *History, Civil and Commercial, of the British West Indies* (London: John Stockdale, 1793), book 4, 87: "the people of Whidah, or Fida . . . are called generally in the West Indies *Papaws*, and are unquestionably the most docile and best-disposed Slaves that are imported from any part of Africa". Whidah, or Whydah, was the slave-trading port Ouidah, in modern Benin.
5. That is, from modern Ghana to Cameroon.
6. The ferocity and independence of the "Cormantees" (elsewhere variously spelt Coromantee, Koromantyn, etc.), from modern Ghana, were legendary. Compare Edwards, *History*, book 4, ch. 3, page 316 below.
7. Probably Elmina, one of the principal slaving ports on the Gold Coast.

8. Unidentified. Edwards associates them with the "Eboes" and says they were "accustomed to the shocking practice of feeding on human flesh"; *History, Civil and Commercial*, book 4, 88.

9. The baffling problem of dirt-eating, also known as *mal d'estomac* or pica, was recognized, in some cases at least, as an extreme form of slave resistance; see B.W. Higman, *Slave Populations of the British Caribbean, 1807–1834* (Baltimore: Johns Hopkins University Press, 1984), 294–98. John Williamson, in *Medical and Miscellaneous Observations, Relative to the West Indies* (Edinburgh: n.p., 1817), 2:264, commented that slaves who were "ill-disposed to the master's will" would sometimes deliberately "resort to dirt-eating, and thus produce disease, and at length death".

10. *chlorotic*: suffering from "the green sickness", probably a form of anaemia.

11. Poetic name for a doctor, from the Homeric name for Apollo in his role as physician of the gods.

12. [Author's note:] Plantations that have no bells, assemble their Negroes by sounding a conch shell.

13. Scottish coal miners not only worked under deplorable conditions throughout the eighteenth century but were also bound in a state of serfdom little short of chattel slavery.

14. [Author's note:] A river in Hungary, on whose banks are found mines of quicksilver.

15. [Author's note:] The negroe-conjurors, or Obia-men, as they are called, carry about them a staff, which is marked with frogs, snakes, &c. The blacks imagine that its blow, if not mortal, will at least occasion long and troublesome disorders. A belief in magic is inseparable from human nature, but those nations are most addicted thereto, among whom learning, and of course, philosophy have least obtained. As in all other countries, so in Guinea, the conjurors, as they have more understanding, so are they almost always more wicked than the common herd of their deluded countrymen; and as the negroe-magicians can do mischief, so they can also do good on a plantation, provided they are kept by the white people in proper subordination.

16. *Iërne*: Ireland

17. [Author's note:] The orange tree.

18. [Author's note:] This is a sort of rude guitar, invented by the Negroes. It produces a wild pleasing melancholy sound.

EDWARD THOMPSON (1739–86)

Sailor's Letters (1766)[1]

Thompson's lively letters date from his service on the West Indies station and elsewhere as a very young naval officer. He returned in 1779–81 in command of the frigate *Hyaena*, and his further West Indian experiences and observations are reflected in his *Nauticks; or, Sailor's Verses* (1783). Although shocked by the harsh conditions and cruel punishments suffered by the slaves, he does not condemn the slave system as such in his letters, but his outspoken criticism of the white creoles, especially the women, made him a principal target in James M. Adair's rambling "Defence of the Proprietors of the British Sugar Colonies, against Certain Malignant Charges", in his *Unanswerable Arguments against the Abolition of the Slave Trade* (1790). Adair, a Scottish physician and judge in Antigua for many years, was incensed not only by Thompson's comments on creole society generally but also, more justifiably, by his frequent jibes against Scotsmen.

Letter XXIII

Antigua, September 22, 1756.

. . . All the good living is amongst the planters in the country, where, if you are a Scotsman, you may be well entertained. The planter struts a petty king amidst his slaves, and has his black seraglio: – in general, they are haughty, ignorant, and cruel, which arises from that despotick government over their poor slaves, who are whipped, and drove by the lash, like cattle. The greatest part of the estates on the island are conducted by overseers, the most of which are Scotsmen; who perhaps have been transported to Virginia, and from thence escaped to rule here . . . .

Letter XXIV

English Harbour in the island of Antigua,

October 21, 1756.

. . . We have a general visit every Sunday from the negros of the different parts of the island, who hold, in all other places as well as here, their markets on the Sabbath, – being the only day of relaxation they are indulged with by the tyrants they are slaves to: the disagreeable smell of their bodies is so great, that I have smelt, when the wind set from that quarter, a negro market a mile or more. But bad smells don't hurt the sailor's appetite, each man possessing a temporary lady, whose pride is her constancy to the man she chooses, and in this particular they are strictly so. I have known 350 women sup and sleep on board on a Sunday evening, and return at day break to their different plantations. I don't know what to compare this charcoal seraglio to: in numbers we beat the Turk; – in constancy the world; –but, in beauty, we submit to the fair Circassians.[2] These poor slaves bring with them fruit, vegetables and milk, which they exchange for bread and beef. The planters generally allow them a small barren spot of ground, which as soon as they have well tilled, they take to themselves, and give them another: they live in wretched thatched hovels, and after their daily labour, sleep on a board: their fires are in the middle of their huts, which have no chimneys, the smoak creating warmth, and also keeps out the musquitos: – their dress, in general, is no more than a cloath round the middle, – unless the mistresses of great Dons, who wear silks and calicoes . . . .

Letter XXV

Barbadoes, December 5, 1756.

. . . The inhabitants are more easy, hospitable and kind, than on the other islands; – but yet have that volatile spirit so peculiar to the *Creole*. The cruel tyranny exercised over the slaves, is shocking to humanity: – a most horrid instance of which, was acted here the other day by a mistress to her female slave: the girl had committed some trivial domestick error; upon which, she commanded four of her servants to hold her down to the ground, while she absolutely exulted in smiles, and dropped hot sealing wax on the different parts of the back, till the poor creature expired in the most excruciating tortures. – Was you accustomed to live with the planter's ladies, you would not be surprised at any cruelty, for they are taught in their very infancy, to flog with a whip the slave that offends them. The negros, in general, come from the coast of Guinea, which makes their manners and superstitions alike, – altho' I never knew they had the least idea of any worship, till I was acquainted by Doctor Hill of this place, who told me he had many African negros brought him in the hypocondriack state, which neither medicine nor advice could palliate, and that he had no other recourse in such cases, but in sending for a negro priest, who would persuade the patient, after having exercised a number of legerdemain tricks, that he had extracted toads, serpents and birds from his body, – which being concealed about him, he produces them at pleasure; – after such an operation, you'll see the superstitious wretch revive, and in a few days, return in spirits to his labour. They very often, in their thefts, meet with a string of rags hung out to frighten the birds from fresh-sown seed; – this they call their god *Obia*,[3] who, they believe, has detected them, – and is very often a means of their confessing the crime they have committed, or becoming splenetic; imagining that all their food is poison, which operates so strongly on their weak minds, as even to kill them in a few months. In all climates, and in all ages, ignorance and superstition have gone hand in hand, and wherever they have predominantly prevailed, they have effectually ruined the people . . . .

Letter XXVIII

St. Kitts, June 13, 1757

Altho' we sail this day with 170 sail of ships for England, yet I nevertheless write to you, imagining they may delay our passage. In nine months cruising, our success has only been three prizes, for which I've received about three pounds: – thus, enriched and honoured, we leave these islands, and yet, before we absolutely depart, I must give you a general character of these people. The *Creoles* are a volatile, haughty, ignorant people; fond of dress, pomp and pageantry, and slaves to all the *Cardinal Vices* . . . The women, in general, unhappily cherish a low pride; few are acquainted with good breeding, and more unacquainted with modesty. – Swearing in a vulgar corrupted dialect at their slaves in general; . . . and ogling and intriguing no where more common: – which in a great measure may be attributed to the men, who carry on amours with their ladie's slaves, and the less private, the more *degagé* and genteel.[4] I cannot forbear sending you a few lines written here, in answer to Mr Ulton's verses in praise of these people.[5]

THE CREOLE

To see a tyrant in an abject state,
Too mean to live, aspiring to be great.
Does it not shock the truly nobler mind,
To see such monsters mingl'd with mankind!
Thus have I seen a wood of spreading trees,   5
Strip'd of their foliage by th'autumnal breeze,
Their leaves by various winds puff'd ev'ry way,
And mixt promiscuous, wither and decay.

    There turn, my MUSE, and view that sunny hill,
Where whisp'ring zephyrs turn a little mill!   10
There view the sons of Africk's golden shore,
Drove by the lash, and working in their gore:
There view the *Creole* ruling with a nod,

The man forgetting, struts a *Demi-god!*
Forbear ye western sons, nor thus despise   15
The slave you make, whom Heaven made as wise!
"God with an equal eye beholds us all,
The planter perish, or the negro fall!"[6]
Had Heaven bestow'd you an imperial ray,
Would Heaven have hid it in plebeian clay?   20
O wretched pride! spun through life's wretched span;
Is not the slave, tho' black, a Heaven form'd man?
Do not the breezes, which refresh proud you,
Visit the hut, and fan the negro too?
Does nature, *Creole*, own thy empty sway,   25
Will not the ass before a CÆSAR bray?
O cease, vain reptile, give the black his due,
"The world was made for Scots and NEGROES too!"[7]
Are they not forc'd in chains from Gambia's shore
By you to taste of LIBERTY no more?   30
But should we ask, How came *MacDuggle* here?
Mute rests the tongue, and thunder-struck's the ear:
Obnoxious to the law for some damn'd crime,
He flies from England to some savage clime.
With an impartial eye survey the two,   35
The captive negro's just, – but what are you?
Shame, like a whirlwind, swallow up your pride,
Or Heaven, from better men, – your clan divide.
But how could ULTON prostitute his muse,
To praise an isle, unworthy his abuse!   40
To praise a frothy, wretched race, earth's scum,
And seat an Angel with an Absolom!
I love the poet, but the theme in rhime,
Is much beneath the Prior of the time.

    We are happily setting sail from this land, – to one flowing with milk and honey.

                        I am, &c.

Notes

1. Edward Thompson, *Sailor's Letters. Written to Select Friends in England, During his Voyages and Travels in Europe, Asia, Africa, and America. From the year 1754 to 1759* (London: T. Becket, P.A. De Hondt, W. Flexney, and J. Moran, 1766).

2. Thompson's judgement in favour of the "fair" Circassians was purely aesthetic. In an erotic lyric by Thompson, titled "The Nigro Naiad" and dated St Kitts, 1781, a black girl is preferred to "Fanny blooming fair" as an object of sexual desire, specifically because of her "swart" beauty (*Nauticks: or Sailor's Verses*, n.pl., 1783).

3. The terms *obia* and *obi* were often misunderstood by Europeans as referring to a god.

4. James Adair responds to Thompson's reference to concubinage in his criticism of Luffman (see page 143n3), in *Unanswerable Arguments against the Abolition of the Slave Trade* (London: J.P. Bateman, 1790).

5. Adair, *Unanswerable Arguments,* says the author (whom he knew) was named Hulton, but I have not traced either the writer or the poem to which Thompson refers. The quotations in the text are presumably taken from it.

6. Quotation adapted from Pope, *Essay on Man*, 1.86–88: "Heav'n; / Who sees with equal eye, as God of all, / A hero perish, or a sparrow fall."

7. Ibid., 4.145–46: "This world 'tis true, / Was made for Caeser, but for Titus too".

JOHN SINGLETON (FL. 1767–77)

A General Description of the West-Indian Islands (1767)[1]

Singleton was a member of Lewis Hallam's English acting company, which performed in Jamaica in 1755–58 and toured Jamaica and the eastern Caribbean in the 1760s.[2] He writes in book 4 of having spent "a series of indulgent years" in Barbados and of enjoying the hospitality of plantation owners on various islands. In book 2 he declares his indebtedness as a poet to Grainger's *Sugar-Cane*, and the poem "mingles a Graingeresque approbation of West- Indian life with shallow pity for the slave".[3] Singleton's abhorrence of the slave trade is unqualified but the poem otherwise is riddled with self-contradictions. It oscillates between praise for the innate nobility of the African slaves, condemnation of their "savage" and "perverse" dispositions, and compassion for the "torments" they endure at the hands of cruel masters. Singleton's rhetoric seems to be underpinned neither by pro- nor anti-slavery sentiment as such, but rather by an almost pathological aversion to "the negro race" itself and to the idea of any physical contact between whites and blacks; even mulattos are to be avoided because of the "odious source" of their colour (book 4, lines 552–59). In a later version of the poem, *A Description of the West-Indies* (1776), the text was abbreviated by severe pruning of its long descriptions and by removal of passages which might have caused offence to white West Indians resident in England.

Book III (lines 495–577)

Description of the burial of a slave in the Virgin Islands

[The preceding lines describe the passionate grief displayed at
European funerals after a hurricane killed a number of white
inhabitants.]

Ah me! how diff'rently th' untutor'd slave,
To no philosophy indebted, views
The obsequies of his departed friend,
And with his calm deportment puts to shame
The boasted reason of the polish'd world: 5
A moment dries his manly eye, untaught
To melt at death, the necessary end
Of all terrestrial things. His creed (the voice
Of nature) keeps him firm, nay, gives him joy,
When he considers (so the sages teach   10
Of Afric's sun-burnt realms) that the freed soul
Soon as it leaves its mortal coil behind,
Transported to some distant world, is wrapt
In bliss eternal. There the man begins,
With organs more refin'd, to live again,   15
And taste such sweets as were deny'd him here,
The sweets of liberty: Oh glorious name!
Oh pow'rful soother of the suff'ring heart!
That with thy spark divine can'st animate
Unletter'd slaves to stretch their simple thoughts   20
In search of thee, beyond this gloomy vale
Of painful life, where all their piteous hours
Drag heavily along in constant toil,
In stripes, in tears, in hunger, or in chains:
These are the ills which they rejoice to fly;   25
Unless, by partial chance, their lot is cast
Beneath some kind indulgent master's sway,

Whose hand, like their good genius, feeds their wants,
And with protection shields their hapless state.
    But see what strange procession hither winds,   30
With long-continued stream, through yonder wood!
Like gentle waves hundreds of sable heads
Float onwards, still they move, and still they seem
With unexhausted flow to keep their course.
    In calm succession thus th' unruffled main   35
Rolls on its peaceful waters to the shore,
With easy swell, wave gliding over wave,
Till the spectator can no longer count
Their breaks incessant, but the numbers past
Are in succeeding numbers quickly lost.   40
Behold the white-rob'd train in form advance
To yonder new-made grave: Six ugly hags,
Their visage seam'd with honorary scars,
In wild contorsive postures lead the van;
High o'er their palsied heads, rattling, they wave   45
Their noisy instruments; whilst to the sound
In dance progressive their shrunk shanks keep time.
With more composure the succeeding ranks,
Chanting their fun'ral song in chorus full,
Precede the mournful bier, by friendly hands   50
Supported: Sudden stops the flowing line;
The puzzled bearers of the restive corps
Stand for a while, fast rooted to the ground,
Depriv'd of motion, or, perhaps, impell'd
This-way, or that, unable to proceed   55
In course direct, until the troubled dead
Has to some friend imparted his request;
That gratify'd, again the fun'ral moves:
When at the grave arriv'd the solemn rites
Begin; the slave's cold reliques gently laid   60
Within their earthy bed, some veteran
Among the sable Archimages,[4] pours

Her mercenary panegyric forth,
In all the jargon of mysterious speech,
And, to compose the spirit of the dead,   65
Sprinkles his favourite liquor on the grave.
This done, the mourners form a spacious ring,
When sudden clangours, blended with shrill notes,
Pour'd forth from many a percing pipe, surprize
The deafen'd ear   70
Thus do these sooty children of the sun,
"Unused to the melting mood," perform
Their fun'ral obsequies, and joyous chaunt,
In concert full, the requiem of the dead;
Wheeling in many a mazy round, they fill   75
The jocund dance, and take a last farewell
Of their departed friend, without a tear.

Book IV (lines 393–439)[5]

Advice most humbly offer'd to the consideration of the inhabitants
[of Barbados]

                    Know then, ye fair,
Among your plagues I count the negro race,
Savage by nature. Art essays in vain   80
To mend their tempers, or to tune their souls
In unison with ours: No doctrines touch
Their callous senses; no instruction wakes
Their drowsy faculties, nor bends their will,
Perverse and obstinate, to reason's lure.   85
Cruel and fierce, no admonitions tame
The brutal disposition of their souls;
Nor can "philosophy's sweet milk" e'er quench
The flame that ever and anon springs up
To curse their beings, and to torture ours.   90

Then take, ye fair, the counsels of the muse,
Since for your peace, your happiness she sings.
If in the hymeneal state ye live,
And to your loves a happy offspring rise,
Should Nature to the mother's tender breast   95
The flowing streams of nutriment refuse,
Or sickness lessen her maternal care,
O! rather use all art the babes to rear,
Than e'er condemn them to the sable pap's
Infectious juice! for, with the milky draught,   100
The num'rous vices of the fost'ring slave
Deep they imbibe, and, with their life's support,
Draw in the latent principles of ill;
Which, brooking no controul, in riper years,
Grow with their growth, and strengthen with their strength.   105
Nor, when the babes to prattling years arrive,
Let fondling parents, or relations dear,
Teach the apt tongue an horrid oath to lisp,
Or phrase obscene; nor frame the ductile lips
Of innocence to utterance vile and base.   110
Taint not the minds with cruelty and rage,
Nor wantonly indulge a savage joy
To practice torments on the hapless slave;
Such dispositions ill become your sex,
Which but disgrace the rougher character   115
Of boist'rous man, the lord of all below,
Of man, whom your soft charms in bondage hold.
Exert your empire then, when rage hath rais'd
A storm which only beauty can allay;
Oh! then let meek compassion strongly plead   120
In the moist eye, then drop the melting tear,
And let a look, soft as the new-born babe's,
Disarm th' impending hand, and save the wretch,
Crouching beneath the vengeance of his lord.

Notes

1. John Singleton, *A General Description of the West-Indian Islands, . . . from Barbados to Saint Croix. Attempted in Blank Verse* (Barbados: n.p., 1767).
2. Richardson Wright, *Revels in Jamaica 1682–1838* (New York: Dodd, Mead and Co., 1937), 38–40; Errol Hill, *The Jamaican Stage 1655–1900: Profile of a Colonial Theatre* (Amherst: University of Massachusetts Press, 1992), 76–77; Krise, *Caribbeana,* 261.
3. Sypher, *Guinea's Captive Kings,* 173.
4. [Author's note:] I.e. chief magicians among the Obeah negroes. – *This word is often used by Spencer.* [Archimage is the name of the powerful enchanter in books 1 and 2 of Spenser's *Faerie Queene.*]
5. The whole of this section (lines 389–652) was omitted from the London edition.

EDWARD LONG (1734–1813)

The History of Jamaica (1774)[1]

Edward Long was descended from four generations of Jamaican landowners. He was educated in England but went out to Jamaica in 1757 to take over a prosperous estate in Clarendon parish inherited from his father. He married the daughter of another plantation owner and was a member of the Jamaican Assembly from 1761 until ill-health forced him to leave in 1769. In England he campaigned vigorously through articles and pamphlets on behalf of the pro-slavery Committee of West India Merchants and Planters, but his most influential work was *The History of Jamaica*, "an invaluable vademecum to the social, economic, and political life" of the colony, combining "encyclopaedic detail with polemics and propaganda".[2] In spite of his political bias and his dogmatic insistence on the moral and intellectual inferiority of African slaves, his close observation of their behaviour, customs and beliefs makes the long chapter abridged below an important source of information.

Of the Creole Slaves and African Negroes in Jamaica

The *general* character of our Creole slaves may be summed up in the words of an old proverb, "Like master, like man." They are capable of being made diligent, and moderately faithful; or the reverse, just as their dispositions happen to be worked upon. It cannot be doubted, but the far greater part of them are more inclined to a life of idleness and ease, than a life of labour: yet the regular discipline to which they are inured from their infancy, becomes habitual and natural to them, as it does to soldiers, sailors, and school-boys; and, like the latter, their principal address is shewn in finding out their master's temper, and playing upon it so artfully as to bend it with most convenience to their own purposes. They are not less studious in sifting their master's representative, the overseer; if he is not too cunning for them, which they soon discover after one or two experiments, they will easily find means to over-reach him on every occasion, and make his indolence, his weakness, or sottishness, a sure prognostic of some comfortable term of idleness to them: but, if they find him too intelligent, wary, and active, they leave no expedient untried, by thwarting his plans, misunderstanding his orders, and reiterating complaints against him, to ferret him out of his post: if this will not succeed, they perplex and worry him, especially if he is of an impatient, fretful turn, till he grows heartily sick of his charge, and voluntarily resigns it. An overseer therefore, like a premier minister, must always expect to meet with a faction, ready to oppose his administration, right or wrong; unless he will give the reins out of his hands, and suffer the mobility to have things their own way; which if he complies with, they will extol him to his face, contemn him in their hearts, and very soon bring his government into disgrace. But such a man, if he is gifted with good-nature and humanity, will easily get the better in every struggle; for these are qualities which the Negroes prize in their superiors above all others . . . . I shall not attempt to give a complete description of all the customs and manners of our Creole Negroes, since many of them are not worth recording; and, in consequence of their frequent intermixture with the native Africans, they differ but little in many articles.

In their tempers they are in general irascible, conceited, proud, indolent, lascivious, credulous, and very artful. They are excellent dissemblers, and skilful flatterers. They possess good-nature, and sometimes, but rarely, gratitude. Their memory soon loses the traces of favours conferred on them, but faithfully retains a sense of injuries; this sense is so poignant, that they have been known to dissemble their hatred for many years, until an opportunity has presented of retaliating; and, in taking revenge, they shew a treachery, cowardice, and deliberate malice, that almost exceed credibility. A stupid insensibility of danger often gives them the specious appearance of dauntless intrepidity; though, when once thoroughly made sensible of it, none are more arrant cowards. A blind anger, and brutal rage, with them stand frequently in place of manly valour. The impressions of fear, naturally accompanied with cunning and wariness, make them always averse to any other mode of engaging with an enemy, than by ambuscades, and surprize . . . .

They are in general excellent marksmen at a standing shot, their eye quick, and sight so clear, that they seldom miss; yet their vision (as I have before remarked) is the worst possible for the regular position of any thing. They cannot place a dining-table square in a room; I have known them fail in this, after numberless endeavours; and it is the same in other things. So that such as are bred carpenters and bricklayers, are often unable, after many tedious and repeated trials with the rule and plumb-line, to do a piece of work straight, which an apprentice-boy in England would perform with one glance of his eye in a moment. It is somewhat unaccountable, too, that they always mount a horse on the off-side. Their ideas seem confined to a very few objects; namely, the common occurrences of life, food, love, and dress: these are frequent themes for their dance, conversation, and musical composition.

The African, or imported Negroes, are almost all of them, both men and women, addicted to the most bestial vices, from which it is the more difficult to reclaim them, as they are grown inveterately confirmed from their very infancy. In Guiney they are taught to regard a dram, as one of the chief comforts of life; they grow up in this opinion: and I have seen some of them forcing the precious liquor down the throats of their children, or *pickaninnies*, with the same eagerness that indulgent mothers shew, when they cram their little favourite with sugar-plumbs. In thieving they are thorough adepts, and perfectly accomplished. To set eyes on any thing, and endeavour to possess it, is with them intirely the same. From this cause it happens, that, upon their being brought into the plantations, they are soon engaged in quarrels, which sometimes are attended with fatal consequences; for, when they are prompted to revenge, they pursue it against one another with so much malevolence and cruelty, that the punishment exacted is generally beyond all proportion greater than the offence can possibly merit . . . .

The Creole Blacks differ much from the Africans, not only in manners, but in beauty of shape, feature, and complexion. They hold the Africans in the utmost contempt, stiling them, "salt-water negroes," and "Guiney birds;" but value themselves on their own pedigree, which is reckoned the more honourable, the further it removes from an African, or transmarine ancestor. On every well-governed plantation they eye and respect their master as a father, and are extremely vain in reflecting on the connexion between them. Their master's character and repute casts, they think, a kind of secondary light upon themselves, as the moon derives her lustre from the sun; and the importance he acquires, in his station of life, adds, they imagine, to their own estimation among their neighbour Negroes on the adjacent estates. Their attachment to the descendants of old families, the ancestors of which were the masters and friends of their own progenitors, is remarkably strong and affectionate. This veneration appears hereditary, like clanships in the Scotch Highlands; it is imbibed in their infancy, or founded perhaps in the idea of the relation which subsisted between, and connected them in, the bond of fatherly love and authority on the one side, and a filial reverence and obedience on the other; nor is this effect, however it arises, unmixed with somewhat of gratitude, for the favours and indulgencies conferred on their predecessors; some fruits of which they themselves have probably enjoyed by devise; for, even among these slaves, as they are called, the black grandfather, or father, directs in what manner his money, his hogs, his poultry, furniture, cloaths, and other effects and acquisitions, shall descend, or be disposed of, after his decease. He nominates a sort of trustees, or executors, from the nearest of kin, who distribute them among the legatees, according to the will of the testator, without any molestation or interruption, most often without the enquiry, of their master; though some of these Negroes have been known to possess from 5ol. to 200l. at their death; and few among them, that are at all industrious and frugal, lay up less than 20 or 30l. For in this island they have the greatest part of the small silver circulating among them, which they gain by sale of their hogs, poultry, fish, corn, fruits, and other commodities, at the markets in town and country.

They in general love their children, though sometimes they treat them with a rigour bordering upon cruelty. They seem also to feel a patriotic affection for the island which has given them birth; they rejoice at its prosperity, lament its losses, and interest themselves in the affairs and politics that are the talk of the day. Whoever has studied their disposition and sentiments attentively, will be of opinion, that, with mild and humane usage, they are more likely to become the defenders than the destroyers of their country. As a large share of vanity and pride may be observeable among them, so the better sort appear sensible to shame. I have known a very considerable number of them on a plantation kept in due decorum for several years, with no other discipline than keen and well-timed rebukes; and my observations have tended to confirm me in opinion, that our Creole Blacks (for I speak of them only) may, with a very moderate instruction in the Christian rules, be kept in good order, without the whip. Rash correction has often rendered them stubborn, negligent, and perverse, when they might have been influenced chearfully to perform every thing required of them, by judiciously working on their vanity; by bestowing seasonable rewards and encomiums on their praise-worthy conduct, and by stinging reproaches for their misdemeanors. There are many artifices to be practised with the greatest success; such as, degrading for a while from some employment esteemed among them a post of distinction, and authority; holding them up to the ridicule of their fellow Blacks, and the like. What they endure, upon these occasions, has nothing in it of that sense of vile abasement, which corporal inflictions are apt to produce; and whenever corporal punishment is carried to extreme, it is sure to excite a hearty and indelible contempt and abhorrence for the inflictor . . . .

The superstition of these Blacks is carried to very singular lengths, although the more polished among them believe in a future state of reward and punishment; . . . They firmly believe in the apparition of spectres. Those of deceased friends are *duppies*; others, of more hostile and tremendous aspect, like our raw-head-and-bloody-bones, are called *bugaboos*. The most sensible among them fear the supernatural powers of the African *obeah-men*, or pretended conjurors; often ascribing those mortal effects to magic, which are only the natural operation of some poisonous juice, or preparation, dexterously administered by these villains. But the Creoles imagine, that the virtues of baptism, or making them Christians, render their art wholly ineffectual; and, for this reason only, many of them have desired to be baptized, that they might be secured from *Obeah*.

Not long since, some of these execrable wretches in Jamaica introduced what they call the *myal dance*, and established a kind of society, into which they invited all they could. The lure hung out was, that every Negroe, initiated into the myal society, would be invulnerable by the white men; and, although they might in appearance be slain, the obeah-man could, at his pleasure, restore the body to life. The method, by which this trick was carried on, was by a cold infusion of the herb *branched colalue;*[3] which, after the agitation of dancing, threw the party into a profound sleep. In this state he continued, to all appearance lifeless, no pulse, nor motion of the heart, being perceptible; till, on being rubbed with another infusion (as yet unknown to the Whites), the effects of the colalue gradually went off, the body resumed its motions, and the party, on whom the experiment had been tried, awoke as from a trance, entirely ignorant of any thing that had passed since he left off dancing. Not long ago, one of these myal men, being desirous of seducing a friend of his to be of their party, gave him a wonderful account of the powerful effects produced by the myal infusion, and particularly that it rendered the body impenetrable to bullets; so that the Whites would be perfectly unable to make the least impression upon them, although they were to shoot at them a thousand times. His friend listened with great attention, but seemed to doubt the truth of it exceedingly; but, at length, proposed to the other, that, if he was willing to stand a shot, he should be glad to make the experiment; and, if it turned out as he pretended, he himself would then most readily consent to be a myal man. To this the other agreed, not imagining, perhaps, that matters would come to extremity; or else convinced in his own mind of the reality of what he asserted. Having prepared himself, he stood up to receive the shot. His friend fired, and killed him dead. This accident, with the circumstances leading to it, were soon made known; and, for some time, brought the priests and their art into great disrepute among all their converts . . . .

The Negroes wear the teeth of wild cats, and eat their flesh, as a charm for long life; for they hold the vulgar opinion, that a cat has nine lives. Thus, by assimilation of the cat's flesh and juices into their own, they imagine they can ensure longevity, and a power of sustaining great fatigues. Many a poor grimalkin has fallen a victim to this strange notion. Bits of red rag, cats teeth, parrots feathers, egg-shells, and fish-bones, are frequently stuck up at the doors of their houses when they go from home leaving any thing of value within (sometimes they hang them on fruit-trees, and place them in corn-fields), to deter thieves. Upon conversing with some of the Creoles upon this custom, they laughed at the supposed virtue of the charm, and said they practised it only to frighten away the salt-water Negroes, of whose depredations they are most apprehensive. Their funerals are the very reverse of our English ceremony. The only real mourners are the husband, wife, or very near relations of the deceased; yet even these sometimes unite their voices to the general clamour or song, whilst the tears flow involuntarily down their cheeks. Every funeral is a kind of festival; at which the greater part of the company assume an air of joy and unconcern; and, together with their singing, dancing, and musical instruments, conspire to drown all sense of affliction in the minds of the real mourners. The burthen of this merry dirge is filled with encomiums on the deceased, with hopes and wishes for his happiness in his new state. Sometimes the coffin-bearers, especially if they carry it upon their heads, pretend that the corpse will not proceed to the grave, notwithstanding the exertion of their utmost strength to urge it forwards. They then move to different huts, till they come to one, the owner of which, they know, has done some injury to, or been much disliked by, the deceased in his life-time. Here they express some words of indignation on behalf of the dead man; then knock at the coffin, and try to sooth and pacify the corpse: at length, after much persuasion, it begins to grow more passive, and suffers them to carry it on, without further struggle, to the place of repose. At other times, the corpse takes a sudden and obstinate aversion to be supported on the head, preferring the arms; nor does it peaceably give up the dispute, until the bearers think proper to comply with its humour. The corpse being interred, the grave is but slightly overspread with earth. Some scratch up the loose mould, with their backs turned to the grave, and cast it behind them between their legs, after the manner of cats which have just exonerated. This, they say, is done, to prevent the deceased person from following them home. When the deceased is a married woman, the husband lets his beard remain unshaved, and appears rather negligent in his attire, for the space of a month; at the expiration of which, a fowl is dressed at his house, with some messes of good broth, and he proceeds, accompanied by his friends, to the grave. Then begins a song, purporting, that the deceased is now in the enjoyment of compleat felicity; and that they are assembled to rejoice at her state of bliss, and perform the last offices of duty and friendship. They then lay a considerable heap of earth over the grave, which is called *covering it*; and the meeting concludes with eating their collation, drinking, dancing, and vociferation. After this ceremony is over, the widow, or widower, is at liberty to take another spouse immediately; and the term of mourning is at an end . . . .

They have good ears for music; and their songs, as they call them, are generally *impromptus*, without the least particle of poetry, or poetic images, of which they seem to have no idea. The tunes consist of a *solo* part, which we may style the recitative, the key of which is frequently varied; and this is accompanied with a full or general chorus. Some of them are not deficient in melody; although the tone of voice is, for the most part, rather flat and melancholy. Instead of choosing panegyric for their subject-matter, they generally prefer one of derision, and not unfrequently at the expence of the overseer, if he happens to be near, and listening: this only serves to add a poignancy to their satire, and heightens the fun. In the crop season, the mill-feeders entertain themselves very often with these *jeux d'esprit* in the night-time; and this merriment helps to keep them awake.

Their *merry-wang* is a favourite instrument, a rustic guitar, of four strings. It is made with a calibash; a slice of which being taken off, a dried bladder, or skin, is spread across the largest section; and this is fastened to a handle, which they take great pains in ornamenting with a sort of rude carved work, and ribbands.

The *goombah*, another of their musical instruments, is a hollow block of wood, covered with sheep-skin stripped of its hair. The musician holds a little stick, of about six inches in length, sharpened at one end like the blade of a knife, in each hand. With one hand he rakes it over a notched piece of wood, fixed across the instrument, the whole length, and crosses with the other alternately, using both with a brisk motion; whilst a second performer beats with all his might on the sheep-skin, or tabor.

Their tunes for dancing are usually brisk, and have an agreeable compound of the *vivace* and *larghetto*, gay and grave, pursued alternately. They seem also well-adapted to keep their dancers in just time and regular movements. The female dancer is all languishing, and easy in her motions; the man, all action, fire, and gesture; his whole person is variously turned and writhed every moment, and his limbs agitated with such lively exertions, as serve to display before his partner the vigour and elasticity of his muscles. The lady keeps her face towards him, and puts on a modest demure look, which she counterfeits with great difficulty. In her paces she exhibits a wonderful address, particularly in the motion of her hips, and steady position of the upper part of her person: the right execution of this wriggle, keeping exact time with the music, is esteemed among them a particular excellence; and on this account they begin to practise it so early in life, that few are without it in their ordinary walking. As the dance proceeds, the musician introduces now and then a pause or rest, or dwells on two or three *pianissimo* notes; then strikes out again on a sudden into a more spirited air; the dancers, in the mean while, corresponding in their movements with great correctness of ear, and propriety of attitude; all which has a very pleasing effect.

In the towns, during Christmas holidays, they have several tall robust fellows dressed up in grotesque habits, and a pair of ox-horns on their head, sprouting from the top of a horrid sort of visor, or mask, which about the mouth is rendered very terrific with large boar-tusks. The masquerader, carrying a wooden sword in his hand, is followed with a numerous croud of drunken women, who refresh him frequently with a sup of aniseed-water, whilst he dances at every door, bellowing *John Connú!* with great vehemence; so that, what with the liquor and the exercise, most of them are thrown into dangerous fevers; and some examples have happened of their dying. This dance is probably an honourable memorial of John Conny, a celebrated cabocero[4] at *Tres Puntas*, in *Axim*, on the Guiney coast; who flourished about the year 1720. He bore great authority among the Negros of that district. When the Prussians deserted Fort Brandenburgh, they left it to his charge; and he gallantly held it for a long time against the Dutch, to whom it was afterwards ceded by the Prussian monarch.

Notes

1. Edward Long, *History of Jamaica,* 3 vols. (London: T. Lowndes, 1774), 2:404–25.
2. K. Morgan, *Oxford Dictionary of National Biography* (Oxford: Oxford University Press, 2004).
3. [Author's note:] This herb is a species of *solanum,* . . . very common in the lowlands of Jamaica . . . . In regard to the other infusion, which puts an end to its operation, we can only conjecture . . .
4. *cabocero*: caboceer, the headman of a West African village or tribe (*Oxford English Dictionary*). For the history of these famous masquerades see Olive Senior, *Encyclopedia of Jamaican Heritage* (Kingston: Twin Guinep Publishers, 2003), s.v. "Jonkonnu".

JAMAICA: A POEM (1777)[1]

Nothing is known about the author of these poems apart from a few self-references in the preface and text. He states that *Jamaica: A Poem* was written at the age of eighteen. He had gone out to Jamaica "at a very early period" in his life, ambitious to make his fortune as a planter, but he was repelled by his discovery of the working of the slave system. Though "captivated by the beauty of the Island" he was "disgusted with the severity of the inhabitants, the cruelty of the planters, and the miseries of the slaves". The poem is notable as one of the earliest abolitionist protests to be cast in verse form; the apparent allusion in part I (below) to Grainger's *Sugar-Cane* suggests that it was the immediate target of the author's anti-slavery polemic.

Jamaica, Part I. Of the Country, Fruits, &c. [lines 180–89]

The Muse thinks it disgraceful in a Briton to sing of the Sugar-cane, since to it is owing the Slavery of the Negroes

Here could I sing what soils and seasons suit,
Inform the tap'ring arrow how to shoot;
Under what signs to plant the mother cane,

What rums and sugars bring the planter gain;
Teach stubborn oxen in the wain to toil,   5
And all the culture of a sugar soil:
Th' ungrateful task a British Muse disdains,
Lo! tortures, racks, whips, famine, gibbets, chains,
Rise on my mind, appall my tear-stain'd eye,
Attract my rage, and draw a soul-felt sigh;   10
I blush, I shudder at the bloody theme,
And scorn on woe to build a baseless fame.

Jamaica, Part II. Of the Inhabitants [lines 11–77]

Then first, O Muse! attempt the motly fair,
From lank and long, to short and woolly hair;
From white to black, thro' ev'ry mixture run,
And sing the smiling daughters of the sun!
'Tis true, few nymphs with British bloom we boast,   5
No rosy red adorns the tropic toast;[2]
But here the lilly sheds her purest white,
And well-turn'd limbs the panting youth invite!
While sportive Cupids circle round the waist,
Laugh on the cheek, or wanton in the breast!   10
Our sultry sun (tho' fierce in vertic rage)
Ripes the young blood, and nourishes old age;
O'er every limb spreads more than mortal grace,
And gives the body what he robs the face.
Next comes a warmer race, from sable sprung,   15
To love each thought, to lust each nerve is strung;
The Samboe[3] dark, and the Mullattoe[4] brown,
The Mestize[5] fair, the well-limb'd Quaderoon,[6]
And jetty Afric, from no spurious fire,
Warm as her soil, and as her sun – on fire.   20
These sooty dames, well vers'd in Venus' school,
Make love an art, and boast they kiss by rule.
'Midst murm'ring brooks they stem the liquid wave,

And jetty limbs in coral currents lave.   25
In field or household pass the toilsome day,
But spend the night in mirth-enlivening play:
With pipe and tabor woo their sable loves,
In sad remembrance of their native groves;
Or, deck'd in white, attend the vocal halls,   30
And Afric postures teach in Indian balls.
Not always thus the males carouse and play,
But toil and sweat the long laborious day;
With earliest dawn the ardent task begun,
Their labour ends not with the setting sun: 35
For when the moon displays her borrow'd beams,
They pick the canes, and tend the loaded teams,
Or in alternate watch, with ceaseless toil,
The rums distil, or smoaky sugars boil.
Ev'n while they ply this sad and sickly trade,   40
Which numbers thousands with the countless dead,
Refus'd the very liquors which they make,
They quench their burning temples in the lake;
Or issuing from the thick unwholesome steam,
Drink future sorrow in the cooling stream.   45
    Why need I sing the Indian's copper hue,
Broad face, short size, lank hair, and scowling brow,
Unfit for toil? a mild, tho' gallant race,
Inur'd to war, and panting for a chace;
Born free, they scorn to brook a lawless sway,   50
Spurn the dire wretch who'd stripes for toils repay:
They pine! they sicken! hope their native sky,
Their friends, their loves – they languish and they die.
    Here the fond Muse the Caribb[7] race would sing,
The painted people, and the plumag'd king: 55
Their feats in arms; in peace domestic toils;
The happiest people of the fairest isles!
Where thee, *Columbus!*[8] great as injur'd name,
Found a new world, and gain'd an empty fame.

Their sylvan sports along the sea-green shore,   60
What swarms *Domingo*,⁹ what *Jamaica* bore.
But O! how vain the task! the theme how vain,
Their flitting shades still curse the faithless main,
Bare their gor'd breasts, and point at cruel Spain!
    O that the Muse, who makes her cruelties known,   65
Could spurn her crimes, and not detest her own:
But lo! the Afric genius clanks his chains,
And damns the race that robs his native plains!

Jamaica, Part III. [lines 1–116]

Thus far the Muse, when mad'ning at the scene
Of Christian guile, and man enslaving man:
Around my head aërial phantoms rise,
And soothing slumbers seal my tear-stain'd eyes.
    O! pride and glory of a sinking state!   5
Great in thy power, and in retirement great;
Tho' Lawyer, honest; – Courtier, sincere;
Patriot, unstain'd; – uncorrupt tho' a Peer:
Camden! a Bard unknown, would claim thine ear,
And mix the Muse's with the Patriot's tear.   10
    The drowsy god had calm'd my troubled breast,
Charm'd every care and ev'ry limb to rest;
When lo! out-issuing from surrounding night,
The goddess *Liberty* arrests my sight:
A cypress garland round each temple twines,   15
And at her feet the British lion pines.
The sugar-isles with furious frown she eyes,
And I attend while thus the goddess cries:
"Lo! Afric from your furthest shores complains,
Bares her foul wounds, and clanks your cruel chains;   20
Polluted Gambia¹⁰ mourns her country spoil'd,
And wild Zaara's¹¹ fields become more wild:
The peaceful Fauns forsake dishonour'd groves,

And gentle Naiads leave their watry loves!
Your cruelties reach beyond th' Atlantic main,   25
A people sigh, but all their sighs are vain!
These eyes have seen what this tongue can't reveal,
These ears have heard what I would blush to tell;
Whate'er the Briton, or the man could stain,
Or give the Christian, or the Heathen pain!   30
    "Thus Rome of old the barb'rous nations brav'd,
Ev'n Indus saw his tawny sons enslav'd;
Far to the North she spread her proud domain,
And bound ev'n Britain in a gilded chain.
But she who aw'd the world by arms and fame,   35
Now smoaks by slaves, now stands an empty name!
Fear then, like her, to meet an awful doom,
And let your sea-girt shores still think on Rome;
For your green isles, surcharg'd with bosom'd foes,
May yield to slaves, – you feel the captive's woes."   40
This said, – the goddess sheds ambrosial tears,
Spreads her fleet wings, and instant disappears!
    O Planter! be it yours to nurse the slave,
From Afric's coasts waft o'er th' Atlantic wave:
With tender accents smooth the brow of care,   45
And from his bosom banish dark despair:
So may rich sugars fill your roomy stores,
And rums in plenty reach your native shores:
So may no dire disease your stock invade,
But feed contented in the cooling shade!   50
    Oft have I blush'd to see a Christian give
To some black wretch, worn out, and just alive,
A *manumission*[12] *full*, and leave him free,
To brave pale want, disease, and misery!
A poor reward for all his watchful cares,   55
Industrious days, and toil-revolving years!
    And can the Muse reflect her tear-stain'd eye
When blood[13] attests ev'n slaves for freedom die?

On cruel gibbets high disclos'd they rest,
And scarce one groan escapes one bloated breast.   60
Here sable Caesars[14] feel the Christian rod;
There Afric Platos, tortur'd, hope a God:
While jetty Brutus for his country sighs,
And sooty Cato with his freedom dies!

    Britons, forbear! be Mercy still your aim,   65
And as your faith, unspotted be your fame;
Tremendous pains tremendous deeds inspire,
And, hydra-like, new martyrs rise from fire.

    O hapless Afric! still the sport of fate,
Prey of each clime, and haunt of ev'ry state;   70
Lo! borne thro' sultry skies by fav'ring gales,
With ceaseless wishes and extended sails,
The restless merchant seeks thy hapless shore,
Sped by inhuman gain and golden ore!

    Inhuman ye! who ply the human[15] trade,   75
And to the West[16] a captive people lead;
Who brother, sister, father, mother, friend,
In one unnat'ral hapless ruin blend.
Barbarians! steel'd to ev'ry sense of woe,
Shame of the happy source from whence ye flow: 80
The time may come, when, scorning savage sway,
Afric may triumph, and ev'n you obey!

    The Muse, fond wish, would hope some day may give
The world in peace and liberty to live!
Freedom descend! invigorate the whole,   85
And stretch your free domain from pole to pole;
Till the Cane-isles accept your easy reign,
And Gambia murmur freedom to the main!
Till Europe peace to Africa restore,
Till slav'ry cease, and bondage be no more!   90

    O'er the warm South[17] extend your nursing wings,
Till future Incas rise, and future Kings;
Till captive tribes cease to be bought or sold,

And Chili's sons enjoy their native gold:
May Britain first her grateful tribute bring,   95
And all the world consenting Paeans sing!
   Let the gorg'd *East* boast *China*'s beauteous looms,
Golconda's gems, *Sumatra*'s rich perfumes;
The sickly *South*, *Potosi*'s pregnant ore,
Peru's fam'd drugs, and *Chili*'s golden shore;   100
The frozen *North*, *Spitzbergen*'s mighty whale,
Black *Hudson*'s ermine, *Zembla*'s spotted seal:
While the warm West her twice-impregn'd plain,
Twice vertic suns, and man enslaving cane:
Britannia! thine (the mighty boast below)   105
Is in what *freedom*, *commerce*, *health* bestow!
   Hail, only isle! girt by the only shore,
Whose feeling cliffs the captives right restore![18]
Hail, happy shore! wash'd by the only wave
That bears to freedom the desponding slave;   ⸱ 110
Whose awful view unbinds his galling chain,
Whose sacred justice makes his bondage vain!
The joyous Muse could wanton in thy praise,
Proud from the theme to pluck unspotted bays;
Where freedom left her last best lumin'd ray,   115
And lighted Britain to a glorious day! . . .

A Poetical Epistle

. . . From where the sun burns with his fiercest ray,
To where, midst Britain, flows the temp'rate day:
Lo! England's beauties croud upon my soul,
And o'er my mind our former pleasures roll:
When gay with thee, Augusta[19] I survey'd,   5
Or o'er thy *Kensington* enraptur'd stray'd!
   These all are fled! ambition was my aim,
To raise a fortune, or erect a name:
Midst tropic heats, and sickly climes, to scan

The works of Nature, and the ways of man.   10
　　The Muse, when first she view'd the destin'd isle,[20]
(Where slav'ry frown'd, and fortune ceas'd to smile,)
Was forc'd by fate to pass her joyless days,
'Mong men unknown to sympathetic lays.
To see the captive drag the cruel chain,   15
Repaid with tortures, and solac'd with pain;
To give the Afric's fate the pitying tear,
And spurn the slavery that she could not bear.
But soon she scorn'd on human woe to rise,
Nor with a tort'ring hand would stain the bays   20
　　But happy ye, who dwell midst Britain's isle,
Thrice happy men! if fortune deigns to smile.
No sighing slave there makes his heedless moan,
No injur'd Afric echoes forth his groan;
No tort'ring lord ransacks his fruitful mind,   25
Some unthought woe, some unknown rack to find.
　　At each new crime this labours in my breast,
And this each night denies a quiet rest:
Some Afric chief will rise, who, scorning chains,
Racks, tortures, flames – excruciating pains,   30
Will lead his injur'd friends to bloody fight,
And in the flooded carnage take delight;
Then dear repay us in some vengeful war,
And give us blood for blood, and scar for scar.

Notes

1. *Jamaica: A Poem, In Three Parts. Written in that Island, in the Year MDCCLXXVI.*
    To which is annexed, A Poetical Epistle from the Author in that Island to a Friend in
    England (London: William Nicoll, 1777).
2. [Author's note:] *toast*: reigning belle. By these are meant the Whites, or
    Creole Ladies.

3. [Author's note:] The Samboe arises from the cohabitation of a Mullattoe man and a black woman, and *vice versa*.

4. [Author's note:] Mullattoe, from white and black.

5. [Author's note:] Mestize, from white and Quaderoon.

6. [Author's note:] Quaderoon, from white and Mullattoe.

7. [Author's note:] The Aborigines of the West India islands, who were all extirpated by the Spaniards.

8. [Author's note:] C. Columbus was sent home in chains from that very world which he subdued and after the death of his patroness Isabella, treated very harshly by the court of Spain.

9. [Author's note:] Hispaniola.

10. [Author's note:] A river on the coast of Guinea, much frequented by our trading vessels.

11. [Author's note:] A desart tract in Africa.

12. [Author's note:] An instrument in writing used by masters in giving freedom to their slaves.

13. [Author's note:] During what the Planters term rebellion, but what a philosopher would call a brave struggle of an injured people for their lost liberties: During these, the Negroes will die amidst the most cruel torments, with the most obstinate intrepidity.

14. [Author's note:] Names given by the Planters to their slaves.

15. [Author's note:] Guinea trade, execrable not only on account of its inhumanity, but also for the many villainies practised in it.

16. [Author's note:] America.

17. [Author's note:] South America.

18. [Author's note:] Alluding to a famous decision of Lord Mansfield's, concerning the privileges of negroes in England. [In the landmark case of James Somerset in 1771–72, William Murray, Lord Mansfield, as lord chief justice, ruled in favour of the defendant, an enslaved black, on the grounds that slavery was "so odious that nothing can be suffered to support it, but positive law. Whatever inconveniences, therefore, may follow from the decision, I cannot say this case is allowed or approved by the law of England; and therefore the black must be discharged." *Howell's State Trials* (1816) no. 548, vol. 20, col. 82.]

19. *Augusta*: poetic name for London.

20. [Author's note:] Alluding to the author's stay for a few months in the country, as a Planter, after his arrival.

"The Field Negroe; or the Effect of Civilization" (1783)[1]

This poem is printed in *Poems, on Subjects Arising in England, and the West Indies. By a Native of the West Indies.* From internal evidence it appears that the author was born in the West Indies, lived in Antigua in the 1770s, and served at some time as rector of St John's, Nevis, before returning to England.

Say, lovely muse, what thoughts compel
   Thy poet's partial fire
To sound, uncouth, th' Indian shell,
   Or strike the savage lyre? . . .

O, fancy, let me view the toil,   5
   When drooping, faint with pain,
The panting negroe digs the soil
   Of sugar's sweet domain.

And now I see thy *canes* arise,
   Like blades of springing corn;
And now thy *cocoas* meet my eyes,   10
   High waving as in scorn.

Here stand the slaves in even rows,
   And, though the season warms,
They throw, at once, their equal hoes,   15
   Like soldiers under arms.

On skins of goats their children lie,
   Or here and there they run;
And grow, beneath a torrid sky,
   Still blacker in the sun.   20

Hence, then, the polish'd skin, so meek,
   Of shining glossy black; –
The sable plumes are not so sleek
   Upon a raven's back.

O let me steal upon that soil,   25
   So long unbless'd by rain,
Which oft, with never-ceasing toil,
   The negroe digs in vain.[2]

'Twas here, as once I stroll'd along,
   With musing steps and slow,   30
I spied, the other slaves among,
   One leaning on his hoe.

Just by his famish'd side, I think,
   A *yabbah*[3] struck my view;
And, empty quite of meat and drink,   35
   A *calabash*[4] or two.

Poor Arthur was the wretch's name,
   And Guinea gave him breath;
While he to sad Antigua came,
   To meet, he fear'd, his death.   40

That negroe near the burning line
    Had mov'd the swift canoe,
Had stem'd the foamy ocean brine
    With paddle light and true.

Poor Arthur now, aloud cry'd I,   45
    You are not, sure, dismay'd!
Poor Arthur answer'd with a sigh,
    And scratch'd his woolly head.

I begg'd some water of a maid,
    To give the wretch relief;   50
He held it, trembling, to his head,
    Within a plantain leaf.

The sweat ran down his sun-burnt face,
    In troubl'd torrents fast;
While not a breeze, with tepid grace,   55
    Dispell'd it as it past.

I now my silk umbrella spread,
    To screen him from the sun;
And patient held it o'er his head,
    'Till all his work was done.   60

The slave then stoop'd and kiss'd my feet,[5]
    Low prostrate on the ground,
And made his arms in wonder meet
    My fainting knees around!

The bell of noon now open'd wide,   65
    The shell a signal sent;
Poor Arthur rubb'd each awkward side,[6]
    And home his footsteps bent.

But Arthur now has made a hut,[7]
    And little garden wild,   70
Which keeps, contiguous to a gut,
    Himself, his wife, and child.

'Tis there the Jessamine demure,
    And fav'rite flow'ry fence,
Shall ev'ry holiday allure   75
    The negroe's simple sense.

'Tis here, oft as the gentle airs
    At morn and eve renew;
So oft a thrilling music bears,
    To tune the *diddledoe*.[8]   80

There Melancholy lifts her head,
    With soft dejected mien,
And rises from her mountain bed,
    To grace the palmy scene.

On Sunday, oft he joins the throng   85
    Of India's swarthy dames;
On Sunday, oft he sings the song
    Expressive of his flames.

Now Arthur and the youths advance
    With pleasure-smiling mien,   90
He leads, at once, the antick dance,
    And beats the *tamboreen*.

At cudgels[9] now, against all blows
    He nicely guards his head;
And boldly meets a thousand foes,   95
    Beneath the plantain shade.

And now the rank *baba*¹⁰ he throws
   From off his polish'd limbs,
And every day he nicer grows,
   Improving in his whims.   100

A shirt of check that loss supplies,
   And other garbs below;
And rings of horn, of homely guise,
   Compleats the savage beau.

Now faithful to his master's side,¹¹   105
   And takes his nimble course:
He braids his hair, with decent pride,
   And runs beside his horse.

And now we daily hear him sing,
   The merriest and the best: 110
He seems, he moves another thing,
   And portly rears his crest.

Notes

1. "The Field Negroe", in *Poems, on Subjects Arising in England, and the West Indies. By a Native of the West Indies* (London: R. Faulder, 1783), 1–16.
2. [Author's note:] The allusion is here to the island of Antigua, once a flourishing and wealthy colony, but now desolated by a perpetual sun-shine.
3. [Author's note:] An earthen pot or vessel to hold meat, provisions, and the like.
4. [Author's note:] Spoons, bowls, and other utensils for slaves to eat out of are made of them.
5. [Author's note:] Their usual manner of expressing their gratitude for any great and unlooked for act of kindness.
6. [Author's note:] Descriptive of a new negroe, or one who has not been long in the island, after leaving his native country.

7. [Author's note:] Negroes live in huts, on the western side of our dwelling houses; so that every plantation resembles a small town; and the reason why they are seated on the western side, is, that we may breathe the pure eastern air, without being offended with the least nauseous smell. Our kitchens and boiling houses are on the same side, and for the same reason.

8. [Author's note:] The pod in which the seed of the aquafee grows, and which, when blown upon by the mouth or the air, produces a tone.

9. [Author's note:] An amusement common among negroes.

10. [Author's note:] A blanket or loose kind of covering used by the meanest kind of slaves.

11. [Author's note:] It is usual in the West Indies for the slave, who more immediately waits upon his master, to attend him on his journies, and airings on horseback, which he generally does on foot, with an activity and strength, which has, at first, very much surprized the Europeans who have gone to that part of the world. It is considered by them as a mark of distinction, and preferred to the more slavish office of digging the cane holes.

PHILIP FRENEAU (1752–1832)

"To Sir Toby, A Sugar Planter in the interior parts of Jamaica" (1784)[1]

Born into a well-to-do New York family, Freneau absorbed libertarian and patriotic American principles as a student at Princeton, and was esteemed as the poet of the American Revolution. His residence in the West Indies between 1775 and 1978 fuelled his hatred of slavery, while his capture and imprisonment by the British in 1780 inflamed his anti-British feeling. "To Sir Toby", written in 1784, was first printed in the *National Gazette* (21 July 1792) under the title "The Island Field Hand", with a note saying it was written "some years ago at a sugar plantation in Jamaica".[2] It was reprinted in Freneau's *Poems written between the years 1768 & 1794*, the text used here, and in revised form in his collected *Poems*, published in Philadelphia in 1809.

If there exists a Hell – the case is clear –
Sir Toby's slaves enjoy that portion here:
Here are no blazing brimstone lakes – 'tis true,
But kindled Rum full often burns as blue,
In which some fiend, whom nature must detest,   5
Steeps Toby's name, and brands poor Cudjoe's breast.[3]

Here, whips on whips excite a thousand fears,
And mingled howlings vibrate on my ears:
Here Nature's plagues abound, of all degrees,
Snakes, scorpions, despots, lizards, centipees –   10
No art, no care escapes the busy lash;
All have their dues, and all are paid in cash:
[The eternal driver keeps a steady eye
On a black herd, who would his vengeance fly,
But chain'd, imprison'd, on a burning soil,   15
For the mean avarice of a tyrant, toil!]⁴
The lengthy cart-whip guards this tyrant's reign,
And cracks like pistols from the fields of Cane.
    Ye Powers that form'd these wretched tribes, relate,
What had they done, to merit such a fate?   20
Why were they brought from Eboe's⁵ sultry waste,
To see the plenty which they must not taste –
Food, which they cannot buy, and dare not steal,
Yams and potatoes! – many a scanty meal! –
One, with a jibbet wakes his negro's fears,   25
One, to the wind-mill nails him by the ears;
One keeps his slave in dismal dens, unfed,
One puts the wretch in pickle, ere he's dead;
This, from a tree suspends him by the thumbs,
That, from his table grudges even the crumbs!   30
    O'er yon' rough hills a tribe of females go,
Each with her gourd, her infant, and her hoe,
Scorch'd by a sun that has no mercy here,
Driven by a devil, that men call Overseer:
In chains twelve wretches to their labour haste,   35
Twice twelve I see with iron collars grace'd: –
Are these the joys that flow from vast domains!
Is wealth thus got, Sir Toby, worth your pains –
Who would that wealth, on terms like these, possess,
Where all we see is pregnant with distress;   40
Angola's natives scourg'd by hireling hands,

And toil's hard earnings shipp'd to foreign lands?
   Talk not of blossoms and your endless spring –
No joys, no smiles, such scenes of misery bring!
Though Nature here has every blessing spread,   45
Poor is the labourer – and how meanly fed!
Here, Stygian paintings all their shades renew,
Pictures of woe, that Virgil's pencil drew;
Here, surly Charons make their annual trip,
And souls arrive in every Guinea ship   50
To find what hell this western world affords,
Plutonian scourges, and Tartarian lords; –
Where they who pine, and languish to be free
Must climb the tall cliffs of the Liguanee;
Beyond the clouds, in sculking haste repair,   55
And hardly safe from brother butchers there![6]

Notes

1. Philip Freneau, "To Sir Toby", in *Poems Written Between the Years 1768 & 1794* (Monmouth, NJ: n.p., 1795).

2. *Poems* (Philadelphia, 1809) adds "near the City of San Jago de la Vega, (Spanish Town) 1784".

3. [Author's note:] This passage has a reference to the custom of branding the slaves in the islands, as a mark of property.

4. Lines 13–16 were added in *Poems* (1809).

5. *Poems* (1809) footnotes this as "A small Negro Kingdom near the river Senegal", but *Eboe* in Caribbean English refers to a region and people of modern south-eastern Nigeria.

6. [Author's note:] Alluding to the independent negroes in the Blue Mountains; who, for a stipulated reward deliver up every fugitive that falls into their hands. [See Dallas's account of the Maroons, page 185 below.]

JAMES RAMSAY (1733–89)

An Essay on the Treatment and Conversion of African Slaves in the British Slave Colonies (1784)[1]

Ramsay served as a naval surgeon on the West India station and was horrified to discover the squalid and degrading conditions under which slaves were transported across the Atlantic. After leaving the navy in 1759 he was ordained and served as priest and surgeon in the West Indies from 1762 to 1781, mainly on St Kitts, where his concern for the welfare and just treatment of the slaves aroused violent antagonism from local planters and government officials. His *Essay*, based on painstaking study as well as direct observation, is a classic of British anti-slavery literature.

From Sect. V. African Capacity vindicated from Experience

Negroes are capable of learning any thing that requires attention and correctness of manner. They have powers of description and mimickry that would not have disgraced the talents of our modern Aristophanes. The distillation of rum, the tempering of the cane juice for sugar, which may be considered as nice chemical operations, are universally committed to them.

They become good mechanics; they use the square and compass, and easily become masters of whatever business they are put to. They have a particular turn for music, and often attain a considerable proficiency in it without the advantage of a master. Negroe sick nurses acquire a surprizing skill in the cure of ordinary diseases, and often conquer disorders that have baffled an host of regulars. Nor want they emulation, in whatever their observation can reach. Hence our black beaus, black belles, black gamesters, black keepers, black quacks, black conjurers, and all that variety of character, which strikes in their masters, or promises to add to their own dignity or interest. But what can we expect them to attempt in the higher departments of reason? Their slavish employments and condition; their being abandoned to the caprice of any master; the subjection in which it is thought necessary to keep them all; these things depress their minds, and subdue whatever is manly, spirited, ingenuous, independent, among them. And these are weights sufficient to crush a first-rate human genius.

Had it been the lot of a paradoxical Hume, or of a benevolent Kaims,[2] to have cultivated the sugar-cane, under a planter, in one of our old islands; the first probably would have tried to have eked out his scanty pittance of two pounds of flour or grain per week, by taking up the profession of a John Crowman, or conjurer; and doubtless would have got many a flogging for playing tricks with, and imposing on the credulity of his fellows, to cheat them of their allowance. The turn of the other to works of taste might have expressed itself in learning to blow a rude sort of music from his nostril, through an hollowed piece of stick; or, if blessed with an indulgent master, he might have learned to play by ear a few minuets, and fiddle a few country dances, to enable the family and neighbours to pass an evening cheerfully together.

The truth is, a depth of cunning that enables them to over-reach, conceal, deceive, is the only province of the mind left for them, as slaves, to occupy. And this they cultivate, and enjoy the fruits of, to a surprizing degree. I have, as a magistrate, heard examinations and defences of culprits, that for quibbling, subterfuges, and subtilty, would have done credit to the abilities of an attorney, most notoriously conversant in the villainous tricks of his profession. Their command of countenance is so perfect, as not to give the least clue for discovering the truth; nor can they be caught tripping in a story.

Nothing in the turn or degree of their mental faculties, distinguishes them from Europeans, though some difference must appear, if they were of a different or an inferior race.

I had a young fellow, who was a notorious gambler, idler, liar, and man of pleasure; yet so well did he lay his schemes, so plausibly did he on all occasions account for his time and conduct, that I, who could not punish unless I could convince the culprit that I had undoubted proof of his guilt, was hardly ever able to find an opportunity of correcting him. This lad, when he came a boy from Africa, shewed marks of sentiment, and of a training above the common run of negroes. But slavery, even in the mildest degree, and his accompanying with slaves, gave him so worthless, dissipated a turn, that I was obliged to send him out of the family, and have him taught a trade in hopes of his reformation. By this he insensibly acquired a little application, and has since attached himself to a wife. His father, he says, was a man of property, had a large household, and many wives. He was kidnapped.

There is another lad, who could stand without flinching to be cut in pieces by the whip, and not utter a groan.[3] As whipping was a triumph instead of a punishment to him, I was obliged to overlook the most notorious faults, or affect generously to pardon them, rather than pretend to correct them. Yet this proceeds not from insensibility of pain, for if bleeding be prescribed for him when sick, he cries like a child, and shrinks from the operation. About twelve years ago he was caught in a fault, that by the custom of the colony would have justified his master in carrying his punishment to any degree, short of extremity. Pains were taken to set the enormity of it before him, and he was freely pardoned, and his fellows were strictly forbidden ever to upbraid him with it. Since that time he has behaved remarkably well and trust-worthy, and shewn a very uncommon attachment to the family. A third boy, who is sensible as a little lord of every affront to his dignity, could stand with the sullen air of a stoic to receive the severest correction.

In truth, in spite of the disadvantages under which they labour, individuals, on particular occasions, have shewn an elevation of sentiment that would have done honour to a Spartan. The Spectator, No. 215,[4] has celebrated a rude instance in two negroes, in the island of St. Christopher, which on inquiry I find to be true. I will confirm this by the relation of a deed, that happened within these thirty years, for which I have no name. As I had my information from a friend of the master's, in the master's presence, who acknowledged it to be genuine, the truth of it is indisputable. The only liberty I have taken with it, has been to give words to the sentiment that inspired it.

Quashi was brought up in the family with his master, as his play-fellow, from his childhood. Being a lad of towardly parts, he rose to be driver, or black overseer, under his master, when the plantation fell to him by succession. He retained for his master the tenderness that he had felt in childhood for his play-mate; and the respect with which the relation of master inspired him, was softened by the affection which the remembrance of their boyish intimacy kept alive in his breast. He had no separate interest of his own, and in his master's absence redoubled his diligence, that his affairs might receive no injury from it. In short, here was the most delicate, yet most strong, and seemingly indissoluble tie, that could bind master and slave together. Though the master had judgment to know when he was well served, and policy to reward good behaviour, he was inexorable when a fault was committed; and when there was but an apparent cause of suspicion, he was too apt to let prejudice usurp the place of proof. Quashi could not exculpate himself to his satisfaction, for something done contrary to the discipline of the plantation, and was threatened with the ignominious punishment of the cart-whip; and he knew his master too well, to doubt of the performance of his promise.

A negroe, who has grown up to manhood, without undergoing a solemn cart-whipping, as some by good chance will, especially if distinguished by any accomplishment among his fellows, takes pride in what he calls the smoothness of his skin, its being unrazed by the whip; and he would be at more pains, and use more diligence to escape such a cart-whipping, than many of our lower sort would use to shun the gallows. It is not uncommon for a sober good negroe to stab himself mortally, because some boy-overseer has flogged him, for what he reckoned a trifle, or for his caprice, or threatened him with a flogging, when he thought he did not deserve it. Quashi dreaded this mortal wound to his honour, and slipt away unnoticed, with a view to avoid it.

It is usual for slaves, who expect to be punished for their own fault, or their master's caprice, to go to some friend of their master's, and beg him to carry them home, and mediate for them. This is found to be so useful, that humane masters are glad of the pretence of such mediation, and will secretly procure it to avoid the necessity of punishing for trifles; it otherwise not being prudent to pass over without correction, a fault once taken notice of; while by this method, an appearance of authority and discipline is kept up, without the severity of it. Quashi therefore withdrew, resolved to shelter himself, and save the glossy honours of his skin, under favour of this custom, till he had an opportunity of applying to an advocate. He lurked among his master's negroe huts, and his fellow slaves had too much honour, and too great a regard for him, to betray to their master the place of his retreat. Indeed, it is hardly possible in any case, to get one slave to inform against another, so much more honour have they than Europeans of low condition.

The following day a feast was kept, on account of his master's nephew then coming of age; amidst the good humour of which, Quashi hoped to succeed in his application; but before he could execute his design, perhaps just as he was setting out to go and solicit this mediation, his master, while walking about his fields, fell in with him. Quashi, on discovering him, ran off, and the master, who is a robust man, pursued him. A stone, or a clod, tripped Quashi up, just as the other reached out his hand to seize him. They fell together, and wrestled for the mastery, for Quashi also was a stout man, and the elevation of his mind added vigour to his arm. At last, after a severe struggle, in which each had been several times uppermost, Quashi got firmly seated on his master's breast, now panting and out of breath, and with his weight, his thighs, and one hand, secured him motionless. He then drew out a sharp knife, and while the other lay in dreadful expectation, help-less, and shrinking into himself, he thus addressed him. "Master, I was bred up with you from a child; I was your play-mate when a boy; I have loved you as myself; your interest has been my study; I am innocent of the cause of your suspicion; had I been guilty, my attachment to you might have pleaded for me. Yet you have condemned me to a punishment of which I must ever have borne the disgraceful marks; thus only can I avoid them." With these words, he drew the knife with all his strength across his own throat, and fell down dead without a groan, on his master, bathing him in his blood.[5]

Had this man been properly educated; had he been taught his importance as a member of society; had he been accustomed to weigh his claim
to, and enjoy the possession of the unalienable rights of humanity; can any
man suppose him incapable of making a progress in the knowledge of religion, in the researches of reason, or the works of art? Or can it be affirmed,
that a man, who amidst the disadvantages, and gloom of slavery, had
attained a refinement of sentiment, to which language cannot give a name,
which leaves the bulk of polished society far behind, could want abilities to
acquire arts and sciences, which we too often find coupled with a fawning, a
mean, a slavish spirit? Others may, I will not believe it.

Notes

1. James Ramsay, *An Essay on the Treatment and Conversion of African Slaves in the
    British Slave Colonies* (London: James Phillips, 1784), section 5, 243–53.
2. David Hume (1711–76) was "paradoxical" in that he argued against slavery while
    also asserting that negroes were naturally inferior to other human species.
    Lord Kames (Henry Home, 1696–1782) is called "benevolent" in various senses.
    As a moral philosopher he upheld benevolence as opposed to self-interest as a
    mainspring of human action. In the "Preliminary Discourse" to *Sketches of the
    History of Man* (1774) he took a more favourable view of Africans, suggesting
    that their apparent "inferiority" might be due to environmental factors and the
    effects of enslavement. Kames was on the panel of judges in the landmark
    Joseph Knight case (1774), which ruled that the state of slavery was not recog-
    nized in Scotland. In "works of taste" Ramsay alludes to Kames's famous trea-
    tise on aesthetic principles, *Elements of Criticism* (1763).
3. The pro-slavery authors of *An Answer to the Reverend James Ramsay's Essay . . .
    By some Gentlemen of St. Christopher* (Basseterre, St Kitts: n.p., 1784), 92, chal-
    lenged Ramsay on this point. "He mentions another [slave] of his own, who
    would stand to be cut in pieces by the whip. Where slept his boasted humanity,
    while that cruel operation was performing?"
4. See Addison, "A Kind of Wild Tragedy", page 38 above.
5. Ramsay's story was disputed in *An Answer to the Reverend James Ramsay's Essay*,
    92: "Quashie's story is dressed out in fine glaring colours, but unfortunately is
    not agreeable to truth; for the fact was (as We had it from an eye witness) that
    he was pursued for inveigling a female slave from another estate. His master

ran after him, was entangled in some pease, and fell down; but recovered himself, and came near enough, to think, he could dash the old razor out of his
hand, with which he threatened to cut his own throat; but the master missed
his blow, and the slave half executed his threats; he lived several days, long
enough to acknowledge and lament his passion; but 'the glossy honours of his
skin' had before that suffered for repeated insolence and transgressions."

GORDON TURNBULL (FL. 1785–95)

An Apology for Negro Slavery (1786)[1]

Turnbull, a planter in Grenada, was the author of two other works on the West Indies: a manual on plantation management and *A Narrative of the Revolt and Insurrection of the French Inhabitants in the Island of Grenada*, published in Edinburgh in 1795. His *Apology* was intended as a retort to the "horrid and fictitious picture . . . of the state of the negroes in the West-Indies" drawn in the abolitionist tracts of James Ramsay (see above). The extract below describes the treatment of slaves on arrival in the West Indies from Africa and their subsequent "seasoning".

As soon as the ship that brings them is at anchor, the master or surgeon goes on shore to procure fresh provisions, fruit, and vegetables of all kinds, which are immediately sent on board for the slaves. Parties of them are sent on shore at different times, and conducted a little way into the country, where they frequently meet with many natives of their own country, who speak the same language, and sometimes with near and dear relations, who all appear very cheerful and happy. These agreeable and unexpected meetings are truly affecting, and excite the most tender and pleasing sensations in the breasts of the by-standers. It is not uncommon for those newly arrived guests, to mingle in the dance, or to join in the song, with their country people.

If any of them appear dull or desponding, the old negroes endeavour to enliven them, by the most soothing and endearing expressions, telling them, in their own tongue, not to be afraid of the white men; that the white men are very good; that they will get plenty of *yam, yam,* (their general name for victuals) and that their work will be of the easiest kind. By these means, they are perfectly reconciled to the white men, and to a change of country, and of situation, which many of them declare, to be far superior to that which they had quitted. When the day of sale arrives, they not only meet the planter's looks, and answer his enquiries, by means of an interpreter, with great firmness, but they try, by offering their stout limbs to his inspection, jumping to shew their activity, and other allurements, to induce those, whose appearance pleases them, to buy them, and to engage, if possible, a preference in their favour.

In this place, it is certainly proper to observe, that a mode of selling negroes is sometimes practised, which ought to be abolished by a law of the islands where it prevails, as being repugnant to decency, and in some measure to humanity. The custom I mean to reprobate, is the selling a cargo of slaves by what is called a *scramble.* This is shutting them up in the merchant's house, or the area adjoining, and at the beat of a drum, or some other signal, all those who intend to become purchasers, rush on suddenly; or, to use a military phrase, dash upon the astonished and frightened negroes, and endeavour to get hold of, or to encircle in a cord, as many of them as they can. Although the negroes are generally prepared for this, by being pre-informed of what is to happen, yet some of the women and children have been known to expire, from the excess of terror, which is incited by a scene of such confusion and uproar. Nor is it uncommon for the purchasers themselves to go by the ears, and quarrel about the objects of their choice. In justice to the Guinea merchants, let me add, this shocking custom is not frequently practised; and, for their own sake, and for the sake of these fellow-creatures, over whom an all-wise Providence has permitted them to have such power, and for the sake of humanity, let it be utterly abolished.

As soon as the new negroes are brought home to the plantation, if a planter has purchased them they are properly clothed. – A sufficient quantity of wholesome food is prepared, and served to them three times a day. They are comfortably lodged in some room of the manager's own house, or in some other convenient place, where they can be immediately under his eye for a few days. During this time they are not put to any kind of labour whatever, but are regularly conducted to bathe in the river, or in the sea, if it is nigh, twice a day. In the evenings they sing and dance, after the manner of their own nation, together with the old negroes who happen to be from the same country, one or two of whom are commonly instrumental performers in these very noisy, but very joyous assemblies. In a very short time, they are taken into the houses of the principal and best disposed negroes, who adopt one or two of these new subjects into each family, to assist them in all the little domestic offices of cookery, carrying water, wood, &c. This almost the only work they are employed in for the first two or three months, at the expiration of which, they are put to the easiest kind of labour for some months more. Their food is regularly dressed and served to them, as at first, for twelve months, and longer if they desire it. But, after this term, they generally prefer the same allowance that is given to the old settled negroes. By this time, perhaps, many of them are married, (*in their way*) and have houses, gardens, hogs, and poultry of their own. – When the Guinea negroes are purchased young, and are treated in this manner, they become, in two or three years, in every respect, as valuable subjects to their owners, as these *creoles*, who were born, and have lived from their infancy upon the plantations.

Note

1.   Gordon Turnbull, *An Apology for Negro Slavery: or the West-Indian planters vindicated from the charge of inhumanity*, 2nd ed. (London: Stuart and Stevenson, 1786), 21–26.

Remarks upon the Situation of Negroes in Jamaica (1788)[1]

Beckford (cousin of the better-known William Beckford, author of *Vathek*) was born in Jamaica and lived on the island from 1774 to 1786, having inherited four sugar plantations with 910 slaves on his father's death in 1756. This pamphlet is a defence of the West Indian slave system; Beckford argued that "under a kind owner or a benevolent overseer" a well-behaved, industrious slave was in most respects better off than "the generality of labouring poor in England". Under "capricious and inhuman managers", however, their situation was "too lamentable to be described". Such managers would "inflict heavy punishments for the slightest omissions, be constantly upon the watch to detect petty errors, and descend to such instances of low and malignant revenge as would shock the greatest savage that ever enjoyed the sight of human blood". The remedy, Beckford urged, was for all planters to follow best practice in the treatment of slaves: "I am not an advocate for the liberation of the slave. I am an advocate for all that can make him happy; I am an advocate for his removal from his native soil, that he may taste the comforts of protection, the fruits of humanity, and the blessings of religion."

I shall now suppose that the African are assimilated, as it were, from time, connections, and habitudes of custom, with the Creole negroes: I shall therefore, for the better elucidation of my subject, describe their general and specific labours upon a plantation, beginning with their hours of toil, and interventions of rest, and descend to their common recreations, and domestic œconomy; by which means you will be enabled to form some just ideas of the real situation of a slave; and will in consequence, I hope, believe, that it is by no means so dreadful as those, deluded, I fear by a mistaken, although a laudable motive of humanity, may be led to believe. . . .

They generally turn out to work at six o'clock in the morning, and continue unremittingly employed until the time of breakfast, which is generally between the hours of nine and ten. For this meal they are allowed half an hour, but three quarters or more is the general average. They then continue upon the hoe till dinner time, that is, until twelve or one o'clock; and perhaps the medium of these hours is the general time of vacancy all over the Island. Although this be called the time of refection, and is with the overseer and the white people upon the plantation that period of the day which is set aside for this particular purpose; yet in this interval the negroes seldom make a meal, but are rather inclined to indulge their leisure in conversation with their fellows, or to loiter away the time in useless inactivity untill the shell[2] prepares them for a renovation of toil. They are allowed for a nominal dinner one hour and a half, but it generally arrives at, or exceeds two, before they all assemble; and if the spot upon which their labour be called, be at any distance from their houses, the time is proportionally elonged. They seldom continue in the field, out of crop, after sun-set, which is never later than seven, so that from this hour until six the ensuing morning they may call their time their own; a part of which they consume in broken sleep, the rest in supper and a preparation for breakfast at the matin summons; so that the negroes can absolutely command between thirteen and fourteen hours a day, out of crop, besides the accidental vacancies during the rainy seasons, without mental care or bodily exertion; and where is the labourer in England who can resign himself to rest, and be soothed by these reflections . . . .

In crop time the labour of the negroes is more constant, I will not say that it is more severe. The situation of the tiers (or those who collect and bind up the canes for carriage) is that which I have been the most often led to compassionate; for as they are too weak for the labours of the big gang,

one would of course imagine that they were entitled to some indulgence –
on the contrary they are oftentimes kept in the field from morning to night[3]
without the privilege of retiring from their work, or enjoying that interval
of rest from the ardours of the mid-day sun, which other negroes expect
invariably to enjoy. To oppress the weak with toil is impolitic and inhuman;
but as labour in the West Indies is not always apportioned to strength, it cannot be wondered at, if exertions without power, and weakness without
indulgence, so frequently fail.

To enter into a detail of the continued labour of a negro would be as
tedious as to trace the exertions of a hedge-man from morning to night; the
first works with vacancy, the last with thought. So soon as the day shall
close, the one has not any thing to do but to prepare for supper, and for rest.
An omission of his labour is not attended with a loss of bread to himself, his
wife, and children; a fit of sickness is not followed by an expence, which the
labour of seven days in the week will not discharge; he is not deprived of
sleep by the anticipation of want, nor alarmed in his dreams by the ideal
summons of an attorney, nor does he dread that utmost reach of meanness
and oppression, that *ne plus ultra* of vindictive justice, that confines misfortunes to the horrors of a jail, and sinks the sufferer, his family, and hopes to
irremediable misery, and eternal despair . . . .

A slave, from his situation commands protection; and before he can sink
his master must fall; nay, he is by law considered as a fixture, as a vegetable
upon the soil, which the hand of power cannot eradicate, and which must
either flourish, or wither upon the spot. The necessitous labourer in
England meets with no compassion for inability, no indulgence from age, no
feeling from despair: he must pay, or starve; and if he die insolvent his
friends are not assured that he will find a Christian burial . . . .

Where is the man in ten thousand who can say, that he can lay himself
down to rest with a healthy body, and unruffled mind; or awake without the
dread of some anticipated, and over hanging affliction? These comforts are
left to those whom humanity pities, and whose situation religion condemns.
As negroes are not acquainted with anticipation, they are relieved from one
of the greatest curses that human nature can experience: if punishment
come, it is sudden at least, and unexpected; and the impression of sorrow
wears away with that of the lash . . . .

[Beckford reflects on the privations, hardships and insecurity which, he supposes, typify the lives of Africans in their native land, before turning to the consolations of transportation to a West Indian plantation.]

That they leave a bad climate for one that is better, for one in which their natural wants may be as easily provided, and without that risk and labour which must attend a life of constant warfare, can hardly be denied. If they have wives, children, and connections upon the property, those attachments are encouraged and preserved from interest,[4] that *primum mobile* of the actions of men: they are not subject to the chance of war, nor does the breast of the mother beat with constant trepidation for the danger of a husband or the loss of a child; nor is she subject to the mortification of seeing them snatched from her bosom to undergo eternal banishment, or suffer the anticipation of death. The comforts of certainty in a domestic life at least she may gain by an alteration of her state, and console herself with seeing the same protection extended to those she loves which she enjoys, and that the chances in her favour are, that they will not ever be disjoined. I firmly believe that there is not a description of people in the world, less occupied by uneasy sensations, who are more disposed to be, and who really are, more happy than the generality of negroes after the toil of the day is over, when assembled in their huts, conversing over their fires, and anticipating the pleasures of the approaching meal, (which generally consists of pottage, highly seasoned, and is such as may be considered a luxury in any climate) and of these the generality of them partake, to their utmost wish, at least twice a day. I do not think them a greedy people, they have no appearance of haste in eating, will chearfully let others enjoy their mess, and are fond of extending, particularly at night, the hours of refection. The women in general drink nothing but water, or sugar and water as a treat – the men will almost all indiscriminately swallow drams when they can get them, and even indulge in spirit to intoxication; but yet it is not often that riots ensue, and if they do happen, they are easily quelled. They seem sensible, if it be sudden, of a small indulgence, and I think they do not abuse great ones if caution be used in the time of concession. I have known a little grog, sugar and water, an unexpected herring, or a piece of salt fish give them spirits for the remainder of the day, and an afternoon allowed almost transport them. They are particularly fond of tobacco, and as it chears them in their labour, and is not attended with bad consequences, a present of a little every now and then when they deserve it, would be but a trifling expence to an estate. They ought not to be refused the participation of harmless recreations; why not make them as contented as their situations will allow? A good-natured man not only gains by their enjoyment, but adds felicity to his own mind: where the master is determined to be easy, it is not likely that his negroes will be wretched. They should rejoice at each others happiness, and sympathise with each others misery: the first should teach the last to consider themselves as men. A good slave will be attached to a good master from principle, and where he has been entrusted with the preservation of his life, he has never, as far as I have been able to learn, been found a traitor. As confidence begets service, so should service be attended with gratitude. Make a negro estimable in his own eyes, and he will be faithful and just in yours.

Notes

1. William Beckford, *Remarks upon the Situation of Negroes in Jamaica, impartially made from local experience of nearly thirteen years in that island* (London: T. and J. Egerton, 1788).
2. [Author's note:] Upon some estates the negroes are summoned to work, or to a relaxation from toil, by the blowing of a shell, and upon some by the ringing of a bell.
3. [Author's note:] Of this I have seen many instances; nay, I could mention some properties upon which the poor negroes were employed in cutting canes during the hours of common vacancy at noon; and who have been moreover obliged to labour on a Sunday. A practice as indecent as inhuman!
4. That is, it is in the master's interest to maintain and increase (through child-bearing) his stock of slaves.

OLAUDAH EQUIANO (1745–97)

The Interesting Narrative of the Life of Olaudah Equiano (1789)[1]

The first chapters of Equiano's autobiography relate that he was born in 1745 in Nigeria, kidnapped at the age of eleven and sent as a slave to Virginia. Recently discovered documents suggest that this was a fiction, and that he was actually born in South Carolina, but the authenticity of his narrative otherwise has been confirmed.[2] He was purchased as a boy by an English naval officer and taken to England, where he was renamed Gustavus Vassa after the famous Swedish patriot-king. After service in the Royal Navy with his master in the Seven Years' War he was sold to the captain of a ship sailing to the West Indies. On arrival in Montserrat in 1763, Equiano was sold to a new master, "Mr. Robert King, a quaker, and the first merchant in the place", who proved to be exceptionally humane. Eventually, by shrewd trading on his own account while sailing on his master's ships in the Caribbean and to and from America, Equiano saved sufficient money to buy his freedom in 1766.

From Chapter V.

Arrives at Montserrat, where he is sold to Mr. King – Various interesting instances of oppression, cruelty, and extortion, which the author saw practised upon the slaves in the West Indies during his captivity from the year 1763 to 1766 – Address on it to the planters.

Mr. King soon asked me what I could do; and at the same time said he did not mean to treat me as a common slave. I told him I knew something of seamanship, and could shave and dress hair pretty well; and I could refine wines, which I had learned on shipboard, where I had often done it; and that I could write, and understood arithmetic tolerably well as far as the Rule of Three. He then asked me if I knew any thing of gauging; and, on my answering that I did not, he said one of his clerks should teach me to gauge.[3]

Mr. King dealt in all manner of merchandize, and kept from one to six clerks. He loaded many vessels in a year; particularly to Philadelphia, where he was born, and was connected with a great mercantile house in that city. He had besides many vessels and droggers[4] of different sizes, which used to go about the island[5] to collect rum, sugar and other goods. I understood pulling and managing those boats very well; and this hard work, which was the first that he set me to, in the sugar seasons used to be my constant employment. I have rowed the boat, and slaved at the oars, from one hour to sixteen in the twenty-four; during which I had fifteen pence sterling per day to live on, though sometimes only ten pence. However this was considerably more than was allowed to other slaves that used to work often with me, and belonged to other gentlemen on the island: those poor souls had never more than nine-pence a day, and seldom more than six-pence, from their masters or owners, though they earned them three or four pisterines:[6] for it is a common practice in the West Indies for men to purchase slaves, though they have not plantations themselves, in order to let them out to planters and merchants at so much a piece by the day, and they give what allowance they choose out of this produce of their daily work to their slaves for subsistence; this allowance is often very scanty. My master often gave the owners of these slaves two and a half of these pieces per day, and found the poor fellows in victuals himself, because he thought their owners did not feed them well enough according to the work they did. The slaves used to like this very well, and, as they knew my master to be a man of feeling, they were always glad to work for him in preference to any other gentleman; some of whom, after they had been paid for these poor people's labours, would not give them their allowance out of it. Many times have I seen these unfortunate wretches beaten for asking for their pay; and often severely flogged by their owners if they did not bring them their daily or weekly money exactly to the time; though the poor creatures were obliged to wait on the gentlemen they had worked for sometimes more than half the day before they could get their pay; and this generally on Sundays, when they wanted the time for themselves. In particular, I knew a countryman of mine who once did not bring the weekly money directly that it was earned; and though he brought it the same day to his master, yet he was staked to the ground for his pretended negligence, and was just going to receive a hundred lashes, but for a gentleman who begged him off fifty. This poor man was very industrious, and by his frugality had saved so much money, by working on shipboard, that he had got a white man to buy him a boat, unknown to his master. Some time after he had this little estate, the governor wanted a boat to bring his sugar from different parts of the island; and, knowing this to be a negro-man's boat, he seized upon it for himself, and would not pay the owner a farthing. The man on this went to his master, and complained to him of this act of the governor; but the only satisfaction he received was to be damned very heartily by his master, who asked him how dared any of his negroes to have a boat. If the justly-merited ruin of the governor's fortune could be any gratification to the poor man he had thus robbed, he was not without consolation. Extortion and rapine are poor providers; and some time after this the governor died in the King's Bench,[7] in England, as I was told, in great poverty. The last war[8] favoured this poor negro-man, and he found some means to escape from his Christian master; he came to England, where I saw him afterwards several times. Such treatment as this often drives these miserable wretches to despair, and they run away from their masters at the hazard of their lives. Many of them, in this place, unable to get their pay when they have earned it, and fearing to be flogged, as usual, if they return home without it, run away where they can for shelter, and a reward is often offered to bring them in dead or alive. My master used sometimes, in these cases, to agree with their owners, and to settle with them himself; and thereby he saved many of them a flogging.

Once, for a few days, I was let out to fit a vessel, and I had no victuals allowed me by either party; at last I told my master of this treatment, and he took me away from it. In many of the estates, on the different islands where I used to be sent for rum or sugar, they would not deliver it to me, or any other negro; he was therefore obliged to send a white man along with me to those places; and then he used to pay him from six to ten pisterines a day. From being thus employed, during the time I served Mr. King, in going about the different estates on the island, I had all the opportunity I could wish for to see the dreadful usage of the poor men; usage that reconciled me to my situation, and made me bless God for the hands into which I had fallen.

I had the good fortune to please my master in every department in which he employed me; and there was scarcely any part of his business, or household affairs, in which I was not occasionally engaged. I often supplied the place of a clerk, in receiving and delivering cargoes to the ships, in tending stores, and delivering goods: and, besides this, I used to shave and dress my master when convenient, and take care of his horse; and when it was necessary, which was very often, I worked likewise on board of different vessels of his. By these means I became very useful to my master, and saved him, as he used to acknowledge, above a hundred pounds a year. Nor did he scruple to say I was of more advantage to him than any of his clerks; though their usual wages in the West Indies are from sixty to a hundred pounds current[9] a year.

I have sometimes heard it asserted that a negro cannot earn his master the first cost;[10] but nothing can be further from the truth. I suppose nine tenths of the mechanics throughout the West Indies are negro slaves; and I well know the coopers among them earn two dollars a-day; the carpenters the same, and oftentimes more; as also the masons, smiths, and fishermen, &c. and I have known many slaves whose masters would not take a thousand pounds current for them. But surely this assertion refutes itself; for, if it be true, why do the planters and merchants pay such a price for slaves? And, above all, why do those who make this assertion exclaim the most loudly against the abolition of the slave trade? So much are men blinded, and to such inconsistent arguments are they driven by mistaken interest! I grant, indeed, that slaves are sometimes, by half-feeding, half-clothing, overworking, and stripes,[11] reduced so low, that they are turned out as unfit for service, and left to perish in the woods, or expire on a dunghill.

My master was several times offered by different gentlemen one hundred guineas for me; but he always told them he would not sell me, to my great joy: and I used to double my diligence and care for fear of getting into the hands of those men who did not allow a valuable slave the common support of life. Many of them even used to find fault with my master for feeding his slaves so well as he did; although I often went hungry, and an Englishman might think my fare very indifferent; but he used to tell them he always would do it, because the slaves thereby looked better and did more work.

While I was thus employed by my master, I was often a witness to cruelties of every kind, which were exercised on my unhappy fellow slaves. I used frequently to have different cargoes of new negroes in my care for sale; and it was almost a constant practice with our clerks, and other whites, to commit violent depredations on the chastity of the female slaves; and these I was, though with reluctance, obliged to submit to at all times, being unable to help them. When we have had some of these slaves on board my master's vessels to carry them to other islands, or to America, I have known our mates to commit these acts most shamefully, to the disgrace, not of Christians only, but of men. I have even known them gratify their brutal passion with females not ten years old; and these abominations some of them practised to such scandalous excess, that one of our captains discharged the mate and others on that account. And yet in Montserrat I have seen a negro-man staked to the ground, and cut most shockingly,[12] and then his ears cut off bit by bit, because he had been connected with a white woman who was a common prostitute: as if it were no crime in the whites to rob an innocent African girl of her virtue; but most heinous in a black man only to gratify a passion of nature, where the temptation was offered by one of a different colour, though the most abandoned woman of her species.

One Mr. D—— told me that he had sold 41,000 negroes, and that he once cut off a negro-man's leg for running away – I asked him, if the man had died in the operation, how he as a Christian could answer for the horrid act before God? and he told me, answering was a thing of another world; what he thought and did were policy. I told him that the Christian doctrine taught us to do unto others as we would that others should do unto us. He then said that his scheme had the desired effect – it cured that man and some others of running away.

Another negro-man was half hanged, and then burnt, for attempting to poison a cruel overseer. Thus by repeated cruelties are the wretched first urged to despair, and then murdered, because they still retain so much of human nature about them as to wish to put an end to their misery, and retaliate on their tyrants! These overseers are indeed for the most part persons of the worst character of any denomination of men in the West Indies. Unfortunately, many humane gentlemen, by not residing on their estates, are obliged to leave the management of them in the hands of these human butchers, who cut and mangle the slaves in a shocking manner on the most trifling occasions, and altogether treat them in every respect like brutes. They pay no regard to the situation of pregnant women, nor the least attention to the lodging of the field negroes. Their huts, which ought to be well covered, and the place dry where they take their little repose, are often open sheds, built in damp places; so that, when the poor creatures return tired from the toils of the field, they contract many disorders, from being exposed to the damp air in this uncomfortable state, while they are heated, and their pores are open. This neglect certainly conspires with many others to cause a decrease in the births as well as in the lives of the grown negroes. I can quote many instances of gentlemen who reside on their estates in the West Indies, and then the scene is quite changed; the negroes are treated with lenity and proper care, by which their lives are prolonged, and their masters profited. To the honour of humanity, I knew several gentlemen who managed their estates in this manner; and they found that benevolence was their true interest. And, among many I could mention in several of the islands, I knew one in Montserrat[13] whose slaves looked remarkably well, and never needed any fresh supplies of negroes; and there are many other estates, especially in Barbadoes, which, from such judicious treatment, need no fresh stock of negroes at any time. . . .

[Equiano gives specific examples of leniency but notes (citing published evidence) that in spite of such exceptions the general "stock of negroes" constantly needed replenishment because of the annual decrease in the slave population throughout the British West Indian colonies.]

While I was in Montserrat I knew a negro man, named Emanuel Sankey, who endeavoured to escape from his miserable bondage, by concealing himself on board of a London ship: but fate did not favour the poor oppressed man; for, being discovered when the vessel was under sail, he was delivered up again to his master. This *Christian master* immediately pinned the wretch down to the ground at each wrist and ancle, and then took some sticks of sealing wax, and lighted them, and dropped it all over his back. There was another master who was noted for cruelty; and I believe he had not a slave but what had been cut, and had pieces fairly taken out of the flesh: and after they had been punished thus, he used to make them get into a long wooden box or case he had for that purpose, in which he shut them up during pleasure.[14] It was just about the height and breadth of a man; and the poor wretches had no room when in the case to move.

It was very common in several of the islands, particularly in St. Kitt's, for the slaves to be branded with the initial letters of their master's name, and a load of heavy iron hooks hung about their necks. Indeed on the most trifling occasions they were loaded with chains, and often instruments of torture were added. The iron muzzle, thumbscrews, &c. are so well known, as not to need a description, and were sometimes applied for the slightest faults. I have seen a negro beaten till some of his bones were broken, for only letting a pot boil over. I have often asked many of the men slaves (who used to go several miles to their wives, and late in the night, after having been wearied with a hard day's labour) why they went so far for wives, and why they did not take them of their own master's negro women, and particularly those who lived together as household slaves? Their answer has ever been –'Because when the master or mistress choose to punish the women, they make the husbands flog their own wives, and that they could not bear to do.' Is it surprising that usage like this should drive the poor creatures to despair, and make them seek a refuge in death from those evils which render their lives intolerable – while

> With shudd'ring horror pale, and eyes aghast,
> They view their lamentable lot, and find
> No rest![15]

This they frequently do. A negro-man on board a vessel of my master, while I belonged to her, having been put in irons for some trifling misdemeanor, and kept in that state for some days, being weary of life, took an opportunity of jumping overboard into the sea; however, he was picked up without being drowned. Another, whose life was also a burden to him, resolved to starve himself to death, and refused to eat any victuals: this procured him a severe flogging; and he also, on the first occasion which offered, jumped overboard at Charles Town,[16] but was saved.

Nor is there any greater regard shewn to the little property than there is to the person and lives of the negroes. I have already related an instance or two of particular oppression out of many which I have witnessed; but the following is frequent in all the islands. The wretched field-slaves, after toiling all the day for an unfeeling owner, who gives them but little victuals, steal sometimes a few moments from rest or refreshment to gather some small portion of grass, according as their time will permit. This they commonly tie up in a parcel; either a bit's worth (six-pence) or half a bit's-worth; and bring it to town, or to the market to sell. Nothing is more common than for the white people on this occasion to take the grass from them without paying for it; and not only so, but too often also, to my knowledge, our clerks, and many others, at the same time have committed acts of violence on the poor, wretched, and helpless females; whom I have seen for hours stand crying to no purpose, and get no redress or pay of any kind. Is not this one common and crying sin to bring down God's judgment on the islands? He tells us the oppressor and the oppressed are both in his hands; and if these are not the poor, the broken-hearted, the blind, the captive, the bruised, which our Saviour speaks of, who are they?[17] One of these depredators once, in St. Eustatia, came on board of our vessel, and bought some fowls and pigs of me; and a whole day after his departure with the things, he returned again, and wanted his money back: I refused to give it; and, not seeing my captain on board, he began the common pranks with me; and swore he would even break open my chest and take my money. I therefore expected, as my captain was absent, that he would be as good as his word: and he was just proceeding to strike me, when fortunately a British seaman on board, whose heart had not been debauched by a West India climate, interposed and prevented him. But had the cruel man struck me I certainly should have defended myself at the hazard of my life; for what is life to a man thus oppressed? He went away, however, swearing; and threatened that whenever he caught me on shore he would shoot me, and pay for me afterwards.

The small account in which the life of a negro is held in the West Indies, is so universally known, that it might seem impertinent to quote the following extract, if some people had not been hardy enough of late to assert that negroes are on the same footing in that respect as Europeans. By the 329th Act, page 125, of the Assembly of Barbadoes,[18] it is enacted 'That if any negro, or other slave, under punishment by his master, or his order, for running away, or any other crime or misdemeanor towards his said master, unfortunately shall suffer in life or member, no person whatsoever shall be liable to a fine; but if any man shall out of *wantonness, or only of bloody-mindedness, or cruel intention, wilfully kill a negro, or other slave, of his own, he shall pay into the public treasury fifteen pounds sterling.*' And it is the same in most, if not all, of the West India islands. Is not this one of the many acts of the islands which call loudly for redress? And do not the Assembly which enacted it deserve the appellation of savages and brutes rather than of christians and men? It is an act at once unmerciful, unjust, and unwise; which for cruelty would disgrace an assembly of those who are called barbarians; and for its injustice and *insanity* would shock the morality and common sense of a Samaide[19] or Hottentot.

Shocking as this and many other acts of the bloody West India code at first view appear, how is the iniquity of it heightened when we consider to whom it may be extended! Mr. James Tobin, a zealous labourer in the vineyard of slavery, gives an account[20] of a French planter of his acquaintance, in the island of Martinico, who shewed him many mulatttoes working in the fields like beasts of burden; and he told Mr. Tobin these were all the produce of his own loins! And I myself have known similar instances. Pray, reader, are these sons and daughters of the French planter less his children by being begotten on black women? And what must be the virtue of those legislators, and the feelings of those fathers, who estimate the lives of their sons, however begotten, at no more than fifteen pounds; though they should be murdered, as the act says, *out of wantonness and bloody-mindedness!* But is not the slave trade entirely a war with the heart of man? And surely that which is begun by breaking down the barriers of virtue, involves in its continuance destruction to every principle, and buries all sentiments in ruin!

I have often seen slaves, particularly those who were meagre, in different islands, put into scales and weighed; and then sold from three-pence to six-pence or nine-pence a pound. My master, however, whose humanity was shocked at this mode, used to sell such by the lump. And at or after a sale even those negroes born in the islands it is not uncommon to see taken from their wives, wives taken from their husbands, and children from their parents, and sent off to other islands, and wherever else their merciless lords choose; and probably never more during life see each other! Oftentimes my heart has bled at these partings; when the friends of the departed have been at the water-side, and, with sighs and tears, have kept their eyes fixed on the vessel till it went out of sight.

A poor Creole negro I knew well, who, after having been often thus transported from island to island, at last resided in Montserrat. This man used to tell me many melancholy tales of himself. Generally, after he had done working for his master, he used to employ his few leisure moments to go a fishing. When he had caught any fish, his master would frequently take them from him without paying him; and at other times some other white people would serve him in the same manner. One day he said to me, very movingly, 'Sometimes when a white man take away my fish I go to my maser [*sic*], and he get me my right; and when my maser by strength take away my fishes, what me must do? I can't go to any body to be righted;' then, said the poor man, looking up above, 'I must look up to God Mighty in the top for right.' This artless tale moved me much, and I could not help feeling the just cause Moses had in redressing his brother against the Egyptian.[21] I exhorted the man to look up still to the God on the top, since there was no redress below. . . .

Nor was such usage as this confined to particular places or individuals; for, in all the different islands in which I have been (and I have visited no less than fifteen) the treatment of the slaves was nearly the same; so nearly indeed, that the history of an island, or even a plantation, with a few such exceptions as I have mentioned, might serve for a history of the whole. Such a tendency has the slave-trade to debauch men's minds, and harden them to every feeling of humanity! For I will not suppose that the dealers in slaves are born worse than other men – No; it is the fatality of this mistaken avarice, that it corrupts the milk of human kindness and turns it into gall. And, had the pursuits of those men been different, they might have been as generous, as tender-hearted and just, as they are unfeeling, rapacious and cruel. Surely this traffic cannot be good, which spreads like a pestilence, and taints what it touches! which violates that first natural right of mankind, equality and independency, and gives one man a dominion over his fellows which God could never intend! For it raises the owner to a state as far above man as it depresses the slave below it; and, with all the presumption of human pride, sets a distinction between them, immeasurable in extent, and endless in duration! Yet how mistaken is the avarice even of the planters. Are slaves more useful by being thus humbled to the condition of brutes, than they would be if suffered to enjoy the privileges of men? The freedom which diffuses health and prosperity throughout Britain answers you – No. When you make men slaves you deprive them of half their virtue, you set them in your own conduct an example of fraud, rapine, and cruelty, and compel them to live with you in a state of war; and yet you complain that they are not honest or faithful! You stupify them with stripes, and think it necessary to keep them in a state of ignorance; and yet you assert that they are incapable of learning; that their minds are such a barren soil or moor, that culture would be lost on them; and that they come from a climate, where nature, though prodigal of her bounties in a degree unknown to yourselves, has left man alone scant and unfinished, and incapable of enjoy-ing the treasures she has poured out for him! – An assertion at once impious and absurd. Why do you use those instruments of torture? Are they fit to be applied by one rational being to another? And are ye not struck with shame and mortification, to see the partakers of your nature reduced so low? But, above all, are there no dangers attending this mode of treatment? Are you not hourly in dread of an insurrection? Nor would it be surprising: for when

> ———— No peace is given
> To us enslav'd, but custody severe;
> And stripes and arbitrary punishment
> Inflicted – What peace can we return?
> But to our power, hostility, and hate;
> Untam'd reluctance, and revenge, though slow.
> Yet ever plotting, how the conqueror least
> May reap his conquest, and may least rejoice
> In doing what we most in suffering feel.[22]

But by changing your conduct, and treating your slaves as men, every cause of fear would be banished. They would be faithful, honest, intelligent and vigorous; and peace, prosperity, and happiness, would attend you.

Notes

1. Olaudah Equiano, *The Interesting Narrative of the Life of Olaudah Equiano, or Gustavus Vassa, The African. Written by Himself*, 3rd ed. (London: n.p., 1790), 117–48.
2. See Vincent Carretta, *Equiano the African: Biography of a Self-made Man* (Atlanta: University of Georgia Press, 2005).
3. *gauge*: measure the capacity of a container.
4. *droggers*: coasting vessels, originally peculiar to the West Indies.
5. In later editions, "and other places" was added.
6. [Author's note:] These pisterines are of the value of a shilling. [The words "a day" was added in later editions.]
7. *King's Bench*: the prison for debtors in London.
8. *last war*: the American Revolution, 1775–83.
9. *current*: in local currency. The Jamaican pound at this time was worth about three-fifths of a pound sterling.
10. *first cost*: the price paid by the master for the slave.
11. *stripes*: whippings.
12. *cut most shockingly*: castrated.
13. [Author's note:] Mr. Dubury, and many others, in Montserrat.
14. *during pleasure*: as long as the master pleased.
15. John Milton, *Paradise Lost*, 2.616–18 (slightly altered).
16. *Charles Town*: Charleston, South Carolina.
17. See Luke 4:18.
18. The act was passed in 1688.
19. *Samaide*: Samoyed, one of a Mongolian race living in Siberia.
20. [Author's note:] In his 'Cursory Remarks'. [See James Tobin, *Cursory Remarks upon the Reverend Mr. Ramsay's Essay* (London: G. and T. Wilkie, 1785), 38n: "I have actually had a French planter pointed out to me, who took a pride in boasting, that at least one third of his field gang were the produce of his own loins."]
21. Referring to the occasion during the captivity of the Jews in Egypt, when Moses killed an Egyptian whom he discovered striking "an Hebrew, one of his brethren" (Exodus 2:11–12).
22. Beelzebub's speech to the fallen angels in Milton, *Paradise Lost*, 2.332–40 (slightly altered).

R.C. DALLAS (1754–1824)

A Short Journey in the West Indies (1790)[1]

Robert Charles Dallas, a prolific writer and friend of the poet Byron, was born in Kingston, Jamaica. *A Short Journey* was published anonymously, but Dallas's authorship was established in the *Jamaica Journal* by Michael Ashcroft, who also provides detailed information about the extensive Dallas connections in Jamaica.[2] Robert Dallas's father, a Scottish doctor, went to Jamaica in 1730 and acquired an estate in the parish of Port Royal, which he named Dallas Castle. His mother's forebears had been planters on the island since the seventeenth century. The author's family left Jamaica in 1764, but Dallas returned in 1778 to deal with financial troubles besetting the estate, and he stayed for a few years. *A Short Journey* is a semi-fictionalized account of his observations during that period. Ashcroft suggests that Dallas concealed his authorship to avoid offending his Jamaican relatives and acquaintances with his vigorous attacks on the slave system. Personal and place names are also disguised: Dallas Castle estate appears as "Transit Castle"; the humane "Philanthropos" (perhaps an imaginary figure) is spokesman for enlightened Jamaican opinion, and "Eugenio" is the friend in England to whom the book is addressed.

[Reception of the new master at his estate][3]

An estate put in trust is like a consumptive patient gone to the hot-wells, where hundreds perish for one that is restored. Trustees are careless physicians, little interested in the fate of the patient, whose distemper, say they, was beyond the reach of art before he came under our hands. Even so I found the estate my father had left in this island, in the last stage of its disorder. A small debt, not one-fifth part of its value, had encreased, since his death, under the care of its physicians, to almost its whole value.

"Massa," said old Cudjoe to me, some days after my arrival, "you no dey go in a plantation? all you nega dey come down, if you no go see 'em soon. You been tan here in a dis country, so long you no shame for no go see dem yet?" Very true, Cudjoe, said I to him, I ought to be ashamed of myself. Well, old man, we'll set out to-morrow morning. "Gar a mighty in a top! Massa, dem nega dey go run mad wid joy for see you."

Cudjoe is a character, and I must make him known to you: having worn the livery of old Massa, as he calls my father, he thought he had a right to wear mine, and claimed it the very day after I arrived. He made another claim on the score of his long attachment and fidelity; nothing less than the Saturnalian freedom for every month as well as December. –

> Age libertate Decembri,
> (Quando ita majores voluerunt) utere; narra.[4]

He speaks his mind, and advancing years have had their wonted effect upon his tongue. He loves to talk, and I love to hear him talk. Our colloquies would divert you, could I remember them verbatim, for his remarks are often proverbial, and his allusions keen and novel.

The language of the negroes is more expressive than I could have supposed, and conveys their ideas most forcibly. Cudjoe has gained experience, and he tells old stories with humour. As to his person, it is a little moulded like La Mancha's knight – as lean as you can well conceive; as erect, but not quite so tall, as Quixote: his features, however, do not continue the resemblance – the prominency of his nose being at its lower end, in shape like the ace of clubs, and one of his eyes a little cocked; but archness, rather than disgust, is the effect it produces, and, with the good-natured smile natural to him, gives a pleasant cast to his countenance; so that, when he combs his woolly hair – *he's as tight a lad to see to, as* NEVER *stept in leathern shoe.*[5] Put him now into a stone-colour coat, with orange cape and cuffs, a striped waistcoat and breeches, neatly buttoned at the knees; give him neither stocking nor shoe, but a black stock and a fine frill, and you have a complete figure of Cudjoe, an old beau black footman. He serves me as well, and perhaps better than a young negro would; but his great desire to attend me, was the chief recommendation I had of him.

We got up very early to profit of the sun's absence. Transit Castle is seventeen miles beyond Spanish Town, and Spanish Town is fourteen from Kingston . . . .

TRANSIT CASTLE.

OS HOMINI SUBLIME DEDIT[6] – two hundred beings of this description have been at my feet, in spite of all my efforts to restrain them from humbling themselves so low. "Are you not our master? Are you not our old master's son? We belong to you, we are your negroes, we are your poor faithful slaves." They kissed my shoes again and again, and sung and showed extravagant joy. They all remained about the house the rest of the day. I made it a point to talk to every one of them by turns, at which they were delighted, and threw out expressions as if they esteemed me a being of a superior order. I marked my repugnance at this servility of mind to Philanthropos. – "I do not wonder at it, said he; yet is it more pardonable in the ignorance and fears of a slave, than in the avarice and ambition of a statesman. Chains and tortures put the poor negroes constantly in mind of their dependence on their master, and finding flattery, and every species of servility, powerful means of soothing the overseers that are placed immediately over them, it gradually becomes a part of their character. It has been so through all ages; servility is the attendant of slavery: would to God, all the causes of slavery were eradicated!" . . .

[Disciplinary practices][7]

On my excursion to *Ratoon Rock*, where I was invited to pass some days by a few choice spirits, to whom I was formerly known, I was struck in going through a capital town with the sight of a file of negroes chained to one another, and with the sound of the echoing cattle-whip. Runaways, and negroes that are found *straying*, and do not give an account of themselves, or cannot, from not knowing how to speak English, are taken up and put into the workhouse: – in this situation their labour is supposed to be so much harder than is their common lot, that negroes are often sent hither by their masters and mistresses as a punishment for the faults they commit; and, according to the supposed heinousness of their guilt, the correction (that is the torture) of the cattle-whip is superadded. These unhappy wretches (I have reckoned near a hundred linked to the same chain) are employed to dig and carry stones, remove rubbish, and to perform all the most fatiguing offices of the public. The chain being fixed about the leader, is carried round the bodies of the followers, leaving a sufficient distance to walk without treading on each other's heels, and to each it is secured by a padlock.

As soon as they are thus yoked, within the walls of the workhouse, the gate is thrown open, and the *poor animals* are driven out by a negro *Driver*, attended by a white *Driver*, both with cattle-whips in their hands: – sometimes the white *Driver* rides on a mule.

You may imagine that, in the great number of persons thus fastened to each other, without the least attention to the difference of age or strength, it is not very probable that an equal pace among them can be kept up through the day as they move about.

They are set off upon a brisk walk, almost approaching to *a trot*, and woe be to those whom fatigue first forces to flag: – the never-ceasing sound of the cattle-whip long keeps a regularity in the slight sinking curve of the intervening links of the chain, but, *naturam expellas furca tamen usque recurret*,[8] nature will return, the feebler will begin to pull upon the stronger, the intervening links will lose their regular curve: here they become stretched to their utmost, there they sink nearly to the ground, the weak add the weight of their exhausted limbs to the strong, and the strong tread upon the heels of the weak. – This the Drivers *remedy* as much as possible, by their cattle-whips, till Nature, quite worn out, is at last driven back to the workhouse.

I observed, that many of their bodies were terribly gashed and mangled. – One of them had an instrument about his neck they call a pot-hook, it was made of iron, and had worked his collar-bone raw.

I have seen things of this kind, in wood, put about the throats of hogs on

English farms, to prevent their going through hedges: what purpose it was to serve round the neck of a man I could not divine, but I was informed by Philanthropos, that it was to prevent such as were disposed to run away from making their way easy through the woods . . . .

I have not lost my natural abhorrence to cruelty, yet I see it practised with much less impatience than I did, and I have only to pray, that I may not feel an inclination to turn *driver* myself, before I have the satisfaction of taking my dear Eugenio by the hand. On my arrival at Ratoon Rock, I found my old acquaintance so deeply engaged in consultation, that they scarcely welcomed me, before they resumed their deliberations upon a subject very interesting to them, and to which I was allowed to listen . . . . One of the gentlemen suspected that the horses had been taken out of the stable and rode in the night; another was sure of it; a third swore it with horrid imprecations; and a fourth was for finding the truth out immediately, by putting the stable boy upon the picket till he acknowledged all he knew of the matter. The sentiment of the last was adopted, and the boy was instantly called in: he was a fine youth about seventeen years old, a mulatto, and supposed to be the son of the same father as his masters. The poor boy approached with dismay in his countenance; he was questioned and cross-questioned; he was sworn at, he was counselled to declare what he knew – he protested, that if the horses had been rode it was without his knowledge: this only brought forth vollies of oaths, abuse, and threats, and an immediate recourse to the torture: a cord was run round one of his wrists and thrown over a beam, by which he was suspended, while his foot was placed on a pointed stake fixed in the ground, the other arm and leg swung off with the body from its poise. This he bore a considerable time, protesting himself ignorant of the cause of his punishment; at last the torture became insupportable, and he promised confession if they would take him down; he was accordingly taken off the picket, and the rope slackened; he was now desired to tell the truth: "Well, Massa," said he, after resting a little while, "if I must tell the truth, I assure you, Massa, I don't know anything about it." He was immediately hoisted to his former position, where a second proof made him *more reasonable*, and he was ready to declare *all*, if they would but take him down again; but no relief was to be granted now, until he first mentioned the negroes who had been riding the horses. He was asked if it was not Alexander, or Jupiter, Marlborough, or Ned, and the last name vibrating on his distended nerves, he roared out "Ned, Ned, Massa." – While he still swung upon the picket, many more questions were put to him about Ned, who being thus *fully convicted*, the poor accuser and evidence was let down. It is impossible for me to describe to you, the vehemence of passion that succeeded, when Ned was brought to face his accuser, who again flinched from the charge, which he said was but the effect of pain; on which both he and Ned were now picketed, and it ended with their charging one another, and both confessing themselves guilty: the consequence was, that they were carried into the field, and I heard the gentlemen say, that they stood by while these poor creatures received a *hundred lashes* each from the cattle-whip, to the repetition of which, they were determined to be again spectators the next day.

I made the best of my way from Ratoon Rock. – Shall I add, that I afterwards heard that cruelty not being satisfied with the cattle-whip, poor Ned was stripped of his livery, degraded to a field negro, and for six months dug cane-holes, weeded, and cut down the crop with a fifty pound weight fastened to his body.

Notes

1. R.C. Dallas, *A Short Journey in the West Indies, in which are interspersed, curious anecdotes and characters* (London: n.p., 1790).
2. Michael Ashcroft, "Robert Charles Dallas", *Jamaica Journal* 44 (1980): 94–101.
3. Dallas, *Short Journey*, 1:66–83.
4. *Age . . . narra*: "Come, use the freedom allowed in December (as our fathers ordained); speak" in Horace, *Satires*, 1.2.4–5, referring to the Roman custom of Saturnalia, when slaves were given licence to speak and act freely. See Robert Dirks, *The Black Saturnalia: Conflict and Its Ritual Expression on British West Indian Slave Plantations* (Gainesville: University of Florida Press, 1987).
5. A versified rendering (source untraced) of Shakespeare's "As proper men as ever trod upon neat's leather", in *Julius Caesar*, 1.1.27.
6. *os homini sublime dedit*: Ovid, *Metamorphoses*, 1.85, from his account of the creation. God or Nature "gave man an uplifted gaze" and ordered him to stand

upright and turn his face to heaven, as distinct from downward-looking animals.

7. Dallas, *Short Journey*, 2:59–74.

8. *Naturam . . . recurret*: "you may drive out Nature with a pitchfork but she will always return", Horace, *Epistles*, 1.10.24.

JOHN LUFFMAN (FL. 1776–1820)

A Brief Account of the Island of Antigua (1789)[1]

Luffman lived for three years in Antigua, pursuing his occupation as surveyor, cartographer and engraver: his maps of Antigua and other islands in the West Indies were highly valued in the eighteenth century. His anti-slavery views seem to have been formed independently of the public movement for abolition of the slave trade. When he received news of the opening of the campaign in London he greeted it with enthusiasm (Letter XXVIII, 7 February 1788), condemning the "traffic to Africa for human flesh and blood", in typically forthright language, as "the most abominable, the most to be abhorred of any species of commerce ever carried on by our countrymen", and "a disgrace to those excellent laws we boast, and to the enlightened age we live in". Luffman like Edward Thompson was pilloried by James Adair for his so-called malignant charges against the planters of Antigua (see headnote to Thompson, page 61 above).

LETTER XI.

To ———.

St. John's, Antigua,
Jan. 28, 1787.

Dear Sir,

To be the manager of an estate of an absentee, in this isle, I am well satisfied is one of the best situations in it, altho' their stipends amount to no more than from eighty to one hundred pounds sterling, per ann. and, notwithstanding the necessaries and superfluities of life are considerably dearer than at London; yet, however paradoxical it may appear, when I tell you this discription of men sport several dishes at their tables, drink claret, keep mulatto mistresses, and indulge in every foolish extravagance of this western region, it is nevertheless strictly true. But as you would naturally ask, by what means this expensive manner of living is supported? It is thus I answer – These people, Sir, raise on the grounds of their employers, stock of every kind, suitable to our markets, which they feed principally with the grain, &c. belonging to the estate on which they live; they also grow exotics, as well as the vegetables natural to this climate; and, to complete the system, planned with so much wisdom and justice, they employ the slaves belonging to the plantation to vend such produce. There are of these men, or at least their wives [some?] who occupy the time from twelve to twenty negroes daily on this business to the manifest injury of their masters, and emolument of themselves. The adage which I have often heard applied to masters of vessels and their owners, may, with the alteration of two words, be applicable to these men – "Fat managers and lean employers," for I am very certain, to be manager of, and attorney[2] to an estate of a non-resident, is better than to be its owner, the first, receiving benefits without the least risque, while the latter is subject to every loss without receiving the advantages which ought, consistent with justice, to be his and not his servants. But here I must observe, that many of these gentlemen managers, as well as the overseers under them, contribute in a great degree, to stock the plantation with mulatto and mestee slaves; it is impossible to say in what numbers they have such children, but the following fact is too often verified, "that, as soon as born, they are despised, not only by the very authors, under God, of their being, but by every white, destitute of humane and liberal principles," such is the regard paid to the hue of complexion in preference to the more permanent beauties of the mind.[3]

I remain, &c. &c.

[The extract below is preceded by a second-hand account of the methods by which slaves were acquired in Africa and the vile conditions under which they were shipped across the Atlantic. Luffman's description of their arrival in the West Indies, however, is based on personal observation.]

LETTER XIX.

St. John's, Antigua,
July 6, 1787.

. . . Thus are the degraded sons of Africa brought to the West-Indian shores; and they are treated in the following manner on their arrival here, previous to the day of sale: As soon as the anchor is over the vessel's side, and the captain gone on shore to give in his account of the cargo, the slaves are brought upon deck (having been shaved some days before they made the land), where they are cleansed from the stench and vermin contracted on the passage, and their skins rubbed with oil or grease, to give them a sleek appearance. This business being done, they are sent on shore, under the care of some petty officers and seamen, to the merchant to whom the cargo is consigned, who deposits them altogether in an empty store or warehouse, contiguous to the wharfs, when after being advertised for sale, and walked about the town, preceded by a drum beating and flag flying, for the purpose of attracting the attention of the inhabitants to the persons about to be sold; and when the merchant has sent written notices of the time of such sale to the planters or others, whom he thinks likely to become purchasers, the sale is announced by a trumpet sounding, while the ship's ensign, or some other flag is displayed from a window, or from the top of the place where the Negroes are deposited; and so eager are the whites to see these ill-fated people, that the doors of such receptacles are crowded almost as much as those of the theatre, when the immortal Garrick, or the inimitable Siddons, were to represent the finest passages from our greatest and most favored poets.

The purchasers of slaves are as particular in examining them before they strike a bargain, as a butcher, at Smithfield market, when dealing for sheep. As soon as bought, they are walked to the respective plantations of their owners, where the hoe is frequently put into hands, hitherto unused to labor, and as soft as the finest lady's in Europe. These cargoes average from thirty-seven to forty pounds sterling per head.

LETTER XXIV.

St. John's, Antigua,
Nov. 9, 1787.

Dear Sir,

The punishments inflicted on slaves, in this island, are various and torment-ing. The picket,[4] is the most severe, but as its consequences are well known in Europe, particularly among the military, I shall speak no further upon it, than to say it is seldom made use of here, but many other cruelties equally destructive to life, though slower in their operations, are practised by the unfeeling, which is the thumb-screw, a barbarous invention to fasten the thumbs together, which appears to cause excruciating pain. The iron neck-lace, is a ring, locked or riveted about the neck; to these collars are fre-quently added what are here termed pot-hooks, additions, resembling the hooks or handles of a porridge-pot, fixed perpendicularly, the bent or hooked parts turning outwards, which prevents the wearers from laying down their heads with any degree of comfort. The boots are strong iron rings, full four inches in circumference, closed just above the ancles, to these some owners prefix a chain, which the miserable sufferers, if able to work, must manage as well as they can, and it is not unfrequent to see in the streets of this town, at mid-day, negroes chained together by these necklaces as well as by the boots, when let out of their dungeon for a short time to breathe the fresh air, whose crime has been endeavoring to gain that liberty by running away, which they well knew could never be otherwise obtained from their owners. The spurs are rings of iron, similar to the boots, to which are added spikes from three to four inches long, placed horizontally. A chain fastened about the body with a padlock, is another mode of tormenting this oppressed race of beings. A boy who has not yet seen his fourteenth year, passes by my house several times in a day, and has done so for these six months past, with no other cloathing; he also lays upon his chains, and although they are as much in point of weight as he ought reasonably to carry, yet he is obliged, through the day to fetch water from the country pond at the distance of half a mile from the house of his mistress, who is an old widow-woman. To the chains thus put on, a fifty pounds weight is sometimes added, as an appendage; this is undoubtedly a prudent measure, and admirably well calculated to keep the slave at home; as it must of course prevent the object thus secured, from escaping the rigor of his destiny. The bilboes, severe floggings, and sundry other methods of torturing these unhappy people, as best suits the caprice or inventive cruelty of their own-ers or employers, are here inflicted. The public whipper is a white man, who executes his office by a negroe deputy, and the price for every flogging is two bits.

However hurtful or disgusting the aforementioned punishments are to those who have minds fraught with humanity, every application to the mag-istrates to prevent the exercising such severities on these unfriended people, must be ineffectual while there is no existing law in the island code enabling them to take cognizance of the correction of slaves by their proprietors. I could therefore presume to advise those, to whom the power of making laws for the good government of the British empire, both at home and abroad, is delegated, to enact a law for establishing a committee of human-ity, composed of men of liberal principles, and such, no doubt, can be found, not only in this island, but also in all those under the British govern-ment, who should have entire controul in all cases between the master and the slave. To these men all complaints should be made, and by them and them only, should punishments be directed; an act of such a nature, would, I trust, not only be applauded by all good men, but bring on the authors of it, the blessings of Heaven, and the gratitude of a numerous body of unfor-tunate fellow creatures.

Slaves, for criminal offences, have within these few years, been admitted to a trial by a jury of six white men, at which proceedings two justices pre-side as judges. They are seldom hanged, unless for murder, it being the inter-est of the owners of such as are convicted, to get them off, the country allowing the masters but half the appraised value of such as are executed; they are therefore in mitigation generally flogged under the gallows, and sometimes sent off the island to be sold . . .[5]

LETTER XXV.

St. John's, Antigua,
Dec. 8, 1787.

Dear Sir,

Slaves are not permitted to marry consequently take one anothers words, and change their husbands and wives (as they term them) when, and as often as they please. Baptism is allowed by some owners, but the slave must pay the priest for executing his office and the price is a dollar. Negroes and colored people are not buried in the same church-yard as the whites, even if free; the distinction, and the superiority which the European race claim over the African, are extended as far as they can possibly go: to the grave! but there they must cease, and the hereafter, when the reign of human pride is over, will be directed according to the fear we have had of God, and the love we have borne one another during our earthly state of trial.

Negroe funerals, particularly such as are of old Creole families, or in esteem among their fellows, are numerously attended; I have seen from one to two hundred men, women, and children, follow a corpse, decently dressed in white, which dress has been recommended to them by the Methodist and Moravian preachers, whose meetings are crouded by these people, and to whose discourses they listen with seeming attention. If the party deceased has been christened, and their friends can afford to pay for the ringing of the church bell, they may have that ceremony performed, as also the burial service, the first of these is sometimes done, the latter very seldom. The body is mostly enclosed in a wooden shell or coffin, which, during the procession to the grave, is covered with a sheet, by way of pall, and such as have it in their power, bring liquor, fruit, &c. to the house of their deceased uncle or aunt, brother or sister, (the common appellations, whether related in consanguinity or not) which are consumed by the company while things are getting into readiness. Before I leave the subject of negroe burials, I cannot avoid remarking to you, one, among many other singularities, possessed by these people, as it will shew in what manner they feel, and express their feelings: when one of their brotherhood dies, as they suppose by ill-usage; as soon as the body is brought out of the place where it was deposited, taken upon the shoulders of the bearers, and has remained in that situation a few seconds, they (the bearers) begin to reel and stagger about surprisingly, going in zig-zags, and hurrying from one side of the street to the other, as if forced by some supernatural impulse, when after carrying on this joke for sometime, and probably tired themselves with their retrograde motions, one or two of the mourners walk up to the head of the coffin, and talk in a low voice to their departed brother or sister, the purport of which is to request the deceased to go in an orderly manner to the place of interment; to see them thus agitated gives great trouble to their friends, who are very sorry for what has happened, and that Gorramitee, (the negroe manner of expressing God Almighty) will punish those who have done them ill. This exordium always appeases the defunct, who then goes *quietly* to interment . . .

LETTER XXX.

St. John's, Antigua,
March 14, 1788.

Dear Sir,

Negroes are very fond of the discordant notes of the banjar, and the hollow sound of the toombah. The banjar is somewhat similar to the guittar, the bottom, or under part, is formed of one half of a large calabash, to which is prefixed a wooden neck, and it is strung with cat-gut and wire. This instrument is the invention of, and was brought here by the African negroes, who are most expert in the performances thereon, which are principally their own country tunes, indeed I do not remember ever to have heard anything like European numbers from its touch. The toombah is similar to the tabor, and has gingles of tin or shell; to this music (if it deserves the name) I have seen a hundred or more dancing at a time, their gestures are extravagant, but not more so than the principal dancers at your Opera-house, and, I believe, were some of their steps and motions introduced into the public amusements at home, by French or Italian dancers, they would be well received; I do not mean, by the bye, to indicate that the movements of these sables are altogether graceful, but their agility and the surprising command of their limbs, is astonishing; this can be accounted for only by their being habituated to a warm climate, where elasticity is more general than in the colder latitudes: The principal dancing time is on Sunday afternoons, when the great market is over (the nature and utility of which I propose to give you in my next), in fact Sunday is their day of trade, their day of relaxation, their day of pleasure, and may, in the strictest sense of the words, be called the negroes holiday . . .

LETTER XXXI.

St. John's, Antigua,
March 28, 1788.

Dear Sir,

In my last I promised you an account of the Sunday market, and will now perform that promise. This market is held at the southern extremity of the town, on the land of John Otto Baijer, Esq; between three roads, leading to Five Islands, Bermudian Valley, and English Harbour, and is about as large again as the Royal Exchange;[6] here an assemblage of many hundred negroes and mulattoes expose, for sale, poultry, pigs, kids, fruit, and other things; they begin to assemble by daybreak, and the market is generally crouded by ten o'clock; this is the proper time to purchase, for the week, such articles as are not perishable: The noise occasioned by the jabber of the negroes, and the squalling and cries of the children basking in the sun, exceeds any thing I ever heard in a London market: The smell is also intolerable, proceeding from the strong effluvia, naturally arising from the bodys of these people, and from the stinking salt-fish and other offencibles sent for sale by hucksters, which the negroes will buy, even when in the last stage of rottenness, to season their pots with, and I do not exaggerate when I say that the nostrills will receive the fragrance of this place, when at the distance of a full quarter of a mile from it, to leeward. About three o'clock business is nearly over, when the hucksters shops are filled, and their doors crouded, and new rum grog is swilled in large quantities to the benefit of the retailers and destruction of the negroes; some, as I before wrote you, dance, others play at dice (as they call it) with small shells, and frequently lose, not only every dog[7] that they have been working for through the day, but so great is their love of play, that the very trifling clothes from their backs is a forfeit to their mischance. It is not uncommon for them, when intoxicated, to turn out to fight in Otto's pasture (adjoining the market); they are not confined to rules, like the gentlemen brutes with you, but give their blows – how, and where they can, generally open handed, and it is all fair to pull each others wool, kneel upon, beat when down, or indeed whatever they have power to do, to the hurt of their adversary. They are punishable by law for fighting, but the law seldom interferes. The sight of a gun, or a white man, laying about him with a whip, will disperse them immediately; and a negroe durst not return a blow, under the forfeiture of their right hand.

This rigid law was introduced, I learn, to prevent the insurrection of slaves; which, about fifty years ago, had nearly proved fatal to the white inhabitants of this island.[8]

Notes

1. John Luffman, *A Brief Account of the Island of Antigua, together with the customs and manners of its inhabitants, as well white as black: as also an accurate statement of the food, cloathing, labor, and punishment, of slaves. In Letters to a Friend. Written in the Years 1786, 1787, 1788* (London: T. Cadell, 1789).
2. [Author's note:] An Attorney for an estate, receives from half a guinea, to a guinea, for every hogshead of Sugar he ships.
3. Adair comments on this sentence: "You are a *modest* man, Mr. L. or you would have boasted of the share you had in stocking plantations. Probably you was a *married* man, and therefore only stocked in the legal way; which you intimate few husbands in that country are contented with doing. Now, Sir, I believe (though I will not swear that any husband is guilty of infidelity in that country) that your countrymen are as much suspected of wandering from home as the native [Antiguan] *whites*. I know not what you mean by *despising* spurious progeny: I believe they are not much respected by their parents any where; but parental affection to those children is more frequent in the West Indies, than in

your country; and their parents often purchase their freedom, and treat them with great tenderness"; James Adair, *Unanswerable Arguments against the Abolition of the Slave Trade* (London: J.P. Bateman, 1790), 99–100.

4. This punishment was evidently in use in Jamaica at about this time: see the description in Dallas's *Short Journey* (page 132 above).

5. Adair comments at length on this letter. His main concern is to defend the treatment of slaves by creole as opposed to non-native whites, claiming that "*Europeans* to my certain knowledge, are much severer task-masters than the natives of the country, vulgarly called *Creoles*". While he "never heard that either the *picket* or *thumb-screw* were used in Antigua", he concedes that they might have been used by "the *hucksters* [small traders], most of them *Europeans* . . . because I can conceive them to be capable of any act of cruelty. I sat, as one of the *Judges*, on one of those fellows, an *Englishman*, who had destroyed one of his slaves by the most deliberate and repeated acts of cruelty; and yet fine and imprisonment were all the punishment the laws would permit us to inflict. Shocked at this rare instance of barbarity, and not being a member of the Legislature, I entreated some of the gentlemen of that body . . . to have a law passed to have such crimes made *capital*"; *Unanswerable Arguments*, 103–5.

6. The commercial trading centre of London.

7. *dog*: name of a copper coin used in some West Indian islands.

8. A major conspiracy by a group of African slaves, supported by some creoles, was uncovered in Antigua in 1736. The slaves intended to kill all the whites, and to set up an Asante-type kingdom under a slave called Court, known to his followers as Tackey. He and eleven other ringleaders were summarily tried and executed, and a savage programme of executions and deportations followed. See Michael Craton, *Testing the Chains: Resistance to Slavery in the British West Indies* (Ithaca: Cornell University Press, 1982), 120–22.

M.H.

"The Poor Negro Beggar's Petition and Complaint" (1791)[1]

This poem appeared in *The Bee, or Literary Weekly Intelligencer*, a magazine published in Edinburgh under the editorship of James Anderson, whose anti-slavery views are reflected in its generous selection of articles and poems about slavery and detailed reports of parliamentary debates on the slave trade. Anderson's own *Observations on Slavery*, published in Manchester in 1789, proposed the complete abolition of slavery within ten years. Nothing is known about "M.H.", but his or her account of the cruel practice which prompted the poem contains details not given in other sources,[2] suggesting that the author visited or resided in Jamaica.

SIR,

I am sorry to have it in my power to assure you, that the story which gave rise to the following lines, is not fictitious, but a real fact, that happened in the Island of Jamaica, not many years ago. The man who perpetrated the deed, a Scotchman too, is, I believe, alive in that Island at this time. It was the practice of this man, from deliberate system, to work out his slaves with hard labour; and when the doctor reported that they were no longer able to work, nor any hopes remained of their recovery, they were ordered to be carried immediately to the *launch*, an inclined plane made of several boards fastened together, whose lower extremity pointed over the edge of a precipice several hundred feet in height, that hung over a deep ravine on his plantation. This was, in general, a pretty certain launch into eternity, though, in the present case, it failed. Nossak had been declared by the Doctor incapable of any further service, and was ordered, as usual, to the launch. The poor fellow begged hard that he might not be carried to the launch, as he said he was not dead: – But nothing could prevail with his inhuman master. Like his fellows, he must take his fate; but, by a kind of miracle, he escaped with life, and made a shift to crawl away from the foot of the rocks. Some of his black friends fell in with him, had compassion on him, and used means for his recovery. Some time after, the merciless wretch who had caused him to be launched over the precipice, was somewhat surprized at seeing his slave, whom he had believed to be in the other world, begging in one of the streets of a neighbouring town; but had the modest assurance to wish to reclaim him as his property. The poor fellow's story, however, prevailed, even in the West Indies, to make all agree in thinking he had got a full discharge from his service: And the tyrant owner seeing the general indignation rising high against him, was glad, at length, to make his escape from the mob as quickly as possible, though no public vengeance overtook him.

If I shall be told this story cannot be true, because it is contrary to the laws provided for the safety of the negroes, I answer, that I dispute not about the law; but that the fact is literally true, I do maintain, and am ready to prove it upon the most undeniable evidence, should it be necessary. – And this I aver, though I am no friend to the abolition of the slave-trade.

The negroes themselves made up a ballad in their own way, which they used to sing at their public merry makings, the chorus of which was,

Massa, Massa, no launch, –

Massa, no dead yet, – or something to that purpose, which I am sorry I did not then take down. These gave rise to the following lines:

The Poor Negro Beggar's Petition and Complaint.

O Massa, poor negro! God Almighty you bless:
O Massa, poor negro! in utmost distress.

Much beating, much lashing, poor Nossak endur'd;
No toil, no submission, good usage insur'd.
Provisions were bad; our allowance was small;   5
Hard work; no relief for poor Nossak at all.
Sick, sick, and not able to stand to the hoe;
"Given up by the doctor, to the launch he must go,"
Said my master, unfeeling, and sent me away,
Though I pleaded, intreated, – "O let me but stay.   10
"O Massa, no launch, me no dead, me no dead,
No launch, me grow well again, Massa," I said.
He was deaf to my cries; – so dragg'd to the rock,
From the plank I was launched, – the terrible shock!
I got fast asleep, but awaking again,   15
Alas! I awoke to much sorrow and pain;
My legs they were broke, – all my body much bruis'd;
No hope; even death to relieve me refus'd;
Dry bones of poor negroes were scatter'd around;
Like me they were launch'd; but sweet death they had found;   20
Had escap'd, exulting, from slavery and pain;
Their spirits high soaring had cross'd the wide main,
To visit the land of their fathers and brothers;
To salute the lov'd souls of their sisters and mothers.
O death! why so slow? – but why should I complain,   25
Since the launch has releas'd me from collar and chain?[3]
O Massa, a bit[4] on poor Nossak bestow,
God Almighty you bless, no distress may you know.
Here laid on a dunghill, poor Nossack must lie;
No eye drops a tear; no breast heaves a sigh;   30
But death shall release me from sorrow and pain;
Then my dear native home I'll revisit again.

Notes

1. "M.H.", "The Poor Negro Beggar's Petition and Complaint", *The Bee, or Literary Weekly Intelligencer* 3 (18 May 1791): 63–65.
2. See "Take Him to the Gulley", page 428 below.
3. [Author's note:] To the iron chain which they wear constantly, a half hundred weight is appended, to prevent their running away during the night; and the collar has long spikes running out in every direction, to prevent their laying down their heads to rest.
4. *bit*: a Jamaican coin of small value.

BRYAN EDWARDS (1743–1800)

"Ode on seeing a Negro-Funeral" (1793)[1]

Edwards is best known for his monumental *History, Civil and Commercial of the British West Indies* (1793). He went out to Jamaica in 1759 to live with his uncle, Zachary Bayly, a leading figure in Jamaican society. On his uncle's death in 1769 he inherited several sugar plantations with at least 1,500 slaves; he remained in Jamaica, off and on, until 1792. He then settled in England as a West India merchant, was elected a Member of Parliament in 1796 and campaigned vigorously against abolition of the slave trade. He was nevertheless relatively humane and enlightened in his attitude towards slavery. While regarding the slave system as indispensable on historical, social and economic grounds, he recognized the slave trade as unjust and cruel in itself, leading him to the paradoxical belief that "nothing is more certain than that the Slave Trade may be very wicked, and the planters in general very innocent."[2]

This "Ode" was printed in his *History* in a footnote to an account of slaves' funeral songs, which he describes as

> all of the heroick or martial cast; affording some colour to the prevalent notion, that the Negroes consider death not only as a welcome and happy release from the calamities of their condition, but also as a passport to the place of their nativity; a deliverance which, while it frees them from bondage, restores them to the society of their dearest, long-lost, and lamented relatives in Africa. But I am afraid that this, like other European notions concerning the Negroes, is the dream of poetry; the sympathetic effusion of a fanciful or too credulous imagination.

The footnote adds: "Perhaps it was some such imagination that gave rise to the following little poem, now published for the first time – the production of early youth". Edwards must mean "published in England", since it had previously appeared, with minor variations, in his *Poems, written chiefly in the West Indies*, published in Kingston, Jamaica, in 1792. Another version, the text used here, survives in manuscript, inscribed on a blank page of what appears to be a trial edition, privately printed in Bath as *Poetical Essays, Written chiefly in the West-Indies.*[3] The third stanza does not appear in either of the printed versions, perhaps because Edwards thought it politic to moderate his anti-slavery tone at a critical stage in the first slave-trade debate.

Mahali dies! o'er yonder plain
His bier is borne; the sable train
   By youthful virgins led.
Daughters of injur'd Afric, say
Why raise ye thus th' heroic lay,   5
   Why triumph o'er the dead?

No tear bedews their fixed eye:
Lo! now[4] the Hero lives, they cry; –
   Releas'd from slav'ry's chain:
Beyond the billowy surge he flies,   10
And joyful views his native Skies,
   And long lost bow'rs again!

Happy, brave Chief! to reach the shore!
– Europe's false Sons shall now no more
   Thy freeborn limbs confine;   15
Waste in hard toil thy manhood's bloom,
And, harder, thy sad offspring doom
   To wretchedness like thine!

On *Koromantyn's* palmy soil,
Heroic deeds and martial toil,   20
   Shall fill each glorious day;
Love, fond and faithful, crown thy nights,
And artless joys,[5] – unmixt delights,
   Past cruel wrongs repay.

Nor lordly pride's hard avarice[6] there,   25
Alone, shall Nature's bounties share, –
   To all her Children free:
For thee the dulcet reed shall spring;
His milky bowl[7] the *Coco* bring,
   Th' *Anana* bloom for Thee.   30

Hark Warriors! tis our Afric's God! –[8]
He wakes; – He lifts th' avenging rod,
   And speeds th' important hours![9]
From *Niger's* golden stream he calls,
Fair Freedom comes! – Oppression falls;   35
   And vengeance now[10] is ours!

Soon, Christian, thou,[11] in wild dismay,
Of Afric's ruthless rage[12] the prey,
   Shalt roam[13] th' affrighted wood;
Transform'd to Tygers, fierce and fell,   40
Thy race shall prowle with savage yell,
   And glut their rage for blood!

But soft; – Beneath yon *Tam'rind* shade,
Now let the Hero's limbs be laid;
   Sweet slumbers bless the brave!   45
There shall the breezes waft perfume,
Nor livid light'nings[14] blast the bloom,
   That decks Mahali's grave!

Notes

1. Edwards, *History, Civil and Commercial*, 2:85–87.
2. Ibid., 2:40.
3. Undated, but on internal evidence earlier than the *Poems* of 1792. The unique copy of this work is in Edinburgh University Library.
4. "'Tis now" in the 1793 version.
5. 1793: "And bliss unbought"
6. 1793: "stern avarice"
7. 1793: "balmy bowl"
8. 1793: "The thunder, hark! 'Tis Afric's God,"
9. 1793: "impatient hours;"
10. 1793: "vengeance yet"
11. 1793: "Now, Christian, now,"
12. 1793: "proud revenge"
13. 1793: "Go roam"
14. 1793: "vivid lightnings"

JOHN MARJORIBANKS (1759–96)

Slavery: An Essay in Verse (1792)[1]

The author, a soldier and minor poet, was stationed in Jamaica from 1784 to 1787, but it is clear from his earliest work, *Trifles in Verse*, published in Kelso in 1784, that he was opposed to slavery even before he set foot in the West Indies. First-hand observation turned him into a fierce and untiring critic of the slave system, and references to slavery abound in his writings during and after his service in Jamaica. *Slavery* is inscribed "Stoneyhill Barracks, Liguanea, Oct. 1786" and prefaced by a "Letter" from the author to the secretary of the Edinburgh Society for Promoting the Abolition of the African Slave Trade, explaining that although the account of slavery given in the poem accords exactly with evidence published by the Society, it was written before the society existed. He presumably delayed publishing it until after leaving Jamaica, for fear of arousing the wrath of local slave owners or the disapproval of his senior officers. The text is given here in full since it is available only in abridged form in other modern sources. Marjoribanks later wrote a long poem "The Deliverance of Africa", dated April 1792, applauding Wilberforce's bill for abolition of the slave trade.

Britannia's heroes for fair Freedom fought,
And gain'd, at length, the prize they nobly sought.

On our brave ancestors did Freedom smile,
And fix'd her empire in their happy isle.
There still she flourishes in all her charms,   5
Each heart enlivens, and each bosom warms.
    Ungrateful men! to whom such boons she gave!
Who dare whole nations of mankind enslave!
From the rich ports, where she triumphant reigns,
Forth fly the fleets that carry freights of chains!   10
From peaceful counting-houses edicts pour,
Afric's wide realms rapaciously to scour.
By Freedom's sons o'er distant oceans borne,
Are helpless wretches from their country torn!
In noisome cells, where fell Distemper glows,   15
A favour'd part *Death* frees from future woes!
Or happy they, who in the friendly deep
Fly from their tyrants to eternal sleep!
    What horrid fears must haunt th' untutor'd mind
(Too *just*, alas!) of torments yet behind!   20
On shocking feasts must savage fancy brood,[2]
Where pale Europeans prey on human food!
His bloody limbs, yet quiv'ring on the board,
Glut the keen stomach of his ruthless lord!
Or on the shrine of vengeful gods he lies;   25
And, in atonement for a Christian, dies!
Yes! every slave must yield a master food,
Who slowly fattens on his vital blood!
Blest, if at once his cruel tortures ceas'd,
And gave white cannibals a short liv'd feast!   30
Yes! Afric's sons must stain the bloody shrine!
But all those victims, Avarice, are *thine!*
On Mercy's God those tyrants dare to call;
But Av'rice only is their lord of all!
To him their rites incessantly they pay;   35
And waste for him the Negro's life away!
    "But hear!' say you. Philosophy will hear;

Whoever argues, he will lend an ear.
"On their own shore those wretches *Slaves* we found,[3]
And only mov'd them to a fairer ground.   40
Captives in war they met this wayward fate;
Or Birth had doom'd them to a servile state.
Oft they are convicts, sentenc'd for their crimes
To endless exile from their native climes.
With plants they knew not on those sterile lands,   45
Here are they nourish'd by our friendly hands;
Of our own properties we give them share,
And food or raiment never cost them care.
On them no debts, no difficulties prey,
Not Britain's peasants half so blest as they!"   50
Hold, impious men! the odious theme forbear!
Nor with such treason wound a Briton's ear!
The British peasant! healthy, bold, and *free!*
Nor wealth, nor grandeur, half so blest as he!
The state of life, for *happiness the first*,[4]   55
Dare you compare with this the *most accurs'd*
You found them slaves – but who that title gave!
The God of Nature never form'd a slave!
Tho' Fraud, or Force acquire a master's name,
Nature and Justice must remain the same!   60
He who from thieves their booty, conscious, buys,
May use an argument as sound and wise:
That he conceives no guilt attends his trade,
Because the booty is already made.
    For your own honour, name not Afric's wars!   65
Ye, whose curs'd commerce rais'd those civil jars!
Each petty chief, whose tribes were drain'd for you,
For *your vile traffic* roams in quest of new;
For you in guiltless blood imbrues his hands,
And carries havoc o'er his neighbour's lands!   70
They whom the feebler rage of war may spare,
A harder fate from you and Slavery share!

For you – *sole instigators to the wrong,*[5]
The brutal victor hurries them along.
From Afric's far interior regions driven,   75
To you – and Anguish are those wretches given!
   Nor yet are you, for any *righteous cause,*
The *executioners of Afric's laws*;
Th' *atrocious criminals* I oft have view'd,
European Justice has so far pursu'd;   80
Emblems of Innocence they met my eyes,
In soft simplicity and young surprise![6]
   But I, alas! may spare my idle strains,
Which ne'er can wrest them from European chains!
For Int'rest speaks in language far too strong,   85
Either to heed a sermon, or a song!
Yet happy I, and not in vain I write,
If I could render but their chains more light;
Could I but wipe one tear from SLAVERY's eye,
Or save his heart one agonising sigh!   90
   Grant then your plea: – "Necessity demands
The toil of foreign slaves' unwilling hands."
Yet no necessity could e'er excuse,
The more than savage cruelty you use![7]
"Those creatures are so obstinate," you say,   95
"That but from punishment they will obey;
No kindness soothes; no gratitude they know" –
Ah! little gratitude, indeed, they owe!
Ere you this virtue to their race denied,
Th' effects of kindness might have well been tried!   100
   Come, now, reflect what *tender* modes you take
To make those beings labour – *for your sake!*
First, then, you are so generous and good
To give them time to rear a *little* food;
On the same selfish principle, of course,   105
You feed *(far better though)* your mule or horse,

Small is the portion, poor the granted soil,
Till'd by the Negroe's restless Sabbath's toil!
What loud applause a master must deserve,
Not to permit his property[8] to *starve!*   110
   But worn by toils he can no more renew,
The helpless wretch is turn'd adrift by you![9]
Ye, who destroyed, refusing to sustain
The few unhappy days that yet remain!
To render misery itself more hard,   115
You term it Favour, Freedom, and Reward:
Can we your generosity deny –
Who grant your victims – *liberty to die!*
   Soon as the trembling crew are landed *here,*
Their quiv'ring flesh the burning pincers fear;   120
Proudly imprinting your degrading brand
On men created by your Maker's hand!
A dreadful specimen, we may suppose,
This *warm* reception gives of future woes!
   Ere the poor Savage can yet understand   125
The haughty language of a foreign land;
Ere he conceive your meaning, or your view,
The whip directs him what he is to do.
No sex, no age, you ever learn'd to spare,
But female limbs indecently lay bare;   130
See the poor mother lay her babe aside,[10]
And stoop to punishment she must abide!
Nor midst her pangs, her tears, her horrid cries,
Dare the sad husband turn his pitying eyes.
   Amongst your numbers, do we never meet   135
Villains so most atrociously complete,
Who, with curs'd accuracy, count the days,
The hours of labour pregnancy delays;
Who Nature's wond'rous work attempt to spoil
By stripes, by terrors, and excess of toil.[11]   140
   Agualta's[12] stream by rains become a flood,

Once by its side a fearful female stood;
Th' attempt to cross it was a certain death –
To tarry worse, perhaps – her tyrant's wrath!
Some anxious hours, *unwilling*, did she stay;   145
Then thro' the less'ning torrent fought her way.
Prostrate she lay before her despot's feet,
Imploring mercy she was not to meet!
For ah! the ruffian's heart was hard as steel!
No pity *he* had e'er been known to feel!   150
While the lash tore her tir'd and tortur'd frame,
The pangs of labour prematurely came.
She clasp'd her murder'd infant to her breast;
Stretch'd her fore limbs, and sunk in endless rest![13]
    Your ingenuity we must confess,   155
In finding various methods to distress:
See the wretch fasten'd to an emmet's nest,
Whose stings in myriads his whole frame molest!
Or smear'd with cowheage[14] all his body o'er,
His burning skin intolerably sore!   160
Chains, hooks, and horns, of every size and shape,
Mark those who've once attempted an escape.
A sister isle first us'd, but *this* improves,
That curs'd invention call'd Barbadoes Gloves.[15]
For your own sakes, your malice and your whim   165
But *rarely* sacrifice a Negroe's limb.
Unless a Slave of sedentary trade,
(A luckless Taylor well may be afraid);
Where there's no great occasion for a pair,
You may lop off the leg he has to spare.[16]   170
Were there a surgeon – and there may be such,[17]
Whose heart compassion had the power to touch;
Who dar'd the horrid office to decline,
Your laws condemn him in a heavy fine.[18]
    If int'rest teaches you their limbs to spare,   175
Immediate[19] *murders* must be still more *rare*.

Tho' 'tis this selfish sentiment alone
That oft deters you to destroy *your own.*
But should your passions hurry you away
Another person's property to slay,   180
The guilt's consider'd in a venial light,
The proof is difficult; the sentence slight.[20]
Nay, Malice, safe, may find a thousand times
When no *white evidence* can prove his crimes.
Since, 'tis establish'd by your partial laws,   185
No slave bears witness in a *white* man's cause.[21]
'Tis said your equitable laws confine
The Negroe's punishment to *thirty-nine.*[22]
A specious sound! – which never gave redress,
Since who the dev'l can prove when you transgress.   190
Or curs'd pretences you can find, with ease,
For nine and thirties num'rous as you please.
A jealous mistress finds a ready sham
To give a handsome maid the sugar dram;[23]
With her fair hands prepares the nauseous draught,   195
And pours the scalding mixture down her throat;
Closely confin'd for mad'ning nights and days,
Her burning thirst no liquid drop allays.
Nay, well I know a proud revengeful dame,
Who gave a dose too loathsome here to name.[24]   200
It must be own'd you *all* do wond'rous well,
Yet still in *torturing* the fair excel.
What strange inventions has their genius found,
(Impell'd by Jealousy) to plague and wound!
And in *those modes* we should the least suppose   205
That *female delicacy* would have chose.
    Bad is at best the Slave's most easy state!
Yet some are destin'd to a harder fate.
Villains there are, who, doubly bent on gain,
Most nicely calculate the toil and pain;   210
Who fix the time (Oh! Heav'n! why sleeps thy wrath?)

They may, *with profit*, work their gangs to death.
"Whether shall we," those precious scoundrels say,
"Grasp Fortune quickly, or make long delay?
A hundred slaves we have no fund to buy;   215
The strength of *half that number* let us try,
With *mod'rate toil*, from practice it appears
These slaves might live, perhaps, a dozen years;
To us, you know, the matter will be even,
If we can make as much of them in seven."[25]   220
The price of property they only weigh,
Regardless, else, what *lives they take away!*
    In mild Britannia many of you dwell,
Where tortur'd Slavery ne'er is heard to yell.
You fly wherever Luxury invites,   225
And Dissipation crowns your days and nights;
The dire reflection never meets your view,
What pangs, what bloodshed, buy those joys for you!
Your injur'd slaves, perhaps, you *never saw;*[26]
And doubt the picture I *so truly* draw.   230
Such would not willingly, I hope, impose
The last extremity of human woes.
But, if from Freedom's land you never stray'd,
By false descriptions you may be betray'd.
Self-interested men have met your ear;   235
I, *without int'rest*,[27] will be more sincere!
Wretches by want expell'd from foreign climes;[28]
Escap'd from debts, or justice due their crimes;
The base, the ignorant, the ruffian steer,
And find a desperate asylum *here.*   240
Abject and servile tho' themselves they be
To those above them but in one degree;
O'er the subordinate, sad, sable crew
They have as absolute controul as you.
Men uninform'd, uncultivated, rude,   245
Whose boist'rous passions ne'er have been subdu'd;

Whose tempers, never naturally mild,
Care and misfortune render still more wild;
Their furious hearts a short relief procure,
To wreak on others more than they endure;   250
By such caprice are Negroes doom'd to bleed,
The Slaves of Slavery – They are low indeed!
   He who has made an independence *here*,
At home in splendor hurries to appear;
London, or Bath, with lying fame resounds,   255
"A fresh Creole! – worth Fifty Thousand Pounds!"
Tho' ten he knows the limit of his store,
He must keep up the figure first he wore.
Thoughtless, he riots in the gay career;
And finds himself half ruin'd in the year.   260
Duns grow importunate – and friends but cool;
Back to Jamaica comes the bankrupt fool.
First goes the Pen;[29] the Polink;[30] worse and worse;
At last the Sugar-work is put to nurse.
He strives with Jews and Marshalls[31] long – in vain –   265
Once thus involv'd, he ne'er gets clear again.
Worse ev'ry year his situation grows,
'Till in a prison he concludes his woes;
Unless, perhaps, a seat at Council-board
A sure protection should for life afford;   270
Or in the Lower House enacting laws –
The laws eluding faster than he draws.
But while he parries off from year to year,
The Negroes' suff'rings are indeed severe!
For their vain lord the most supplies to raise,   275
Ill fed; hard work'd; they know no resting days![32]
Perhaps to greedy jobbers lent on hire,[33]
Who from excess of toil their gain require;
Who have no int'rest in them to preserve;
And if they labour, care not how they starve.   280
Or seiz'd by marshalls, and to market brought;

By various masters families are bought.
Amidst their unregarded sighs and tears,
The wife and husband fall to diff'rent shares;
Their clinging offspring from their arms are tore,   285
And hurried from them, ne'er to meet them more!
    I knew a foetus, in mere wanton play,
Sold from the mother in whose womb it lay.
Unhappy mother! doom'd for months to bear
The luckless burden, thou art not to rear;[34]   290
    What dreadful partings, for Revenge's sake,
Do furious females in a moment make!
Their fav'rite maids, with whom from youth they grew;
As fine their shape, and scarce less fair their hue;[35]
For some slight errror; some unlucky chance;   295
A tea-cup broken; or a lover's glance;
Feel all the fury of their quenchless flame;
And meet the punishments of pain and shame.
The parent's, sister's, ev'ry tender tie –
All are dissolv'd – and round the isle they fly!   300
    Accursed state! where Nature, and where Love,
Rude violations must for ever prove!
You, brutal ravishers! pretend in vain
That Afric's children feel no jealous pain.
Untaught EUROPEANS, with illib'ral pride,   305
Look with contempt on all the world beside;
And vainly think no virtue ever grew,
No passion glow'd beneath a sable hue.
Beings you deem them of inferior kind;[36]
Denied a human, or a thinking mind.   310
Happy for Negroes were this doctrine true!
Were *feelings lost to them – or giv'n to you!*
But Love and Passion ne'er had more controul,
Than o'er the African's hot, haughty soul.
Oft, 'mongst your slaves, a once proud chief we find,   315
Of dauntless courage, and exalted mind;

His body cover'd o'er with many a scar,
Proofs of his prowess in the field of war;
More keen his *mental* than *corporeal* pains,
While his fierce *spirit feels* your lash and chains.   320
In vain the noble pride, which glory gave,
You would subdue, and *"break the stubborn slave."*
Resolv'd to perish by a heroe's hand,
He seeks in suicide his native land.[37]
　　Or, should he take a bolder, juster course,   325
And try to vindicate his rights by force;
Thro' coward numbers you the hero take,
And hell's own torments wait him at the stake.
　　There are, of gentler race and low degree,
Who were not ever *nominally free*.   330
But while they loiter'd on their native soil,
Slight was the nature of th' exacted toil.
Taught but, perhaps, the savage chase to rouse;
Or guard the scanty flocks, or goats to brouse.
Perhaps, the only task they ever knew,   335
To sow the seeds that half spontaneous grew.
No complicated agriculture there;
No modes of luxury made toil severe.
No bloody fields their peaceful nature sought;
But am'rous combats all they ever fought.   340
Thus, slaves, perhaps, in nothing but the name,
They never felt it – till Europeans came –
In happy indolence life slipp'd away,
And ease and sun-shine bless'd them every day.[38]
But when the Christians came, in evil hour,   345
They found the rigour of a tyrant's power;
Some dragg'd by force, and some by fraud beguil'd,[39]
The despot reigns – rich Monarch of a Wild!
　　In dumb despair these helpless wretches pine,
Yet are their feelings *exquisitely fine!*[40]   350
Think you the silent slave beholds, *unmov'd,*

The rape committed on his best-belov'd?
With keenest pangs his am'rous heart is wrung,
Rage fires his soul, tho' fear restrains his tongue.
    Oh! friendless race! for whom I, only, sigh;[41]   355
Who scarce have ever met a pitying eye!
Oh! had I power to melt, by tender strains,
Your lawless lords to mollify your pains!
Could I excite one sympathetic tear,
To make long-lost Humanity appear!   360
Could I but teach them – what they never knew,
The sacred rights which Nature gave to you!
But had I music – magic in my strain,
Music or magic had been giv'n in vain!
    Here the rough planter looks profoundly wise;   365
"A pretty fellow this, indeed!" he cries.
"What would *your* conduct be, I'd gladly know,
Should Chance on you some hundred slaves bestow!
Pray would you set the worthless rascals *free?*
Or would you keep them – *just the same as we?*"[42]   370
    How he would act, till tried, no man can say,
But may temptation still be kept away!
I am an erring man, as well as you,
And might by Av'rice be corrupted too;
But, be *my* conduct whatso'er it might,   375
That ne'er could alter either Wrong or Right.
    Altho' no wealth should e'er be destin'd mine;
Nay, were I doom'd in poverty to pine,
Still with contempt I'd inwardly behold
The greedy tribe whose guilt had purchas'd gold;   380
Content that Fortune may be still denied,
If by the pangs of Innocence supplied!
For *me* be never struggling victim tore
From friends, from freedom, and his native shore!
Give me no fields where fruits luxuriant wave,   385
Whose culture ever curs'd a single slave!

To me how bitter were the sweetest food,
Whose seed was nourish'd by one wretch's blood!
To me no beauties e'er could grace the soil,
That ow'd its tillage to reluctant toil!   390
Nor Flattery's voice, nor Music's notes I'd hear,
Still whips would wound, and shrieks would pierce mine ear!
And, tho' I own'd whate'er was rich or rare,
I'd dream of chains, of exile, and despair!
Then take, ye tyrants, all that gold can grant!   395
Be *mine* the heartfelt rectitude you want!⁴³
    Do your fair fields with pipe or song resound?
No! chains and scourges echo all around!
Thro' verdant meads yon limpid waters flow,
But scarce a freeman there is seen to go!   400
Not gay to me yon gaudy mountain's side,
There sickly Slavery "work'd and wept," and died!
Can I behold yon mansion with a smile?
Unwilling labour rear'd the splendid pile!
Can all Lucinda's outward charms inspire   405
A tender feeling, or a soft desire?
When ev'ry gem the cruel creature wears,
Was bought by streams of blood, and floods of tears.
    If (Heaven avert it!) slaves e'er work'd for me,
Easy, *I think*, their daily tasks should be.   410
With lodging, raiment, and nutritious food,
I'd make their lives *as happy as I could.*
    Again, perhaps, another sage will say,
"This is a traitor, *who receives our pay!*
He, tho' by duty bound to guard our laws,   415
Dares to espouse the slave's rebellious cause!
Should factious Negroes rise against their lord,
Durst he refuse to draw his venal sword?
Is he not then at least as bad as we,
Who helps to *bind* the men he wishes *free?*"   420

The heavy charge I must confess too true;
I am accomplice in the guilt with you!
But distant be the day my weapon draws
Against whoever fights in Freedom's cause!
If Britain bid, obey her servants must;   425
Yet must I sigh – if Britain be unjust!
If by our hands their harmless blood be spilt,
With Britain's lawgivers remains the guilt!
   Statesmen and Patriots! does it well agree
With you – the guardians of the brave and free!   430
For the emolument of sordid trade,
To give such villainies a legal aid?[44]
Be not your pity to one race confin'd;
But rise the benefactors of mankind!
Let Afric's children tread their native shore;   435
And BRITISH RUFFIANS ravage them no more!
The galling chains of Servitude remove,
And leave them all to Liberty and Love![45]

Notes

1. John Marjoribanks. *Slavery: An Essay in Verse . . . Humbly inscribed to Planters, Merchants, And others concerned in the Management or Sale of Negro Slaves* (Edinburgh: J. Robertson, 1792).
2. [Author's note:] The general idea of the new Negroes seems to be, that they are to be devoured. [In chapter 2 of his *Interesting Narrative*, Equiano describes the fears of Africans on board a slave-ship that when they reached Barbados they would be eaten by the merchants who came to inspect them.]
3. [Author's note:] This, and every other argument I have put into their mouths, I have frequently heard planters use. Futile as they are, I believe no better can be found.
4. [Author's note:] I would here be understood to allude to the peasantry of England.

5. [Author's note:] I must here remind the reader that the lines are addressed to
    all concerned in the Slave-Trade; but the planters, for whose use the negroes
    are ultimately intended, may be considered as the original instigators of the
    traffic.

6. [Author's note:] Of the great numbers of new negroes I have seen, a very
    considerable proportion appeared to me to be under 14 years of age.

7. [Author's note:] While I speak of the cruelty practised by planters in general,
    I would not be understood to say that there may not be exceptions.

8. [Author's note:] So they term him; but I deny that, in the sight of God, any
    human being can be the *property* of another.

9. [Author's note:] I have seen several of these unfortunates expire, literally of
    hunger who had been picked up on the road by soldiers; but too late for their
    preservation. I have known a good many others, who had been abandoned
    by their owners, supported for years by the humanity of those poor fellows.

    One old debilitated negro had resided for several years at Stoney-hill
    barracks; and I believe remained there at the time I left the island. He was
    the property of the Honourable (*ex officio*) Paul Phipps, then Custos, or
    Chief Magistrate of Kingston, one of the representatives of that town in the
    House of Assembly, Colonel of the regiment of Saint Andrew's Militia, and
    one of the judges of the Common Pleas of that parish.

    If such an act of deliberate cruelty as the abandoning this helpless wretch,
    could be committed by a man who united in his own person the conspicuous
    characters of a judge, a legislator, a militia commander, and in these several
    capacities, as well as in his private profession as a merchant, uniformly main-
    tained an unblemished reputation; who was, I believe, free from pecuniary
    embarrassments; and who being himself advanced in years, might have been
    expected to have felt some degree of sympathy for the infirmities of age. I
    think I should have been justified from this single instance, (even if a variety
    of others had not fallen under my observation) in inferring that this practice
    of turning out old, or unserviceable slaves to *pick*, as they emphatically term
    it, must be generally prevalent among persons in more obscure stations, of
    less respectable characters, or in more indigent circumstances.

10. [Author's note:] The negro women who have young children, carry them
    fastened on their backs, while they are at work in the field.

11. [Author's note:] To the villainous principle, that it is *cheaper* to purchase
    Guinea negroes, than by better usage, and lighter labour, to encourage popu-
    lation among those of *this* country, may, in a great measure, be ascribed the
    necessity of so vast an annual importation from Africa.

12. [Author's note:] Agualta, a rivulet which takes its rise in the Liguanéa mountains. It is vulgarly known by the name Wag-water.

13. [Author's note:] This happened during my residence *here*, within a little more than a mile of the spot where I now sit: viz. on Norbrook mountain; the property of Mr. Long, compiler of the History of Jamaica. Stoney-hill, 16th October, 1786. [Marjoribanks doubtless expects readers to note the irony of this location; for Long's contempt for slaves as voiced in his *History of Jamaica*, see pages 74–75 above.]

14. *cowheage*: cow-itch, a stinging plant.

15. [Author's note:] Slips of wood are placed between every two fingers, and the whole screwed or wedged close together, so as to give a most exquisite torture. I have known this infernal machine kept on house slaves for many days together.

16. [Author's note:] The reason assigned to a gentleman of my acquaintance, by his overseer, for cutting off the leg of one of his negroes in his absence; was, that the fellow having run off, he thought this the most effectual method of preventing his trying it a second time; adding, that as *he was a taylor*, the *property* was not a bit less valuable.

17. [Author's note:] I mean, even in the West Indies.

18. [Author's note:] The penalty, I think, is 50l. currency. [In Jamaican currency that would be equivalent to about £30 sterling.]

19. [Author's note:] *Immediate*; in contradistinction to the slow murder of toil and torment.

20. [Author's note:] Generally payment of the price of the negro to his owner. It is then, it may be remarked, as expensive to kill another man's slave as your own. But this does not follow; in the former case, the loss is certain; in the latter, the fact must be proved (which is often impossible) before the damages can be incurred.

21. [Author's note:] Not only slaves, but free negroes, and people of colour, are excluded. They are, however, admitted as evidences *against each other*.

22. [Author's note:] As there is seldom more than one white man in the field the futility of this law is clear. (Original note, 1786). For the same reason it is obvious that the late Act of Assembly of Jamaica, in favour of slaves, must be ineffectual. (Feb. 1792).

23. [Author's note:] An equal mixture of rum and salt.

24. [Author's note:] A lady of my acquaintance caused a slave, in presence of her family and strangers, to swallow a glass of rum mixed with human excrement.

25. [Author's note:] This diabolical practice is called *driving* a gang. I have repeat-
     edly heard calculations made on this subject, with all the coolness and accu-
     racy of an innkeeper estimating the probable expenditure of post-horses.

26. [Author's note:] Many proprietors of estates in this country have never been
     in the island.

27. [Author's note:] At least, no other than the interest of humanity.

28. [Author's note:] The life of a *book-keeper* is, in general, such a complication of
     drudgery and disease, pride and poverty, despotism and servility, that no man
     of birth, education, spirit, or sensibility would, if previously acquainted with
     its nature, ever engage in it. That there are, however, among this class of men
     some unfortunate people of the above description is certain (though, as mat-
     ters are now conducted, they could not well be possessed of less essential
     qualifications). But a far greater proportion of them are low and illiterate (for
     it is far from requisite that a *book-keeper* should be able to read), many of
     them are desperadoes, fraudulent bankrupts, jail-birds, deserters from the
     troops, run-away seamen, and other vagabonds of all countries and denomi-
     nations. Several of them inlisted in the 19th regiment, and rejoiced greatly at
     their change of situation. [The 19th was the infantry regiment in which
     Marjoribanks himself was serving.]

29. [Author's note:] The villa. [In Jamaican terminology this was a country house
     or estate, as distinct from a plantation.]

30. [Author's note:] A mountain farm for raising provisions and stock. [*Polink*
     was a variant of *palenque* in Jamaican English.]

31. *Marshalls*: legal officers.

32. [Author's note:] Indeed, some of them do; but the Sunday, which they ought
     to be allowed to work for themselves, is generally styled a resting day. When
     the master is hard pushed, I believe there may be found instances of the
     negroes being cheated out of a great part even of this their own day.

33. [Author's note:] Bad as the situation of slaves is in general, it will easily be
     credited that those on bankrupt estates (of which God knows, there is no
     scarcity) are more peculiarly wretched. But the most super-eminently miser-
     able of the human race are, undoubtedly, the negroes belonging to *jobbing
     gangs*. Should the person who hires them, dispose of a negro; should he
     shoot him through the head, or stab him to the heart; he would, I dare say, be
     obliged to pay the price of him to his owner. But it does not appear that he is
     liable to replace those who may be left by accidental, or natural deaths – and
     no death, surely, is so *perfectly natural* – none, I will aver, so frequent, in job-
     bing gangs, as from the effects of hunger, want of accommodation, violent

blows, excessive labour, severe flogging, and every other possible species of cruelty and bad treatment.

34. [Author's note:] The bargain was struck in hearing of the unfortunate mother.

35. [Author's note:] The ladies are generally attended by girls of colour, who, frequently, are their own near relations; in the third or fourth generation, many of them are almost as fair as Europeans.

36. [Author's note:] I have often heard planters, talking of their negroes, very gravely style them their *Cattle*.

37. [Author's note:] This is more particularly the case with the high spirited, (or, as the planters call them, the sulky, contumacious) Coromantees. I never conversed with any African negro, who did not seem to consider *death* as a *certain pass to Guinea*.

38. [Author's note:] The two blessings they seem most to relish. – To *sleep* in the sun, they consider as one of the highest luxuries. This state of ease and tran- quillity appeared, from their artless accounts, to have been the original lot of most of the Guinea negroes I have interrogated on the subject.

39. [Author's note:] This also is from the information I have often received from African slaves.

40. [Author's note:] If I have not had proofs sufficient to warrant this assertion, they have at least been such as to carry to my own mind the fullest convic- tion of its truth.

41. [Author's note:] Thank Heaven! *this* is no longer the case! I have now the pleasure to see thousands of my fellow Britons espouse the cause of this injured race of men, who appeared to me, at the time the above lines were written, to be for ever abandoned by the rest of the human species.

42. [Author's note:] I have frequently had these, and the like *knock me down* arguments dashed into my teeth.

43. [Author's note:] This is not addressed to planters in general (among whom there are undoubtedly many men of integrity); but the speculators in human blood *only*.

44. [Author's note:] Supposing (which yet remains to be proved) that the African Slave-Trade is actually of commercial advantage to Great Britain.

45. [Author's note:] If the reader imagine I here recommend the romantic, and as yet impracticable, scheme of emancipating the Negroes in the West- Indies; he greatly misunderstands me. My wishes (however obscurely they may be expressed,) though when first formed, not encouraged by the slight- est or most distant hopes of gratification; did then, as now, perfectly coincide

with what I conceive to be the laudable views of the societies since instituted, for the abolition of the trade to Africa for slaves; the meliorating the condition of those already in the islands; and, perhaps, in time, the gradual establishment of their freedom.

[Marjoribanks's disclaimers sound disingenuous. His writings strongly suggest that he found the slave system as such intolerable, but he may have been persuaded by the Edinburgh abolitionists that the campaign against the slave trade depended for its success on reassuring supporters of the powerful West Indian lobby that it was not a prelude to emancipation.]

HENRY EVANS HOLDER (FL. 1788–92)

Fragments of a Poem (1792)[1]

The author, named on the title age as the Rev. H.E. Holder of
Bristol, was a native of Barbados. He had previously written a
defence of slavery and the slave trade in *A Short Essay on the Subject
of Negro Slavery, with particular reference to the island of Barbados*,
published in London in 1788. The passage below is a brief extract
from Holder's long and furious verse diatribe against "Major"
Marjoribanks (Holder evidently confuses the author of *Slavery* with
his father, Major John Marjoribanks) and other anti-slavery writers.
The poem is dedicated to "the West-Indian Merchants and Planters"
whom Holder, writing as one "personally concerned in the injury
sustained, as being a West Indian", seeks to vindicate against "the
infamous attacks which have been made, and are now making,
against the West-Indians, by the misguided and the licentious of
this country [Britain]".

. . . And are you sure, Reformer, fiery red!
That what you give is worth acceptance?
Can you suppose that freedom is a boon
Where competence is wanting? Can the Black
Hail you his benefactor, when you give   5

A name, and strip him of realities?
When you curse him with a *fancied* liberty,
And leave him to endure the many cares
Which people each domestic head and heart,
To rear a tender offspring, and provide   10
For tott'ring age and fell infirmity? . . .
　　But who, you'll say, shall guard the wretched slave
From tyrant-cruelty and bloody scourge?
Believe me he requires no hand to guard,
No interference from your mad'ning zeal: . . .   15
The voice of interest will be heard aloud;
Nor yet in any state of life more loud,
Than when she teaches ev'ry master's heart,
That all his wealth is center'd in his slave, . . .
　　But after all, when this great work is done,   20
When you have fill'd this hemisphere with rage,
Against the children of the Western world,
Can you look up to GOD, and boldly say,
My motive was to serve his creatures,
And further his designs of genial love? . . .   25
But hang your heads, and smite your guilty breasts,
As you confess, because you can't deny,
That pride, or vanity, or envy mean,
Or malice fell, or private views, first arm'd
Your zeal; and shame has since impell'd you on,   30
Your cruel work of darkness to complete . . . .

Note

1.　Henry Evans Holder, *Fragments of a Poem, intended to have been written in conse-quence of reading Major Marjoribanks's Slavery* (Bath: R. Cruttwell, 1792).

John Gabriel Stedman (1744–97)

Narrative of a Five Years' Expedition against the Revolted Negroes of Surinam (1796)[1]

Stedman, an officer in the Scots Brigade (a mercenary unit) from 1761 to 1783, volunteered to serve in the campaign to suppress the rebel slaves of Suriname, then a Dutch colony. The vivid narrative of his experiences, including his common-law marriage to Joanna, an enslaved woman, was written in 1790 but not published until 1796. Handsomely illustrated with engravings by William Blake and others that were based on drawings made by Stedman himself, the *Narrative* became famous as one of the most detailed personal accounts of West Indian slave society published in the eighteenth century. The discovery of Stedman's original manuscript in 1978, however, showed that his text had been substantially and systematically altered for publication without his knowledge, distorting his reflections on race and slavery in order to moderate his condemnation of the slave system as practised in Suriname.[2] Stedman opposed the abolition of slavery, advocating instead more just and humane treatment of the enslaved. Nevertheless the publisher John Johnson believed "that the *Narrative* (with its numerous chilling eyewitness accounts of barbaric tortures of slaves and its graphic accompanying illustrations) would, even in its edited form, stand as one of the strongest indictments ever to appear against plantation slavery", and contemporary reviews confirmed his belief.[3] The text here is from the 1796 edition.

Barbarity of a Planter[4]

[During a period of inaction after his arrival at the town of Paramaribo in Suriname early in 1773, Stedman was invited to stay on a coffee plantation belonging to a Mr Macneyl.]

At our arrival on the estate Sporkesgift, I had the pleasure to be the spectator of an instance of justice which afforded me the greatest satisfaction.

The scene consisted in Mr. Macneyl's turning the overseer out of his service, and ordering him to depart from the plantation in an inferior boat, called a *ponkee*,[5] to Paramaribo, or to wherever he thought proper; which was instantaneously put in execution. The cause of his disgrace was having, by bad usage and cruelty, caused the death of three or four negroes. His departure was made completely joyful to all the slaves by an holiday, which was spent in festivity by dancing and clapping hands on a green before the dwelling-house windows.

The overseer's sentence was the more ignominious and galling as, at the time of his receiving it, a negro foot-boy, who was buckling his shoes, was ordered back, and he was desired to buckle them himself . . . . But I should be guilty of partiality, did I not relate one instance, which throws a shade over the humanity even of my friend Macneyl.

Having observed a handsome young negro walk very lamely, while the others were capering and dancing, I inquired into the cause of his crippled appearance; when I was informed by this gentleman, that the negro having repeatedly run away from his work, he had been obliged to hamstring him, which operation is performed by cutting through the large tendon above one of the heels. However severe this instance of despotism may appear, it is nothing when compared with some barbarities which the task I have undertaken will oblige me, at the expence of my feelings, to relate . . . .

As we were still in a state of inaction, I made another excursion, with a Mr. Charles Ryndorp, who rowed me in his barge to five beautiful coffee estates, and one sugar plantation, in the Matapaca, Paramarica, and Werapa Creeks, the description of which I must also defer to another occasion; but on one of which I saw a scene of barbarity which I cannot help relating.

The victim of this cruelty was a fine old negro slave, who, having been as he thought undeservedly sentenced to receive some hundred lashes by the lacerating whips of two negro-drivers, in the midst of the execution pulled out a knife, which, after having made a fruitless thrust at his persecutor the overseer, he plunged up to the haft in his own bowels, repeating the blow till he dropped down at the tyrant's feet. For this crime he was, being first recovered, condemned to be chained to the furnace which distills the *kill-devil*,[6] there to keep in the intense heat of a perpetual fire night and day, being blistered all over, till he should expire by infirmity or old age, of the latter of which he had but little chance. He shewed me his wounds with a smile of contempt, which I returned with a sigh and a small donation: nor shall I ever forget the miserable man, who, like Cerberus, was loaded with irons, and chained to everlasting torment. As for every thing else I observed on this little tour, I must acknowledge it to be elegant and splendid, and my reception hospitable beyond my expectation: but these Elysian Fields could not dissipate the gloom which the infernal furnace had left upon my mind . . . .

We now once more, on the sixth of April, returned safe to Paramaribo, where . . . dining at the house of my friend Mr. Lolkens, . . . I was an eyewitness of the unpardonable contempt with which negro slaves are treated in this colony. His son, a boy not more than ten years old, when sitting at table, gave a slap in the face to a grey-headed black woman, who by accident touched his powdered hair, as she was serving in a dish of kerry [curry]. I could not help blaming his father for overlooking the action; who told me, with a smile, that the child should no longer offend me, as he was next day to sail for Holland for education; to which I answered that I thought it almost too late. At the same moment a sailor passing by, broke the head of a negro with a bludgeon, for not having saluted him with his hat. – Such is the state of slavery, at least in this Dutch settlement!

General description of the African negroes[7]

All negroes firmly believe the being of a *God*, upon whose goodness they rely, and whose power they adore, while they have no fear of death, and never taste food without offering a libation . . . . Perceiving that it was their custom to bring their offerings to the wild cotton-tree, I enquired of an old negro, why they paid such particular reverence and veneration to this growing piece of timber. 'This proceeds (said he) from the following cause: having no churches nor places built for public worship (as you have) on the Coast of Guinea, and this tree being the largest and most beautiful growing there, our people, assembling under its branches when they are going to be instructed, are defended by it from the heavy rains and scorching sun.[8] Under this tree our gadoman, or priest, delivers his lectures; and for this reason our common people have so much veneration for it, that they will not cut it down upon any account whatever."

No people can be more superstitious than the generality of negroes; and their *Locomen*, or pretended prophets, find their interest in encouraging this superstition, by selling them *obias*, or amulets, . . . as some hypocrites sell absolution in Europe, for a comfortable living. These people have also amongst them a kind of *Sybils*, who deal in oracles; these sage matrons dancing and whirling round in the middle of an assembly, with amazing rapidity, until they foam at the mouth, and drop down as convulsed. Whatever the prophetess orders to be done during this paroxysm, is most sacredly performed by the surrounding multitude; which renders these meetings extremely dangerous, as she frequently enjoins them to murder their masters, or desert to the woods; upon which account this scene of excessive fanaticism is forbidden by law in the colony of Surinam, upon pain of the most rigorous punishment: yet it is often practised in private places, and is very common among the Owca and Seramica negroes . . . . It is here called the *winty-play*, or the dance of the mermaid, and has existed from time immemorial . . . .[9]

If savage nations be commonly generous and faithful, they are not, however, without their dark shades; and among these, the most conspicuous is a proneness to anger and revenge. I never knew a negro indeed forgive those who had wilfully offended him. The strength of this passion can only be equalled by their gratitude; for, amongst them, it may be truly said, that

> A generous friendship no cold medium knows,
> But with one love, with one resentment glows.

Their abominable cruelties also, like those of all barbarous nations, are truly shocking. In the colony Berbice, during the late revolt, they made no scruple of cutting up their mistresses with child, even in their master's presence, with many other savage devices too dreadful to relate.[10] – In the art of poisoning, not even the *Accawaw* Indians are more expert; they can carry it under their nails, and by only dipping their thumb into a tumbler of water, which they offer as a beverage to the object of their revenge, they infuse a slow but certain death.[11] Whole estates, as well as private families, have become the victims of their fury, and experienced their fatal vengeance, even putting to death scores of their own friends and relations, with the double view of depriving their proprietors of their most valuable possessions.[12] These monsters are distinguished by the name of *Wissy-men*, perhaps from *wise*, or knowing, and by their fatal genius carry destruction to a most dreadful length before they are detected.

All barbarous and uneducated people have indistinct notions of property; nor can we wonder that slaves, who in their own persons suffer the most flagrant violation of every right, should be disposed to retaliate. The slaves on the plantations are therefore too commonly thieves, plundering whatever they can lay their hands upon with impunity; nor can any bounds be set to their intemperance, especially in drinking. I have seen even a negro girl empty a china-bowl at one draught, containing two bottles of claret, which I had given by way of experiment, till she could no more stand . . . .

But from these deformities of character I will now relieve the attention of the reader, and proceed in justice to dispel the gloomy cloud, by introducing the sunshine of their virtues.

Their genius has already been treated of, so has their gratitude; which last they carry to such a length, that they will even die for those who have shewn them any particular favour. Nothing can exceed the fidelity and attachment they have for those masters who use them well, which proves that their affection is as strong as their hatred. Negroes are generally good-natured, particularly the *Coromantyn*, and those of *Nago*.[13] They are also susceptible of the tender passion, and jealousy in their breasts has produced the most dreadful effects. The delicacy of these people deserves likewise to be noticed; I do not remember, amongst the many thousands I have seen during several years residence among them, ever to have observed even an offer to kiss a woman in public. Maternal tenderness for their children is also natural to the females, for in general, during the two years which they usually suckle them, they never cohabit with their husbands; this they consider as unnatural, and prejudicial to the infants . . . .

The negroes are likewise spirited and brave, patient in adversity, meeting death and torture with the most undaunted fortitude. Their conduct, in the most trying situations, approaching even to heroism; no negro sighs, groans, or complains, though expiring in the midst of surrounding flames. Nor do I remember, upon any occasion whatever, to have seen an African shed a tear, though they beg for mercy with the greatest earnestness when ordered to be flogged for offences which they are conscious deserve to be punished; but if they think their punishment unmerited, immediate suicide is too often the fatal consequence, especially among the *Coromantyn* negroes, who frequently, during the act of flagellation, throw back their heads in the neck, and *swallow their tongue*, which chokes them upon the spot, when they drop dead in the presence of their masters. But when negroes are sensible of having deserved correction, no people can be more humble, or bear their unhappy fate with greater resignation.

[Stedman concludes with an idealized account of the lives of the enslaved under a humane owner, and of their "instrumental music and dancing". He gives a detailed description of musical instruments, continuing as follows.][14]

I will only add, that they always use full or half measure, but never triple time, in their dancing music, which not unlike that of a baker's bunt,[15] when he separates the flour from the bran, sounding *tuckety-tuck* and *tuckety-tuck* ad perpetuum. To this noise they dance with uncommon pleasure, and most times foot it away with great art and dexterity . . . .

Every Saturday evening, the slaves who are well treated close the week, with an entertainment of this kind, and generally once a quarter are indulged with a grand ball, to which the neighbouring slaves are invited; the master often contributing to their happiness by his presence, or at least by sending a present of a few jugs of new rum.

At these grand balls the slaves are remarkably neat, the women appearing in their best chintz petticoats, and many of the men in fine Holland trowsers. So indefatigable are they at this diversion, that I have known the drums continue beating without intermission from six o'clock on Saturday night till the sun made its appearance on the Monday morning; thus had passed six-and-thirty hours in dancing, cheering, hallooing, and clapping of hands. The negroes dance always in couples, the men figuring and footing, while the women turn round like a top, their petticoats expanding like an umbrella; and this they call *waey cotto*. During this, the bystanding youths fill about the liquor, while the girls encourage the performance, and wipe the sweat from the brows and sides of the unwearied musicians.

It is indeed upon the whole astonishing to see with what good-nature and even good manners these dancing societies are kept up, of which I repeat they are so fond, that I have known a newly-imported negro, for want of a partner, figure and foot it for nearly the space of two hours, to his shadow against the wall.

Notes

1. John Gabriel Stedman, *Narrative of a Five Years' Expedition against the Revolted Negroes of Surinam in Guiana on the Wild Coast of South America from the years 1772 to 1777*, 2 vols. (London: J. Johnson, and J. Edwards, 1796).
2. See Richard Price and Sally Price, eds., *Stedman's Surinam: Life in an Eighteenth-century Slave Society* (Baltimore: Johns Hopkins University Press, 1992), lvii–lxii.
3. Ibid., lxi.
4. Stedman, *Narrative*, 55–58.
5. [Author's note:] A *ponkee* is a flat-bottomed boat of four or six oars, something like a square-toed shoe: sometimes it has a tilt [tent], and sometimes not.
6. [Author's note:] *Kill-devil* is a species of rum which is distilled from the scum and dregs of sugar cauldrons. This is much drunk in this colony and the only spirits allowed the negroes; many Europeans also, from a point of economy, make use of it, to whom it proves no better than a slow but fatal poison.
7. Stedman, *Narrative*, 364–68.

8. The original version reads: "Do not you Christians pay the same homage to your Bibles &c? We well know that our tree is but a wooden log covered with leaves of green, nor is your book assuredly any more than a piece of lumber composed of leaves of paper." Price and Price, *Stedman's Surinam*, 263.

9. "Spirit possession was (and remains) a core feature of Afro-Suriname religious behavior. Today *winti* has become the general name for coastal Afro-Suriname religion". Ibid., 335n263.

10. There was a major slave rebellion in 1763 in Berbice, then a Dutch colony adjacent to Suriname. Stedman describes further atrocities in a long footnote.

11. [Author's note:] After the most scrupulous enquiry, and even ocular demonstration, I can assert the above as literally true.

12. Followed in original version by "and at once delivering those Negro slaves whom they love best from under the lash of their tyranny". Price and Price, *Stedman's Surinam*, 266.

13. *Nago*: "the Ewe word for Nigerian Yorubas". Ibid., 324n96.

14. Stedman, *Narrative*, 377–78.

15. *bunt*: a tool for sifting meal.

R.C. DALLAS (1754–1824)

The History of the Maroons (1803)[1]

Dallas's *History* is presented in the form of letters to a friend. Letters I–III take the narrative from 1655 down to the treaty of 1739, which brought to an end eighty years of guerrilla warfare waged by the Maroons against English settlers and soldiers. Under this treaty the Maroons were granted possession of land and certain legal rights and freedoms, subject to conditions which included the obligation to capture or kill rebels, to fight alongside the British forces against foreign invaders and to send back any runaway slaves who fell into their hands. Later legislation strengthened the inducements to capture runaways (see below). Maroon towns, Dallas explains, "consisted of a certain number of families collected together under a chief", supervised by a resident white superintendent, but all internal disputes were arbitrated by the chiefs, to whom the Maroons "looked up with implicit confidence, and whom they usually obeyed without argument". Letter IV describes the Maroons of Trelawny Town as the author knew them in the period leading up to the Second Maroon War of 1795–96. Dallas is noticeably less critical of the slave system than he was in his earlier work, for reasons given in the preface.

From Preface[2]

It is well known to my friends, that I early professed my abhorrence of the cruelties attendant upon the state of slavery, and of slavery itself, as it appeared to me in my youth. Lest the tendency of my sentiments in these volumes should expose me to the charge of inconsistency, I beg leave to observe, that it is not my opinions but things that are changed; I am still an enemy to cruelty. Previous to the French revolution, I was an enthusiast for freedom, but I very soon after learned to substitute the words happiness and order, for liberty and right. The former are unequivocal and proceed from God; the latter are ambiguous, and too often become means in the hands of the devil and his agents.

From Letter IV.

Maroon Towns. – Trelawny Town described. – The persons of the
Maroons. – Laws relative to the Maroons.

Having made you acquainted with the origin of the Maroons, and their establishment as a body of free people in the interior of the island of Jamaica, let us take a respite from war, and view them as settled peaceably in their towns. Of these there were five; Trelawny-town, Accompong-town, Scot's Hall, Charles-town, and Moore-town, situated in different parts of the island from the eastern to the western extremity. . . . I will not enter into a separate description of these places, but speak chiefly of Trelawny-town, as being the most considerable, and that which will make the most conspicuous figure in the sequel of our history.[4]

We have seen, that by the treaty made with Cudjoe,[5] 1500 acres of land in the parish of Trelawny were granted to him, and the body of Maroons under his command. On this land stood the town, about 20 miles to the south-east of Montego Bay. Let your imagination help me to convey you up to immense mountains, successively towering one above the other, presenting tangled forests or immense precipices of barren rock. . . .

On the acclivity of the mountain, and on a scite extremely unequal, every where rising and sinking abruptly, the Maroon habitations were disposed without any attention to regularity; each house, for the convenience of a sloping ground to carry off the floods occasioned by heavy rains, being placed on a little ridge or hillock, differing in height from the others; and between these ridges, in various directions, run gullies, or channels, formed by the torrents, in irregular courses. The spots on which the houses were erected, had by degrees lost all the mould with which they had been covered, and presented barren eminences of clay. Here and there, in patches, where the sweepings of the ashes from the houses had been collected, and also on the ground below their hogsties, which were appurtenances to every house, some clumps of plantain trees, and smaller vegetables were nourished by the manure. . . . The houses were in general small cottages covered with thatch, or a long grass called Foxtail; and were without flooring, the ground within, and in the piazzas, with which most of the houses were provided, being trodden with a mixture of ashes into a firm and compact substance. Some habitations, however, belonging to the chiefs, were roofed with shingles, and several had floored rooms. . . .

The Maroons, for their provisions, cultivated, on sufferance, land adjoining to the tract, conceded to them by the treaty. Of the 1500 acres of which their territory consisted, a third was merely rock, about a hundred acres worth cultivating, and the rest of it was over-run with a species of fern and Foxtail grass, which are certain indications of a poor soil. Besides their ground provisions, the Maroons had a stock of cattle; and they kept mares, from which they bred horses for sale. These fed in the woods, and on neighbouring heaths . . . .

It is not to be doubted that the climate of these mountains, which is seldom less than ten degrees cooler than the low lands of the island, the mode of life of the inhabitants, the constant exercise of their limbs in ascending and descending, and their custom of exploring the vast mountains and precipices of the interior of the country in pursuit of the wild boar, contributed to produce the strength and symmetry in which the Maroons of Trelawny Town and Accompong Town, who were the same race of men, far excelled the other negroes of every description in Jamaica. In character, language, and manners, they nearly resembled those negroes, on the estates of the planters, that were descended from the same race of Africans, but displayed a striking distinction in their personal appearance, being blacker, taller, and in every respect handsomer; for such of them as had remained in slavery had intermixed with Eboe negroes and others, imported from countries to the southward of Africa, people of yellow complexions, with compressed features, and thick lips, who were in every respect inferior to themselves. . . .

They possessed most, if not all, of the senses in a superior degree. They were accustomed, from habit, to discover in the woods objects, which white people, of the best sight, could not distinguish; and their hearing was so wonderfully quick, that it enabled them to elude their most active pursuers; they were seldom surprised. They communicated with one another by means of horns; and when these could scarcely be heard by other people, they distinguished the orders that the sounds conveyed. It is very remarkable, that the Maroons had a particular call upon the horn for each individual, by which he was summoned from a distance, as easily as he would have been spoken to by name, had he been near. . . . It has been said that their sense of smelling *is obtuse, and their taste depraved.* With respect to the former, I have heard, on the contrary, that their scent is extremely prompt, and that they have been known to trace parties of runaway negroes to a great distance by the smell of their fire-wood; and as to the latter, they are, like other negroes, fond of savoury dishes, jirked hog, and ringtail pigeons, delicacies unknown to an European table. . . . I know not whence the word *jirked* is derived, but it signifies cutting or scoring internally the flesh of the wild hog, which is then smoked, and otherwise prepared in a manner that gives it a very fine flavour. . . .

After the treaty with Cudjoe, the Maroons became the subject of successive laws, consisting of regulations respecting run-aways, trials, punishments, making roads, and a variety of minute affairs. Being careless whether they brought in a run-away alive, or only his head, a law was passed, with great policy, allowing, besides the usual reward, mile-money for every run-away produced alive. Inveigling slaves and harbouring run-aways, were punishable by transportation; that is, the offender was sold to foreigners on other islands, or on the continent of America. Though a concourse of slaves in their towns was forbidden, the Maroons might have dances among themselves whenever they pleased, and, provided the dances were in the day-time, with a small number of slaves. They were not to quit their town without leave; and, if they staid seven days beyond the time allowed them, they were liable to be taken up and sent home for trial. They were not permitted to purchase or possess slaves. No party in pursuit of run-aways was to consist of more than twelve men, including officers, except on particular occasions; or to go without written orders from the Superintendant; nor were the party to remain out more than twenty days. No Maroons were to be employed by any white person without a written agreement; and debts due to or from them were to be determined by two magistrates in a summary way. Their persons were protected from whipping, or other ill-treatment. They were bound to repair the roads leading to their town once a-year, on being ordered by the Superintendant, for which they were to be paid. Lastly, there was a law which, in consideration of their increasing population, gave them the liberty of relinquishing their rights as Maroons, and residing in any other part of the island except the Maroon towns, no longer subject to the Superintendant, but enjoying the privileges of free people. In which case they were bound to enlist in the militia.

To some of these laws very little attention was paid. The Maroons bought slaves without any notice being taken of it. Parties of them were suffered to wander about the island, and many of them formed temporary connexions with the female slaves on the different plantations in the country. Whole families of them left their towns, and were permitted to establish themselves on the back settlements of the planters, without complying with the forms required by the law respecting such removals . . . . From the neglect of this law, it is evident that it was not passed with a view of encouraging the Maroons to disperse and lose the existence of a distinct community, which it has been imagined would have been beneficial to the island, but merely to give them room, their limits becoming unequal to their increase. Whether their extinction, as a distinct body, would have been beneficial, is highly problematical. The war of 1795 would not have taken place; but who can say what other communities of the slaves might have been formed in the woods and mountains, and what other wars might have been the consequence? It is very probable that assemblages of fugitives would have been formed in the woody and almost inaccessible retreats of the country, had it not been for the frequent scowering of the woods by the Maroons, in search of run-away negroes. These assemblages would in time have formed new

Maroon bodies, as difficult to subdue as the former; and so far more dangerous than the original Maroons were in their outset, that their connexion
with the slaves would have been more general. It is very well known, that
notwithstanding the vigilance and activity with which fugitives were pursued by the Maroons, a small body of them did actually establish themselves
in the mountains, where they had raised huts, and made provision-grounds,
on which some had lived for upwards of twenty years. This body, called the
Congo Settlement, was discovered in the late war by a party of Maroons
crossing the country, and was dispersed, some of the negroes returning to
the estates to which they formerly belonged, and others surrendering with
the Maroons at the termination of the war.

Notes

1. R.C. Dallas, *The History of the Maroons, from their origin to the establishment of
   their chief tribe at Sierra Leone* (London: T.N. Longman and O. Rees, 1803).
2. Ibid., 1:xi–xii.
3. Ibid., 1:78–101.
4. Later letters give a detailed account of the second Maroon War (1795–96),
   waged between the Trelawny Maroons and the British forces, which ended
   with the deportation of 568 Maroons to Halifax, Nova Scotia.
5. Cudjoe was the Maroon leader in 1739.

GEORGE PINCKARD (1768–1835)

Notes on the West Indies (1806)[1]

As physician to the army, Pinckard travelled extensively in the West Indies in 1796–98 and recorded his observations in a series of letters. This was not just a formal convention: in the preface he explains that these were originally private letters written in the form of a daily journal, and not intended for publication. They thus give a refreshingly candid record of the author's changing impressions. Graphic accounts of the maltreatment of slaves, which provided valuable ammunition for the anti-slavery movement, are offset by sympathetic descriptions of their cheerful recreations and contentment under a humane master. However, Pinckard became convinced that the slave system was fundamentally pernicious and that abolition of the slave trade, though imperative, should be only a stage in the progress towards emancipation. The text used here is from the first edition; the second edition, published in London in 1816, was extensively revised, at the expense of the immediacy of the first.

Barbadoes, Feb. [1796][2]

Sunday is a day of festivity among the slaves. They are passionately fond of dancing, and the sabbath offering them an interval from toil, is, generally, devoted to their favorite amusement; and, instead of remaining in tranquil rest, they undergo more fatigue, or at least more personal exertion, during their gala hours of Saturday night and Sunday, than is demanded from them, in labor, during any four days of the week.

They assemble, in crowds, upon the open green, or in any square or corner of the town, and, forming a ring in the centre of the throng, dance to the sound of their beloved music, and the singing of their favorite African yell. Both music and dance are of a savage nature. I have wished myself a musician, that I might take down for you the notes of their songs; which are very simple, but harsh and wholly deficient in softness and melody. . . .

The instrumental parts of the band consist of a species of drum, a kind of rattle, and their ever-delighting Banjar. The first is a long hollow piece of wood, with a dried sheep skin tied over the end; the second is a calabash containing a number of small stones, fixed to a short stick which serves as the handle; and the third is a coarse and rough kind of guitar. While one negro strikes the Banjar, another shakes the rattle with great force of arm, and a third sitting across the body of the drum, as it lies lengthwise upon the ground, beats and kicks the sheep skin at the end, in violent exertion with his hands and heels, and a fourth sitting upon the ground at the other end, behind the man on the drum, beats upon the wooden sides of it with two sticks. Together with these noisy sounds, numbers of the party of both sexes bawl forth their dear delighting song with all possible force of lungs; and from the combination, and *tout ensemble* of the scene, a spectator would require only a slight aid from fancy to transport him to the savage wilds of Africa. On great occasions the band is increased by an additional number of drums, rattles, and voices.

The dance consists of stamping of the feet, twistings of the body, and a number of strange indecent attitudes. It is a severe bodily exertion – more bodily indeed than you can well imagine, for the limbs have little to do in it. The head is held erect, or, occasionally, inclined a little forward – the hands nearly meet before – the elbows are fixed, pointing from the sides – and the lower extremities being held rigid, the whole person is moved without lifting the feet from the ground. Making the head and limbs fixed points, they writhe and turn the body upon its own axis, slowly advancing towards each other, or retreating to the outer parts of the ring. Their approaches, with the figure of the dance, and the attitudes and inflexions in which they are made, are highly indecent; but of this they seem to be wholly unconscious, for the gravity – I might say the solemnity of countenance, under which all this passes, is peculiarly striking, indeed almost ridiculous. Not a smile – not a significant glance, nor an immodest look escapes from either sex: but they meet, in very indecent attitudes, under the most settled, and unmeaning gravity of countenance. Occasionally they change the figure by stamping upon the feet, or making a more general movement of the person, but these are only temporary variations; the twistings and turnings of the body seeming to constitute the supreme excellence of the dance.

For the most part only two enter the ring at a time, but, occasionally, as many as three or four! each making a small contribution to the band at the time of stepping into the circle. They circle, violently, together until one is tired, and when this escapes from the circle another assumes the place, thus continuing to follow, one by one, in succession, so as frequently to keep up the dance, without any interval, for several hours . . . .

As I was looking on at one of these dances I observed a soldier's wife, from the north of Tweed, gazing with curiosity and astonishment, amidst the throng: and seeing her features marked with dissatisfaction and surprize, I asked her what she thought of the African dance. *"Oot,"* said she *"tis an unco way o' spending the Sabbath night"*. – And on my asking her if there were any as pretty woman in the Highlands of Scotland, she, instantly, replied *"whether or not – they smell better."*

Negro funeral.[3] [same date]

At the gate of the burying ground the corpse was taken from the hearse, and borne by eight negroes, not upon their shoulders, but upon four clean white napkins placed under the coffin. The body was committed to the grave, immediately, on reaching it, without either prayer or ceremony; and the coffin, directly, covered with earth. In doing this, much decent attention was observed. The mould was not shovelled in roughly with the spade, almost disturbing the dead, with the rattling of stones and bones upon the coffin, but was first put into a basket, and then carefully emptied into the grave; an observance which might be adopted in England very much to the comfort of the afflicted friends of the deceased.

During this process an old negro woman chanted an African air, and the multitude joined her in the chorus. It was not in the strain of a hymn, or solemn requiem, but was loud and lively, in unison with the other gaieties of the occasion.

Many were laughing and sporting the whole time with the fishermen, who danced and gambolled, during the ceremony, upon the neighbouring graves. From the moment the coffin was committed to the earth, nothing of order was maintained by the party. The attendants dispersed in various directions, retiring or remaining, during the filling up of the grave, as inclination seemed to lead.

When the whole earth was replaced several of the women, who had staid to chant, in merry song, over poor Jenny's clay, took up a handful of the mould, and threw it down again upon the grave of their departed friend, as the finishing of the ceremony, crying aloud *"God bless you, Jenny! good-by! remember me to all friends t'other side of the sea, Jenny! Tell 'em me come soon! Good-by, Jenny, good-by! See for send me good - - - - to-night Jenny! Good-by, good night, Jenny, good-by!"* All this was uttered in mirth and laughter, and accompanied with attitudes and gesticulations expressive of any thing but sorrow or sadness.

From the grave-digger we learned that poor Jenny had been a washer-woman, and that the females who had, so merrily, sounded her requiem, had been her sud-associates. They had full faith in Jenny's transmigration to meet her friends, at her place of nativity; and their persuasion that death was only a removal from their present to their former home – a mere change from a state of slavery to a state of freedom – did not barely alleviate, but wholly prevented the natural grief and affliction arising from the loss of a friend. They confidently expected to hear from poor Jenny, or to know her influence, in the way they most desired, before morning.

Stabroek [Guiana], May 6 [1796][4]

Unfortunately I am now enabled to speak of the punishment of a slave . . . Happening to call one morning upon a lady at Stabroek, in company with several Europeans who had been my fellow-passengers hither, we were scarcely seated before we heard the bleeding clang of the whip, and the painful cries of a poor unfortunate black. The lady of the house, more accustomed to scenes of slavery than ourselves, pointing to the spot, as if it were a pleasant sight for strangers, or something that might divert us, asked, with apparent glee, if we saw them *"flogging the negre?"* Truly we saw the whole too clearly. A poor unhappy slave was stretched out naked upon the open street, tied down with his face to the ground before the fiscal's door, his two legs extended to one stake, his arms strained out, at full length, to two others in form of the letter Y, and, thus secured to the earth, two strong-armed drivers,[5] placed at his sides, were cutting his bare skin, by turns, with long heavy-lashed whips, which, from the sound, alone, without seeing the blood that followed, conveyed the idea of tearing away pieces of flesh at every stroke.

I am extremely happy to be able to relieve you from this painful scene, by presenting to you one of a very opposite nature – one in which every feeling of your heart will warmly participate. A party of recently arrived Europeans went to dine at "Arcadia;" the plantation of a Mr. Osborn, about eight miles from Stabroek. Five slaves were sent, with a handsome covered boat to fetch us, in which we had a most pleasant sail, about six miles up the river. and, then, coming into a canal which led to the estate, we were drawn about two miles further, by the negroes running at the side of the canal . . . singing all the way, and pulling, in merry tune, together . . . .

[After dinner at Arcadia, the party is taken to a plantation belonging to Osborn's neighbour, Mr Dougan.]

I know not whether, upon any occasion, since my departure from England, I have experienced such true and heart-felt pleasure as in witnessing the high degree of comfort and happiness enjoyed by the slaves of "Profit." Mr. Dougan not only grants them many little indulgences, and studies to make them happy, but he fosters them with a father's care; and they, sensible of his tenderness towards them, look to their revered master as a kind and affectionate parent; and, with undivided – unsophisticated attachment, cheerfully devote, to him, their labour and their lives . . . .

The slaves of Mr. Dougan are not only fed, and clothed, and tenderly watched in sickness, without any personal thought or concern; but each has his appropriate spot of ground, and his cottage, in which he feels a right as sacred as if secured to him by all the seals and parchments of the Lord High Chancellor of England, and his court.

Happy and contented, the slave of "Profit" sees all his wants supplied. Having never been in a state of freedom, he has no desire for it. Not having known liberty, he feels not the privation of it; nor is it within the powers of his mind either to conceive or comprehend the sense we attach to the term. Were freedom offered to him he would refuse to accept it, and would only view it as a state fraught with certain difficulties and vexations, but offering no commensurate good. "Who gib me for gnyhaam Massa," he asks, "if me free?" "Who gib me clothes!" "Who send me a doctor when me sick?"

With industry a slave has no acquaintance; nor has he any knowledge of the kind of comfort and independence which derive from it. Ambition has not taught him that, in freedom, he might escape from poverty – nor has he any conception that by improving his intellect he might become of higher importance in the scale of humanity. Thus circumstanced, to remove him from the quiet and contentment of such a bondage, and to place him amidst the tumults and vicissitudes of freedom, were but to impose upon him the exchange of great comparative happiness, for much of positive misery and distress . . . .[6]

The cottages and little gardens of the negroes exhibited a degree of neatness, and of plenty, that might be envied by free-born Britons, not of the poorest class. The huts of Ireland, Scotland, France, Germany, nay many, even of England itself, bear no comparison with these. In impulsive delight I ran into many of them, surprizing the slaves with an unexpected visit, and, verily, I say the peasantry of Europe might envy these dwellings of slavery. They mostly consist of a comfortable sitting room, and a neat, well-furnished bed-chamber. In one I observed a high bedstead, according to the present European fashion, with deep mattresses, all neatly made up, and covered with a clean white counterpane; the bed-posts, drawers, and chairs bearing the polish of well-rubbed mahogany. I felt a desire to pillow my head in this hut for the night, it not having fallen to my lot, since I left England, to repose on so inviting a couch. The value of the whole was ten-fold augmented by the contented slaves being able to say, "All this we feel to be our own." . . . Were all masters kind and humane as Mr. Dougan, and his neighbour, the peasants of Europe, although blessed with freedom, might sigh, in vain, for the happiness enjoyed – by slaves!

A regular sale of negroes

Stabroek, May 8 [1797][7]

The poor Africans, who were to be sold, were exposed, naked, in a large empty building, like an open barn. Those, who came, with intention to purchase, minutely inspected them; handled them; made them jump, and stamp with their feet, and throw out their arms and their legs; turned them about; looked into their mouths; and, according to the usual rules of traffic with respect to cattle, examined them, and made them shew themselves in a variety of ways, to try if they were sound and healthy. All this was distressful as humiliating, and tended to excite strong aversion and disgust; but a wound, still more severe, was inflicted on the feelings, by some of the purchasers selecting only such as their judgment led them to prefer, regardless of the bonds of nature, and affection! The urgent appeals of friendship and attachment were unheeded; sighs and tears made no impression; and all the imploring looks, and penetrating expressions of grief were unavailing. Hungry commerce corroded even the golden chains of affection; and sordid interest burst every tie of nature asunder . . . .

A whole host of painful ideas rushed into my mind at the moment. In sad contemplation all the distorted images of this abhorrent traffic presented themselves to my recollection. The many horrors and cruelties, I had so often heard of, appeared in their worst shape before me; and my imagination was acutely alive to the unmerited punishment sometimes inflicted – the incessant labour exacted – the want of freedom – and all the catalogue of hardships endured by slaves. I endeavoured to combat the effect of these impressions by attaching my mind to opposite images. The kind treatment of negroes under humane masters occurred to me; I recollected the comfort and harmony of the slaves I had lately seen at "Profit." I contemplated their freedom from care, and the many anxieties of the world; and I remembered the happiness and contentment expressed in their songs and merry dances: but – all in vain! The repugnant influence would not thus be cheated. With such distress, before my eyes, all palliatives were unavailing. The whole was wrong, and not to be justified. I felt that I execrated every principle of the traffic. Nature revolted at it; and I condemned the whole system of slavery under all its forms and modifications.

When purchased, the slaves were marked by placing a piece of string, or of red or white tape round their arms or necks. One gentleman, who bought a considerable number of them, was proceeding to distinguish those he had selected, by tying a piece of red tape round the neck, when I observed two negroes, who were standing together entwined in each others arms, watch him with great anxiety. Presently he approached them, and after making his examination affixed the mark only to one of them. The other, with a look of unerring expression, and, with an impulse of marked disappointment, cast his eyes up to the purchaser seeming to say – "and will you not have me too?" – then jumped, and danced, and stamped with his feet, and made other signs to signify that he, also, was sound and strong and worthy his choice. He was, nevertheless, passed by unregarded; upon which he turned, again, to his companion, his friend, his brother, whichever he was, took him to his bosom, hung upon him, and, in sorrowful countenance expressed the strongest marks of disappointment and affliction. The feeling was mutual: – it arose from reciprocal affection. His friend participated in his grief, and they both wept bitterly. Soon afterwards on looking round to complete his purchase the planter, again, passed that way, and not finding any one that better suited his purpose, he, now, hung the token of choice round the neck of the negro whom he had before disregarded. All the powers of art could not have effected the change that followed. More genuine joy was never expressed. His countenance became enlivened. Grief and sadness vanished, and flying into the arms of his friend, he caressed him with warm embraces, then skipped, and jumped, and danced about, exhibiting all the purest signs of mirth and gratification. His companion, not less delighted, received him with reciprocal feelings – and a more pure and native sympathy was never exhibited. Happy in being, again, associated, they now retired apart from the crowd, and sat down, in quiet contentment, hugging and kissing the red signal of bondage, like two attached and affectionate brothers – satisfied to toil out their days, for an unknown master, so they might but travel their journey of slavery together.

Barbarous murder of a slave. Conduct of the gang at the funeral of their murdered brother

Mahaica [Guiana], August [1798][8]

Two unhappy negroes, a man and a woman, having been driven by cruel treatment to abscond from the plantation Lancaster, were taken a few days since, and brought back to the estate, when the manager, whose inhuman severity had caused them to fly from his tyrannic government, dealt out to them his avenging despotism with more than savage brutality. Taking with him two of the strongest drivers, armed with the heaviest whips, he led out these trembling and wretched Africans, early in the morning, to a remote part of the estate, too distant for the officers to hear their cries; and there, tying down first the man, he stood by, and made the drivers flog him with may hundred lashes, until, on releasing him from the ground, it was discovered that he was nearly exhausted: and in this state the inhuman monster struck him on the head, with the butt end of a large whip, and felled him again to the earth; when the poor negro, escaping at once from his slavery and his sufferings, expired at the murderer's feet. But not satiated with blood, this savage tyrant next tied down the naked woman, on the spot by the dead body of her husband, and with the whips, already deep in gore, compelled the drivers to inflict a punishment of several hundred lashes, which had nearly released her also from a life of toil and torture.

Hearing of these acts of cruelty, on my return from the hospital, and scarcely believing it possible that they could have been committed, I went immediately to the sick-house to satisfy myself by ocular testimony: when, alas! I discovered that all I had heard was too fatally true; for, shocking to relate, I found the wretched and almost murdered woman lying stark-naked on her belly, upon the dirty boards, without any covering to the horrid wounds which had been cut by the whips, and with the still warm and bloody corpse of the man extended at her side, upon the neck of which was an iron collar, and a long heavy chain, which the now murdered negro had been made to wear from the time of his return to the estate . . . .

[Pinckard continues with a detailed description of the woman's "shocking and distressful" condition and that of another slave still suffering from injuries inflicted a fortnight earlier.]

The following day we witnessed the preparations for the funeral of their murdered brother, by his fellow slaves. It was conducted in their usual manner, not with the afflicting solemnity of the Christian rites, but with all the mirthful ceremonies of an African burial, forming a scene of gaiety, which consisted of music, dancing, singing, and loud noise. They all seemed to rejoice more in his escape from pain and misery, than they sorrowed for his loss.

The body being put into the coffin, and every thing made ready for proceeding to the grave, the corpse was taken out of the sick-house into the yard, and there placed very carefully upon the heads of two robust negroes, who carried it as far as the house, and then, halting under the window of the manager's room, they set the coffin upon the ground, and the whole gang of slaves danced and sang, and played their music round it, in loud gambols, for nearly two hours; beating at intervals, with great violence, against the door and window-shutters, and threatening vengeance upon the murderer of their companion. The manager expecting that they would break into the house to massacre him, and feeling, no doubt, that he merited death from their hands, was seized with sad alarm, and breaking from his hiding place, ran abruptly into the mess-room, imploring the protection of the officers, and looking a ghastly figure of terror. I could not but remark the effect of his sudden appearance among us. Not an officer of the whole mess separated his lips in reply to him. The general feeling seemed to say – a wretch so cruel can deserve no compassion . . . . His fears had magnified the danger, for although the slaves were clamorous, we did not observe among them any marks of violence which evinced a disposition forcibly to break into the house. They at length concluded their dance, then replacing the coffin upon the heads of the two negroes, and observing much ceremony with regard to the position of the corpse, they proceeded towards the place of interment. On leaving the court yard, they used the precaution of going round the house, in order to avoid carrying the body across the manager's window – not, as you will suppose, from any sense of delicacy towards him, but from some superstition regarding the spirit of the dead slave. As they moved on, two women tapped gently at the sides of the coffin, as if to appease the corpse, or soften its wrath while passing the murderer's abode. The manager felt highly relieved by their departure; but they had not gone far before the whole party suddenly faced about, and came running back to the house, the two negroes who were carrying the corpse turning round and round with it upon their heads a number of times in the yard, while many of the gang beat and kicked against the door, and the window-shutters of the manager's room, shouting and crying aloud for vengeance: upon which one of the book-keepers, an old man who had been long upon the estate, went out and joined in the crowd, and exerting his influence to appease them, again led them away, when they went dancing, singing, and beating their music to the place of burial. After a short time, the gang returned again into the court yard, having left their companion to seek peace in the grave. The busy dance was now resumed, and they hooted and hissed at the manager, and beat loudly at his door and window, continuing their shoutings and clamour until dark, when they all retired quietly to their huts.

Notes

1. George Pinckard, *Notes on the West Indies: during the expedition under the command of the late General Sir Ralph Abercromby* (London: Longman, Hurst, Rees, and Orme, 1806).
2. Ibid., 1:263–68.
3. Ibid., 1:272–74.
4. Ibid., 2:200–209.
5. [Author's note:] Slaves so termed from being promoted to the distinguished office of following their comrades, upon all occasions, with a whip at their backs, as an English carter follows his horses.
6. In a letter of 11 February 1797, Pinckard reports a dialogue with a female slave illustrating again the state of helpless dependency which he found among creole slaves (*Notes*, 3:252–55). Cf. Mrs Carmichael's "Conversations with Native Africans", page 282 below.
7. Pinckard, *Notes*, 2:217–22.
8. Ibid., 3:65–70.

EDWARD RUSHTON (1756–1814)

"The Coromantees" (1824)[1]

Rushton became familiar with the West Indies as a young man. He first visited Jamaica as an officer on a merchant ship, but later served on a slave-trading vessel, where he observed with horror the conditions under which slaves were transported on the Middle Passage. He stated in the preface to *West-Indian Eclogues* (see page 365 below) that he had "resided several years in the West-Indies". After his return to England in the 1770s he became well-known as an energetic campaigner against slavery and the slave trade. The story on which the following poem was based was presumably real (otherwise the rhetorical appeal in lines 71–75 would be invalid), but I have failed to trace it. Rushton may have heard it from William Rathbone, to whom he inscribed a copy of his *Poems*,[2] addressing him as "the Friend of Liberty, and of Man". Rathbone, a Liverpool merchant and sturdy abolitionist, had extensive trading connections with the West Indies. The poem was first published posthumously in *Poems and Other Writings by the late Edward Rushton* (1824), the text used here, but evidently belongs to the period 1793–1807, between the outbreak of war with France and abolition of the slave trade.

On the wing for Barbadoes, and sweeping along
  Before a brisk easterly gale,

An African trader with wretchedness stored,
With his crew half destroy'd and contagion on board,
   Beheld on his quarter a sail.   5

It was war, and the tri-colour'd flag soon appear'd,
   And a row of nine-pounders were shewn;
And now the poor slaves under hatches were placed,
And the British oppressors beheld themselves chased
   By a force far exceeding their own.   10

Now all their light sails to the turbulent wind
   The tars with despondency gave,
While around the keen dolphin, more brilliantly dress'd
Than the tropical morn or the humming-bird's breast,
   Made the flying-fish skim o'er the wave.   15

The master who saw that his flight was in vain,
   That the powers of his seamen were broke,
Now ordered each resolute negro with speed,
From his loathsome abode and his chains to be freed,
   And thus to the sufferers he spoke: –   20

"Yon bark, oh! ye warriors, belongs to a race
   "Who laugh at the gods you adore,
"Who will torture your frames, and enjoy your deep groans,
"Who will roast you, and boil you, and pick all your bones,
   "And your names shall be heard of no more.   25

"Then say, oh! ye negroes, ye Coromantees,
   "Whose prowess green Africa knows,
"Say, will you submit to this cannibal band,
"And be swallowed up quick – or, with musket in hand,
   "Say, will you these miscreants oppose?"   30

"Give us arms," cried a slave who had once been a chief,
    And whose scars shew'd acquaintance with blood,
"Give us arms, and those sharks that infest the blue main,
"Those vultures that feast on the flesh of the slain,
    "Shall pay, dearly pay for their food."   35

"Yes, yes, give us arms," the stern negroes exclaimed,
    And their eye-balls ferociously glared.
And now fore and aft, like the seamen array'd,
Undaunted the fast sailing French they survey'd,
    And stood for the conflict prepared.   40

The foe now approaches, the battle begins,
    And the bravest are stunn'd by the roar;
Deep immersed in thick smoke, every sinew is strain'd,
And they tug, and they shout, and the strife is maintain'd
    Amidst crashings, and groanings, and gore.   45

Now the French try to board, but their daring design
    The slaves like fierce tigers oppose;
Where danger appears like a torrent they sweep,
And the fearless assailants now plunge in the deep,
    Or expire on the decks of their foes.   50

With their sails all in tatters, exhausted, repell'd,
    Lo! the Frenchmen sheer off in despair;
While the English, all joyous, behold them retire,
Shake the hands of the negroes, their courage admire,
    And both with wild shouts rend the air.   55

Though the master exults, yet the conquering slaves
    Fill his soul with a thousand alarms;
Now he whispers the mates, and the brandy appears,

The dance is proposed, and received with three cheers,
    And the Africans lay down their arms.   60

As the sharks, all voracious, in Congo's broad stream,
    Quickly dart human flesh to devour,
So the mates and the master soon seize on their prey,
And soon to the arm-chest those weapons convey
    Which bend groaning millions to power.   65

And now the bashaws give their fears to the gale,
    And resume their imperious tone;
And now the poor negroes again are confined,
Again are their limbs to the deck-chains consign'd,
    And again in their fetters they groan.   70

Oh Britons! behold in these Coromantees
    The fate of an agonized world,
Where, in peace, a few lordlings hold millions in chains,
Where, in war, for those lordlings men open their veins,
    And again to their dungeons are hurl'd!   75

But the period approaches when poor prostrate man
    Shall enjoy what the Deity gave;
When the oculist Reason shall touch his dim eyes,
With a soul all abhorrence the sufferer shall rise,
    And undauntedly throw off the slave.   80

Notes

1. Edward Rushton, *Poems and Other Writings by the late Edward Rushton*, ed. William Shepherd (London: Effingham Wilson, 1824), 72–76.
2. Published London: T. Ostell, 1806, and now in the Liverpool University Library.

Part 2.

From Abolition to Emancipation, 1808–1834

"Slaves in Barbadoes", reprinted from J.A. Waller, *A Voyage in the West Indies* (London: Sir R. Phillips and Co., 1820). Courtesy of the Trustees of the National Library of Scotland.

JOHN STEWART (D. 1832)

An Account of Jamaica (1808)

Stewart's authorship of this anonymous work is well attested. He speaks in the preface of a "residence of twenty-one years in Jamaica" (that is, 1787–1808), on the basis of which he aims "to exhibit a picture of society and manners in this island" and "an account of the slaves, their character, customs, condition, and treatment". Writing just after the abolition of the slave trade, he claims to be neutral on the question of the continuation of slavery itself. Though he lived in Edinburgh from 1809 onwards, Stewart continued to own properties in Jamaica with upwards of 180 slaves, and he appears to have revisited the island at least once after 1808. He later published a substantially revised version of *An Account* under the title *A View of the Past and Present State of the Island of Jamaica*, published in Edinburgh in 1823, in which he supported a gradualist approach to the ending of slavery rather than immediate emancipation. Stewart's observations on slave conditions and treatment were nevertheless trusted as fair-minded by anti-slavery campaigners in Britain, and his 1823 book was frequently cited as a reliable record. The earlier account, however, reflects his Jamaican experience more directly, and is therefore the text preferred here.

Former condition and treatment of the slaves.

Present ameliorated condition and treatment. – Routine of their work.[2]

In former times, the condition and treatment of the poor negro was truly deplorable; particularly when he had the misfortune to fall into the hands of a barbarous master or manager. He might torture him in various ways, he might wound, maim, or even kill him, and all the punishment he was liable to for this savage exercise of authority, was the payment of a pecuniary fine! The author has heard of one wretch who used to set his dogs upon those of his negroes who displeased him, and feast his eyes with the spectacle of the animals worrying them: and of another, who, when his negroes became useless by age or disease, ordered them to be precipitated into the cavern of a rock! This man was an incredible monster of inhumanity, and was so notorious throughout the island, that there is still a general song among the negroes relative to him, the burthen of which is a poor negro, while he is dragging to this horrible fate, exclaiming, *'Massa me no dead yet!'*[3] It is said that one of those poor wretches escaped by miracle from this dungeon of death, not having been materially hurt by the fall, and afterwards recovered; but that evil mischance bringing him one day in the way of his diabolical master, he claimed him; though the unhappy negro justly pleaded that he had now no further title to him, as he had *'thrown him away.'* . . . In the time of these men, it was not an unusual thing, when a negro ran away, to pay so much to a Maroon to produce him dead or alive; that is, under the pretence that the fugitive had made resistance, the Maroon killed him, and cut off his head, which he brought in his wallet to the master, who had it set up in some conspicuous part, as an example, *in terrorem*, to the rest of his slaves!

But these horrible times are now past, and the negro slave is as completely protected against violence and murder, as the white man. Within these late years, one or two white men have been executed in Jamaica for the murder of their own negroes; and one infatuated man, of opulent fortune and respectable family, was lately obliged to fly to a foreign country, in order to avoid a like fate, for having, in a fit of passion and inebriety, killed his negro servant. There is a complete code of laws, called the consolidated slave law, now existing in this island, chiefly for the protection of the slaves. A white man, who beats and abuses a negro, is equally liable to be prosecuted and punished, either by a magistrate, or the owner of the slave, as if he thus treated a white man like himself. The evidence of a slave is, however, not admissible against a white man: it is conceived, that such admissions would open a door to much perjury and abuse of this prerogative; for the slaves, who do not consider it any great sin or shame to tell the grossest falsehoods, would, also, not scruple to confirm such falsehood with the solemnity of an oath; they have no other opinion of *'Buckra swear,'* as they call the oath of the white people, than that it is a mere empty form of words, unless they have been baptized as Christians; but they regard their own mode of taking an oath as most solemn and binding; this however can only be administered by one negro to another . . . .

Formerly the slaves on the estates were cruelly and injudiciously made to perform much supernumerary work, at improper times. After the labours of crop were over, and they should have enjoyed a little additional respite, they were, on many properties, harassed to a shameful degree. Not even the light of heaven circumscribed their labours, but they were made to work for hours after it was dark, and for hours before the light dawned in the morning. At present their labour is light, and this supernumerary toil is no longer exacted. On a property which has five hundred acres of land in cultivation (including pasture and provisions) there are two hundred slaves, about half of which number are constantly employed in the agricultural duties of the estate, and manufacturing the produce. In England, an estate of this extent would be cultivated by the tenth of this number. It is true, the mode of cultivation is here different. This proportion shews at least that the work the slaves here perform is far from being excessive. The routine of their daily work is as follows: They assemble in the fields at day break; about ten in the forenoon, they are allowed about half an hour to eat their breakfast, which is brought out into the fields by the negro cooks; at one they go to dinner, and in about two hours after are again assembled in the fields (either by a bell, or, as is most usual, by the sound of a conque-shell, which is heard at a very great distance); and they draw off from work in the twilight of the evening . . . . The negroes are formed into different gangs, according to their age and strength. The first gang consists of the ablest hands (of both sexes) on the estate; the second gang of less able hands, and boys and girls; and the third, or small gang, of children from eight to twelve years of age, who are employed in weeding the young plant-canes, and such other light work. The two principal gangs are followed by black drivers, as they are called, who superintend the work under the book-keepers, and carry whips, as instruments of occasional correction, which it is the duty of the book-keeper, in the absence of the overseer, to see they do not unnecessarily or maliciously inflict, and only in a moderate degree. It were perhaps to be wished, that this instrument were laid aside, at least only used in cases of marked delinquency, and a mode of common correction, less revolting, substituted; for, however seldom this instrument may be used, it is in itself a disgusting and unnatural thing, and the very sound of it must be the reverse of music to the ears of a man of sentiment and feeling.

General character of the negroes.
Various tribes of them that come to the West Indies.[4]

The negroes are crafty, artful, and plausible; not often grateful for small services; but frequently deceitful and over-reaching; of a more mild and pacific disposition than the North American savage, and more timid and cowardly; not so easily roused to fierceness and revenge; but, when once those passions are awakened, equally cruel and implacable; they are avaricious and selfish, obstinate and perverse, giving all the plague they can to their white rulers; little ashamed of falsehood, and strongly addicted to theft. Some of these dispositions doubtless originate in, and are fostered by, the nature of their situation and treatment; and would probably spring up in an European breast, if sunk and degraded by a state of servile bondage. The negro has, however, some good qualities mingled with his unamiable ones. He is patient, cheerful, and commonly submissive, capable, at times, of grateful attachments, where uniformly well treated, and kind and affectionate towards his kindred and offspring. The affection and solicitude of a negro mother towards her infant, is indeed ardent even to enthusiasm. The crime of infanticide, so shocking to nature, so horrible in idea, yet unfortunately not unknown to nations calling themselves civilized, was perhaps never heard of among the negro tribes: and yet it is said that, prompted by avarice, the African father will sometimes sell his children to the Europeans! It is not an easy matter to trace with an unerring pencil the true character and dispositions of the negro, they are often so ambiguous and disguised; and there will occur examples that bid defiance to analogy. The dispositions of some are a disgrace to human nature; while others there are whose good qualities would put many of their rulers to the blush. . . . It is also to be observed, that there is a marked difference in the dispositions of the different tribes of Africans who are *imported* into this country. The Eboe is crafty, saving, and industrious, artful and disputative in driving a bargain, and suspicious of being over-reached by others with whom he deals. The Eboe may be called the Jew of the negro race, though they sometimes say that they are like the Scotch; a very large proportion of which nation reside in this part of the world, and generally succeed, by their diligence, their perseverance, their economy, and industry, in their respective pursuits. The Coromantee is fierce, savage, violent, and revengeful. This tribe has generally been at the head of all insurrections, and was the original parent-stock of the Maroons. The Congo, Chamba, Mandingo, &c. are of a more mild and peaceable disposition. The Mandingoes are a sort of Mahometans, though they are too ignorant to understand any thing of the Alcoran, or of the nature of their religion. Some of them, however, can scrawl a few Arabic characters, but without understanding, or being able to explain, much of their meaning. Probably they are scraps from the Alcoran, which they have been taught by their imans, or priests. The Creole negroes are, of course, the descendants of the Africans, and may be said to possess in common the mingled dispositions of their parents or ancestors. But they affect a greater degree of *taste and refinement* than the Africans, boast of their good fortune in being born a Creole, and the farther they are removed from the African blood, the more they pride themselves thereon. There is a variety of shades between the black and the white; as Sambos, Mulattos, Quadroons, and Mestees, beyond which last the distinction of colour is lost.

Metaphysical and religious ideas of the negroes.
Funerals. – Music. – Thoughts on converting them to Christianity. – Obeah.

The ideas of the negroes cannot be expected to extend to abstract and metaphysical subjects. Of the existence and attributes of a Deity, of a future state, and of duration and space, they have but imperfect notions. They cannot dilate and subdivide their conceptions into minuter distinctions and more abstract combinations; yet they will often express, in their own way, a wonderfully acute conception of things. These conceptions they sometimes compress into short and pithy sentences, something like the sententious proverbs of the Europeans, to which many of them bear an exact analogy. These sayings often convey an astonishing force and meaning; and would, if clothed in a more courtly dress, make no despicable figure even among those precepts of wisdom which are ascribed to the wisest of men. When they wish to imply, that a peaceable man is often wise and provident in his conduct, they say, '*Softly water run deep:*' when they would express the oblivion and disregard which follows us after death, they say, '*when man dead grass grow in him door;*' and when they would express the humility which is the usual accompaniment of poverty, they say, '*Poor man never vex.*' . . .

The African negroes, whatever theological notions they may bring with them from Africa, generally agree in believing in the existence of a Supreme Being, whom they also consider as the distributor of rewards and punishments, for good or evil actions, in a future life. But their ideas in other respects are peculiar and fanciful. They think, that for some unexpiated guilt, or through some unaccountable folly of the primitive black pair to whom they owe their origin, servitude was the unfortunate lot assigned to them; while dominion was given to the more favoured whites. The poor creatures cherish the hope, that after death they shall first return to their native country, and enjoy again the loved society of kindred and friends, from whom they have been torn away in a luckless hour, and who would be so hard-hearted as to deprive them of the sweet consolation! It is true, this idea is, on their first arrival, sometimes carried to such a length, as, combined with their terrors, to produce acts of suicide. . . .

At their funerals they use various ceremonies; among which is the practice of pouring libations, and sacrificing a fowl on the grave of the deceased; a tribute of respect they afterwards occasionally repeat. During the whole of the ceremony, many fantastic motions and wild gesticulations are practised, accompanied with a suitable beat of their drums, and other rude instruments, while a melancholy dirge is sung by a female, the chorus of which is performed by the whole of the other females with admirable precision, and full toned, and not unmelodious voices. This species of barbarous music is indeed more enchanting to their ears than all the most exquisite notes of a Purcell or a Pleyel; and however delighted they might appear to be with the finest melody of our bands, let them but hear at a distance the uncouth sounds of their own native instruments, and they would instantly fly from the one to enjoy the other. When taught to sing in the European style, the negro girls have an expression and melody little inferior to the finest voice of a white female.

When the deceased is interred, the plaintive notes of sympathy and regret are no longer heard; the drums resound with a livelier beat, the song grows animated and cheerful; dancing and apparent merriment commences, and the remainder of the night is spent in feasting and riotous debauchery. Previous to the interment of the corpse, it is pretended that it is endowed with the gift of speech, and the friends and relatives alternately place their ears to the lid of the coffin to hear what the deceased has to say. This generally consists of complaints and upbraidings for various injuries, treachery, ingratitude, injustice, slander, and in particular, the non-payment of debts due to the deceased; this latter complaint is sometimes shewn by the deceased in a more *cogent* way than by mere words; for on coming opposite to the door of the negro debtor, the coffin makes a full stop, and no persuasion nor *strength* can induce the deceased to go forward peaceably to his grave, till the money is paid; so that the unhappy debtor has no alternative but to comply with this demand, or have his creditor palmed on him as a lodger for some time. . . .

[Stewart argues that attempts to convert slaves to Christianity had been ineffective, mainly because the missionaries sent to Jamaica were generally unfit for the task, but also because of opposition from the planters. The latter begrudged allowance of time to the slaves on Sundays for "religious exercises and attendance", thinking it should be spent working on their provision grounds to support themselves and their families.]

It has been said, that the mind of the negro is too rude and barbarous to receive, with its desired effect, the principles and maxims of Christianity.

Perhaps the experiment was never yet properly tried; at least most of the itinerant preachers who have worked in this vineyard, have not, as before observed, been the most respectable or judicious characters. One of these, it is said, instead of inculcating the Christian virtues, directed a long dissertation, to his sable congregation, on slavery, and assimilated their condition to that of the oppressed Israelites, who at length escaped from the bondage of their unjust task-masters. A few such preachers as this in the island, would soon light up a flame, which neither their *eloquence* not their *sanctity* could extinguish! . . .

There is one good effect which the simple persuasion of his being a Christian produces on the mind of the negro; it is an effectual antidote against the spells and charms of his native superstition. One negro who desires to be revenged on another, if he fears a more open and manly attack on his adversary, has usually recourse to *obeah*. This is considered as a potent and irresistible spell, withering and palsying, by undescribable terrors, and unwonted sensations, the unhappy victim! Like the witches' cauldron in Macbeth, it is a combination of all that is hateful and disgusting; a toad's foot, a lizard's tail, a snake's tooth, the plumage of the carrion crow, or vulture, a broken egg-shell, a piece of wood fashioned into the shape of a coffin, with many other nameless ingredients, compose the fatal mixture. It will of course be conceived, that the practice of *obeah* can have little effect, without a negro is conscious that it is practised upon him, or thinks so; for as the sole evil lies in the terrors of a perturbed fancy, it is of little consequence whether it is really practised or not, if he only imagines that it is. An *obeah* man or woman upon an estate, is therefore a very dangerous person; and the practice of it is made a felony by the law. But numbers may be swept off by its infatuation, before the practice is detected; for, strange as it may appear, so much do the negroes stand in awe of these wretches, so much do they dread their malice and their power, that, though knowing the havock they have made, and are still making, many of them are afraid to discover them to the whites; and others, perhaps, are in league with them for sinister purposes of mischief and revenge. A negro under this infatuation can only be cured of his terrors by being made a Christian; refuse him this indulgence, and he soon sinks a martyr to imagined evils. The author knew an instance of a negro, who being reduced by the fatal influence of *obeah* to the lowest state of dejection and debility, from which there were little hopes of his recovery, was surprisingly and rapidly restored to health and to spirits, by being baptized a Christian: so wonderful are the workings of a weak and superstitious imagination. But, though so liable to be perverted into an instrument of malice and revenge, *obeah*, at least a sort of it, may be said to have its uses. When placed in the gardens and grounds of the negroes, it becomes an excellent guard or watchman, scaring away the predatory run-away, and mid-night plunderer, with more effective terror than gins and spring guns. It loses its effect, however, when put to protect the gardens and plantain-walks of the *Buckras*!

Notes

1.   John Stewart, *An Account of Jamaica, and its Inhabitants. By a Gentleman, long resi-dent in the West Indies* (London: Longman, Hurst, Rees, and Orme, 1808).
2.   Ibid., 224–31.
3.   See the song "Take Him to the Gulley", page 428.
4.   Stewart, *Account*, 234–37.
5.   Ibid., 247–58.

MATTHEW GREGORY LEWIS (1775–1818)

Journal of a West India Proprietor (1834)[1]

Lewis won fame as a writer early in life with his sensational Gothic novel *The Monk* (1795). On the death of his father in 1812 he inherited two estates in Jamaica with nearly four hundred slaves. His *Journal of a West India Proprietor* is an eloquent, richly informative record of visits he made in 1815–16 and 1817–18 in order to see to his plantations and investigate the condition of the slaves. By West Indian standards, Lewis was a liberal, enlightened slave owner, and he was a friend of Wilberforce. His attitude towards his slaves was sympathetic but paternalist and condescending; he thought the hardships of slavery were exaggerated by the abolitionists and was opposed to immediate emancipation. Lewis left England on 11 November 1815 on board *Sir Godfrey Webster*, landed in Jamaica on 1 January 1816 and travelled to his Cornwall estate the next day.

1816. – January 1.[2]

At length the ship has squeezed herself into this champagne bottle of a bay! Perhaps, the satisfaction attendant upon our having overcome the difficulty, added something to the illusion of its effect; but the beauty of the atmosphere, the dark purple mountains, the shores covered with mangroves of the liveliest green down to the very edge of the water, and the light-coloured houses with their lattices and piazzas completely embowered in trees, altogether made the scenery of the Bay wear a very picturesque appearance. And, to complete the charm, the sudden sounds of the drum and banjee, called our attention to a procession of the *John-Canoe*,[3] which was proceeding to celebrate the opening of the new year at the town of Black River. The John-Canoe is a Merry-Andrew dressed in a striped doublet, and bearing upon his head a kind of pasteboard house-boat, filled with puppets, representing, some sailors, others soldiers, others again slaves at work on a plantation, &c. The negroes are allowed three days for holidays at Christmas, and also New-year's day, which being the last is always reckoned by them as the festival of the greatest importance. It is for this day that they reserve their finest dresses, and lay their schemes for displaying their show and expense to the greatest advantage; and it is then that the John-Canoe is considered not merely as a person of material consequence, but one whose presence is absolutely indispensable. Nothing could look more gay than the procession which we now saw with its train of attendants, all dressed in white, and marching two by two (except when the file was broken here and there by a single horseman), and its band of negro music, and its scarlet flags fluttering about in the breeze, now disappearing behind a projecting clump of mangrove trees, and then again emerging into an open part of the road, as it wound along the shore towards the town of Black River . . . .

It seems that, many years ago, an Admiral of the Red was superseded on the Jamaica station by an Admiral of the Blue;[4] and both of them gave balls at Kingston to the '*Brown Girls;*' for the fair sex elsewhere are called the 'Brown Girls' in Jamaica. In consequence of these balls, all Kingston was divided into parties: from thence the division spread into other districts: and ever since, the whole island, at Christmas, is separated into the rival factions of the Blues and the Reds (the Red representing also the English, the Blue the Scotch), who contend for setting forth their processions with the greatest taste and magnificence. This year, several gentlemen in the neighbourhood of Black River had subscribed very largely towards the expenses of the show; and certainly it produced the gayest and most amusing scene that I ever witnessed, to which the mutual jealousy and pique of the two parties against each other contributed in no slight degree. The champions of the

rival Roses, – the Guelphs and the Ghibellines, – none of them could exceed
the scornful animosity and spirit of depreciation with which the Blues and
the Reds of Black River examined the efforts at display of each other. The
Blues had the advantage beyond a doubt; this a Red girl told us that she
could not deny; but still, 'though the Reds were beaten, she would not be a
Blue girl for the whole universe!' On the other hand, Miss Edwards (the mistress of the hotel from whose window we saw the show), was rank Blue to
the very tips of her fingers, and had, indeed, contributed one of her female
slaves to sustain a very important character in the show; for when the Blue
procession was ready to set forward, there was evidently a hitch, something
was wanting; and there seemed to be no possibility of getting on without it
– when suddenly we saw a tall woman dressed in mourning (being Miss
Edwards herself) rush out of our hotel, dragging along by the hand a
strange uncouth kind of a glittering tawdry figure, all feathers, and pitchfork, and painted pasteboard, who moved most reluctantly, and turned out
to be no less a personage than Britannia herself, with a pasteboard shield
covered with the arms of Great Britain, a trident in her hand, and a helmet
made of pale blue silk and silver. The poor girl, it seems, was bashful at
appearing in this conspicuous manner before so many spectators, and hung
back when it came to the point. But her mistress had seized hold of her, and
placed her by main force in her destined position. The music struck up; Miss
Edwards gave the Goddess a great push forwards; the drumsticks and the
elbows of the fiddlers attacked her in the rear; and on went Britannia willy-
nilly!

The Blue girls called themselves 'the Blue girls of Waterloo.'[5] Their
motto was the more patriotic; that of the Red was the more gallant: –
'Britannia rules the Day!' streamed upon the Blue flag; 'Red girls forever!'
floated upon the Red. But, in point of taste and invention, the former carried it hollow. First marched Britannia; then came a band of music; then the
flag; then the Blue King and Queen – the Queen splendidly dressed in white
and silver (in scorn of the opposite party, her train was borne by a little girl
in red); his Majesty wore a full British Admiral's uniform, with a white satin
sash, and a huge cocked hat with a gilt paper crown upon the top of it.
These were immediately followed by 'Nelson's car,' being a kind of canoe
decorated with blue and silver drapery, and with 'Trafalgar' written on the

front of it; and the procession was closed by a long train of Blue grandees (the women dressed in uniforms of white, with robes of blue muslin), all Princes and Princesses, Dukes and Duchesses, every mother's child of them.

The Red girls were also dressed very gaily and prettily, but they had nothing in point of invention that could vie with Nelson's Car and Britannia; and when the Red throne made its appearance, language cannot express the contempt with which our landlady eyed it. 'It was neither one thing nor t'other,' Miss Edwards was of opinion. 'Merely a few yards of calico stretched over some planks – and look, look, only look at it behind! you may see the bare boards! By way of a throne, indeed! Well, to be sure, Miss Edwards never saw a poorer thing in her life, that she must say!' And then she told me, that somebody had just snatched at a medal which Britannia wore round her neck, and had endeavoured to force it away. I asked her who had done so? 'Oh, one of the Red party, *of course!*' The Red party was evidently Miss Edwards's Mrs. Grundy. John Canoe made no part of the procession; but he and his rival, John Crayfish (a personage of whom I heard, but could not obtain a sight), seemed to act upon quite an independent interest, and go about from house to house, tumbling and playing antics to pick up money for themselves.

A play was now proposed to us, and, of course, accepted. Three men and a girl accordingly made their appearance; the men dressed like the tumblers at Astley's,[6] the lady very tastefully in white and silver, and all with their faces concealed by masks of blue silk; and they proceeded to perform the quarrel between Douglas and Glenalvon,[7] and the fourth act of 'The Fair Penitent.'[8] They were all quite perfect, and had no need of a prompter. As to Lothario, he was by far the most comical dog that I ever saw in my life, and his dying scene exceeded all description; Mr. Coates himself might have taken hints from him! As soon as Lothario was fairly dead, and Calista had made her exit in distraction, they all began dancing reels like so many mad people, till they were obliged to make way for the Waterloo procession, who came to collect money for the next year's festival; one of them singing, another dancing to the tune, while she presented her money-box to the spectators, and the rest of the Blue girls filling up the chorus. I cannot say much in praise of the black Catalani;[9] but nothing could be more light, and playful, and graceful, than the extempore movements of the dancing girl.

Indeed, throughout the whole day, I had been struck with the precision of their march, the ease and grace of their action, the elasticity of their step, and the lofty air with which they carried their heads – all, indeed, except poor Britannia, who hung down hers in the most ungoddess-like manner imaginable. The first song was the old Scotch air of 'Logie of Buchan,' of which the girl sang one single stanza forty times over. But the second was in praise of the Hero of Heroes; so I gave the songstress a dollar to teach it to me, and drink the Duke's health. It was not easy to make out what she said, but as well as I could understand them, the words ran as follows: –

'Come, rise up, our gentry, . . .' [see page 438]

– and then there came something about green and white flowers, and a Duchess, and a lily-white Pig, and going on board of a dashing man of war; but what they all had to do with the Duke, or with each other, I could not make even a guess. I was going to ask for an explanation, but suddenly half of them gave a shout loud enough 'to fright the realms of Chaos and old Night,' and away they flew, singers, dancers, and all. The cause of this was the sudden illumination of the town with quantities of large chandeliers and bushes, the branches of which were stuck all over with great blazing torches: the effect was really beautiful, and the excessive rapture of the black multitude at the spectacle was as well worth witnessing as the sight itself.

I never saw so many people who appeared to be so unaffectedly happy. In England, at fairs and races, half the visiters at least seem to have been only brought there for the sake of traffic, and to be too busy to be amused; but here nothing was thought of but real pleasure; and that pleasure seemed to consist of singing, dancing, and laughing, in seeing and being seen, in showing their own fine clothes, or in admiring those of others. There were no people selling or buying; no servants and landladies bustling about; and at eight o'clock, as we passed through the market-place, where was the greatest illumination, and which, of course, was most thronged, I did not see a single person drunk, nor had I observed a single quarrel through the course of the day; except, indeed, when some thoughtless fellow crossed the line of the procession, and received by the way of a good box of the ear from the Queen or one of her attendant Duchesses. Every body made the same remark to me; 'Well, sir, what do you think Mr. Wilberforce would think of the state of the negroes, if he could see this scene?' and certainly, to judge by this one specimen, of all beings that I have yet seen, these were the happiest.

January 2.[10]

At four o'clock this morning I embarked in the cutter for Savannah La Mar, lighted by the most beautiful of all possible morning stars . . . .

The distance was about thirty miles, and soon after nine o'clock we reached Savannah La Mar, where I found my trustee, and a whole cavalcade, waiting to conduct me to my own estate; for he had brought with him a curricle and pair for myself, a gig for my servant, two black boys upon mules, and a cart with eight oxen to convey my baggage. The road was excellent and we had not above five miles to travel; and as soon as the carriage entered my gates, the uproar and confusion which ensued sets all description at defiance. The works were instantly all abandoned; every thing that had life came flocking to the house from all quarters; and not only the men, and the women, and the children, but, 'by a blind assimilation,' the hogs, and the dogs, and the geese, and the fowls, and the turkeys, all came hurrying along by instinct, to see what could possibly be the matter, and seemed to be afraid of arriving too late. Whether the pleasure of the negroes was sincere may be doubted; but certainly it was the loudest I ever witnessed; they all talked together, sang, danced, shouted, and, in the violence of their gesticulations, tumbled over each other, and rolled about upon the ground. Twenty voices at once enquired after uncles, and aunts, and grandfathers, and great-grandmothers of mine, who had been buried long before I was in existence, and whom, I verily believe, most of them only knew by tradition. One woman held up her little naked black child to me, grinning from ear to ear; – 'Look, Massa, look here! him nice lilly neger for Massa!' Another complained, – 'So long since none come see we, Massa; good Massa, come at last.' As for the old people, they were all in one and the same story: now they had lived once to see Massa, they were ready for dying to-morrow, 'them no care.'

The shouts, the gaiety, the wild laughter, their strange and sudden bursts of singing and dancing, and several old women, wrapped up in large cloaks, their heads bound round with different-coloured handkerchiefs, leaning on a staff, and standing motionless in the middle of the hubbub, with their eyes fixed upon the portico which I occupied, formed an exact counterpart of the festivity of the witches in Macbeth. Nothing could be more odd or more novel than the whole scene; and yet there was something in it by which I could not help being affected; perhaps it was the consciousness that all these human beings were my *slaves*; – to be sure, I never saw people look more happy in my life; and I believe their condition to be much more comfortable than that of the labourers of Great Britain; and, after all, slavery, in *their* case, is but another name for servitude, now that no more negroes can be forcibly carried away from Africa, and subjected to the horrors of the voyage, and of the seasoning after their arrival: but still I had already experienced, in the morning, that Juliet was wrong in saying 'What's in a name?' For soon after my reaching the lodging-house at Savannah La Mar, a remarkably clean-looking negro lad presented himself with some water and a towel: I concluded him to belong to the inn; and, on my returning the towel, as he found that I took no notice of him, he at length ventured to introduce himself, by saying, – 'Massa not know me; *me your slave!*' – and really the sound made me feel a pang at the heart. The lad appeared all gaiety and good humour, and his whole countenance expressed anxiety to recommend himself to my notice; but the word 'slave' seemed to imply, that, although he did feel pleasure then in serving me, if he had detested me he must have served me still. I really felt quite humiliated at the moment, and was tempted to tell him, – 'Do not say that again; say that you are my negro, but do not call yourself my slave.'

January 6.[11]

This was the day given to my negroes as a festival on my arrival. A couple of heifers were slaughtered for them: they were allowed as much rum, and sugar, and noise, and dancing as they chose; and as to the two latter, certainly they profited by the permission. About two o'clock they began to assemble round the house, all drest in their holiday clothes, which, both for men and women, were chiefly white; only that the women were decked out with a profusion of beads and corals, and gold ornaments of all descriptions; and that while the blacks wore jackets, the mulattoes generally wore cloth coats; and inasmuch as they were all plainly clean instead of being shabbily fashionable, and affected to be nothing except that which they really were, they looked twenty times more like gentlemen than nine tenths of the bankers' clerks who swagger up and down Bond Street . . . . I had particularly invited 'Mr. John-Canoe' (which I found to be the polite manner in which the negroes spoke of him), and there arrived a couple of very gay and gaudy ones. I enquired whether one of them was 'John-Crayfish;' but I was told that John-Crayfish was John-Canoe's rival and enemy, and might belong to the factions of 'the Blues and the Reds;' but on Cornwall they were all friends, and therefore there were only the father and the son – Mr. John-Canoe, senior, and Mr. John-Canoe, junior . . . .

The John-Canoes are fitted out at the expense of the rich negroes, who afterwards share the money collected from the spectators during their performance, allotting one share to the representator himself; and it is usual for the master of the estate to give them a couple of guineas apiece . . . .

The dances performed to-night seldom admitted more than three persons at a time: to me they appeared to be movements entirely dictated by the caprice of the moment; but I am told that there is a regular figure, and that the least mistake, or a single false step, is immediately noticed by the rest. I could indeed sometimes fancy, that one story represented an old duenna guarding a girl from a lover; and another, the pursuit of a young woman by two suitors, the one young and the other old; but this might be only fancy. However, I am told, that they have dances which not only represent courtship and marriage, but being brought to bed. Their music consisted of nothing but Gambys (Eboe drums), Shaky-shekies, and Kitty-katties: the latter is nothing but any flat piece of board beat upon with two sticks, and the former is a bladder with a parcel of pebbles in it. But the principal part of the music to which they dance is vocal; one girl generally singing two lines by herself, and being answered by a chorus. To make out either the rhyme of the air, or meaning of the words, was out of the question. But one very long song was about the Duke of Wellington, every stanza being chorussed with,

> 'Ay! hey-day! Waterloo!
> Waterloo! ho! ho! ho!'

I too had a great deal to do in the business, for every third word was 'massa;' though how I came there, I have no more idea than the Duke.

The singing began about six o'clock, and lasted without a moment's pause till two in the morning; and such a noise never did I hear till then. The whole of the floor which was not taken up by the dancers was, through every part of the house except the bed-rooms, occupied by men, women, and children, fast asleep. But although they were allowed rum and sugar by whole pailfuls, and were most of them *merry* in consequence, there was not one of them drunk; except indeed, one person, and that was an old woman, who sang, and shouted, and tossed herself about in an elbow chair, till she tumbled it over, and rolled about the room in a manner which shocked the delicacy of even the least prudish of the company. At twelve, my agent wanted to dismiss them; but I would not suffer them to be interrupted on the first holiday that I had given them; so they continued to dance and shout till two; when human nature could bear no more, and they left me to my bed, and a violent headache.

February 24.[12]

[This was a regular "play-day" at which Lewis announced that he was going to give them three additional play-days every year, and extra days off to cultivate their grounds.]

The poor creatures overflowed with gratitude; and the prospective indulgences which had just been announced, gave them such an increase of spirits, that on returning to my own residence, they fell to singing and dancing again with as much violence as if they had been a pack of French furies at the Opera. The favourite song of the night was,

'Since massa come, we very well off;'

which words they repeated in chorus, without intermission (dancing all the time), for hours together; till, at half-past three, neither my eyes nor my brain could endure it any longer, and I was obliged to send them word that I wanted to go to bed, and could not sleep till the noise should cease . . . . So instantly the drums and gumbies left off beating; the children left off singing; the women and men left off dancing; and they all with one accord fell to kicking, and pulling, and thumping about two dozen of their companions, who were lying fast asleep on the floor. Some were roused, some resisted, some began fighting, some got up and lay down again; but at length, by dint of their leading some, carrying others, and rolling the remainder down the steps, I got my house clear of my black guests about four in the morning.

Notes

1. Matthew Gregory Lewis, *Journal of a West India Proprietor, kept during a residence in the island of Jamaica* (London: John Murray, 1834).
2. Ibid., 50–59.
3. *John-Canoe*: the usual nineteenth-century spelling of Jonkonnu in British-authored texts. See Senior, *Encyclopedia*, s.v. "Jonkonnu", for the history of these masquerades. For a critical reading of Lewis's report, see Donna Heiland, "The *Unheimlich* and the Making of Home: Matthew Lewis's *Journal of a West Indian Proprietor*", in *Monstrous Dreams of Reason: Body, Self, and Other in the Enlightenment*, ed. Laura J. Rosenthal and Mita Choudhury (Lewisburg, PA: Bucknell University Press, 2002), 173–74.
4. Until 1864 the Royal Navy was divided into three squadrons named Red, Blue and White.
5. For stories about Wellington and Bonaparte still in circulation among the blacks of Jamaica in the 1840s, see D'Costa and Lalla, *Voices in Exile*, 110–11.
6. Astley's Amphitheatre, or circus, founded in 1774, was one of the principal shows in London.
7. *Douglas and Glenalvon*: principal characters in John Home's highly successful romantic tragedy *Douglas*, first performed in Edinburgh in 1756 and in London in 1757. For slave performances of western drama, see Hill, *Jamaican Stage*, 237–39.
8. Nicholas Rowe's popular tragedy *The Fair Penitent*, first performed on the London stage in 1703, was constantly revived throughout the eighteenth century and later. Lothario and Calista are the main protagonists; Robert Coates, an amateur actor, played Lothario in a performance in London in 1811.
9. *Catalani*: the Italian soprano Angelica Catalani (1780–1849) was a leading opera singer in London from 1806 to 1814.
10. Lewis, *Journal*, 59–62.
11. Ibid., 73–81.
12. Ibid., 192–93.

"ACCOUNT OF THE CHRISTMAS RACKET AMONG THE NEGROES IN JAMAICA" (1810)[1]

This little-known description of the celebrations at Falmouth in 1809–10 illustrates the performance of these masquerades as part of the annual routine of slave life in town. Falmouth was then a thriving seaport, rivalling Montego Bay in importance. The description was sent in a letter from "an intelligent friend in the West Indies" to "C.F.B." in Edinburgh, who submitted it to the editor of the *Scots Magazine* as evidence that the slaves enjoyed at least a few days of free recreation during the year "to lighten the chain of slavery". C.F.B. offered to supply further letters "to shew that the situation of these unfortunate beings is not now so deplorable as the generality of people imagine", but no further contributions appeared.

Falmouth, Jamaica.

3d May 1810.

My Dear C. – About a fortnight before Christmas last, I was awakened one morning before day, with a very unusual sound of mirth. I heard a drum beating, and, as near as I could conjecture, about three or four dozen of voices singing, La, la, la, in great style. On inquiry, I found that it was a parcel of Black wenches, marching up and down, beginning the Christmas racket.[2] Now, you must know, that at that merry season, the Negroes have four days entirely to themselves, namely, Christmas day, the day before, the day after, and New Year's day; during that time they are *free*, and a pretty sort of freedom they make of it.

To prepare for this momentous period is the business of the whole year; every penny is scraped together, by begging, borrowing, and stealing. In Falmouth there are two parties, the Blues and the Reds, and the whole of the business is, which of these shall excel in dress, numbers, *beauty*, and fine singing; their masters and mistresses are also brought into the scrape; for example, Mr ———'s is a Blue house, that is, all our negroes are of the Blue party, and must of course be of the same colour. The Negroes of our next neighbour may be Reds; that again is called a Red house: with the Whites it is merely a nominal distinction, but with the Browns and Blacks it is a serious affair.

About a fortnight before Christmas, then, the Negro wenches begin to prepare. They get up long before day, shoulder their water-buckets, and off to the tank for water. The tank is a reservoir, which stands in the middle of the town, like your public wells in Edinburgh; but instead of minding their business, down go the buckets. The Blues collect in one corner; the Reds in another; and there they begin. Some stout Negro man joins each party, who can beat, and rattles away at their head on an old drum, keeping time to their voices; this continues till after day-break, when they are obliged to muster up their scattered utensils, and trudge home. This is what I call the rehearsal, and the nearer it draws to Christmas, the more assemble, and the longer the said rehearsal lasts.

The much wished for morning dawns at last, to the great joy of the whole black race, and to the great annoyance of all lovers of peace and good order. Buckra's (white person) house is left to take care of itself; out set the Negroes, one and all, to the jubilee, and about daylight the damnable uproar begins; drums, fifes, tambourines, fiddles, and voices, La, la, la. I pulled on my clothes last Christmas morning, and set out determined to see the *dust*. I followed the sound of the hurricane that was nearest me, and met the Blues plump in the face. Lord have mercy on us, such a sight! They were dressed exactly alike: first and foremost, a white muslin turban, spangled with silver, was twisted round their curly locks; in the front of which stuck something like a feather, and beneath peeped their round and black faces, as 'Fair as the star of the morning.'[3] Their necks were uncovered; and to mark their colour, they each wore a short spencer[4] of light blue silk, or Persian,[5] tastefully trimmed with white, and bound at the bottom with an orange-coloured sash, tied in a large knot behind, with the ends hanging down to their heels, likewise adorned with spangles. A short white muslin petticoat, with a wrought border, white stockings, and fancy shoes and gloves, made up the dress. In the front marched the drummer; on each side of him a standard bearer (men) carrying, one a silk flag of light blue, and the other a white, famously decorated. Round these were collected all the idlers, or mobility, some playing on one thing, some another, all keeping good time. Close following came the Queen, (each party have a King and Queen,) supported on each side by a *maid of honour*, glittering in finery; after her followed the principal ladies, two and two, arm in arm; betwixt them, again, marched the rest, in regular succession, two and two, according to their size, the smallest bringing up the rear. The drums beat and the ladies sing. The glittering colours wave in the sun-beams, and the multitude rejoice. The Reds follow the same order, only red is their predominant colour.

You will naturally ask where do slaves get all this? I'll tell you: the Mulattos take a principal part in the fray. The elderly brown women in Falmouth, many of whom are well to do, head the different parties in private, regulate the ceremonies, and purchase the dresses out of their own purse, while the young brown girls make them; and to such a height is the spirit of emulation carried, that the brown woman who headed the Reds last year, said publicly, that, 'before the Blues should gain the day, she would sell a Negro, and spend every farthing of the money.' In this order, then, and with the greatest glee imaginable, do the two parties parade up and down, from one corner of the town to the other, all day. The first day of the year is the last and grand exhibition, and it is then that the great trial of strength takes place, and the King makes his appearance. In the forenoon it is not known who will gain the day, for many additions take place on both sides. About five in the evening both parties make their appearance complete. The music comes first; then comes the King, superbly dressed in blue or red, covered with gold or silver lace, a sword at his side, and a cocked hat. On his right walks *her Majesty*; on his left the chief maid of honour. Immediately behind comes his Majesty's chief officer, with other two principal dames on each arm; and so on in succession, a gentleman being now placed between each two ladies, all attired in court dresses. The King and his retinue are generally the handsomest young Negroes in the town. The King himself is always a free black. Immediately at dusk, a thousand candles are lighted up, and the procession moves by candle light. About seven each party takes their station before the principal house of their colour. The Blues last year encamped before our door, and the King made the piazza the hall of audience. The Reds were almost opposite at another house. In our piazza a table was set forth covered. On it stood a cake six stories high, round, each story smaller as it drew towards the top, powdered over with sugar, and on each side of it stood half a dozen of Madeira, glasses, &c. &c. At this table sat their Majesties attended, and the piazza was perfectly full of people of all descriptions. Mr and Mrs ———, and some company which we had that day at dinner, came all down to pay their respects. They drank a glass of wine with the sovereigns, and marched up stairs again. The rest at this time had formed a circle at the door, and there they dance, surrounded by the candle holders and an immense mob. At ten the procession moves off in order; the King and Queen are escorted to their abode; he bows, and she curtsies to their subjects; the subjects bow in return. Three loud cheers are given; the drums beat, and the colours wave. Their majesties retire. The candles are put out, and I conclude my letter.

Notes

1. "Account of the Christmas Racket among the Negroes in Jamaica", *Scots Magazine and Edinburgh Literary Miscellany*, n.s. 81 (March 1818): 213–15.
2. *racket*: social gathering.
3. From the description of an Israelite maiden in a biblical epic by the American poet Timothy Dwight, *The Conquest of Canaan* (1785), book 4, line 135: "Fair as the star of the morn, a lovely maid".
4. *spencer*: jacket.
5. *Persian*: a thin, soft silk material.

JOHN AUGUSTINE WALLER (FL. 1807–22)

A Voyage in the West Indies (1820)[1]

The author was stationed in the West Indies as a naval surgeon in 1807–10. He lived mainly in Barbados but visited several of the Leeward Islands and spent some months in charge of military hospitals on the French island of Marie Galante after its capture by the British. Generalizing boldly but unreliably on limited experience, he found "the state of society and manners" in the French colonies superior to the English. Working and living conditions for slaves, he found, were "much upon a par" in the two colonies, but the French were again superior in providing education for the slaves.[2] His description of English conditions divides the enslaved into "field slaves" and "house slaves", beginning with the former.

In the English islands, their education is neglected: the natives do not even take the pains to instruct them in the principles of the Christian religion, or take any care to have their children baptized. Indeed, in general, they set their faces against all the attempts to instruct them which have been made by the Methodists and Moravians, particularly in the island of Barbadoes. In the French islands, the case is very different. The slaves are very carefully instructed in the principles of religion; and I have been much gratified by observing their serious and decent behaviour at church. There, at least, they seem to feel themselves men, the offspring of one common Father, and entitled to the same blessings as their masters. They have a constant custom here,[3] which no Christian can look upon with indifference. Every night, when the negroes have finished their task, they return home together, each with a bundle of grass or guinea-corn on his head, for the supply of their cattle; they then proceed to some open space on the estate, where, forming a large circle, each one throws down his load, and sits down upon it. Then the best instructed negro on the estate (and they never want persons capable of the office), stands up in the middle, as their officiating minister; when, in a double choir, they begin to sing their evening-hymn, the man in the centre, with one or two others, beginning the first stanza, which is repeated in chorus by all the rest, male and female: thus it is continued to the end of the hymn. The effect is very sweet on a still night, the echo of the strain reverberating from the neighbouring ravines. After the hymn, two or three short sentences, with responses, are recited; and the man in the centre concludes the devotion by a short prayer, the rest all kneeling. The same kind of religious exercise takes place in the morning before they go to work.

The circumstance of being Christians, and instructed in the sublime principles of that religion, conduces much to the comfort of these people. It teaches them that they are men, and equally under the protection of the common Father of mankind with their masters. It imparts to them a hope of a blessed immortality; and, if they suffer oppression here, they have the assurance of being heard at last before an equitable tribunal, where every man will be rewarded according to his works. The English planters allow their slaves to continue Pagans from generation to generation, and even seem to dread the introduction of moral and Christian instruction. There are, no doubt, exceptions to this rule; but it is, in fact, the predominant principle. The French slaves, therefore, are in some respects incomparably in a better condition than the English, as they are regarded and treated like brethren and Christians.

The next class of slaves comprises artizans, or domestic servants, whom they call house slaves. The first of these are such as have learned some trade, as carpenters, coopers, taylors, &c. They are very valuable to their owners, not only for the work they do in the family, but for the great profit which their labour brings in, and the hire which they fetch when let out to work. A slave of this description frequently sells for five hundred pounds. It often happens that the stock of some small estate is disposed of by auction, and every week the Barbados Gazette teems with advertisements such as the following:

'To be sold by public vendue,[4] at ———, on ——— next, the whole of the live stock, late the property of ———, consisting of four mules, two asses, a cow, a washerwoman, and an excellent cooper.'

This association of articles appears the more strange, as the slaves are universally the last of the catalogue. I recollect one instance in this style: 'Two mules, three goats, a sow with eight pigs, and a fine healthy young woman with four children.' The slaves, like other articles at an auction, are mounted on a table for inspection, and their limbs and body undergo a close examination by the purchasers, to see that they labour under no disease.

The other class of house slaves do the duties of domestic servants; and, as a number of them are retained in every respectable house, they have little to do, and live well. They are lazy enough, and their morals in general are very loose. An English servant-girl in London would for the most part do the work of fourteen female slaves. They are well treated, I may say, upon the whole, though they often suffer, and that not a little, from the caprice of their masters and mistresses. From their debauched habits, the females are continually producing an offspring from white men, and this causes the coloured race (Mulattos, Mustees, &c.) to increase in a degree which may be thought dangerous to the safety of the colonies. These persons are generally well-informed, being brought up from their infancy among the whites; and, as they acquire all the habits and vices of the Europeans, they look down with contempt upon their ignorant and uncivilized brethren. The young Mulatto and Mustee females frequently procure their freedom and that of their offspring, as the reward of their prostitution and fidelity. At Barbadoes, however, this cannot be done under a very considerable sum of money. Three hundred pounds currency is the lowest price at which a young female slave can obtain her manumission. Each of her children must be freed separately, at a very exorbitant price, whence it frequently happens that the children of a free woman are her slaves. I was greatly astonished at this circumstance, having never heard of it till some time after my arrival at

Barbadoes. I one day received a visit from a very respectable looking woman, who waited upon me at my apartments in the hospital, and, after some preamble, laid open the motive of her visit. I should not, on my first arrival, have taken her for a woman of colour; but I was now sufficiently accustomed to the features of these people, to perceive that she was a Mustee.[5] She informed me that she had always lived very respectably as the *chère amie* of an officer of rank, who had been long dead; he had purchased her, and died of the fever, leaving her a female child; that, before his death, he had made her free, but that her daughter was not included in the manumission, and was her slave, left to her by will; that she had bestowed some expense and great pains on her education; that her daughter was virtuous, had refused some good offers because she did not feel a mutual passion, and that she (the mother) could not think of forcing her inclination. I was at a nonplus to divine what this story would lead to; but the good woman at length put me out of suspense, by informing me that I had seen and several times spoken to her daughter, and she thought, as I was not yet provided with what is here considered an essential part of the establishment of every unmarried man, that I ought not to let slip the opportunity of possessing a girl who was greatly attached to me, and whose person was very superior to the generality of women of colour. The terms on which she proposed to part with her daughter were the following: That I should purchase her from her mother at 120*l.* currency, which, she said, was twenty pounds less than what she would fetch, if sold at a public vendue; and that I should engage to give her her freedom before I quitted the colony. She observed also, as a greater inducement, that there would be no need to purchase the freedom of her children, as she was herself of the last degree of colour that could be enslaved, and that her children would necessarily be free, and entitled to all the privileges of white people. Surprised as I was at this strange proposal, I was still more so, on ascertaining who the girl was; for I had indeed frequently spoken to her, and noticed her, but never suspected her to be a person of colour, much less a slave, for she was of as fair a complexion as any European, with beautiful brown long hair, and possessed all the manner and accomplishments of a young lady.

It is amongst this class that the yoke of slavery is most severely felt; for, as I observed before, they are more intelligent in proportion to their intercourse with the whites, and are, from nature, tinctured with a great degree of curiosity. They are well apprised of the situation of affairs in St. Domingo, and there is some reason to think, that, in the British colonies, these people will effect one day a revolution which will astonish Europe. I particularize the British colonies, as the slaves are no where, perhaps, so harshly treated as by the English and Dutch. I know not how the French slaves were treated prior to the Revolution; but, at the present moment, their situation is unquestionably very far superior to that of the English. They are not degraded to an inferior order of beings, nor kept at such a mortifying distance as in the British and Dutch colonies.

Notes

1. John Augustine Waller, *A Voyage in the West Indies* (London: Sir R. Phillips and Co., 1820), 89–95.
2. Ibid., 88–91.
3. *here*: on Marie Galante.
4. *vendue*: sale by auction.
5. *mustee*: offspring of a white and a mulatto (mixed black and white) parent.

C.S.

"Negro Slavery" (ca. 1821)

The following poem was published in Manchester as a single sheet, perhaps intended for distribution in support of the emancipation cause. It is signed "C.S. *Rio, Demerara*."

Negro Slavery
Lines written on witnessing the separation of an African
negro and his wife, having been sold to different masters.

I saw the two parted
That ne'er had been parted before –
They spoke not, but quite broken-hearted,
Grasp'd the hand they would never grasp more; –
As the calm the dread torrent concealing,
Subdued was each token of feeling
Save a tear, – but they dash'd it away;
'Twas a moment of torturing sadness,
Too strong for the bosom to bear:
It burst, – and the loud cry of madness,
Was heard through the tremulous air.
As they rush'd from the arms of each other,
I met the poor African's eye:
The remembrance no time can e'er smother,
It reproach'd me that mine was so dry.

THOMAS COOPER (1791/2–1880)

Facts illustrative of the condition of the Negro slaves in Jamaica
(1824)[1]

Cooper, a Unitarian missionary, lived on Georgia estate in Hanover parish from 1817 to 1821. The main part of this tract was printed by Zachary Macaulay in his compilation of abolitionist writings, *Negro Slavery*, published in London in 1823. In publishing it separately in 1824 (the text used here), Cooper made a few small changes but retained the third-person narrative form. An important purpose of his self-styled "tract" was to show that, in spite of legislation in 1816 designed to improve the treatment of slaves in the West Indies, conditions had not materially improved. Cooper was violently attacked over his report in the Jamaican press by a group of local planters.

General Treatment

The gangs always work before the whip, which is a very weighty and powerful instrument. The driver has it always in his hand, and drives the Negroes, men and women, without distinction, as he would drive horses or cattle in a team. Mr. Cooper does not say that he is always using the whip, but it is known to be always present, and ready to be applied to the back or shoulders of any who flag at their work, or lag behind the line. The driver, who is generally a Black man, has the power not only of thus stimulating the slaves under him to exertion, by the application of the whip to their bodies while they are proceeding with their work; but, when he considers any of them to have committed a fault deserving of a more serious notice, he has the power also of prostrating them (*women* as well as men) on the ground, causing them to be held firmly down, by other Negroes,[2] who grasp the hands and legs of their prostrate companion, when he may inflict upon the bare posteriors such a number of lashes as he may deem the fault to have merited; the whole number which he may inflict at one time, without the presence of the overseer, being, by the Slave Act of 1816,[3] limited to ten. One of the faults which the driver most frequently punishes in this way, is that of coming late to the field either in the morning or after dinner. Those who arrive after the fixed time are pretty sure to get a few, perhaps five or six lashes. Mr. and Mrs. Cooper, before whose window the scene took place, on one occasion, saw three or four old women come too late; they knew they were to be whipped, and as soon as they came up, threw themselves down on the ground to receive the lashes: some of them received four, others six lashes. These minor punishments, Mr. Cooper says, are very frequent. He believes that seldom a day passes without some occurring; and he has heard of as many as sixty Negroes being flogged in one morning, for being late.

More serious punishments are only inflicted by the authority of the overseer; and the mode of their infliction is usually the same as has been already described. Whether the offender be male or female, precisely the same course is pursued. The posteriors are made bare,[4] and the offender is extended prone on the ground, when the driver, with his long and heavy whip, inflicts, under the eye of the overseer, the number of lashes which he may order; each lash, when the skin is tender and not rendered callous by repeated punishments, making an incision on the buttocks, and thirty or forty such lashes leaving them in a lacerated and bleeding state. Even those that have become the most callous, cannot long resist the force of this terrible instrument, when applied by a skilful hand, but become also raw and bloody; indeed, no strength of skin can withstand its reiterated application.

These punishments are inflicted by the overseer, WHENEVER HE THINKS THEM TO HAVE BEEN DESERVED. He has no written rules to guide his conduct, nor are the occasions at all defined on which he may exercise the power of punishment. *Its exercise is regulated wholly and solely by his own discretion.* An act of neglect or of disobedience, or even a look or a word supposed to imply insolence, no less than desertion or theft or contumacy, may be thus punished; and they may be and in a thousand instances are, without trial, at the *mere pleasure and fiat of the overseer.* Doubtless, any slave may, *after having been punished,* complain of his overseer to the attorney of the estate, or to a magistrate; but such complaint often does him more harm than good.[5]

The law professes to limit the number of lashes which shall be given at one time, to thirty-nine; but neither this law, nor any other which professes to protect the slave, can be of much practical benefit to him: it cannot, under existing circumstances, be enforced. A Negro, especially one who is the slave of an absentee proprietor, may be considered as entirely in the power of the overseer, who is his absolute master, and may be at the same instant his lawgiver, accuser, and judge; and may not only award sentence, but order its execution. And supposing him to act unjustly, or even cruelly, he has it in his power to prevent any redress from the law. The evidence of a thousand slaves would avail nothing to his conviction; and, even if there were any disposition in the inferior Whites to inform, or to bear testimony against him, he has only to take care that the infliction does not take place in their presence . . . .

The law permits the Negroes to make their complaints to magistrates. In one case several Negroes went to complain to a magistrate of their want of houses, or proper accommodation. Mr. Cooper saw them, on that occasion, at the magistrate's door. The magistrate, however, told him it would never do to interfere in such matters, for, if they did, there would be no getting on between masters or overseers, and magistrates; and, with respect to these complainants, what he did was to desire them to return home and trust to their master's kindness: and Mr. Cooper thought that, all things considered, he could not well have done otherwise.[6]

Two women who were pregnant, desired to quit the field during rain, on account of their pregnancy. The overseer refused them permission. They went to complain of this refusal to a magistrate, but were stopped in their way by a neighbouring overseer, and by him thrown into the stocks until he sent them back to their own overseer, who put them again into the stocks on their own estate, and had them flogged. Of this proceeding they complained to the attorney. The attorney was of opinion that the overseer had acted with undue severity; but he considered the women to have been highly to blame for attempting to complain to the magistrate; whereas, he said, they ought in the first instance to have complained to him.

It is common for Negroes, who have been guilty of what is deemed a serious offence, to be worked all day in the field, and during the intervals of labour, as well as during the whole night, to be confined, with their feet fast in the stocks. In the case of one Negro, who was so confined for some weeks, Mrs. Cooper begged hard to obtain a remission of his punishment, but did not succeed. Another Negro, belonging to the estate, was a notorious runaway. Being taken, he was flogged in the usual manner, as severely as he well could bear, and then made to work in the field. During the interval of dinner-time he was regularly placed in the stocks, and in them also he was confined the whole night. When the lacerations, produced by the flogging he had received, were sufficiently healed, he was flogged a second time. While the sores were still unhealed, one of the book-keepers told Mr. Cooper that maggots had bred in the lacerated flesh. . . .

An old African Negro, well known to Mr. Cooper, who appeared to possess a sound and superior mind, and was reckoned the best watchman on the estate, was placed to watch the provision-grounds for the use of the overseer's house. These were robbed, and the robbery being imputed to his neglect, he received a very severe flogging. The old man declared (Mr. Cooper does not vouch for the truth of the excuse) that he could not help what had happened, the grounds being too extensive for him to guard them effectually, so that while he was on one side of them, the Negroes could easily steal on the other. This flogging made a great alteration in the old man, and he never seemed well after it. In two or three weeks another robbery occurring, he received a still more severe flogging than before. One morning, while Mr. and Mrs. Cooper were at breakfast, they heard a groaning, and going to the window, saw this poor man passing along in a state which made Mrs. Cooper shrink back with horror. Mrs. Cooper went out to him, and found his posteriors, which were completely exposed, much lacerated, and bleeding dreadfully. He seemed much exhausted. He attempted to explain the case, but was incapable from fatigue and suffering. A Negro boy was standing by; the old man pointed to him, and said, 'Massa, him tell you'. The poor old man from this time was never well or cheerful, and he soon afterwards died.

Notes

1. Thomas Cooper, *Facts illustrative of the condition of the Negro slaves in Jamaica* (London: J. Hatchard and Son, 1824), 16–23.
2. [Author's note:] It is said that, in Demerara and some other places, the offender is not always held down by his or her fellow-slaves, but is, in some instances, tied down to four stakes.
3. The Consolidated Slave Law, 1816.
4. [Author's note:] It is well known that the Negroes will make a song out of any thing. On one occasion, I listened to a party of old women, boys, and girls, singing the following in our kitchen: *O massa! O massa! on Monday morning they lay me down, And give me thirty-nine on my bare rump. O massa! O massa!*
5. [Author's note:] It makes the overseer jealous of him: sometimes even to inflict an additional punishment. Hence many slaves get weary of complaining to any one.
6. [Author's note:] On another occasion, I saw a gang of fifteen to twenty Negroes, who belonged to a small settler in Hanover, come from a magistrate, to whom they had been to complain, that the cloth which they had just received from their master was rotten, and not fit to give to them, or such as the law allowed. They had the cloth with them, and the magistrate confessed that their complaint was just, but he could not interfere in so invidious a matter.

ROBERT WEDDERBURN (1762–1835/6)

The Horrors of Slavery (1824)[1]

Wedderburn, son of an African-born slave by a white Scottish planter, was freed at birth and given an elementary education. He served as a boy in the British Navy and went to England in 1778. Licensed as a dissenting preacher, he was a vigorous participant in working-class radicalism and was imprisoned for his activities. In 1817 he published a periodical, *The Axe Laid to the Root*, subtitled *An Address to the Planters and Negroes of the Island of Jamaica*, which is notable for "its sustained attempt to integrate the prospect of slave revolution in the West Indies with that of working-class revolution in England".[2] While in prison in 1822 he was visited by Wilberforce, to whom he dedicated *The Horrors of Slavery*.

From Life of the Rev. Robert Wedderburn

I was born in the island of Jamaica, about the year 1762, on the estate of a Lady Douglas, a distant relation of the Duke of Queensbury. My mother was a woman of colour, by name ROSANNA, and at the time of my birth a slave to the above Lady Douglas. My father's name was JAMES WEDDER-BURN, Esq. of Inveresk, in Scotland, an extensive proprietor, of sugar estates in Jamaica . . .

I must explain at the outset of this history – what will appear unnatural to some – the reason of my abhorrence and indignation at the conduct of my father. From him I have received no benefit in the world. By him my mother was made the object of his cruel lust, then insulted, abused, and abandoned . . .

My grandfather was a staunch Jacobite, and exerted himself strenuously in the cause of the Pretender, in the rebellion of the year 1745. For his aiding to restore the exiled family to the throne of England, he was tried, condemned, and executed. . . . For this act of high treason, our family estates were confiscated to the King, and my dear father found himself destitute in the world, or with no resource but his own industry. He adopted the medical profession; and in Jamaica he was Doctor and Man-Midwife, and turned an honest penny by drugging and physicing the poor blacks, where those that were cured, he had the credit for, and for those he killed, the fault was laid to their own obstinacy. In the course of time, by dint of *booing* and *booing*,[3] my father was restored to his father's property, and he became the proprietor of one of the most extensive sugar estates in Jamaica. While my dear father was poor, he was chaste as any Scotchman, whose poverty made him virtuous; but the moment he became rich, he gave loose to his carnal appetites, and indulged himself without moderation, but as parsimonious as ever. My father's mental powers were none of the brightest, which may account for his libidinous excess. It is a common practice, as has been stated by Mr. Wilberforce in parliament, for the planters to have lewd intercourse with their female slaves; and so inhuman are many of these said planters, that many well-authenticated instances are known, of their selling their slaves while pregnant, and making that a pretence to enhance their value. A father selling his offspring is no disgrace there. A father selling his prettiest female slaves for purposes of lust, is by no means uncommon. My father ranged through the whole of his household for his own lewd purposes; for they being his personal property, cost nothing extra; and if any one proved with child – why, it was an acquisition which might one day fetch something in the market, like a horse or pig in Smithfield. In short, amongst his own slaves my father was a perfect parish bull; and his pleasure was the greater, because he at the same time increased his profits.

I now come to speak of the infamous manner with which JAMES
WEDDERBURN . . . entrapped my poor mother in his power. My mother
was a lady's maid, and had received an education which perfectly qualified
her to conduct a household in the most agreeable manner. She was the
property of Lady Douglas, whom I have before mentioned; and prior to the
time she met my father, was chaste and virtuous. After my father had got his
estate, he did not renounce the pestle and mortar, but, in the capacity of
Doctor, he visited Lady Douglas. He there met my mother for the first time,
and was determined to have possession of her. His character was known;
and therefore he was obliged to go *covertly* and *falsely* to work. In Jamaica,
slaves that are esteemed by their owners have generally the power of
refusal, whether they will be sold to a particular planter, or not; and my
father was aware, that if *he* offered to purchase her, he would meet with a
refusal. But his brutal lust was not to be stopped by trifles; my father's conscience would stretch to any extent; and he was a firm believer in the doctrine of 'grace abounding to the chief of sinners.' For this purpose, he
employed a fellow of the name of Cruikshank, a brother doctor and
Scotchman, to strike a bargain with Lady Douglas for my mother; and this
scoundrel of a Scotchman bought my mother for the use of my father, in
the name of another planter, a most respectable and highly esteemed man. I
have often heard my mother express her indignation at this base and treacherous conduct of my father – a treachery the more base, as it was so calm
and premeditated. . . .

From the time my mother became the property of my father, she
assumed the direction and management of his house; for which no woman
was better qualified. But her station there was very disgusting. My father's
house was full of female slaves, all objects of his lusts; amongst whom he
strutted like Solomon in his grand seraglio, or like a bantam cock upon his
own dunghill. My good father's slaves did increase and multiply, like Jacob's
kine; and he cultivated those talents well which God had granted so amply.
My poor mother, from being the housekeeper, was the object of their envy,
which was increased by her superiority of education over the common herd
of female slaves. While in this situation, she bore my father two children,
one of whom, my brother James, a millwright, I believe, is now living in
Jamaica, upon the estate. Soon after this, my father introduced a new concu-

bine into his seraglio, one ESTHER TROTTER, a free tawny, whom he placed over my mother, and to whom he gave the direction of his affairs. My brother COLVILLE[4] asserts, that my mother was of a violent and rebellious temper. I will leave the reader now to judge for himself, whether she had not some reason for her conduct. Hath not a slave feelings? If you starve them, will they not die? If you wrong them, will they not revenge? Insulted on one hand, and degraded on the other, was it likely that my poor mother could practise the Christian virtue of humility, when her Christian master provoked her to wrath? She shortly after became again pregnant; and I have not the least doubt but that from her rebellious and violent temper during that period, that I have inherited the same disposition – the same desire to see justice overtake the oppressors of my countrymen – and the same determination to lose no stone unturned, to accomplish so desirable an object. My mother's state was so unpleasant, that my father at last consented to sell her back to Lady Douglas; but not till the animosity in my father's house had grown to such an extent, that my uncle, Sir JOHN WEDDERBURN,[5] my father's elder brother, had given my mother an asylum in his house, against the brutal treatment of my father. At the time of sale, my mother was five months gone in pregnancy; and one of the stipulations of the bargain was, that the child which she then bore should be FREE from the moment of its birth. I was that child. When about four months old, the ill-treatment my mother had experienced had such an effect upon her, that I was obliged to be weaned to save her life. Lady Douglas, at my admission into the Christian church, stood my godmother, and as long as she lived, never deserted me. She died when I was about four years old.

From my mother I was delivered over to the care of my grandmother, who lived at Kingston, and who earned her livelihood by retailing all sorts of goods, hard or soft, smuggled or not, for the merchants of Kingston. My grandmother was the property of one JOSEPH PAYNE, at the east end of Kingston; and her place was to sell his property – cheese, checks, chintz, milk, gingerbread, etc; in doing which, she trafficked on her own account with the goods of other merchants, having an agency of half-a-crown in the pound allowed her for her trouble. No woman was perhaps better known in Kingston than my grandmother, by the name of 'Talkee Amy,' signifying a chattering old woman. Though a slave, such was the confidence the merchants of Kingston had in her honesty, that she could be trusted to any amount; in fact she was the regular agent for selling smuggled goods.

I never saw my dear father but once in the island of Jamaica, when I went with my grandmother to know if he meant to do anything for me, his son. Giving her some abusive language, my grandmother called him a mean Scotch rascal, thus to desert his own flesh and blood; and declared, that as she had kept me hitherto, so she would yet, without his paltry assistance. This was the parental treatment I experienced from a Scotch West-India planter and slave-dealer.

When I was about eleven years of age, my poor old grandmother was flogged for a witch by her master, the occasion of which I must relate in this place. Joseph Payne, her master, was an old and avaricious merchant, who was concerned in the smuggling trade. He had a vessel manned by his own slaves, and commanded by a Welchman of the name of Lloyd, which had made several profitable voyages to Honduras for mahogany, which was brought to Jamaica, and from thence forwarded to England. The old miser had some notion, that Lloyd cheated him in the adventure, and therefore resolved to go himself as a check upon him. Through what means I know not, but most likely from information given by Lloyd out of revenge and jealousy, the Spaniards surprised and captured the vessel; and poor old Payne, at seventy years of age, was condemned to carry stones at Fort Homea, in the Bay of Honduras, for a year and a day; and his vessel and his slaves were confiscated to the Spaniards. On his way home he died, and was tossed overboard to make food for fishes. His nephew succeeded to his property; and a malicious woman-slave, to curry favour with him, persuaded him, that the ill-success of old Payne's adventures was owing to my grandmother's having bewitched the vessel. The old miser had liberated five of his slaves before he set out on his unlucky expedition; and my grandmother's new master being a believer in the doctrine of Witchcraft, conceived that my grandmother had bewitched the vessel, out of revenge for not being liberated also. To punish her, therefore, he tied up the poor old woman of seventy years and flogged her to that degree, that she would have died, but for the interference of a neighbour. Now, what aggravated the affair was, that my grandmother had brought up this young villain from eight years of age, and, till now, he had treated her as a mother. But my grandmother had full satisfaction soon afterwards. The words of our blessed Lord and Saviour Jesus Christ were fulfilled in this instance: 'Do good to them that despitefully use you, and in so doing you shall heap coals of fire upon their heads.' This woman [the slave who betrayed her] had an only child, which died soon after this affair took place (plainly a judgment of God); and the mother was forced to come and beg pardon of my grandmother for the injury she had done her, and solicit my grandmother to assist her in the burial of her child. My grandmother replied, 'I can forgive you, but I can never forget the flogging;' and the good old woman instantly set about assisting her in her child's funeral, it being as great an object to have a decent burial with the blacks in Jamaica, as with the lower classes in Ireland. This same woman, who had so wickedly calumniated my grandmother, afterwards made public confession of her guilt in the market-place at Kingston, on purpose to ease her guilty conscience, and to make atonement for the injury she had done . . . .

[After the death of Lady Douglas, Rosanna was promised her freedom by her new master. But he reneged on his promise and sold her to a doctor whose wife ill-treated her to such an extent that "she resolved to starve herself to death". The doctor, alarmed at the thought of losing the £110 he had paid for her, resold her to another doctor, who proved equally savage.]

I have seen my poor mother stretched on the ground, tied hands and feet, and FLOGGED in the most indecent manner, though PREGNANT AT THE SAME TIME!!! her *fault* being the not acquainting her mistress that her master had *given her leave to go to see her mother in town*! So great was the anger of this Christian Slave-Dealer, that he went fifteen miles to punish her while on the visit! Her master was then one BOSWELL; his chief companion was CAPTAIN PARR, who *chained a female Slave to a stake, and starved her to death*! Had it not been for a British Officer in the Army, who had her dug up and proved it, this fact would not have been known. *The murderer was sentenced to transport himself for one year.* He came to England, and returned in time – this was *his punishment*.

Notes

1. Robert Wedderburn, *The Horrors of Slavery; exemplified in the Life and History of the Rev. Robert Wedderburn* (London: n.p., 1824). Reprinted in Iain McCalman, ed., *The Horrors of Slavery and Other Writings by Robert Wedderburn* (Edinburgh: Edinburgh University Press, 1991), 45–51, the text used here, by kind permission of the editor.

2. McCalman, *Horrors*, 18.

3. [McCalman's note:] *booing and booing*: making a fuss; a great deal of noise, probably derived from Cobbett.

4. Andrew Colville, or Colvile, was a legitimate son of James Wedderburn; he changed his name in 1814 in order to gain an inheritance through his mother's line. He angrily disputed Robert's claim to be James Wedderburn's son.

5. Sir John Wedderburn was master of a black slave, Joseph Knight, whom he brought back from Jamaica. Knight became famous as the subject of a landmark court case in 1774 which established the illegality of slavery in Scotland.

"THE AFRICAN AND CREOLE SLAVE CONTRASTED" (1825)[1]

This poem from the *Trinidad Gazette* was reprinted in L.M. Fraser's *History of Trinidad* (1896), "not for its merits as a piece of poetry" but to show "one of the many curious arguments" put forward for retaining slavery.

The son of Afric's savage coast regard,
His tatoo'd body, his high cheeks deep scar'd,
His lengthy jaw, his bilious eye of lead,
His acts of awkwardness, his heavy tread;
His gait ungraceful, melancholy air,   5
His grotesque gesture, and incessant stare;
His tongue unwieldy; halting voice, whose sound
Mocks ev'ry language, does each word confound.
Next view, when dancing, his distorted mien,
View (if thy nerves admit it void of pain,)   10
His features, body, muscles, limbs, that try
With vile contortion to distress the eye;
Mark, how when o'er him passion holds her sway,
His lineaments the Cannibal betray.
    Whether he be of Moco's savage race,   15
Or Eboe's saddened looks o'ercloud his face,
Or sulky Beby, or Arada wild,

Or Coromantin's sanguinary child,
Or less fierce Whidah, or Angola tall,
The traits enumerated suit them all.[2]   20
    His Creole offspring to inspect begin,
His form of symmetry and glossy skin,
A form, whose mould full oft might not disgrace,
Thy master hand, Canova great, to trace.
Not his bold laugh, rapidity of talk,   25
His unembarrass'd, even graceful walk –
Oft I regret this stooping gait of mine,
And envy, Creole! the firm step of thine.
His features mark – o'er which incessant play,
The laugh of carelessness, or smiles e'er gay: 30
What tho' those jolly lineaments declare,
There is no depth of thought or wisdom there.
That education ne'er refined each sense,
A happier gift is his – contented ignorance.
    What tho' proud learning ne'er illumed his mind,   35
Yet, to him, Nature has been far more kind,
For she with cunning hath his judgment lit,
And given him humour and a ready wit.
    What tho' light *Vestris* ne'er bestow'd his care
T'instruct his feet to quiver in the air,   40
Yet when arise the Drum and Shack-shack's notes,
And when the chorus singers strain their throats,
Then mixing grace, agility and ease,
His steps e'en European taste might please.
    Contrast the form of Guinea's offspring wild,   45
With his less fierce, more happy, Creole child,
And then pronounce (but void of falsehood's wiles)
If the debasing bondage of these isles,
Or savage freedom of his native coast,
(If freedom e'er was his) degrade man most.   50
Black as the stigma is, that brands the fame,
And weds th'oppressor's with the Planter's name –

E'en at whose sounds, Hypocrisy her eyes
Upturns with pious horror to the skies,
Yet Planters rear a race which will aspire   55
With pity and contempt to view it's Afric sire.

Notes

1. "The African and Creole Slave Contrasted", *Trinidad Gazette* (June 1825). Reprinted in L.M. Fraser, *History of Trinidad* (Port of Spain: Government Printing Office, 1896), 2:194.
2. These were standard West Indian labels for the various "nations" of enslaved Africans; see Grainger, *Sugar-Cane*, pages 51–52 above. Not mentioned by Grainger are the Beby (unidentified) and Arada (from Dahomey).

Sketches and Recollections of the West Indies (1828)[1]

The preface indicates that the author was a public official in Dominica from about 1795 to 1805. His design in writing was to influence opinion on "the great question of slave emancipation" by giving a just and accurate picture of life in the West Indies based on "long personal observation and experience", and to warn of "the probable effects of imparting, at too early a period, the boon of freedom to a yet uncivilized race." In spite of its partisan character the text is useful as a relatively rare description of plantation life in pre-emancipation Dominica.

Visits to the Country and Tour around Dominica

After the termination of the hurricane months, I accompanied one of my young friends, on a tour of inspection, to the different plantations under his charge, in the absence of his uncle, lately sailed for England . . . .

Proceeding to the field [at one estate], we found the slaves in great glee, singing and encouraging each other. The overseer and manager reported favourably of the greater part; and some few, who had transgressed, were forgiven, on promise of better behaviour. A dram was given to each of the men, and some little presents to the women; and meat for Sunday's dinner was ordered to be distributed amongst the gang, which consisted of 160, all healthy and happy. Many were anxious inquirers about 'old Massa,' and whether he had arrived 'in a England,' and 'when he come back.' – 'Young Massa good too – he come and see awee [us] again, when crop time come: – we make plenty sugar, Massa.'

We walked or rode over the greater part of the estate. The cane pieces shewed luxuriant growth, and were nearly fit to cut down; but crop time seldom comes before Christmas. The provision-grounds, grass plots, cattle, mules, &c. all appeared in good condition.

The hospital contained only three or four inmates; one, an old man of eighty, who had been a driver on the estate, for many years, on the occasions of the attorney visiting the estate, long after he had been excused from work, on account of his age and feebleness; but he was now confined to bed. – The Africans are extremely attentive to, and careful of, their old people: to be *old*, secures the kind offices and care of their friends, and of all who know them; and negroes vie with each other, in displaying their kindness to their father or mother, *aunty* or *sissy*, for by all these affectionate appellations do they designate them, though not at all related. – This old man (Harry) was unable to be out, but his first inquiry of us was – 'How old Massa? – I neber see him again – me go dead soon now – God bless Massa – he always good to Harry, and to dem people here – we know Massa long time – he one good man, old Massa.' . . .

We were now called on *to hold a Matrimonial Court*, and to hear appeals from an ill-used wife, or a jealous husband. – The negroes are mostly married – some regularly by the clergyman, or justice of the peace, but the greater part only tacitly, and during the agreement of the parties. . . .

The first case was that of Fidele, a stout negro wench, with three pickininnies, i.e. children, at her feet, who accused her husband of having deserted her, for another wife on a neighbouring plantation, to whom he carried away all the poultry and provisions, and on whom he bestowed not only his company, but also the finery which Fidele thought herself entitled to.

The refractory husband admitted, that he now preferred Adelaide to Fidele, who had teazed him with her jealous fits, and *too much talk*, and driven him, he said, from his own house, and made manager no love him any more, and threaten to flog him. We found, however, that the lady was careful of her children, and willing to receive her deserter back again; and as he was made sensible of the risk he ran of losing his other fair, from whom he was much away, and of incurring the manager's and attorney's displeasure, he promised to take leave of Adelaide, and henceforth live at home.

An old fellow of sixty, having lately entered into the connubial state with a young girl, who might have been his *grand-daughter*, complained, that *too much sweetheart came after Sally*, and that she no longer love *him own husband*. Sally's story was equally ready, and given with much candour and *naïveté*. She said, the old man had prevailed on her to *hab him*, and promised her plenty of fine dress – but that she really no love him – then, young negroes come tell her he go die soon, and want her take them, and *neber* mind old man. She no do so – but this make old man jealous, and he want beat Sally, his poor wife, *for noting*. – We dismissed this case, with admonishing Sally to be kind to her husband; to allow of no followers, during his lifetime, and to choose a more *suitable* helpmate next; to which the distressed wife replied – *me neber hab old husband again – he no good for young girl – him jealous too much.*

A third case still awaited our decision, which was one of some difficulty *to the bench*. A young girl, of the Congo nation, who had been but lately imported, and could hardly make herself understood, appeared in tears, and in great distress. Having called one of her countrymen to act as interpreter, she proceeded to tell us, that having been taken as the wife of a negro, belonging to the manager, then living on the estate, but since, gone to work in Roseau, she had completely *lost sight of him*, and now applied to Massa, to restore her husband. This poor girl was, evidently, much attached to her husband, who was a truant only from necessity, as the distance precluded his often coming to see her. It was therefore settled, that the manager should recall him, and that he should be hired to work on the estate, or sold to it, if the proprietor agreed to purchase him.

[Plantation Life and Society]

Besides exercising the militia on Sundays, I found that it was the custom of the West Indies to hold weekly markets on that day, when the negroes from the different estates and plantations bring their pigs, poultry, fruits, and vegetables for sale. They are then all dressed in their gayest attire; they are allowed the day entirely to themselves; and only those who come from a considerable distance are required to have written or printed passports from their owners. Many of them are enabled to realize considerable sums of money, and to furnish their houses with every thing they require for comfort and convenience, as well as to appear in excellent clothes . . . .

In addition to the Sunday drills and markets, every new comer views with astonishment the negro dances, which are also held on the Sabbath, in the open air, generally on the river side, or wherever the public attention is most likely to be drawn. In the most frequented walks or rides about the town, all the slaves who can attend are sure to be found assembled . . . in their gayest attire; the sable beauties, in gowns white as snow, with turbans, (their universal and favourite head-dress,) composed of Bandana handkerchiefs; – whilst the men are perfect beaus – Sunday dandies even – in their way. No Bond-street exquisite can be at more pains in making his toilet than Jack, Tom, Dick, and Harry, before they proceed to this great scene of enjoyment on Sunday evening. When the novice is brought to witness it for the first time, and is asked if there are happier meetings in England; or if the working classes there are better dressed, or display livelier symptoms of happiness; he is obliged to allow, that in none of these respects are they superior to the slave population, keeping holiday before him. Their dances (John-John) and their music are alike simple. The former has more resemblance to what is called setting, or jigging, in the English country-dance, than to the waltz.[2] Only one couple dance at a time; and it is astonishing to see how many excellent dancers are ready to succeed each other on the turf. The whites, and people of colour, as well as the negroes, are uncommonly fond of dancing; the heat of the climate serves to operate as a stimulus to this healthful and amusing exercise. The music consists generally of a sort of drum, called a tom-tom; the gamboy; and a pipe, a reed of the Bamboo tree, on which they play very sweetly; with the addition, frequently, of castanets and a tambourin. Their dances commence at four or five o'clock on the Sunday evenings, and are concluded at sunset, between six and seven, as there is scarcely any twilight in the West Indies. The negroes then retire to their different abodes, contented, peaceable and happy. – It is not unusual to see, amongst the spectators, many of the first white people in the colony.[3] The English sailors, dressed in holiday attire, and frequently more than half-seas over, are generally of the party. On these occasions, Jack thinks it incumbent on him to step forward and select his sable or yellow partner; and the perfect good humour with which the negroes receive these very noisy and boisterous heroes of the ocean, and allow them to mix in their dances, never fails to conciliate Jack and his associates. Sometimes, however, the white gentlemen assembled to witness these happy holiday folks – such scenes being rather uncommon in Hyde Park or Kensington-gardens – are obliged to interfere to restore blackie his partner. Not unfrequently, the sailor may be seen striving with all his might to imitate the dancing of the negroes. He begins by saluting his partner; and after, perhaps in vain, doing his best to get into the proper step and motion, he is at last obliged to resort to his own mode, and to conclude by whisking his partner round in the waltz style, until his giddy head can no longer direct his heels, and he fairly falls, at full length, amidst the cheers of his messmates, and the surrounding spectators!

Notes

1. *Sketches and Recollections of the West Indies. By a Resident* (London: Smith, Elder, and Co., 1828).
2. [Author's note:] At the time to which these remarks chiefly apply, reels were the favourites; to these, have succeeded the country-dance, and even the quadrille; and, in some of the colonies, so *refined* has the taste of the slave-population become, that their amusements are varied by the introduction of *private theatricals.* – Think of a *black* Juliet!
3. *first white people*: Europeans of the highest rank.

Marly; or, A Planter's Life in Jamaica (1828)[1]

From the preface it appears that the author of this novel, like his hero, Marly, worked on a plantation as a "book-keeper", the junior position among whites on an estate, whose responsibility was to supervise the work of the slave gangs. The fictional plot, he explains, is top-dressing for a documentary work intended to "detail the actual occurrences on a sugar estate" and show "the real state of slavery", with the object of establishing a truthful position between extreme pro- and anti-slavery representations.[2] The following passage describes the response of an overseer (Mr Adams) to the demand of the estate manager (the attorney) to increase productivity without employing extra labour.

The overseer, accordingly, gave instructions to the drivers to perform a certain quantity of work each day, by means of which, he calculated that more work would be got through in a given space. This mode of tasking the people did well enough for a few days; but, as if fate was determined to thwart the overseer and the attorney, the first week had not elapsed, when no less than three of the strongest of the negresses, stated, that they were with pickeniny, and the doctor having corroborated their statement, they ceased working – a slave woman in that condition being freed from work, till a month or two after her accouchement. This was only a prelude to the impediments which contributed to obstruct the overseer's calculations: for, the wet season soon setting in, several of the negroes complained of sickness, and in consequence were sent to the hot-house.[3] Each of these circumstances had the tendency to weaken the gangs, already too weak for performing the work required of them; and in addition to these uncalculated incidents, the wet weather considerably retarded the forwarding of the work among the ratoons.[4] Besides too, the people became very much dissatisfied, at being put off their ordinary routine of working. They were of a race, and in that stage of society, in which men are strongly bigotted to what they have been accustomed to from their youth upwards. Innovations on their habitual manner of labour, was thought by them to be oppression; but Adams having imagined that the work could not otherwise be got through, than with this alteration, of tasking each gang to perform a given quantity in a day, he insisted, without any regard to the sentiments or discontent of the negroes, on its being done. Though, in comparison with their ordinary work, it was laborious, the negroes complained more of the circumstances of being tasked, than they did of the additional labour; saying, 'Dat it hab no be good for him neger, to see what massa hab for him to do. Him neger should work as him negers ebery day work. It bad for him neger to savey what him always hab to work.' In this manner they expressed their disapprobation – they did not complain of the quantity, but only of the mode, and that solely because it was at variance with their former habits, and in consequence they could not reconcile themselves to the change . . . .

The negroes, however unwilling, were obliged to perform their allotted task, which they did not accomplish without much grumbling at the Busha. The women were the organs, through whom the discontent of the gangs was expressed; because, entertaining less fear of a flogging than the men, they were more bold and open in their murmurings, and in shewing their dissatisfaction. Few of them, in comparison with their numbers, underwent punishment, though many times richly deserving it. This mode of working, continued for a week or thereby, without its being apparent that the people could perform the required labour; for, when the days happened to be very wet, or even when there was only a trifling shower, the negroes, if they did not run for shelter, stood bolt upright, with the intention of keeping themselves dry, and for the time work ceased; and it was useless to endeavour to drive them from a custom acknowledged by ages: for, they would not alter their position, do what you would, till the rain was over. One day, after the space allotted for dinner had elapsed, the overseer visited Marly and his gang, during a drizzling shower (a circumstance rather uncommon in Jamaica), when he observed the pickeniny mothers coming to the field. There might be six or eight of these mothers, who were allowed ten minutes additional to the other negroes, to come to the field in the morning, and in the afternoon. They generally, however, took a little more than the prescribed time; but on this afternoon, whether it was owing to the rain, or some other cause, which prevented them, they were considerably later, and the overseer, who had once before checked them for a similar fault, now seemed determined to make an example of them. He, therefore, without any preamble, being equally aware with Samuels [the previous overseer], that the negroes don't like speakee and floggee too, ordered them to be laid down one after the other, when each received the gentle admonition of nine lashes. At first, they were indignant at the idea of receiving punishment, saying, 'dat de Busha floggee them for him's pickeniny mummas getting pickeninies for massa,' meaning the proprietor. They were indeed very little hurt; but, being indignant against the overseer, for the pain which, as they conceived, he had made them unjustly suffer, they reviled him with every opprobrious epithet, which the talkee talkee slang dictionary would have contained, had it been written. The overseer, though abused with this most scurrilous language, lengthened out by the true Creole drawl, enough in all conscience to have provoked the patience of a Job, bore it for a short time apparently without concern; but his choler at last getting up, he hurried to his mule; the whole gang immediately on his back being turned, joining in the usual chorus on such occasions, of, – 'I don't care a damn, oh! – I don't care a damn, oh!'

Next morning, the overseer was with the gang as soon as Marly. He appeared as if determined to observe himself, that the negroes turned out pointedly to their time, in order that he might have the work of cleaning finished in the course of the week, preparatory to commencing the planting of new canes. Unfortunately, seven or eight of Marly's people were late, and these were chiefly old men and women. As they came in, the overseer ordered them to be laid down and punished. Each of them received a dozen of lashes. Marly could not help feeling pity for these unfortunate and truly miserable creatures, the most of whom, were, from their age, apparently tottering on the brink of eternity. They sang out repeatedly for mercy, but the overseer was relentless; notwithstanding their withered posteriors were staring him in the face, showing them to be objects of compassion more than of punishment. Finding that their most compassionate and importunate exclamations were unable to move his tenderness, and that the driver continued using his whip, several of them amidst the cries under the torture of the heavy lash, exclaimed, 'No man pities him poor old neger, but Massa above,' meaning God. What rendered it still more distressing to Marly, whom custom had not yet rendered callous to such sights, was the piteous aspects of the children of several of them, who were spectators of their mothers' and fathers' galling and degrading sufferings, without daring to complain. The last who was laid down, was the mother of the overseer's boy, one of the youngest of the whole. She also very naturally pleaded for mercy, and in this plea, she was aided by her son, who no doubt thought he was entitled to use more liberty with the Busha than the others, crying for forgiveness for his mumma. Finding that their conjoined importunities were ineffectual, he furiously sprung at the overseer, as if he would force him to comply; and before the latter was aware of his intention, his face was scratched till the blood followed. She, notwithstanding, received her dozen. But, although the Busha must have pretty keenly felt the smart of the scratches on his face, and was evidently enraged, it seemed, however, that even *he* felt indignant at the idea of ordering a boy of twelve or fourteen years of age to be punished, merely for shewing the strong and natural affection he bore to his mother . . . ; he, therefore, instantly mounted his mule and rode off, the boy holding on as usual by the tail, cheered with the customary song, of, – 'I don't care a damn, oh!' The overseer's anger had nearly evaporated, before he reached home, for his boy only received a cuff or two on the side of the head, and an admonition to behave better in future, under the pain of being placed in one of the gangs as a field negro.

Notes

1. *Marly; or, A Planter's Life in Jamaica* (Glasgow: Richard Griffin and Co., 1828), 153–57.
2. See Karina Williamson, ed., *Marly; or, A Planter's Life in Jamaica* (Oxford: Macmillan Education, 2005), xvii–xviii, 2–4.
3. *hot-house*: estate infirmary.
4. *ratoons*: sugar canes sprouting from the roots of the previous crop, which had to be pruned.

ASHTON WARNER (CA. 1807–31)

Negro Slavery Described by a Negro (1831)[1]

Warner's narrative was recorded by the writer Susanna Strickland (later known by her married name, Moodie). Her introduction explains that Warner "had recently made his escape from slavery in the West Indies", had been in England for three months, "endeavouring to establish his claims to freedom", and was living in poverty, "suffering under severe illness". In recording his story, Strickland says, she "adhered strictly to the simple facts, adopting wherever it could conveniently be done, his own language, which, for a person in his condition, is remarkably expressive and appropriate." She points out that, owing to the "peculiar circumstances" under which he was enslaved, he was exempt from "the cruel and degrading punishments which form a prominent and characteristic feature in the discipline of a West India sugar-plantation", but that his testimony was thereby the more valuable, since it was "neither dictated by revenge nor by an egotistical desire to recount his own sorrows". Warner died while his relatively short narrative was in press. It occupies less than fifty pages of the book; the following is an abridgement of the first part.

I was born in the Island of St. Vincent's, and baptized by the name of Ashton Warner, in the parish church, by the Rev. Mr. Gildon. My father and mother, at the time of my birth, were slaves on the Cane Grove estate, in Bucumar Valley, then the property of Mr. Ottley. I was an infant at the breast when Mr. Ottley died; and shortly after the estate was put to sale, that the property might be divided among his family. Before Cane Grove was sold, my aunt, Daphne Crosbie, took the opportunity of buying my mother and me of Mr. Ottley's trustees.[2] My aunt had been a slave, but a favoured one. She had money left her by a coloured gentleman of the name of Crosbie, with whom she lived, and whose name she took. After his death she went to reside at Kingston. Finding it a good thing to be free, aunt Daphne wished to make all her friends free also, particularly the slaves on the estate where she was born, and with whom she had shared, in her early days, all the sorrows of negro servitude. She had a large heart, and felt great kindness for her own people; but her means were not equal to her good wishes. . . .

Whilst I lived with my aunt at Kingston I was very happy. I had no heavy tasks to do; and she was as careful over me as if she had been my own mother, and used to keep me with her in the house, that I might not be playing about in the streets with bad companions. My mother made sausages and *souse*,[3] and I used to help her to carry them to gentlemen's houses for sale. This was light labour to her, for she had been a field slave, kept at hard work, and driven to it by the whip. I am sure our best days were spent with my dear aunt; nor did she make us alone happy; all the money she could save went to purchase the freedom of slaves who had formerly been her companions in bondage at Cane Grove, or to make their condition better. There was not a person upon the island who did not speak well of Daphne Crosbie; black or white it was all the same. She bore a good character until the day she died.

I lived with my aunt till I was ten years old, when I was claimed as a slave belonging to the Cane Grove estate, by Mr. Wilson. This was a hard and unjust claim; but Mr. Wilson said, that though my mother was sold I was not – that the best slaves had been sold off the estate – that I was *his* property, and he would claim me wherever I was to be found. Now, he was wrong in all this, and I can prove to you, in two short minutes, that I did not belong to him. When my aunt manumitted my mother and me, Mr. Wilson had not yet bought the estate; and in the Island of St. Vincent's it has always been a customary rule that the young child at the breast is sold as one with its mother, and does not become separate property till it is five or six years old; so that Mr. Wilson's claim was very unjust and oppressive.[4] . . .

[Warner by this time had been apprenticed to a cooper, Pierre Wynn, a "kind good master" with whom he worked for two or three months before his whereabouts were discovered by Wilson's agent. The estate manager was then sent to remove him by force.]

When the manager came into the yard, he said, 'Which is Ashton?' I answered, quite innocently, not suspecting any mischief, 'I am Ashton.' Directly I said so the manager caught hold of me by the back of my neck. I did not know why he held me. I did not know what to think – I could not get my breath to speak – I was dreadfully frightened, and trembled all over. The other men got hold of me, and held me fast. Then they led me away to Mr. Dalzell, Mr. Wilson's attorney, and shut me up in his office till Mr. Wilson came. Mr. Dalzell was afraid that I would try to make my escape, and to make sure of me one man kept watch at the window and another at the door. When Mr. Wilson came in he did not know me, and asked who I was. One of the men told him that I was Ashton. He said, 'Very well, keep him here till I am ready to send him down to the estate.' He then came up to the place where I was standing, and examined me from head to foot; then turned to Mr. Dalzell, and began talking to him about me. I was too young, and too much frightened at being stolen away, to remember much of their discourse; but I am very sure that I shall never forget that day.

Before Mr. Wilson left the office, my mother and Daphne Crosbie came to hear what was being done with me, and why I had been taken away. But all they said was of no use; they could do no good where there was no justice to be had. Mr. Wilson insisted that I was a slave, and *his* slave, and he would have it so, in spite of my mother's tears and my aunt's entreaties . . . .

The manager then put me into a boat, and took me down to the estate. . . . It was Saturday, and I was not set to work till the Monday morning. I was very sad, and wished very much to run away. I could not bear the thought of being a slave, and I was very restless and unhappy.

On the Monday morning, John, the head cooper, took me down to the sugar works to help him; but I had no heart to work – I did nothing but think how I might run away. I was not knowing enough, however, to make my escape; and, after consulting with myself a long time, I found it would be the best plan to make myself as patient as I could. But still I was always thinking of my mother and aunt, and of Pierre Wynn, and the home I had been taken from. The estate of Cane Grove was in the middle of a deep valley, near the sea shore. Mr. Wilson's house stood upon the brow of the hill, and overlooked the whole sugar plantation. He had about three hundred slaves, and was considered one of the severest masters in the whole island.

The manager put me under the charge of John, the cooper. He was a black man, and a slave; but he was very cruel to those of his own colour who were placed under him. I had not been with him many days before he gave me a proof of this. He ordered me to go to the plantation and cut a bundle of faggots from some trees which had been lately felled. This was at noon, when the sun was at the hottest. Owing to the great heat I was a long time making up my bundle. When I brought it home, he was angry with me because I had not cut more, and said that he knew that I had been playing and idling away my time, instead of minding my work. I told him that I had worked as hard as I could, but the heat was so great that I had no strength to chop more. He seized hold of me, and, holding me fast with one hand, he took a piece of wood from the bundle, and struck me over the head again and again, till I was quite stunned with the pain, and the blood flowed from the wound. I went crying to the manager, and complained of the cooper's cruelty. He was not so harsh a man as John, and he told him that he had done wrong; for he knew that Mr. Wilson did not wish me to be treated severely. This was not from any liking he had to me above the rest of the slaves; but Mr. Wilson, having no just claim to me, was fearful that ill usage would induce me to make my escape. I did not suspect this then, but I knew it when I grew older. After John had treated me in this way, I went to live with a slave on the estate called Ben: I slept at his place, and only worked with John, in the coopers' yard, during the day.

The first time I was trusted to leave the estate, John's wife took me with her to Kingston on Sunday morning (which is the slaves' market-day) to sell some Indian corn. I carried the Indian corn to market in an open basket on my head, just as it had been gathered in the long ears. I had, that day, a great desire to see my mother and aunt, which became stronger and stronger the nearer we drew to Kingston. As we went along, I asked the cooper's wife to let me go home and speak to my people. I was so earnest about it, and pressed her so hard, that at last she said she would let me go if I would promise to come back soon. In the market, however, I met my mother, and John's wife gave me into her charge. Oh, I was so glad to see her! – so full of joy after our long, long parting; and when I saw with her a boy of my own age, called William, who had been my play-fellow, and whom I loved as if he had been my brother, and thought I should never see again, I could contain myself no longer, but burst into tears. William was as glad to see me as I was to see him, and we went home together. I told him, as we went along, all that had happened to me since I was stolen away, and how much I disliked being a slave. I was so happy with my friends all that day that I quite forgot my promise to the cooper's wife. I went out to play with William: he took me on board the ship to which he belonged; and, when John's wife came to my aunt's to take me home with her, I was no where to be found: and she was obliged, though much against her will, to return without me. When asked by the manager what had become of me, she told him that I was lost. He was very angry with her for letting me out of her sight; and, thinking that I had taken this opportunity to run away, he ordered some of his people to go to Kingston early in the morning and bring me back. One of the slaves set off before it was light in search of me. But, as my mother and aunt had persuaded me not to run away, but to return to the estate, and be a good and dutiful lad to my master till they could obtain justice for me, – as soon as the day broke I bade them good-bye, and went back to Cane Grove. The slave who had been sent to find me missed me upon the road, and was the whole day looking for me about the town.

The next morning, Mr. Wilson rode up to the cooper's shop, and askd me where I had been; and why I did not come home on the Sunday night, as I had promised? I told him that I went to see my mother, and that I did not mean to stay long away. He did not say many angry words to me; but he told me, the next time I went to Kingston, and wished to see my mother, I must ask his leave, and he would give me a paper to show that I had it. But I never had an opportunity to come to him for a pass: he went away suddenly to England, and I never saw him again.

Mr. Wilson left me to the care of Mr. Donald, his manager, and Mr.

Dalzell, his attorney, who always treated me very well – though I was still held unjustly as a slave. But some time afterwards Mr. Donald was discharged from the estate, because he had not made enough of sugar; and it was reported by some person to Mr. Wilson that he was too indulgent to the slaves, and did not work them hard enough. Another manager came in his place, called Mr. John McFie, who was a very severe task-master, and worked the slaves much harder. Under him my condition became considerably worse. One day he sent and called me to his house, and said that, as there was not sufficient job-work for me about the homestall, I must take a hoe and join the field gang. If the sentence of death had been passed upon me, I could not have felt more stunned. I shall never forget it! I knew that if I was sent to the field it would make me destroy myself – for it is always counted by negroes who have been above it, the worst of all punishements – the lowest step of disgrace – to be placed in the field gang. It is a dreadful state of slavery. I have often seen it – I may say I have *felt* it, though never in my own person. God mercifully spared me that trial. I declare before Almighty God that I would far rather die than submit to it; and, when the manager threatened to send me to the field, I felt so ill and desperate that I did not care for life. But I did not answer a word. If I had spoken my thoughts, he would have had me flogged on the spot. I turned away in silence, with the salt water in my eyes. He saw that it would not do to drive me desperate, and he soon sent after me and ordered me to another task. On another occasion, when something had offended him, Mr. McFie once more threatened to send me to the field; but he never went so far as actually to force me to take the hoe. Had he done so, I can scarcely tell what would have been the consequence. I think it would have been my destruction.

As I have spoken of the condition of the field negroes as being so much worse than that of the mechanics among whom I was ranked on the estate, I shall here endeavour to describe the manner in which the field gang were worked on Cane Grove estate. They were obliged to be in the field before five o'clock in the morning; and, as the negro houses were at the distance of from three to four miles from the cane pieces, they were generally obliged to rise as early as four o'clock, to be at their work in time. The driver is first in the field, and calls the slaves together by cracking the whip or blowing the conch shell. Before five o'clock the overseer calls over the roll; and if any of the slaves are so unfortunate as to be too late, even by a few minutes, which, owing to the distance, is often the case, the driver flogs them as they come in, with the cart-whip, or with a scourge of tamarind rods. When flogged with the whip, they are stripped and held down upon the ground, and exposed in the most shameful manner.

In the cultivation of the canes the slaves work in a row. Each person has a hoe, and the women are expected to do as much as the men. This work is so hard that any slave, newly put to it, in the course of a month becomes so weak that often he is totally unfit for labour. If he falls back behind the rest, the driver keeps forcing him up with the whip. They work from five o'clock to nine, when they are allowed to sit down for half an hour in the field, and take such food as they have been able to prepare over night. But many have no food ready, and so fast till mid-day.

They go to work again directly after half an hour's respite, and labour till twelve o'clock, when they leave off for dinner. They are allowed two hours of mid-day intermission, out of crop time, and an hour and a half in crop time.

During this interval every slave must pick a bundle of grass to bring home for the cattle at night. The grass grows in tufts, often scattered over a great space of ground, and, when the season is dry, it is very scarce and withered, so that the slaves collect it slowly and with difficulty, and are often employed most of the time allowed them for mid-day rest, in seeking for it. I have frequently known them occupied the whole two hours in collecting it.

They work again in gang from two till seven o'clock. It is then dark. When they return home the overseer calls over the roll, and demands of every man and woman their bundles of grass. He weighs with his hand each bundle as it is given in, and, if it be too light, the person who presents it is either instantly laid down and flogged severely with the cart-whip, or is put into the stocks for the whole night. If the slaves bring home no grass, they are not only put into the stocks all night, but are more severely flogged the next morning. This grass-picking is a very sore grievance to the field slaves.

When they are manuring the ground, the slaves are forced to carry the wet manure in open baskets upon their heads. This is most unpleasant as well as severe work. It is a usual occupation for wet weather, and the moisture from the manure drips constantly down upon the faces, and over the body and clothes of the slaves. They are forced to run with their loads as fast as they can; and, if they flag, the driver is instantly at their heels with the cart-whip.

The crop-time usually commences in January and lasts till June, and, if the season is wet, till July. During this season every slave must bring in a bundle of cane-tops for the cattle, instead of a bundle of grass. They then go immediately to the sugar-works, where they have to take up the *mogass* which was spread out at nine o'clock in the morning to dry for fuel to boil the sugar. This mogass is the stalks of the cane after the juice has been squeezed out by the mill. The slaves are employed till ten at night in gathering in the mogass, that it may not be wetted with the dew and rendered unfit for immediate use. The overseer then calls over the roll, and issues orders for a certain spell of them to be up and at the works at one o'clock in the morning. After this the slaves have to prepare their suppers; for, if they have no very aged parents or friends belonging to them, they must do this themselves, which occupies them another hour. Every creature that is capable of work must take a part in the labours of the crop; and no person remains at home but those who are totally unfit for work. Slaves who are too old and weak to go to the field have to make up bundles of mogass, cut grass for the stock, &c.

During this season all the mechanics on the estate are employed to pot the sugar; carpenters, coopers, masons, and rum-distillers, even the pasture boys who tend the cattle, are called in to assist. To the little people are given small tubs to carry the sugar into the curing house; and the grown-up slaves have shovels to fill the tubs for them. When employed in potting the sugar, we did not leave off to get our breakfast till ten or eleven o'clock, and I have known it mid-day before we have tasted food.

The whole gang of field slaves are divided into spells, and every man or woman able to work has not only to endure during crop-time the severe daily labour, but to work half the night also, or three whole nights in the week. The work is very severe and great numbers of the slaves, during this period, sink under it, and become ill; but if they complain, their complaints are not readily believed, or are considered only a pretence to escape from labour. If they are so very ill that their inability to work can no longer be doubted, they are at length sent to the sick-house.

The sick-house is just like a penn to keep pigs in; if you wish to keep yourself clean and decent, you cannot. It is one of the greatest punishments to the slaves to be sent there. When we were hard pressed, and had much sugar to pot, the manager would often send to the sick-house for the people who were sick, or lame with sores, to help us. If they refused to come, and said that they were unable to work, they were taken down and severely flogged, by the manager's order, with the cart-whip. There is nothing in slavery harder to bear than this. When you are ill and cannot work, your pains are made light of, and your complaints neither listened to, nor believed. I have seen people who were so sick they could scarcely stand, dragged out of the sick-house, and tied up to a tree, and flogged in a shocking manner; then driven with the whip to work. I have seen slaves in this state crawl away, and lie down among the wet trash to get a little ease, though they knew that it would most likely cause their death.

People so hardly, so harshly, treated, and so destitute of every comfort, cannot be supposed to work with a willing mind. They have no home which they can well call their own. They are worked beyond their strength, and live in perpetual fear of the whip. They are insulted, tormented, and indecently exposed and degraded; yet English people wonder that they are not contented. Some have even said that they are happy! Let such people place themselves for a few minutes under the same yoke, and see if they could bear it. Such bondage is ruin both to the soul and body of the slave; and I hope every good Englishman will daily pray to God, that the yoke of slavery may soon be broken from off the necks of my unfortunate countrymen for ever.[5]

What made me feel more deeply for the sad condition of the field slaves was the circumstance of my having taken a wife from among them, after I had resided several years on Cane Grove estate. When I was about twenty-one years of age, finding my condition lonely, because I had no friends to manage for me, as the other slaves had, I wished to marry, and have a home of my own, and a kind partner to do for me. Among the field slaves there was a very respectable young woman, called Sally, for whom I had long felt a great deal of regard. At last I asked her to be my wife; and we stood up in her father's house, before her mother, and her uncle, and her sisters, and, holding each other by the hand, pledged our troth as husband and wife, and promised before God to be good and kind to each other, and to love and help each other, as long as we lived. And so we married. And though it was not as white folks marry, before the parson, yet I considered her as much my wife, and I loved her as well, as though we had been married in the church; and she was as careful, and managed as well for me, as if she had been my mother. I could not bear to see her work in the field. It is, as I have already said, a very sad and hard condition of slavery; and the more my wife suffered, the more I wished to be free, and to make her so. When she was with child, she was flogged for not coming out early enough to work, and afterwards, when far advanced in pregnancy, she was put into the stocks by the manager, because she said she was unable to go to the field. My heart was almost broken to see her so treated, but I could do nothing to help her; and it would have made matters worse if I had attempted to speak up for her. She was twice punished in this cruel manner, though the overseer must have known that she was in no condition to work. After our child was born, she was again repeatedly flogged for not coming sooner to the field, though she had stopped merely to attend and suckle the baby. But they had no feeling for the mother or for her child; they cared only for the work. It is a dreadful thing to be a field negro; and it is scarcely less dreadful, if one's heart is not quite hardened, to have a wife, or a husband, or a child, in that condition. On this account I was often grieved that I had taken poor Sally to be my wife; for it caused her more suffering as a mother, while her cruel treatment wrung my heart, without my being able to move a finger, or utter a word, in her behalf.

[Warner eventually ran away from the estate and obtained papers which enabled him to escape to Grenada as a free man. He bitterly lamented the fact that he had to leave behind his wife and child (then four months old), still enslaved, and he continued to live in fear of being recaptured himself by Wilson's agents. After various adventures in the Caribbean, he eventually travelled to England in 1830, where he hoped at last to establish his claim to freedom in law.]

P.S.[6] *Feb 25.* Since the above was put in type, poor Ashton's enfranchisement has been suddenly accomplished by the great Emancipator – DEATH. He was carried off by a rapid inflammatory complaint, and expired this day in the London Hospital, uttering, with his latest breath, some important expressions about the 'King of England,' and 'freedom to the slaves.' *Requiescat!* He is now where 'the wicked cease from troubling and the weary are at rest,' and 'the bondman is free from his master.' 'There the prisoners rest together; they hear not the voice of the Oppressor.'

Notes

1. Ashton Warner, *Negro Slavery Described by a Negro: being the narrative of Ashton Warner, a native of St. Vincent's* (London: Samuel Maunder, 1831), 17–46.
2. A deed of manumission, dated 23 May 1821 and signed with an X by Daphne Crosbie, is quoted in the appendix.
3. [Strickland's note:] *souse*: slices of pig's head, salted and prepared in a particular manner, and sold in the markets by the slaves.
4. [Strickland's note:] This is poor Ashton's own statement. Whether the Colonial *Slave Law* will support his claim for freedom on this ground, is a question which remains to be determined.
5. [Strickland's note:] Such is the impressive language in which Ashton speaks of slavery. The above are his own expressions; for though an uneducated, he is a very intelligent, negro, and speaks remarkably good English. Any reader, who wishes it, may see and converse with himself, by making application through the publisher. – S.S.
6. Susanna Strickland, in Warner, *Negro Slavery*, 65.

MARY PRINCE (CA. 1788–CA. 1832)

The History of Mary Prince (1831)[1]

Mary Prince was both victim and witness of the hardships of slavery under a succession of owners in Bermuda, the Turks Islands and Antigua. In 1828, at the age of about forty, she came to England with her master and mistress, but her ill treatment continued. Her case was taken up by the Anti-Slavery Society and her life story was recorded, at her own request, by Susanna Strickland (later known by her married name, Moodie). Thomas Pringle, secretary to the Anti-Slavery Society, explains in the preface that the narrative, "written out fully, with all the narrator's repetitions and prolixities", was afterwards "pruned" for publication. Nevertheless, he claims, "Mary's exact expressions and peculiar phraseology" were retained as far as possible. He states also that he took pains to verify her story by consulting a person who was resident in Antigua in her time.[2] The narrative begins with Prince's birth and early years, when she lived in the same household as her enslaved mother, serving as personal attendant to her mistress's young daughter, Betsey; she describes it as "the happiest period of my life; for I was too young to understand rightly my condition as a slave". At the age of twelve, however, after the death of her mistress, she and her brothers and sisters were sent away to be sold.

The black morning at length came; it came too soon for my poor mother and us. Whilst she was putting on us the new osnaburgs[3] in which we were to be sold, she said, in a sorrowful voice, (I shall never forget it!) 'See, I am *shrouding* my poor children; what a task for a mother!' – She then called Miss Betsey to take leave of us. 'I am going to carry my little chickens to market,' (these were her very words,) 'take your last look of them; may be you will see them no more.' 'Oh, my poor slaves! my own slaves!' said dear Miss Betsey, 'you belong to me; and it grieves my heart to part with you.' – Miss Betsey kissed us all, and, when she left us, my mother called the rest of the slaves to bid us good bye. One of them, a woman named Moll, came with her infant in her arms. 'Ay!' said my mother, seeing her turn away and look at her child with the tears in her eyes, 'your turn will come next.' The slaves could say nothing to comfort us; they could only weep and lament with us. When I left my dear little brothers and the house in which I had been brought up, I thought my heart would burst . . . .

[Mary and her two sisters, accompanied by their mother, walk to Hamble Town, where they are sold at the "vendue" (slave-market) to different buyers. Mary's new master was Captain I——, who lived at Spanish Point.]

It was night when I reached my new home. The house was large, and built at the bottom of a very high hill; but I could not see much of it that night. I saw too much of it afterwards. The stones and the timber were the best things in it; they were not so hard as the hearts of the owners.[4]

Before I entered the house, two slave women, hired from another owner, who were at work in the yard, spoke to me, and asked who I belonged to? I replied, 'I am come to live here.' 'Poor child, poor child!' they both said; 'you must keep a good heart, if you are to live here.' – When I went in, I stood up crying in a corner. Mrs. I—— came and took off my hat, a little black silk hat Miss Pruden made for me, and said in a rough voice, 'You are not come here to stand up in corners and cry, you are come here to work.' She then put a child into my arms, and, tired as I was, I was forced instantly to take up my old occupation of a nurse. – I could not bear to look at my mistress, her countenance was so stern. She was a stout tall woman with a very dark complexion, and her brows were always drawn together into a frown. I thought of the words of the two slave women when I saw Mrs. I——, and heard the harsh sound of her voice.

The person I took the most notice of that night was a French Black called Hetty, whom my master took in privateering from another vessel, and made his slave. She was the most active woman I ever saw, and she was tasked to her utmost. A few minutes after my arrival she came in from milking the cows, and put the sweet-potatoes on for supper. She then fetched home the sheep, and penned them in the fold; drove home the cattle, and staked them about the pond side;[5] fed and rubbed down my master's horse, and gave the hog and the fed cow[6] their suppers; prepared the beds, and undressed the children, and laid them to sleep. I liked to look at her and watch all her doings, for her's was the only friendly face I had as yet seen, and I felt glad that she was there. She gave me my supper of potatoes and milk, and a blanket to sleep upon, which she spread for me in the passage before the door of Mrs. I——'s chamber.

I got a sad fright, that night. I was just going to sleep, when I heard a noise in my mistress's room; and she presently called out to inquire if some work was finished that she had ordered Hetty to do. 'No, Ma'am, not yet,' was Hetty's answer from below. On hearing this, my master started up from his bed, and just as he was, in his shirt, ran downstairs with a long cow-skin[7] in his hand. I heard immediately after, the cracking of the thong, and the house rang to the shrieks of poor Hetty, who kept crying out, 'Oh, Massa! Massa! me dead. Massa! have mercy upon me – don't kill me outright.' – This was a sad beginning for me. I sat up upon my blanket, trembling with terror, like a frightened hound, and thinking that my turn would come next. At length the house became still, and I forgot for a little while all my sorrows by falling fast asleep.

The next morning my mistress set about instructing me in my tasks. She taught me to do all sorts of household work; to wash and bake, pick cotton and wool, and wash floors, and cook. And she taught me (how can I ever forget it!) more things than these; she caused me to know the exact difference between the smart of the rope, the cart-whip, and the cow-skin, when applied to my naked body by her own cruel hand. And there was scarcely any punishment more dreadful than the blows I received on my face and head from her hard heavy fist. She was a fearful woman, and a savage mistress to her slaves.

There were two little slave boys in the house, on whom she vented her bad temper in a special manner. One of these children was a mulatto, called Cyrus, who had been bought while an infant in his mother's arms; the other, Jack, was an African from the coast of Guinea, whom a sailor had given or sold to my master. Seldom a day passed without these boys receiving the most severe treatment, and often for no fault at all. Both my master and mistress seemed to think that they had a right to ill-use them at their pleasure; and very often accompanied their commands with blows, whether the children were behaving well or ill. I have seen their flesh ragged and raw with licks. – Lick – lick – they were never secure one moment from a blow, and their lives were passed in continual fear. My mistress was not contented with using the whip, but often pinched their cheeks and arms in the most cruel manner. My pity for these poor boys was soon transferred to myself; for I was licked, and flogged, and pinched by her pitiless fingers in the neck and arms, exactly as they were. To strip me naked – to hang me up by the wrists and lay my flesh open with the cow-skin, was an ordinary punishment for even a slight offence. My mistress often robbed me too of the hours that belong to sleep. She used to sit up very late, frequently even until morning; and I had then to stand at a bench and wash during the greater part of the night, or pick wool and cotton; and often I have dropped down overcome by sleep and fatigue, till roused from a state of stupor by the whip, and forced to start up to my tasks.

Poor Hetty, my fellow slave, was very kind to me, and I used to call her my Aunt; but she led a most miserable life, and her death was hastened (at least the slaves all believed and said so,) by the dreadful chastisement she received from my master during her pregnancy. It happened as follows. One of the cows had dragged the rope away from the stake to which Hetty had fastened it, and got loose. My master flew into a terrible passion, and ordered the poor creature to be stripped quite naked, notwithstanding her pregnancy, and to be tied up to a tree in the yard. He then flogged her as hard as he could lick, both with the whip and cow-skin, till she was all over streaming with blood. He rested, and then beat her again and again. Her shrieks were terrible. The consequence was that poor Hetty was brought to bed before her time, and was delivered after severe labour of a dead child. She appeared to recover after her confinement, so far that she was repeatedly flogged by both master and mistress afterwards; but her former strength never returned to her. Ere long her body and limbs swelled to a great size; and she lay on a mat in the kitchen, till the water burst out of her body and she died. All the slaves said that death was a good thing for poor Hetty; but I cried very much for her death. The manner of it filled me with horror. I could not bear to think about it; yet it was always present to my mind for many a day . . . .

One day a heavy squall of wind and rain came on suddenly, and my mistress sent me round the corner of the house to empty a large earthen jar. The jar was already cracked with an old deep crack that divided it in the middle, and in turning it upside down to empty it, it parted in my hand. I could not help the accident, but I was dreadfully frightened, looking forward to a severe punishment. I ran crying to my mistress, 'O mistress, the jar has come in two.' 'You have broken it, have you?' she replied; 'come directly here to me.' I came trembling: she stripped and flogged me long and severely with the cow-skin; as long as she had strength to use the lash, for she did not give over till she was quite tired. – When my master came home at night, she told him of my fault; and oh, frightful! how he fell a swearing. After abusing me with every ill name he could think of, (too, too bad to speak in England,) and giving me several heavy blows with his hand, he said, 'I shall come home to-morrow morning at twelve, on purpose to give you a round hundred.' He kept his word. – Oh sad for me! I cannot easily forget it. He tied me up upon a ladder, and gave me a hundred lashes with his own hand, and master Benjy [his young son] stood by to count them for him. When he had licked me for some time he sat down to take breath; then after resting, he beat me again and again, until he was quite wearied, and so hot (for the weather was very sultry,) that he sank back in his chair, almost like to faint. While my mistress went to bring him drink, there was a dreadful earthquake. Part of the roof fell down, and every thing in the house went – clatter, clatter, clatter. Oh I thought the end of all things near at hand; and I was so sore with the flogging, that I scarcely cared whether I lived or died. The earth was groaning and shaking; every thing tumbling about; and my mistress and the slaves were shrieking and crying out, 'The earthquake! the earthquake!' It was an awful day for us all . . . .

Some little time after this, one of the cows got loose from the stake, and eat one of the sweet-potatoe slips. I was milking when my master found it out. He came to me, and without any more ado, stooped down, and taking off his heavy boot, he struck me such a severe blow in the small of my back, that I shrieked with agony, and thought I was killed; and I feel a weakness in that part [to] this day. The cow was frightened by his violence, and kicked down the pail and spilt the milk all about. My master knew that this accident was his own fault, but he was so enraged that he seemed glad of an excuse to go on with his ill usage. I cannot remember how many licks he gave me then, but he beat me till I was unable to stand, and till he himself was weary.

After this I ran away and went to my mother, who was living with Mr. Richard Darrel. My poor mother was both grieved and glad to see me; grieved because I had been so ill used, and glad because she had not seen me for a long, long while. She dared not receive me into the house, but she hid me up in a hole in the rocks near, and brought me food at night, after every body was asleep. My father, who lived at Crow-Lane, over the salt-water channel, at last heard of my being hid up in the cavern, and he came and took me back to my master. Oh I was loth, loth to go back; but as there was no remedy, I was obliged to submit.

When we got home, my poor father said to Capt. I——, 'Sir, I am sorry that my child should be forced to run away from her owner; but the treatment she has received is enough to break her heart. The sight of her wounds has nearly broke mine. – I entreat you, for the love of God, to forgive her for running away, and that you will be a kind master to her in future.' Capt. I—— said I was used as well as I deserved, and that I ought to be punished for running away. I then took courage and said that I could stand the floggings no longer; that I was weary of my life, and therefore I had run away to my mother; but mothers could only weep and mourn over their children, they could not save them from cruel masters – from the whip, the rope, and the cow-skin. He told me to hold my tongue and go about my work, or he would find a way to settle me. He did not, however, flog me that day.

For five years after this I remained in his house, and almost daily received the same harsh treatment. At length he put me on board a sloop, and to my great joy sent me away to Turk's Island. I was not permitted to see my mother or father, or poor sisters and brothers, to say good bye, though going away to a strange land, and might never see them again. Oh the Buckra people who keep slaves think that black people are like cattle, without natural affection. But my heart tells me it is far otherwise.

We were nearly four weeks on the voyage, which was unusually long. Sometimes we had a light breeze, sometimes a great calm, and the ship made no way; so that our provisions and water ran very low, and we were put upon short allowance. I should almost have been starved had it not been for the kindness of a black man called Anthony, and his wife, who had brought their own victuals, and shared them with me.

When we went ashore at the Grand Quay, the captain sent me to the house of my new master, Mr. D——, to whom Captain I—— had sold me. Grand Quay is a small town upon a sandbank; the houses low and built of wood. Such was my new master's. The first person I saw, on my arrival, was Mr. D——, a stout sulky looking man, who carried me through the hall to show me to his wife and children. Next day I was put up by the vendue master to know how much I was worth, and I was valued at one hundred pounds currency.

My new master was one of the owners or holders of the salt ponds, and he received a certain sum for every slave that worked upon his premises, whether they were young or old. This sum was allowed him out of the profits arising from the salt works. I was immediately sent to work in the salt water with the rest of the slaves. This work was perfectly new to me. I was given a half barrel and a shovel, and had to stand up to my knees in the water, from four o'clock in the morning till nine, when we were given some Indian corn boiled in water, which we were obliged to swallow as fast as we could for fear the rain should come on and melt the salt. We were then called again to our tasks, and worked through the heat of the day; the sun flaming upon our heads like fire, and raising salt blisters in those parts which were not completely covered. Our feet and legs, from standing in the salt water for so many hours, soon became full of dreadful boils, which eat down in some cases to the very bone, afflicting the sufferers with great torment. We came home at twelve; ate our corn soup, called *blawly*, as fast as we could, and went back to our employment till dark at night. We then shovelled up the salt in large heaps, and went down to the sea, where we washed the pickle from our limbs, and cleaned the barrows and shovels from the salt. When we returned to the house, our master gave us each our allowance of raw Indian corn, which we pounded in a mortar and boiled in water for our suppers.

We slept in a long shed, divided into narrow slips, like the stalls used for cattle. Boards fixed upon stakes driven into the ground, without mat or covering, were our only beds. On Sundays, after we had washed the salt bags, and done other work required of us, we went into the bush and cut the long soft grass, of which we made trusses for our legs and feet to rest upon, for they were so full of the salt boils that we could get no rest lying upon the bare boards.

Though we worked from morning till night, there was no satisfying Mr. D——. I hoped, when I left Capt. I——, that I should have been better off, but I found it was but going from one butcher to another. There was this difference between them: my former master used to beat me while raging and foaming with passion; Mr. D—— was usually quite calm. He would stand by and give orders for a slave to be cruelly whipped, and assist in the punishment, without moving a muscle of his face; walking about and taking snuff with the greatest composure. Nothing could touch his hard heart – neither sighs, nor tears, nor prayers, nor streaming blood; he was deaf to our cries, and careless of our sufferings. – Mr. D—— has often stripped me naked, hung me up by the wrists, and beat me with the cow-skin, with his own hand, till my body was raw with gashes. Yet there was nothing very remarkable in this; for it might serve as a sample of the common usage of the slaves on that horrible island . . . .

I think it was about ten years I had worked in the salt ponds at Turk's Island, when my master left off business, and retired to a house he had in Bermuda, leaving his son to succeed him in the island. He took me with him to wait upon his daughters; and I was joyful, for I was sick, sick of Turk's Island, and my heart yearned to see my native place again, my mother, and my kindred . . . .

I was several years the slave of Mr. D—— after I returned to my native place. Here I worked in the grounds. My work was planting and hoeing sweet-potatoes, Indian corn, plantains, bananas, cabbages, pumpkins, onions, &c. I did all the household work, and attended upon a horse and cow besides, – going also upon all errands. I had to curry the horse – to clean and feed him – and sometimes to ride him a little. I had more than enough to do – but still it was not so very bad as Turk's Island . . . .

He had an ugly fashion of stripping himself quite naked and ordering me then to wash him in a tub of water. This was worse to me than all the licks. Sometimes when he called me to wash him I would not come, my eyes were so full of shame. He would then come to beat me. One time I had plates and knives in my hand, and I dropped both plates and knives, and some of the plates were broken. He struck me so severely for this, that at last I defended myself, for I thought it was high time to do so. I then told him, I would not live longer with him, for he was a very indecent man – very spiteful, and too indecent; with no shame for his servants, no shame for his own flesh. So I went away to a neighbouring house and sat down and cried till the next morning, when I went home again, not knowing what else to do . . . .

[In about 1816 Mary Prince was sold to a Mr Wood, who took her to Antigua, where she was again harshly treated. In the hope of paying for her freedom, she saved up money by doing outside work, but Wood always refused to grant her manumission. She also joined the Moravians, through whom she learned to read.]

The way in which I made my money was this. – When my master and mistress went from home, as they sometimes did, and left me to take care of the house and premises, I had a good deal of time to myself, and made the most of it. I took in washing, and sold coffee and yams and other provisions to the captains of ships. I did not sit still idling during the absence of my owners; for I wanted, by all honest means, to earn money to buy my freedom. Sometimes I bought a hog cheap on board ship, and sold it for double the money on shore; and I also earned a good deal by selling coffee . . . .

Some time after I began to attend the Moravian Church, I met with Daniel Jones, afterwards my dear husband. He was a carpenter and cooper to his trade; an honest, hard-working, decent black man, and a widower. He had purchased his freedom of his mistress, old Mrs. Baker, with money he had earned whilst a slave. When he asked me to marry him, I took time to consider the matter over with myself, and would not say yes till he went to church with me and joined the Moravians. He was very industrious after he bought his freedom; and he had hired a comfortable house, and had convenient things about him. We were joined in marriage, about Christmas 1826, in the Moravian Chapel at Spring Gardens by the Rev. Mr. Olufsen. We could not be married in the English Church. English marriage is not allowed to slaves; and no free man can marry a slave woman.

When Mr. Wood heard of my marriage, he flew into a great rage, and sent for Daniel, who was helping to build a house for his old mistress. Mr. Wood asked him who gave him a right to marry a slave of his? My husband said, 'Sir, I am a free man, and thought I had a right to choose a wife; but if I had known Molly was not allowed to have a husband, I should not have asked her to marry me.' Mrs. Wood was more vexed about my marriage than her husband. She could not forgive me for getting married, but stirred up Mr. Wood to flog me dreadfully with the horsewhip. I thought it very hard to be whipped at my time of life for getting a husband – I told her so. She said that she would not have nigger men about the yards and premises, or allow a nigger man's clothes to be washed in the same tub where hers were washed. She was fearful, I think, that I should lose her time, in order to wash and do things for my husband: but I had then no time to wash for myself; I was obliged to put out my own clothes, though I was always at the wash-tub.

I had not much happiness in my marriage, owing to my being a slave. It made my husband sad to see me so ill-treated. Mrs. Wood was always abusing me about him. She did not lick me herself, but she got her husband to do it for her, while she fretted the flesh off my bones. Yet for all this she would not sell me. She sold five slaves whilst I was with her; but though she was always finding fault with me, she would not part with me. However, Mr. Wood afterwards allowed Daniel to have a place to live in our yard, which we were very thankful for.

[The final pages of the *History* concern Mary Prince's experiences in England, concluding as follows.]

I am often much vexed, and I feel great sorrow when I hear some people in this country say, that the slaves do not need better usage, and do not want to be free.[8] They believe the foreign people,[9] who deceive them, and say slaves are happy. I say, Not so. How can slaves be happy when they have the halter round their neck and the whip upon their back? and are disgraced and thought no more of than beasts? – and are separated from their mothers, and husbands, and children, and sisters, just as cattle are sold and separated? Is it happiness for a driver in the field to take down his wife or sister or child, and strip them, and whip them in such a disgraceful manner? – women that have had children exposed in the open field to shame! There is no modesty or decency shown by the owner to his slaves; men, women, and children are exposed alike. Since I have been here I have often wondered how English people can go out into the West Indies and act in such a beastly manner. But when they go to the West Indies, they forget God and all feeling of shame, I think, since they can see and do such things. They tie up slaves like hogs – moor[10] them up like cattle, and they lick them, so as hogs, or cattle, or horses never were flogged; – and yet they come home and say, and make some good people believe, that slaves don't want to get out of slavery. But they put a cloak about the truth. It is not so. All slaves want to be free – to be free is very sweet. I will say the truth to English people who may read this history that my good friend, Miss S——, is now writing down for me. I have been a slave myself – I know what slaves feel – I can tell by myself what other slaves feel, and by what they have told me. The man that says slaves be quite happy in slavery – that they don't want to be free – that man is either ignorant or a lying person. I never heard a slave say so. I never heard a Buckra man say so, till I heard tell of it in England. Such people ought to be ashamed of themselves. They can't do without slaves, they say. What's the reason they can't do without slaves as well as in England? No slaves here – no whips – no stocks – no punishment, except for wicked people. They hire servants in England; and if they don't like them, they send them away: they can't lick them. Let them work ever so hard in England, they are far better off than slaves. If they get a bad master, they give warning and go hire to another. They have their liberty. That's just what *we* want. We don't mind hard work, if we had proper treatment, and proper wages like English servants, and proper time given in the week to keep us from breaking the Sabbath. But they won't give it: they will have work – work – work, night and day, sick or well, till we are quite done up; and we must not speak up nor look amiss, however much we be abused. And then when we are quite done up, who cares for us, more than for a lame horse? This is slavery. I tell it to let English people know the truth; and I hope they will never leave off to pray God, and call loud to the great King of England, till all the poor blacks be given free, and slavery done up for evermore.

Notes

1. Mary Prince, *The History of Mary Prince, a West Indian Slave, Related by Herself* (London: F. Westley and A.H. Davis, 1831).

2. For the nature and authenticity of Prince's *History*, see Ferguson, *Subject to Others*, 281–98, and Gillian Whitlock, "Volatile Subjects: *The History of Mary Prince*", in *Genius in Bondage: Literature of the Early Black Atlantic*, ed. Vincent Carretta and Philip Gould (Lexington: University Press of Kentucky, 2001).

3. *osnaburgs*: loose-fitting garments, made of coarse linen, provided to slaves by their owners.

4. [Editor's note, 1831:] These strong expressions, and all of a similar character in this little narrative, are given verbatim as uttered by Mary Prince. – *Ed.*

5. [Editor's note, 1831:] The cattle on a small plantation in Bermuda are, it seems, often thus staked or tethered, both night and day, in situations where grass abound.

6. [Editor's note, 1831:] A cow fed for slaughter.

7. [Editor's note, 1831:] A thong of hard twisted hide, known by this name in the West Indies.

8. [Editor's note, 1831:] The whole of this paragraph especially, is given as nearly as was possible in Mary's precise words.

9. [Editor's note, 1831:] She means West Indians.

10. [Editor's note, 1831:] A West Indian phrase: to fasten or tie up.

Mrs Carmichael (d. 1885)

Domestic Manners and Social Condition of the White, Coloured and Negro Population of the West Indies (1833)[1]

Alison Carmichael was a younger sister of James Stuart, author of *Three Years in North America* (also published in 1833). She married an army officer who, after retiring from service, acquired plantations in the West Indies, first in St Vincent and later on Laurel Hill estate in Trinidad, where she lived from 1821 to 1826. In the preface to her book she explains that it was written "before the agitation of the West India question by the present government": it was merely "an accumulation of facts; the results of personal experience and attentive observation". As a resolute apologist for West Indian planters, however, she appears confident that her "facts" will undercut the case for emancipation by refuting allegations of the cruelty of slave owners and the misery of the slaves. The reported conversations with enslaved Africans, below, were clearly designed to show their contentment under a benevolent owner. Carmichael was conscientious about recording them with accuracy, but her view of enslaved black people, whether African or creole, as constitutionally lazy, dishonest and deceitful severely limits her capacity to understand their motives and feelings; she seems unaware that her interlocutors might be giving her the answers they perceive she wants.[2] The conversations nevertheless provide some insight into the speech habits and personal experiences of the speakers.

↩

Conversations with native Africans

The subject of the present short chapter, I consider an interesting one, – the detail of conversations, which I had with native Africans. I give their testimony precisely as I received it from them;[3] and in what follows, I beg my readers to keep in view, that I only pledge myself to relate faithfully what was told to me by the negroes themselves. It is impossible for me to vouch for the truth of details coming from a set of people who, as a people, have so little regard for truth. The only way is, to compare the different accounts of negroes of the same national origin; and whenever they do not materially disagree, it is probable that something approaching the truth has been described. I shall also mention the character of the individual as I go along, which ought always to be kept in view . . . .

The details which I present are far from being meant as conveying any apology for the slave-trade, as it existed before the abolition; indeed I never heard the slave-trade mentioned with half the horror in Britain that I have heard it spoken of in the West Indies: and never let it be forgotten that Britain began the slave-trade, – not the colonists; and it is a fact which admits no denial that the British government *forced* the colonists to cultivate the islands by the labour of negro slaves imported from Africa . . . . Of all national iniquities, none surely ever exceeded the slave-trade; but still I feel convinced, from the consistent details of many native Africans, examined at different times and even in different colonies, that the situation of those who were removed to the West Indies, was very greatly improved in every respect . . . .

F. was a native African, an Ebo negro, of uncommonly good character, but not at all clever; – a common field negro, – she had been many years ago offered her freedom as a reward for her faithful services, but declined it, saying she preferred remaining as she was; she worked for some time after this upon the estate, as a nurse, but at the period I speak of, she ceased to be able to do anything: at an early period of her life she had suffered severely from rheumatism, and her joints were much distorted from it; she was also much bent down from old age, and latterly it became difficult to make her contented or happy. She was in many respects savage; and at times insisted upon lying on the floor without any clothes; neither was she willing to have her

head tied with a handkerchief, and her naturally black woolly hair had
become white from age. She would rarely use a spoon for her callalou soup,
which with a little boiled rice was all she relished; and for drink, she liked
weak rum and water: her appearance was anything but pleasing, it was at
times almost disgusting; but she despised and refused all the comforts of civilized life; and a stranger to have seen her, as I daily did, lying on her mat-
tress on the floor, using her hand for a spoon to her soup, and hardly a rag
upon her, might naturally have exclaimed, 'Look at the brutality of this poor
negro's owner!' But had he been conversant with native Africans, he would
have perhaps felt as we did, all the desire to render her comfortable according to our interpretation of the word, but he would no doubt also have
experienced the utter impossibility of convincing her that cleanliness, a few
clothes, and eating her victuals like a civilized being, were real comforts. She
used to say to me, when I spoke to her of such things, 'No tease me, misses,
me one very good nigger; *let me be.*' 'Let me be,' is a frequent expression
among negroes, and they have probably learnt this and other decided
Scotticisms from the number of Scotch managers and overseers.

One day I asked F., 'how big were you when you left Africa?' 'Misses, me
big young woman.' 'How were you taken?' 'Misses, Ebo go war wid a great
grandee massa; him massa take Ebo many, many; tie hand, tie foot, no could
run away, misses: they gie us only so leetle for yam (as she said this, she took
up a splinter of wood, and held it to signify that the food she got was as
insignificant in point of size). Well, misses, they take me mamma too; she
be one nice nigger, fat so; they take her, kill her, fry her, yam her (eat her)
every bit all: dey bringed her heart to me, and force me yam a piece of it.
Well, misses, after dat dey sell me to another grandee for cottons, and he
send me a Guinea coast; and when I comed there, the first buckra I seed,
misses, I started all.' 'Were you afraid of the white man?' 'No, misses, no of
he, but of he colour; look so queer, misses, I axe ye pardon.' 'Did you know
you were going to be sold to a white man?' 'Yes, misses, me happy at dat;
nigger massa bad too much, white massa him better far, Africa no good
place, me glad too much to come a white man's country.' 'Well, what did
you do when you were landed?' 'Old massa buy me, old misses very good;
she make nice bamboo for me (clothing), teached me 'bout God,' said she,
'get me christened; me quite happy; me (said she with much exultation)

never once punished. Old massa love me, old misses love me, me loved dem; me get good husband; me never have sore heart but once, when my H. (her only child) go dead. Misses, oh, she handsome too much: take pain in side, dey do all for her, but God say no; and so she go dead, and so me just take young H——, (a young negro woman, upon the estate, of the same name as her own daughter); she have no daddy or mamma, and me take her for my own, being as I was her god-mamma.' The principal enjoyment of this poor woman was in telling old stories to the family; but the servants were very harsh to her, and I frequently caught the little negroes under a sand-box tree, pelting her while she lay at the open house door, with hard green mangoes which they gathered for the purpose.

I. was a Guinea-coast female negro, of only tolerable character, a common field negro. I asked her when she was brought from Africa? 'When me big woman.' Were your father and mother alive when you left it? 'No, misses, but I had husband and one pic-a-ninny.' And were you not very much grieved when you found yourself away from them? 'Misses, me husband bad too much: beat me one day, two day, tree day, every day. Misses, me husband *here* go beat me too much (meaning if, or when he beats me too much), or when me no really bad, me go a manager, or come a massa, to complaint, and he settle all. Misses, me have one pic-a-ninny in a Guinea; but me have D——, I——, K——, L——, M——, N——, and J——, here; cooper, O—— for husband; he bring me some tick (fuel) often. L. big now – help vorck a provision-ground; little M. she take broom, sweep a house; N. he little too much, but me get fish and bamboo for him. Oh, misses, is Africa good country? No good people say dat surely.'

P., a female field negro, a good character upon the whole, and willing to work; left Africa when not quite grown up, but evidently recollected it perfectly. 'Would you like to go back to your country?' 'Eh, misses, me no like dat. St. Vincent fine country – good white massa dey.' – 'Were you slave or free in Africa?' 'Misses, me one time slave, one time free, just as our grandee massa fight (beat) next grandee massa.' 'And you would rather be here?' 'Yes, misses, I no like me country at all.'

Q., a female field negro, of the very best character, an excellent field-labourer; cheerful, contented, and intelligent, and I can say, affectionate; in manner a perfect savage, yet not rude; for although she never spoke to us without first turning her back, and bursting into a loud fit of laughter, yet she meant no insult by it. Whenever Q. had any request to make to me – and her requests were very numerous – in the dress-making line, she used to come to the door, and turning her back, and laughing as I have described, she stood still, and half turned her head round with a sly smile, until I used to say, 'Well, Q., what do you want?' Then it was always, 'Misses, me just buyed one handkerchief for me, will ye mark me name for me?' or it might be a gown or petticoat, &c. At first Q. was very shy of speaking, but her request once granted, she would turn round and talk with great spirit. Her house was neat and well furnished, according to her ideas of comfort, and she and her husband rarely quarrelled; she could fight when she thought it necessary, just to shew that she was no coward, but she was not given to boxing; and was, and I hope is, in every sense of the word, a good negro.

'What nation are you of, Q?' 'An Ebo.' 'Would you like to go to Africa?' 'Misses, me hope never to see dat country no more; misses, me hear tell dat some white massas go a England, and tell dat nigger wish for go again to Africa, and say dat nigger tink dey go to Africa when dey go dead.' 'Is this not true, Q?' 'Misses, me never hear one nigger say so, me no tink dat; me know very well, God make me above, God make one breath, put one breath in an (all of us); God make us live, God take away breath, we go dead; misses, me notion is, dis breath and life all as one.' – Meaning that without breath we cannot live. 'How old were you when you left Africa?' 'Me big the same as now.' 'Were you free or slave there?' 'Misses, me *born free*. Ebo war with anoder grandee massa – take me, me daddy, me mamma, me husband; sell me, dem, keep me slave to dat grandee massa, no slave to himsel, but to one of him country: me slave to one nigger, massa; he flog me, curse me, use me very bad, me heart-broke; he want calicoes, take me a coast, sell me for calicoes; me dance for joy to get away from nigger massas.' 'And you are now happier than you ever were in Africa?' 'Yes, misses, Africa one bad country.'

R. was a female field negro, rather advanced in life: although only a field negro, she was very much civilized, extremely polite, kind, affectionate, but cunning occasionally; decently attired at all times, extremely gay on holidays, and at church. She was a good work-woman, and her provision grounds were in fine order; she called herself a Roman Catholic, but went to the Methodist chapel almost every Sunday. She was always much respected by the other negroes, as well as by her master and mistress. She had evidently confused notions of Mahomedanism, but says, 'she never hear tell of Mahomet, but knowed there was one good man who came far off from where the sun rise, he tell all people be good.' R. had one great fault, not generally to be found in a female negro of otherwise so exemplary good character: she was fond of having a number of husbands, and of changing them often; I have known her have three different husbands in six weeks. 'What country were you of, R?' 'Misses, me a Mandingo.' Did you like your country? 'Misses, suppose Mandingo be my own country, me no like it.' What were you there? 'Me be waiting maid to a grandee massa's lady; she have fine clothes, necklace, bracelet, rings. Oh! misses, you'd really like to seen her going to church to pray.' Was she kind to you? 'Misses, she flog me too much; pinch me; if me no dress her pretty, she box me ear for me; she handsome too much, clear black kin, so mooth.' What did you get to eat? 'For yam (eatables) misses, me got rice, one leetle river fish – and misses, now and den, when she very good, gie me ripe plantain, and banana.' Which country do you like best? 'Misses, Buckra country very good, plenty for yam (eat) plenty for bamboo (for clothing); Buckra-man book larn (can read) now misses, Buckra-man rise early, – like a cold morning; nigger no like cold.' And I suppose then you'd like to lie in bed in the morning? 'Yes, misses, till sun hot, den go vorck; cold, no good to nigger kin (skin); but misses, me like to go see a cold of England.' Would you? and you know, I added, that if you were in England you would be free. 'Yes, misses, me know that perfect, but me no like to top dey, only see a place, and see many a many white face, and den back to St. Vincent; – misses, is true, no plantain or banana in a England?' Yes, quite true; but there are other fruits that I think as good. 'Eh, eh, misses, noting so good as plantain and banana.'

S. was a second boiler-man, middle aged, with an uncommonly cheerful, frank countenance, good looking, extremely agreeable in his appearance; a negro of the very best possible character, and very intelligent and affection-ate; diligent in his duties, attentive both to his master and to his family; and had only one wife, with whom he had lived in great comfort. He was fond of his children, loved them apparently alike; was kind to his wife, gave her nice dresses, and both of them were civil in their deportment as negroes; no one ever merited the title of a good negro more than S., and the longer I knew him, – indeed up to the moment that I bade him adieu, – I had more and more reason to respect him.

'S. what country did you come from?' 'Ebo, misses.' Do you remember Ebo?' 'Eh, misses, vay well indeed.' Do you like it better than this? 'Misses, me like Ebo well enough den, but me go dead if me go dey now.' How so? 'Misses, noting good a yam (to eat) in Ebo like a here, no salt pork dey, no salt beef, – people dey just go fish in a river, boil a leetle fish, boil a leetle rice, so go yam it,' (then eat it). But you had yams there? 'Misses, only the grandee.' And you were not a grandee? 'No, misses, me free, no slave, but me one poor man dey; me vorck, every day, else eat none.' Whether would you prefer being free in Ebo, or a slave here? 'Misses, Africa no good people, no trust in dem; one slave to-day, you free to-morrow; free to-day, slave to-morrow: your grandee massa make war wid toder massa, (king in their sense of the word), take ye, never mind how great ye be; ye never know how to do vorck, he flog ye; if ye no do a ting, he whip again: noting to yam, but leetle rice. Misses, a me glad too much, when me sent a coast o' Guinea for a Buckra to buy us.'

V. was a common field negro, a quiet but not an intelligent negro, apparently attached to his master, worked well for him, and had his own grounds in very good order; he was not given to fighting; – had many comforts in his house, such as tables, chairs, good bedstead, and crockery-ware, and was always neat and tidy on holidays and Sundays. V. was never in disgrace, and merited the title of a good negro.

What nation are you of V.? 'An Ebo.' Would you like if massa were to free you, and send you to your own country again? 'Eh, eh, misses, me no like dat; me country wicked too much.' They don't eat men in Ebo, do they? 'No, misses, dey no eat men; but raw beast-flesh warm be very nice, me tink dat good yet; S. can tell ye same tory, misses: Ebo eat no men; when Ebo take people in a war from a grandee massa, Ebo no eat 'em: Ebo sell 'em a Guinea coast; – but when Coromantee take a people when they go war with grandee massa, da Coromantee eat all of dem.' How do they eat 'em? 'Misses, me no seed dem eat 'em, but me heared in Ebo 'bout it; and old granny F. tell me 'bout it, when she take by the Coromantees. Dey cook a men in dat place. Misses, Africa wicked too much, me rather go dead afore me go back dey.' Were you slave there or free? 'Me free man one day, slave t'other day; no good people dey, cheat too much.' How old were you when you left Africa. 'Me one big man.'

W. was a carpenter; good tempered, not intelligent, but very indolent. 'What nation are you of?' 'Mandingo.' How old were you when you came to the West Indies? 'One big man.' Do you like St. Vincent, or Africa best? 'Eh, eh, misses, me no one fool, me know better dan dat; Africa one very bad country, dey go vorck poor slave to death; noting for yam, only whip, whip constant; me like where me be.' And were you slave or free in Africa? 'Me one free man, dey take me, carry me in a coast of Guinea, sell me a Buckra capin, me very glad to go wid dem.' 'But had you no friends you were sorry to leave in Africa?' 'Misses, friend to-day, no friend to-morrow; no trust in dey; your daddy want any ting or your mamma, dey go sell de pic-a-ninny, to buy it.'

X. was a faithful working negro, kept his own grounds in high order; was fond of money to hoard it up: he went about in good weather, with hardly a rag to cover him. X. had a good deal of dry humour; he had a very curious and rather savage countenance, and he bore his country's mark upon his chest and also upon his cheeks. He was excessively avaricious, and acted invariably on the principle of trusting no one; he reared poultry very successfully. I believe he was attached to us, yet if I could not produce the exact change to pay him for his fowls, he refused to let me have them, and he was the only negro I ever met with who shewed the slightest want of confidence in this respect towards me. X. made a great deal of money, but what he did with it none could tell. On Sundays, however, he was an amazing dandy, and had his collar so stiff, that he would not have turned his head for the world, lest he should disarrange it. X. never had any settled wife; he tried to get one several times, but they always left him, as they said, 'Cause he so miserly, misses; he plit (split) one black dog if he could,' a coin, value one-sixth of four-pence.

'How old were you when you came to St. Vincent?' 'One big man, so big me be now.' 'What nation were you of?' 'The Mandingo.' 'Were you free or slave?' 'Misses, me be one very great grandee; not one grandee massa, but one great grandee; me hae slave to wash me, me hae yams to eat, fresh pork;

me hae no vorck for do, only me go fire at bird in a bush, for yam: well, misses, one grandee massa send always hunting for people; so dey take me in a bush, make me vorck hard, – me never vorck afore, me no know'd how to vorck; dey flog me, say me no good for noting, send me a Guinea coast, sell me Buckra capin.' 'But surely you would like to go back to Mandingo? 'No, misses, Mandingo one very bad country; me no have vorck too much now, me hae yam, tanias, plantains, every ting very good.'

Y. was a field negro, an uncommon character. He was employed when a young man in a pasture in the upper part of the estate, at some distance from the dwelling-house: he neglected the stock, allowing them to trespass upon the canes in every direction; and there was no possibility of holding any communication with him, – for whenever he saw any white person coming near where he was, he ran like a deer, hid himself in the brush-wood, and defied all pursuit. The pasture he was upon commanded so extensive a prospect, that he had full view of any one who came in that direction. If he saw a human being approach, he made off to one of his hiding places, which was generally on the top of the highest and thickest tree, where he formed a complete bed or hammock of the wild canes, which grew there so luxuriantly. In the course of his sojourning there, he killed four young cattle, besides sundry calves, sheep, and lambs; he skinned, cleaned, and half roasted them, and then covered them over with leaves, for his sustenance. This conduct lasted for two years and a half, when at last he was brought down; he was not punished, but his duty changed; and from that moment, except occasional intoxication, he behaved uncommonly well. Y., from the period I knew him, was a very quiet good negro; he seldom smiled, but was nevertheless very contented; he was uncommonly handsome, and reckoned a first-rate dancer, both of creole and African dances: it was indeed surprising to witness the grace, gravity, and majesty of his demeanour. He was not very intelligent, but a good workman, and kept his grounds in beautiful order; he was not uncivil, but his manners were rather forbidding.

Y., do you recollect your own country? 'Not very much, but me member the ship.' Were you free or slave in your own country? 'Me no know.' Would you like to return to Africa? 'No, misses, every nigger tell me, me country one very bad place; me no wish to leave dis country.' If you were free would you not like to see Africa again? 'No, misses, I'd like to see England, and den come a St. Vincent; me like to see English cold.'

Such are some of the details I received from native Africans. Of their title to credit, let the reader judge. The condition of the Mandingo, or Ebo negro, in his own country, however wretched that condition may be, can be no apology for negro traffic; neither is the contentedness of the African with his condition in the West Indies, any argument against emancipation; but these details and avowals undoubtedly afford the consolation of knowing that the negro has not been made more miserable by the unnatural traffic that deprived him of his home; and some proof, also, that the inhuman conduct of slave proprietors has been exaggerated.

Notes

1. Alison Carmichael, *Domestic Manners and Social Condition of the White, Coloured and Negro Population of the West Indies. By Mrs. Carmichael, Five years a resident in St. Vincent and Trinidad* (London: Whittaker, Treacher, and Co., 1833), 2:299–320.

2. See Philip Baker and Lise Winer, "Separating the Wheat from the Chaff: How Far Can We Rely on Old Pidgin and Creole Texts?", in *St Kitts and the Atlantic Creoles: The Texts of Samuel Augustus Mathews in Perspective*, ed. Philip Baker and Adrienne Bruyn (London: University of Westminster Press, 1999), 106–7.

3. There is no reason to doubt the author's claim. In the preface she apologizes for any "inaccuracies, particularly in Negro language" which might be found, explaining that she had been unable to check the text while it was being printed.

WILLIAM KNIBB (1803–45)

"A Brief Account of a Much-Persecuted Christian Slave" (1834)[1]

The Bow in the Cloud, a collection of pieces by evangelical writers, was edited by Mary Anne Rawson, a member of the Sheffield Women's Anti-Slavery Association. Her aim was to highlight the spiritual aspects of the anti-slavery cause.[2] A prefatory note states that the profits from its sale would be "devoted to the West-Indian Negroes". William Knibb, one of the contributors, was renowned for his energetic activities on behalf of the slaves and for his anti-slavery preaching in Jamaica, where he served as a Baptist missionary from 1825 until his death, apart from brief interludes in England during which he continued to campaign for abolition. He thereby earned the implacable hostility of the planters; he was arrested after the Jamaican slave rebellion of 1831 on a charge of incitement, but the case was thrown out.

A few years ago, one of the slave-members belonging to the Baptist Church at Montego Bay was banished from his home, and sent to the estate where David lived, to be cured of his praying. By the pious conversation of this exiled christian negro, David was brought under serious concern for his soul, which ended in his conversion to God. Acting up to the Christian negro's motto, that 'what good for one negro, good for him brother too,' David spoke to his fellow-slaves about Jesus, and his love in dying for poor sinners. God, who despiseth not the humblest instrument, blessed the efforts of this poor negro, and, in a short time, about thirty on the estate began to pray, and at length built a small hut, in which, after the labours of the day, they might assemble and worship God. Tidings of these things reached the ears of the white persons employed on the estate, and David was summoned before his attorney, and asked whether he was teaching the slaves to pray. On replying in the affirmative, the hut was demolished and burnt, and David was stretched upon the earth and flogged with the cart-whip till his flesh was covered with his blood. Next Lord's-day I missed my faithful deacon at the house of God. His afflicted wife came and told me the sad tale of his sufferings, and informed me, that his hands were bound and his feet made fast in the stocks. Often did I inquire after him, and for him, and the same answer was returned, 'Massa, him in the stocks;' till one morn-ing, as I sat in my piazza, he appeared before the window. There he stood – I have his image now before me – he was hand-cuffed, barefoot, unable to wear his clothes from his yet unhealed back; his wife had fastened some of her garments round his lacerated body. I called him in, and said,

'David, David, what have you done?'
With a look of resignation I shall never forget, he replied,
'Don't ask me, ask him that bring me, massa.'
Turning to the negro who had him in charge, I said,
'Well, what has this poor man done?'
'Him pray, massa,' was the reply, 'and Buchra sending him to the workhouse for punishing.'

I gave him some refreshment, for in the state I have described he had walked thirteen miles under a burning sun, and followed him to that den of cruelty, properly designated a Jamaica inquisition. He was chained to a fellow-slave by the neck, and sent to work on the public roads. The next day I went to visit him again, when I was informed by the supervisor of the workhouse, that he had received orders to have him flogged again, as soon as his back was well enough to bear it. In these chains David remained for months; frequently I saw him, but never did I hear one murmur or one com-plaint, except when he heard that the partner of his joys and sorrows was ill on the estate, and he was forbidden to go and see her.

At the end of three months he was liberated, and returning to the estate, was asked,

> 'Now, sir, will you pray again?'
>
> 'Massa,' said the persecuted disciple, 'you know me is a good slave, but if trouble come for dis, me must pray, and me must teach me broder to pray too.'

Again he was immured in a dungeon, and his feet made fast in the stocks.

Notes

1. William Knibb, "A Brief Account of a Much-Persecuted Christian Slave", in *The Bow in the Cloud; or, The Negro's Memorial. A collection of original contributions, in prose and verse, illustrative of the evils of slavery, and commemorative of its abolition in the British colonies*, ed. Mary Anne Rawson (London: Jackson and Walford, 1834), 188–91.
2. See Ferguson, *Subject to Others*, 265–69.

"THE NEGRO WILL WORK FOR WAGES", FROM *THE BOW IN THE CLOUD* (1834)[1]

Wishing to widen and improve a road from the highway to my residence, which was up a steep and difficult ascent, and indeed scarcely passable, I applied to the master of a jobbing gang, and requested him to state to me the lowest terms for which he would undertake the work: after several interviews and discussions he offered to perform it for the sum of 32*l*. Jamaica currency, prompt payment. Considering this amount too high, I was induced to pursue another plan. Accordingly one day I took a slave, who was driver of a jobbing gang, and after explaining the nature and difficulties of the work, proposed the following question: – 'supposing I was to hire of your master, twelve negroes, and if instead of working them before the whip, I gave each one a fippenny[2] *per* day besides paying the master,[3] how many days would they require to complete the work?' The negro proceeded to examine the nature of the work, when after some time he returned, and replied that if thus rewarded they would do it in ten days, or in eleven at the farthest. Upon this information, I applied to the master, and hired the slaves, who were sent to me on the following Monday. Before, however, appointing them their work, I called them together, and addressed them in the following manner: 'I have hired you of your master to perform certain work, – I shall not allow the whip to be used or even carried by the driver, but if you turn out early in the morning, and work well during the day, I will give each a fipenny for himself; – if any one is late to his work, or indolent in his work, I shall not give him any thing, but will send him home, and obtain another slave in his stead.' When I had thus spoken, one of the negroes, with much good humour, replied, 'Massa, no you talk about sending we home; give we de hammer and make we go work.' They proceeded, and I never recollect to have seen any persons work better or more cheerfully. Frequently, when I went to see how they were getting on, they would indulge in their jokes: 'Massa, you no send we home yet!' referring to my promises to them. One morning I went down about half-past five o'clock; they had been at work half an hour, when with much drollery they said, 'Massa, no you say, if neger no turn out soon, you send him home? Massa no up, him no know when neger come.' And at another time as they were breaking the stones for the road, one remarked, 'Massa, dat fipenny, – him make de stone break. If de hammer only fall upon de stone, him break all to pieces.' I had not occasion to withhold the promised reward from one, nor indeed to find fault with one; and such was the influence which this small sum had upon them, that they completed the work within the specified time, so that it cost me but 13*l*. 15*s*., instead of 32*l*.

Notes

1. "The negro will work for wages: extract from a letter addressed to the editor by a gentleman who has for many years resided in Jamaica", in Rawson, *Bow in the Cloud*, 251–53.
2. [Author's note:] *Fipenny* – a piece of money current in Jamaica.
3. [Author's note:] The sum charged by the master for the hire of each negro, was two-and-sixpence *per diem*.

Letter from a Mother in Jamaica to Her Daughter in Edinburgh (1834)[1]

It appears from the text that the daughter, Sarah Affleck, owned a few slaves, who were kept for hiring out to other employers. Writing less than six weeks before the date of emancipation, Eleanor Affleck's sole interest in the momentous event is financial: she is concerned with the reduction in Sarah's income which will result from introduction of the apprenticeship scheme, and the importance therefore of claiming the compensation due to slave owners from the government.

MS letter 1834

[Address]

Mrs. Sarah Affleck
10 East Adam Street
Edinburgh
per Packet

Greeen Island Hanover Jamaica
24th Jun 1834

My dear Daughter

I had the pleasure to receive your letter of the 24th March a few days ago and am glad to learn that you expected your dispute with Mr. Campbell would be so soon settled and hope you have not been disappointed – In reply to your enquiries respecting your Slaves I have to inform you that they are still on Saltspring[.] There are now living, Jacob, Memha and her two children George & Queen – The hire allowed for them during the lifetime of Mr. Dugald Campbell was £50 Currency per Ann: but I do not know if any valuation for hire has been made since. You are I suppose aware that they will be all free on the 1st of August next – and that you will receive a Compensation from Government – they will after that time be apprentices for six years and work a part of their time for the accommodation of / those who supply them with Houses, Provision Grounds, Clothing &c – so that I am afraid you must not expect much hire for the time to come. You must get some friend to apply for your share of the compensation when the sum is fixed –

I am happy to hear that yourself & family were well – Eliza must now be a young Woman – but what is the reason that you make no mention of your Husband – Is he dead or alive? – Has your Brother's Widow recovered any of his Property?

Since I last wrote to you I have enjoyed very good health and have met with no other misfortunes tho' I find it hard enough to make a living – Your sister Ann begs to be kindly remembered to you & all the family & begs me to say that she has two Children a boy Alexander & a Girl Susan – – With my best wishes for your health & happiness

> I remain
> My dear Daughter
> Your affectionate Mother
> Eleanor Affleck

Note

1.   MS letter, National Library of Scotland.

R.R. MADDEN (1798–1886)

A Twelvemonth's Residence in the West Indies (1835)[1]

Richard Robert Madden, an Irishman, had family connections in Jamaica. In 1833 he was sent out to the island as one of the special magistrates appointed to adjudicate in disputes between apprentices and their masters; he travelled via Barbados and other islands, arriving in Jamaica in January 1834. His vigorous support of the rights of the apprentices alienated the planters to such an extent that Madden felt obliged to resign in November 1834. The narrative is given in the form of a series of letters to various correspondents. In June he set out to find a ruined property named Marley, in the parish of St Mary, which had formerly belonged to his great-uncle.

From Letter XVII, 15 June 1834[2]

After a fatiguing ride in a broiling summer's day, I reached a small plantation in the mountains, where I was informed some of the negroes of my uncle were then living, who had been lately purchased by the proprietor, a Mr. Thomson; and amongst others, an old African negro, who, upwards of forty years ago, had been the favourite waiting-boy of the old gentleman, Dr. Lyons, about whom I was interested in inquiring. I had prepared myself for a very sentimental scene with the old negro. I had pictured to myself the joy of the aged domestic at seeing a descendant of his revered master . . . . But never was there a gentleman of an ardent turn of mind more cruelly disappointed.

The negro was brought before me: he was a hale, honest-looking, grey-headed old man, about eighty.

'Did he remember the old doctor?'

'He remembered him well.'

'Where did he come from?'

'Massa brought him out of a Guinea ship when a piccanini boy: him wait on massa – serve massa very well; him serve massa when young and 'trong; but what use talk of such things now?'

'Did he know what had become of master?'

'Yes, him hear massa die in England.'

'Was he sorry to hear of master's death?'

'No, massa hab plenty of people in England to be sorry for him; him no want poor nigger to be sorry for him.'

'Would he like to see one of master's family?'

'No! him want see nobody.'

'Did he see no resemblance between me and the old doctor?'

'No! him want to see nutten at all of nobody.'

The man was now becoming impatient. I thought it time to awaken his sensibility by telling him at once that I was the nearest relative of old master he had seen for forty years. I was ready to extend my hand for a hearty shake. I was prepared, as I have said before, for an affecting scene; judge of my disappointment –

'For true! you belong old massa: well, what you want here? you come to carry away old stones from Marley – plenty of old stones on grounds at Marley.'

The old man, as he made the concluding observation, gave me a look which I would not willingly meet at the day of judgment. He turned away with the greatest indifference, humming to himself as he toddled towards the garden that sentimental negro air: –

'Hi, massa buckra, sorry for your loss,

Better go to Lunnon town, and buy another oss.'

'He is a surly, sulky old fellow,' said the lady of the house. 'He seems (thought I) an ungrateful old monster: he cares not a straw for the memory of his master; he has not the least regard for one of his descendants.' I now made inquiries into the history of the plantation, for the old doctor had been dead forty years; and his brother, his successor, about thirty-five. And the result of my inquiries was the history of the plunder and the ruins of a property . . . which is the history of hundreds of properties in Jamaica. I had ample grounds for reconsidering my opinion of the old man's ingratitude. I found for many a long year he had no benefits to be grateful for – but great neglect, and many hardships, and, eventually cruelty, to turn the milk of kindly feelings towards his master or his family to gall and bitterness.

Abolition of slavery, 1 August 1834[3]

[Writing from Kingston on 6 August 1834, Madden describes the celebration of this momentous event as he observed it at three city churches, before commenting briefly on its reception outside.]

The 1st of August passed over without the slightest disorder. I did not see a single drunken negro, nor any great appearance of exultation, except that which, in the subdued form of grateful piety, I witnessed in the churches.

In fact, for a great festival, it was as quiet a day as can well be imagined. The only symptoms I saw of turbulent joy was on the part of some negro urchins, who were throwing stones at a drunken sailor, and who, whenever poor Jack made a reel after them, scampered away, shouting most lustily to each other, 'What for you run away? We all free now! buckra can't catch we! hurra for fuss of Augus! hi, hi, fuss of Augus! hurra for fuss of Augus!'

Notes

1. R.R. Madden, *A Twelvemonth's Residence in the West Indies, during the transition from slavery to apprenticeship* (London: James Cochrane and Co., 1835).
2. Ibid., 1:221–23.
3. Ibid., 2:5–6.

A. McL.

"Lady Liberty" (1834)[1]

According to Richard Madden, who printed this emancipation song in an appendix to *Twelvemonth's Residence in the West Indies*, the author was a former planter of St Anne's, Jamaica, who became a schoolmaster and songwriter, using the pen-name "The Fairy of the Hill". Although he showed no signs of insanity, he was committed to the Kingston Madhouse, apparently for political reasons; he told Madden he had been arrested for writing against the apprenticeship system and predicting its failure. Madden "lost no time in placing the particulars of his case before the Attorney-General" but left Jamaica before hearing the outcome. From other sources he learned that the author's "zeal in the cause of negro emancipation made him a marked man; his ballads were adapted to negro tunes, and became very popular with the blacks; one of these songs, called 'Bonnie Lady Mulgrave,' was in the mouth for many weeks of every negro in Kingston." This was probably a satirical song; the Earl of Mulgrave, governor of Jamaica, had made himself unpopular by issuing a proclamation in 1833 announcing the introduction of the Emancipation Bill in Parliament but warning the slaves to remain obedient and orderly in the meantime, on pain of severe punishment if they transgressed. The author sent "Lady Liberty" to Madden in late 1834, describing it as "a recent composition".

Lady Liberty
A Song, by the Fairy of the Hill

Oh, who comes smiling on thy car,
    Aurora, say – so brilliantly?
Who is this other morning-star,
    That dawns with day benignantly?
'Who does not ken her bonnie smile?   5
    She long has pined in jeopardy;
But now I bring to this fair isle
    Your own sweet lady – Liberty!'

Ah, well I ought to ken her smile,
    A mother's smile indeed to me;   10
I ken'd it while a thoughtless child,
    On Scotia's hills sae blithe and free;
Oft with her gamboll'd o'er the hills,
    Ere care approach'd with puberty;
And now she comes to sunny isles,   15
    Our own sweet lady – Liberty!

We'll lead her o'er St. Anna's grove,
    Thro' fairy dells of spicy trees –
The bonny dame! our queen of love,
    Her weary wings at length shall ease: 20
Enthroned on yon Blue Mountain peak,
    View Grandè 'rolling rapidly;'
On Buxton hills the shrine we'll seek
    Of our sweet lady – Liberty!

All hail! all hail! auspicious morn,   25
    That brings our lady o'er the sea;
No more I'll thole[2] the tyrant scorn!
    We'll crush the chains of slavery!
    We swear it by the God of War,

We swear our purpose siccarly![3]   30
And no one shall restrain the car
    Of lovely lady Liberty!

    CHORUS.
Hark, now her song Jamaica sings,
    O'er hill and dale, o'er bower and tree;
We consecrate the land of springs
    To lovely lady Liberty.

Notes

1. A. McL., "Lady Liberty", in Madden, *Twelvemonth's Residence*, 2:331.
2. *thole*: endure.
3. *siccarly*: certainly.

Part 3.

Resistance and Rebellion

"Leonard Parkinson, a Captain of the Maroons", frontispiece to *The
Proceedings of the Governor and Assembly of Jamaica, in regard to the
Maroon negroes* (London: printed for John Stockdale, 1796).
Courtesy of the Trustees of the National Library of Scotland.

RICHARD LIGON (CA. 1585–1662)

A True and Exact History of the Island of Barbados (1657)[1]

> Ligon believed that rebelliousness, cruelty, "fearfulness and false-
> ness" were norms among enslaved Africans, but he also maintained
> that "there are to be found amongst them, some who are as morally
> honest, as conscionable, as humble, as loving to their friends, as any
> that live under the sun".

It has been accounted a strange thing, that the *Negroes*, being more than
double the numbers of the Christians that are there [in Barbados], and they
accounted a bloody people, where they think they have power or advantages; and the more bloody, by how much more fearful than others: that
these should not commit some horrid massacre upon the Christians,
thereby to enfranchise themselves, and become masters of the island. But
there are three reasons which take away this wonder; The one is, they are
not suffered to touch or handle any weapons: the other, That they are held
in such awe and slavery, as they are fearful to appear in any daring act; and
seeing the mustering of our men, and hearing their gun-shot, (than which
nothing is more terrible to them) their spirits are submerged to so low a condition, as they dare not look up to any bold attempt. Besides these, there is a
third reason, which stops all designs of that kind, and that is, They are
fetch'd from several parts of Africa, who speak several languages, and by
that means, one of them understands not another: For, some of them are

fetch'd from Guinny and Binny, some from Cutchew, some from Angola, and some from the river of Gambia[2] . . . .

> [The following passage, describing an attempted mutiny on a plantation, was intended to demonstrate the capacity of slaves for "moral honesty" on occasion.]

It was in a time when victuals were scarce, and plantins were not then so frequently planted, as to afford them enough. So that some of the high spirited and turbulent amongst them, began to mutiny, and had a plot, secretly to be reveng'd on their master; and one or two of these were firemen that made the fires in the furnaces, who were never without store of dry wood by them. These villains, were resolved to make fire to such part of the boyling-house, as they were sure would fire the rest; and so burn all, and yet seem ignorant of the fact, as a thing done by accident. But this plot was discovered, by some of the others who hated mischief, as much as they [the conspirators] lov'd it; and so traduc'd them to their master, and brought in so many witnesses against them, as they were forc'd to confess, what they meant should have been put in act the next night: so giving them condign punishment, the master gave order to the overseer that the rest should have a dayes liberty to themselves and their wives, to do what they would; and withall to allow them a double proportion of victual for three dayes, both which they refus'd; . . . for they told us, it was not sullenness, or slighting the gratuity their master bestow'd on them, but they would not accept any thing as a recompence for doing that which became them in their duties to do, nor would they have him think, it was hope of reward, that made them to accuse their fellow servants, but an act of Justice, which they thought themselves bound in duty to do, and they thought themselves sufficiently rewarded in the act.

Notes

1. Ligon, *True and Exact History*, 46, 53–54.
2. *Guinny*: Guinea; *Binny*: Benin; *Cutchew*: Cacheu in Portuguese Guinea.

Aphra Behn (1640?–89)

Oroonoko: or, The Royal Slave (1688)[1]

In 1663–64 Aphra Behn stayed on a plantation in Suriname, then a British colony. She was involved in local political activities and may have worked as a spy for the British government. Her short novel *Oroonoko*, based on her West Indian experience, became immensely popular. Frequently reprinted, dramatized and imitated for more than a century, it projected a powerful image of a noble slave and, though not itself carrying an anti-slavery message, it supplied ammunition for campaigners against the slave trade. It tells the story of an African prince captured and sold into slavery in Suriname, where he is renamed Caesar. In Suriname he is reunited with his African lover, Imoinda, who had previously also been taken to the colony as a slave. When his request for liberty for Imoinda and himself is denied, he resolves to lead a rebellion.

Taking his opportunity, one Sunday, when all the whites were overtaken in drink, as there were abundance of several trades, and slaves for four years,[2] that inhabited among the negro houses; and Sunday being their day of debauch, (otherwise they were a sort of spies upon Caesar) he went, pretending out of goodness to 'em, to feast among 'em, and sent all his musick, and order'd a great treat for the whole gang, about three hundred negroes, and about an hundred and fifty were able to bear arms, such as they had, which were sufficient to do execution with spirits accordingly: For the English had none but rusty swords, that no strength could draw from a scabbard; except the people of particular quality, who took care to oil 'em, and keep 'em in good order: The guns also, unless here and there one, or those newly carry'd from England, would do no good or harm; for 'tis the nature of that country to rust and eat up iron, or any metals but gold or silver. And they are very unexpert at the bow, which the negroes and Indians are perfect masters of.

Caesar, having singled out these men from the women and children, made an harangue to 'em, of the miseries and ignominies of slavery; counting up all their toils and sufferings, under such loads, burdens and drudgeries, as were fitter for beasts than men; senseless brutes, than human souls. He told 'em, it was not for days, months or years, but for eternity; there was no end to be of their misfortunes: they suffer'd not like men, who might find a glory and fortitude in oppression; but like dogs, that lov'd the whip and bell, and fawn'd the more they were beaten: that they had lost the divine quality of men, and were become insensible asses, fit only to bear: nay, worse; an ass, or dog, or horse, having done his duty, could lie down in retreat, and rise to work again, and while he did his duty, indur'd no stripes; but men, villanous, senseless men, such as they, toil'd on all the tedious week till Black Friday: and then, whether they work'd or not, whether they were faulty or meriting, they, promiscuously, the innocent with the guilty, suffer'd the infamous whip, the sordid stripes, from their fellow-slaves, till their blood trickled from all parts of their body; blood, whose every drop ought to be revenged with a life of some of those tyrants that impose it. *"And why* (said he) *my dear friends and fellow-sufferers, should we be slaves to an unknown people? Have they vanquished us nobly in fight? Have they won us in honourable battle? And are we by the chance of war become their slaves? This would not anger a noble heart; this would not animate a soldier's soul: no, but we are bought and sold like apes or monkeys, to be the sport of women, fools and cowards; and the support of rogues and runagates, that have abandoned their own countries for rapine, murders, theft, and villanies. Do you not hear every day how they upbraid each other with infamy of life, below the wildest salvages?[3] And shall we render obedience to such a degenerate race, who have no one human vertue left, to distinguish them from the vilest creatures? Will you, I say, suffer the lash from such hands?* They all replied with one accord, *No, no, no; Caesar has spoke like a great captain, like a great king.*

Notes

1. Aphra Behn, *Oroonoko: or, The Royal Slave. A True History* (London: Will. Canning, 1688), 59–62.
2. *slaves for four years*: indentured servants.
3. *salvages*: savages.

EDWARD LONG (1734–1813)

The History of Jamaica (1774)[1]

Long gives a detailed history of insurrections in Jamaica, prefaced
by the following strenuous defence of Jamaican planters against the
charge that their cruelty towards their slaves was the main cause of
rebellion.

We are so fond of depreciating our own colonies, that we paint our planters
in the most bloody colours, and represent their slaves as the most ill-treated
and miserable of mankind. It is no wonder therefore that Jamaica comes in
for a large share of abuse; and even our common news-papers are made the
vehicles of it. I read in one of them not long since, "that the cruel usage
inflicted on Negro slaves in Jamaica by their masters, is the reason why
insurrections there are more frequent than in the French or other sugar-
islands." The first enquiry to be made in answer to so invidious a charge is,
whether the fact here asserted be really true? and, 2dly, whether this fre-
quency may not have been owing to some other cause?

Within a few years past, we have heard of them at Hispaniola, at Cuba, at
the Brasils, at Surinam, and Berbice, and at the British islands of Tobago,
Dominica, Montserrat, and St. Vincent. If they should happen oftener at
Jamaica than in the smaller islands, it would not be at all surprizing, since it
has generally contained more Negroes than all the Windward British isles
put together; and its importations in some years have been very great.

For instance, in the year 1764, the importation was 10,223. And from January 1765 to July 1766, one year and an half, 16,760. So large a multitude as 27,000 introduced in the space of two years and an half, furnishes a very sufficient reason, if there was no other, to account for mutinies and plots, especially as no small number of them had been warriors in Afric, or criminals; and all of them as savage and uncivilized as the beasts of prey that roam through the African forests . . . .

The truth is, that ever since the introduction of Africans into the West-Indies, insurrections have occurred in every one of the colonies, British as well as foreign, at times. But the calumniator has not been more erroneous in bringing the charge, than in the reasons assigned to support it; because a faulty indulgence has been one leading cause of the disturbances that have occurred in Jamaica; which is evidently proved by what is set forth in many of the laws passed in consequence of them, restricting several sports, and prohibiting certain festive assemblies, which the Negroes had freely enjoyed before, but were made subservient to the forming and carrying on of dangerous conspiracies. They were formerly allowed to assemble with drums and musical instruments; to dance, drink, and be merry. This was permitted, because it was thought an inoffensive mode of recreation for them. But when these games were afterwards converted into plots, they were with great justice suppressed, as riotous assemblies of people are in England, and for the like reason; that, being perverted from their original intention to wicked and unlawful ends, they became inconsistent with the peace and safety of the community. Such prohibitions (of which there are several) prove undeniably, the great latitude and indulgence, that has been given to the Negroes of this colony; and shew the propriety, and indeed necessity, there has been of laying them under restrictions, when that liberty was abused. The innocent, it is true, were unavoidably involved with the guilty in these restraints; but they have still sufficient pastimes and amusements to divert them, without offending against the public welfare . . . .

The heedless practice formerly of keeping large stands of firearms and cutlasses upon the inland plantations, having only three or four white men upon them, became a strong temptation to any disaffected or enterprizing Africans. It might well be expected, that throwing such magazines and stores of ammunition in their way, was a direct invitation to them to rebel.

The turning many indefensible houses into arsenals for arming mutinous savages, was doubtless the very height of imprudence, tending not only to generate projects of hostility, but to afford the means of conducting them with probable hope of success. Add to this, that many shopkeepers, from a strange spirit of avarice, have been known to sell gunpowder privately to such conspirators, although they must have foreseen the use to which it might be applied; and, to gain a few shillings, even hazarded their own destruction; incredible as this may seem, yet it is certain that such a practice has been carried on, as two laws were passed, one in 1730, the other in 1744, to put a stop to it.

Another cause of conspiracy may have been, a remote hope of some Negroes, who, having heard of the freedom granted to the Maroons after their obstinate resistance of several years, expected, perhaps, that by a course of successful opposition they might obtain the like terms in the end, and a distinct settlement in some quarter of the island.

The vulgar opinion in England confounds all the Blacks in one class, and supposes them equally prompt for rebellion; an opinion that is grossly erroneous. The Negroes, who have been chief actors in the seditions and mutinies, which at different times have broke out here, were the *imported Africans*; and, considering the numbers of them who were banished their country for atrocious misdeeds, and familiarized to blood, massacre, and the most detestable vices, we should not be astonished at the impatient spirit of such an abandoned herd, upon being introduced to a life of labour and regularity. The numbers imported would indeed be formidable, if they continued in a body; but they are soon dispersed among a variety of different estates many miles asunder, by which means they remain a long time ignorant of each other's place of settlement. They often find themselves mixed with many strangers, differing from them in language; and against others they hold a rooted antipathy. But they are chiefly awed into subjection, by the superior multitude of Creole Blacks, with whom they dare not confederate, nor solicit their concurrence in any plan of opposition to the white inhabitants.

The ringleaders of conspiracy have been the native Africans, and of these the *Coromantins* stand the foremost. The Jamaica planters are fond of purchasing Negroes who pass under this name, in preference to those of the other provinces; but the French, and some other West-India colonies, will not knowingly admit them; being sensible of their dangerous tempers and unfitness for the peaceable walk of husbandry.

Note

1. Long, *History of Jamaica*, 2:441–45.

The History, Civil and Commercial, of the British Colonies
in the West Indies (1793)[1]

Edwards was present in Jamaica during the uprising of 1760 known as "Tacky's rebellion". The fullest contemporary account of the event, too long for inclusion here, is provided by Edward Long,[2] but Edwards adds details based on his own first-hand knowledge. He later wrote a report on the part played by Maroons in the suppression of the rebellion.[3] The narrative below appears in a chapter characterizing the different races of enslaved Africans.

Koromantyn Negroes . . . Their ferociousness of disposition displayed by an account of the Negro rebellion in Jamaica in 1760

The circumstances which distinguish the Koromantyn, or Gold Coast, Negroes, from all others, are firmness both of body and mind; a ferociousness of disposition; but withal, activity, courage, and a stubbornness, or what an ancient Roman would have deemed an elevation, of soul, which prompts them to enterprizes of difficulty and danger; and enables them to meet death, in its most horrible shape, with fortitude or indifference. . . . [T]he Gold Coast being inhabited by various different tribes which are engaged in perpetual warfare and hostility with each other, there cannot be a doubt that many of the captives taken in battle, and sold in the European settlements, were of free condition in their native country, and perhaps the owners of slaves themselves. It is not wonderful that such men should endeavour, even by means the most desperate, to regain the freedom of which they have been deprived; nor do I conceive that any further circumstances are necessary to prompt them to action, than that of being sold into captivity in a distant country. I mean only to state facts as I find them. Such I well know was the origin of the Negro rebellion which happened in Jamaica in 1760. It arose at the instigation of a Koromantyn Negro of the name of Tacky, who had been chief in Guiney; and it broke out on the Frontier plantation in St. Mary's parish, belonging to the late Ballard Beckford, and the adjoining estate of Trinity, the property of my deceased relation and benefactor Zachary Bayly, to whose wisdom, activity and courage on this occasion, it was owing that the revolt was not as general and destructive as that which now rages in St. Domingo (1791).[4] On those plantations were upwards of one hundred Gold Coast Negroes newly imported, and I do not believe that an individual amongst them had received the least shadow of ill treatment from the time of their arrival there. Concerning those on the Trinity estate, I can pronounce of my own knowledge, that they were under the government of an overseer of singular tenderness and humanity. His name was Abraham Fletcher; and let it be remembered, in justice even to the rebels, and as a lesson to other overseers, that his life was spared from respect to his virtues. The insurgents had heard of his character from the other Negroes, and suffered him to pass through them unmolested . . . . Having collected themselves into a body about one o'clock in the morning, they proceeded to the fort at Port Maria; killed the centinel, and provided themselves with as great a quantity of arms and ammunition as they could conveniently dispose of. Being by this time joined by a number of their countrymen from the neighbouring plantations, they marched up the high road that led to the interior parts of the country, carrying death and desolation as they went. At Ballard's Valley they surrounded the overseer's house about four in the morning, in which finding all the White servants in bed, they butchered every one of them in the most savage manner, and literally drank their blood mixed with rum. At Esher, and other estates, they exhibited the same tragedy; and then set fire to the buildings and canes. In one morning they murdered between thirty and forty Whites and Mulattoes, not sparing even infants at the breast, before their progress was stopped. Tacky, the Chief, was killed in the woods by one of the parties that went in pursuit of them; but some others of the ringleaders being taken, and a general inclination to revolt appearing among all the Koromantyn Negroes in the island, it was thought necessary to make a few terrible examples of some of the most guilty. Of three who were clearly proved to have been concerned in the murders committed at Ballard's Valley, one was condemned to be burnt, and the other two to be hung up alive in irons, and left to perish in that dreadful situation. The wretch that was burnt was made to sit on the ground, and his body being chained to an iron stake, the fire was applied to his feet. He uttered not a groan, and saw his legs reduced to ashes with the utmost firmness and composure; after which, one of his arms by some means getting loose, he snatched a brand from the fire that was consuming him, and flung it in the face of the executioner. The two that were hung up alive were indulged, at their own request, with a hearty meal immediately before they were suspended on the gibbet, which was erected in the parade of the town of Kingston. From that time, until they expired, they never uttered the least complaint, except only of cold in the night, but diverted themselves all day in discourse long with their countrymen, who were permitted, very improperly, to surround the gibbet.[5]

Notes

1. Edwards, *History, Civil and Commercial*, book 4, 74–79.
2. Long, *History of Jamaica*, 2:447–62.
3. Published in *The Proceedings of the Governor and Assembly of Jamaica, in Regard to the Maroon Negroes* (London: n.p., 1796).
4. A long footnote by Edwards explains the part played by Bayly (his uncle).
5. Edwards was an eyewitness to these hangings; one slave died on the eighth day, the other on the ninth.

RICHARD FULLER

"An Account of *Obi*" (1789)[1]

This account was prepared by Richard Fuller, the agent of Jamaica, drawing substantially on information supplied by Edward Long. Discovery of the involvement of obeah-men in the 1760 rebellion awakened colonial administrators to the subversive powers of the practice.

The term *Obeah*, *Obiah*, or *Obia* (for it is variously written), we conceive to be the adjective, and *Obe* or *Obi* the noun substantive; and that by the words *Obia*-men or women, are meant those who practise *Obi* . . . [Obeah] is now become in Jamaica the general term to denote those Africans who in that island practise witchcraft or sorcery, comprehending also the class of what are called Myal-men, or those who, by means of a narcotick potion, made with the juice of an herb (said to be the branched *Calalue* or species of *Solanum*) which occasions a trance or profound sleep of a certain duration, endeavour to convince the deluded spectator of their power to re-animate dead bodies.

As far as we are able to decide from our own experience and information when we lived in the island, and from the current testimony of all the Negroes we have ever conversed with on the subject, the professors of *Obi* are, and always were, natives of Africa, and none other; and they have brought the science with them from thence to Jamaica, where it is so universally practised, that we believe there are few of the large estates possessing native Africans, which have not one or more of them. The oldest and most crafty are those who usually attract the greatest devotion and confidence; those whose hoary heads, and a somewhat peculiarly harsh and forbidding in their aspect, together with some skill in plants of the medicinal and poisonous species, have qualified them for successful imposition upon the weak and credulous. The Negroes in general, whether Africans or Creoles, revere, consult, and fear them; to these oracles they resort, and with the most implicit faith, upon all occasions, whether for the cure of disorders, the obtaining revenge for injuries or insults, the conciliating of favour, the discovery and punishment of the thief or the adulterer, and the prediction of future events. The trade which these impostors carry on is extremely lucrative; they manufacture and sell their *Obies* adapted to different cases and at different prices. A veil of mystery is studiously thrown over their incantations, to which the midnight hours are allotted, and every precaution is taken to conceal them from the knowledge and discovery of the White people. The deluded Negroes, who thoroughly believe in their supernatural power, become the willing accomplices in this concealment, and the stoutest among them tremble at the very sight of the ragged bundle, the bottle or the egg-shells, which are stuck in the thatch or hung over the door of a hut, or upon the branch of a plantain tree, to deter marauders. In cases of poison, the natural effects of it are by the ignorant Negroes, ascribed entirely to the potent workings of *Obi*. The wiser Negroes hesitate to reveal their suspicions, through a dread of incurring the terrible vengeance which is fulminated by the *Obeah-men* against any who should betray them; it is very difficult therefore for the White proprietor to distinguish the *Obeah professor* from any other Negro upon his plantation; and so infatuated are the Blacks in general, that but few instances occur of their having assumed courage enough to impeach these miscreants. With minds so firmly prepossessed, they no sooner find *Obi set for them* near the door of their house, or in the path which leads to it, than they give themselves up for lost. When a Negro is robbed of a fowl or a hog, he applies directly to the *Obeah* man or woman; it is then made known among his fellow Blacks, that *Obi is set* for the thief; and as soon as the latter hears the dreadful news, his terrified imagination begins to work, no resource is left but in the superior skill of some more eminent *Obeah-man* of the neighbourhood, who may counter-act the magical operations of the other; but if no one can be found of higher rank and ability, or if after gaining such an ally he should still fancy himself affected, he presently falls into a decline, under the incessant horror of impending calamities. The slightest painful sensation in the head, the bowels, or any other part, any casual loss or hurt, confirms his apprehensions, and he believes himself the devoted victim of an invisible and irresistible agency. Sleep, appetite, and cheerfulness forsake him, his strength decays, his disturbed imagination is haunted without respite, his features wear the settled gloom of despondency: dirt, or any other unwholesome substance, become his only food, he contracts a morbid habit of body, and gradually sinks into the grave. A Negro, who is taken ill, enquires of the *Obeah-man* the cause of his sickness, whether it will prove mortal or not, and within what time he shall die or recover? The oracle generally ascribes the distemper to the malice of some particular person by name, and advises to set *Obi* for that person; but if no hopes are given of recovery, immediate despair takes place, which no medicine can remove, and death is the certain consequence. Those anomalous symptoms, which originate from causes deeply rooted in the mind, such as the terrors of *Obi*, or from poisons, whose operation is slow and intricate, will baffle the skill of the ablest physician.

Considering the multitude of occasions which may provoke the negroes to exercise the powers of *Obi* against each other, and the astonishing influence of this superstition upon their minds, we cannot but attribute a very considerable portion of the annual mortality among the Negroes of Jamaica to this fascinating mischief.

The *Obi* is usually composed of a farrago of materials, most of which are enumerated in the Jamaica law,[2] viz. "Blood, feathers, parrot's beaks, dog's teeth, alligator's teeth, broken bottles, grave-dirt, rum, and egg-shells."

[These practices were for a long time regarded by the whites as harmless to their own interests and safety.]

But in the year 1760, when a very formidable insurrection of the Koromantyn or Gold Coast Negroes broke out in the parish of St. Mary, and spread through almost every other district of the island, an old Koromantyn Negro, the chief instigator and oracle of the insurgents in that parish, who had administered the Fetish or solemn oath to the conspirators, and furnished them with a magical preparation which was to render them invulnerable, was fortunately apprehended, convicted, and hung up with all his feathers and trumperies about him; and his execution struck the insurgents with a general panic, from which they never after recovered. The examinations which were taken at that period first opened the eyes of the public to the very dangerous tendency of the *Obeah* practices, and gave birth to the law which was then enacted for their suppression and punishment. But neither the terror of this law, the strict investigation which has ever since been made after the professors of *Obi*, nor the many examples of those who from time to time have been hanged or transported, have hitherto produced the desired effect. We conclude, therefore, that either this sect, like others in the world, has flourished under persecution; or that fresh supplies are annually introduced from the African seminaries.

[A supplementary paper titled "Obeah Trials" quotes from "another Jamaica gentleman"[3] who had been present at the trial of the Koromantyn obeah-man referred to; he gives a similar account of the man but adds a sequel.]

At the place of execution, he bid defiance to the executioner, telling him, that "It was not in the power of the White people to kill him." And the Negroes (spectators) were greatly perplexed when they saw him expire. Upon other *Obeah-men*, who were apprehended at that time, various experiments were made with electrical machines and magic lanterns, but with very little effect, except on one, who, after receiving some very severe shocks, acknowledged that "his master's *Obi* exceeded his own."

Notes

1. Richard Fuller, "Account of *Obi*, attached to the report of the Lords of the Committee of Privy Council on the slave trade", *House of Commons Sessional Papers* (London, 1789). Reprinted in Edwards, *History, Civil and Commercial*, 2:88–99.

2. Act 24, section 10, passed 13 December 1760 by the Assembly of Jamaica. Penalties for practising obeah were severe: "Slaves detected in the practice of Obeah, and being convicted thereof to suffer death or transportation"; *Abridgement of the Laws of Jamaica* (Kingston, Jamaica, 1786).

3. Mr Chisholme, according to the *Sessional Papers*.

THOMAS ATWOOD (D. 1793)

The History of the Island of Dominica (1791)[1]

Atwood spent several years in Dominica, during which he was chief justice of the island. He defended the slave system against the abolitionists and held a low opinion of the character and abilities of the enslaved, Africans and creoles alike.

Of the negro slaves of this island, their rebellion and reduction.

The negros in Dominica, under the description of slaves, are between fifteen and sixteen thousand; but not more than half of that number belongs to the English inhabitants, whose plantations in particular are but thinly furnished with them. This is owing to a variety of causes; and among others, to the rather imprudent conduct of some of the first English settlers, after the country was ceded to Great Britain.[2]

Many of them brought negros who had only been in the capacity of domestics; some, those that were banished from other islands for their crimes, and others purchased negros just brought from Africa, for the purpose of settling their new estates. These were immediately set to work, to cut down massy, hard wood trees, to lop and burn the branches, clear the ground of the roots, and to labour at difficult, though necessary business, for which they were by no means qualified.

The consequences of these great mistakes soon after appeared, for the domestic and new negros labouring in such work as they were not used to, in a climate, which, from the abundance of its woods, was so unsettled, that it rained greatest part of the year; whilst they had only temporary huts covered with the branches and leaves of trees to shelter them in at night, and were subject to many inconveniences in the day-time; this very uncomfortable situation occasioned the death of numbers, and caused others to run away into the woods, where many of them perished.

The increase of runaway negros also owes its origin, in a great measure, to the impolitic conduct of some of the first English settlers: for, during the neutral state of this island, a number of French and Spaniards had settled themselves on the most fertile parts of the sea-coasts, and had raised to themselves very fine sugar and coffee estates. Among these were some Jesuits, who having sugar plantations on the south-east part of the island, they disposed of the same, together with the negros on them, to some of the English new settlers.

Many of the negros so purchased from the Jesuits, either from their attachment to them, or dislike to their new masters, soon after betook themselves to the woods with their wives and children, where they were joined, from time to time, by others from different estates. There they secreted themselves for a number of years, formed companies under different chiefs, built good houses, and planted gardens in the woods, where they raised poultry, hogs, and other small stock, which, with what the sea, rivers, and woods afforded, and what they got from the negros they had intercourse with on the plantation, they lived very comfortably, and were seldom disturbed in their haunts.

They were not, however, often guilty of any material mischief, and had never committed murder till the reduction of the island by the French;[3] but soon after that happened, the depredations of the runaways began to be of a more serious nature; for they robbed, and destroyed the property, and at length killed some of the English inhabitants . . . .

[After repossession of the island by the British, the Legislature issued proclamations "offering a pardon to all that would surrender themselves, except such as had been guilty of murder".]

To these proclamations the runaways paid no manner of attention; but on the contrary, they bid defiance to every measure, and had the audacity to threaten, they would repel any attempts to be made to reduce them. In consequence of this obstinacy of theirs, and their still continued acts of mischief on the plantations, an act of the colony was passed for raising a fund, to be applied to the purpose of forcing them into subjection . . . .

The next step taken by the Legislature for reducing the runaways to obedience was, to raise a body of colony legions, composed of white men, free people of colour, and able negro men belonging to the different plantations, for the purpose of sending them after the runaways into the woods. Three separate encampments, formed by these legions, were established near the haunts of the runaways, against whom operations were immediately commenced; but it was a long time before any material service could be effected against them; they, in the mean while, committing the most daring outrages on the plantations . . . .

The runaways fully acquainted with the measures taken against them, yet confiding in the strength of their numbers, and the difficult access to their camps in the woods, made no offer to surrender themselves; but rather seemed determined to abide by the consequences, and deriding the attempt of reducing them by force, threatened to do still greater mischiefs. They accordingly did as they had threatened, beginning their attack on the plantation of Thomas Osborn, Esq. coming there in the night, and doing considerable damage; in drawing off some rum by the light of their torches, it caught fire, which being communicated to the buildings on the estate, burnt them down to the ground.

Their next attack was soon after on a sugar plantation at Rosalie, belonging to the Lieutenant-governor and other persons in England. There they came also in the night-time, murdered Mr. Gamble, the manager, Mr. Armstrong, carpenter, Mr. Hatton, and Mr. Lile, the overseers, together with the chief negro driver belonging to the estate. Having glutted themselves with murdering these persons, after stripping them of their cloaths, they set fire round the bodies; doing the same to the sugar works, principal buildings, and canes; and committing other considerable damages, to the amount of several thousand pounds.

Elated with their success, and having satiated themselves for that time with murder, plunder, and devastation, they retired to the dwelling-house on the estate, where they regaled on the stock, provisions, and liquors they found in plenty, their chiefs being served in the silver vessels of the Lieutenant-governor, which, together with other valuable articles, to a great amount, they afterwards carried away with them. On this plantation they continued two days, riotting and revelling, blowing conk shells and huzzaing, as for a great victory, having taken the precaution to stop up the roads to the estate by felling large trees, and placing centinels to give them notice, in case of the approach of the legions . . . .

[The legions having proved ineffectual in combating these raids, the initiative was taken up by private individuals, notably John Richardson, a carpenter working at Rosalie estate, who attached himself to one of the legions and persuaded them to attack the camp of "a principal runaway chief" named Balla.]

Mr. Richardson having strengthened this party, with the addition of some trusty negro men of the estate, they set out one evening on their expedition, and having travelled all night through the woods, wading through rapid rivers, crossing over steep mountains, and encountering many difficulties in their way, by noon the next day they came to the mountain whereon was the encampment of Balla. This they ascended with great difficulty, it being cut into steps of a great height above each other, which had been done by the runaways for their own convenience, as being the only possible way to ascend the mountain.

These steps the party were obliged to go up, one after the other, and to have their muskets handed to them, the one on the upper, by him on the step below, till they were all ascended. Mr. Richardson was the first on the landing-place on the top of the mountain, where hiding himself among some bushes, he perceived the runaways going in and out of their houses, preparing their dinners, little expecting such troublesome guests. As soon as the whole of the party had joined him, they rushed on towards the houses, shouting and keeping up a brisk firing from their muskets on the runaways; who, in the greatest dismay and confusion, betook themselves to flight, throwing themselves down the steep sides of the mountain, in their hurry to get out of the way, by which it is probable that several of them were killed.

The party having thus taken possession of the runaway camp, immediately began to destroy it, by setting fire to the houses; but in searching them previous thereto, they found some women and children, among whom was a son of Balla's, who, with the rest, they took prisoners. Whilst searching the houses, the runaways on the opposite mountain, on which they had retired, having recovered a little from their fright, and probably discerning the small number of the party, made several attempts to return and recover their camp, keeping up a smart firing for some time, from the place they were on. But they were discouraged by a well-timed thought of Mr. Richardson's, who, as often as they seemed determined to return, called out the names of the different commanding officers of the legions to attack the runaways, "To the right or left," according to the side on which they kept firing from the opposite mountain. This had the desired effect, making them believe they were surrounded by the legions; the apprehensions of which caused the runaways to abandon the place with the same precipitation they had quitted their camp, leaving it in peaceable possession of the party.

The latter then had leisure to do their business, and to examine the rest of the houses, which they found well furnished with provisions, a vast quantities of cloaths, valuable articles of furniture, and several other things, which they had stolen from the different plantations. Such articles of value as they could carry the party took with them, after destroying such as the fire could not injure, and burning the houses, they descended with their prisoners, and returned home in safety, none of the party being hurt on the occasion.

This was a capital check to the runaways, and reflects great honour on Mr. Richardson; as by his means it was, in a great measure, that the runaways were at that time reduced. For after this action they dispersed, and were so much disheartened, that they never afterwards dared to assemble in any great numbers together; but flying from place to place in the woods, were either killed, taken, or surrendered themselves; and this noted chief, Balla, soon after fell into the hands of a party of the legions, by whom he was killed.

The runaway negros have since then, been seldom heard of in Dominica; for those that were there under another chief, named Farcel,[4] it is imagined have quitted the island, and have retired among the French settlements, or among the Carribbees at Saint Vincent's.

It is computed, that the number of them that were killed, taken, or that surrendered, during this contest, was about one hundred and fifty . . . .

The negro slaves in Dominica are, in general, comfortably situated, and well treated, especially on the plantations; where, if they are industrious, they have the means of living in a manner very different from that deplorable state, which some people in England have been at the pains to represent, as the case in general of slaves in the British islands. They have there as much land as they chuse to cultivate for their own use, are capable of raising great quantities of all manner of ground provisions, garden stuff, and other things, with which they actually supply the markets every Sunday, and some of them to a considerable amount.

They likewise breed hogs, rabbits, fowls, and other small stock for themselves; and many of them, who are careful in raising such provisions, acquire a very comfortable living, exclusive of what is allowed them by their owners. They have, moreover, many opportunities on the plantations to procure other things to sell, or make use of themselves, which are not to be had in many other islands, as plenty of fish in the rivers, crapaux, wild yams, and other articles in the woods; by which, those who are industrious in their leisure hours often make tolerable sums of money . . . .

Notes

1. Thomas Atwood, *The History of the Island of Dominica* (London: J. Johnson, 1791), 224–50.
2. Dominica was ceded to Britain in 1763 under the Treaty of Paris, which ended the Seven Years' War. It was first claimed by France in 1635 but, owing to determined resistance by the Caribs, attempts to colonize it were abandoned in 1660 and it remained officially neutral until 1763.
3. Dominica was occupied by the French from 1778 to 1783.
4. An authorial footnote reports unverified news, received from Dominica after going to press, "that the runaways, under the command of this chief [Farcel], having been joined by a number of other negro slaves, from different plantations of the French inhabitants, have again commenced depredations of a most serious nature in that island".

BENJAMIN MOSELEY (1742–1819)

"Three-fingered Jack" (1799)

Moseley lived in Jamaica from 1768 to 1784, practising as a surgeon-apothecary. His account of the life and death of the legendary Jamaican rebel known as Three-Fingered Jack was the source of a popular novel,[2] a pantomime (performed in 1800) and various chapbook versions circulating in the early nineteenth century. It appears from Jamaican newspaper reports of 1780–81 that Jack was initially the leader of a large gang of runaway Africans who formed a settlement in the Blue Mountains and sustained themselves by robbing travellers and raiding nearby estates. They were said to be "chiefly Congos, and declare they will kill every Mulatto and Creole Negro they can catch".[3] By the end of 1780, however, Jack was hiding out on his own.

I saw the *Obi*[4] of the famous negro robber, Three-fingered Jack, the terror of Jamaica in 1780. The Maroons who slew him brought it to me.[5]

His *Obi* consisted of the end of a goat's horn, filled with a compound of grave dirt, ashes, the blood of a black cat, and human fat; all mixed into a kind of paste. A cat's foot, a dried toad, a pig's tail, a slip of virginal parchment of kid's skin, with characters marked in blood on it, were also in his *Obian* bag.

These, with a keen sabre, and two guns, like *Robinson Crusoe*, were all his *Obi*; with which, and his courage in descending into the plains and plundering to supply his wants, and his skill in retreating into difficult fastnesses, among the mountains, commanding the only access to them, where none dared to follow him, he terrified the inhabitants, and set the civil power, and the neighbouring militia of that island, at defiance, for nearly two years.

He had neither accomplice, nor associate.[6] There were a few runaway negroes in the woods near Mount Lebanus, the place of his retreat; but he had crossed their foreheads with some of the magic in his horn, and they could not betray him. But he trusted no one. He scorned assistance. He ascended above Spartacus. He robbed alone; fought all his battles alone; and always killed his pursuers.

By his magic, he was not only the dread of the negroes, but there were many white people, who believed he was possessed of some supernatural power.

In hot climates females marry very young; and often with great disparity of age. Here Jack was the author of many troubles: – for several matches proved unhappy.

"Give a dog an ill name, and hang him."

Clamours rose on clamours against the cruel sorcerer; and every conjugal mishap was laid at the door of Jack's malific spell of *tying the point*, on the wedding day.

God knows, poor Jack had sins enough of his own to carry, without loading him with the sins of others. He would sooner have made a Medean cauldron for the whole island, than disturb one lady's happiness. He had many opportunities; and though he had a mortal hatred to white men, he was never known to hurt a child, or abuse a woman.

But even Jack himself was born to die.

Allured by the rewards offered by Governor Dalling, in proclamations, dated the 12th of December, 1780, and 13th of January 1781;[7] and by a resolution of the House of Assembly,[8] which followed the first proclamation; two negroes, named Quashee, and Sam (Sam was Captain Davy's son, he who shot a Mr. Thompson, the master of a London ship, at Old Harbour), both of *Scots Hall* Maroon Town, with a party of their townsmen, went in search of him.

Quashee, before he set out on the expedition, got himself christianised, and changed his name to James Reeder.

The expedition commenced; and the whole party had been creeping about in the woods, for three weeks, and blockading, as it were, the deepest recesses of the most inaccessible part of the island, where Jack, far remote from all human society, resided, – but in vain.

Reeder and Sam, tired with this mode of war, resolved on proceeding in search of his retreat, and taking him by storming it, or perishing in the attempt.

They took with them a little boy, a proper spirit, and a good shot, and left the rest of the party.

These three, whom I well knew, had not been long separated from their companions, before their cunning eyes discovered, by impressions among the weeds and bushes, that some person must have lately been that way.

They softly followed these impressions, making not the least noise. Presently they discovered a smoke.

They prepared for war. They came upon Jack before he perceived them. He was roasting *plantains*, by a little fire on the ground, at the mouth of a cave.

This was a scene: – not where ordinary actors had a common part to play.

Jack's looks were fierce and terrible. he told them he would kill them.

Reeder, instead of shooting Jack, replied, that his *Obi* had no power to hurt him; for he was christianised; and that his name was no longer Quashee.

Jack knew Reeder; and, as if paralysed, he let his two guns remain on the ground, and took up only his cutlass.

These two had a severe engagement several years before, in the woods; in which conflict Jack lost the two fingers, which was the origin of his present name; but Jack then beat Reeder, and almost killed him, with several others who assisted him, and they fled from Jack.

To do Three-fingered Jack justice, he would now have killed both Reeder and Sam; for, at first, they were frightened at the sight of him, and the dreadful tone of his voice, and well they might: they had besides no retreat, and were to grapple with the bravest, and strongest man in the world.

But Jack was cowed; for, he had prophesied, that *white Obi* would get the better of him; and, from experience, he knew the charm would lose none of its strength in the hands of Reeder.

Without further parley, Jack, with his cutlass in his hand, threw himself down a precipice at the back of the cave.

Reeder's gun missed fire. Sam shot him in the shoulder. Reeder, like an English bull-dog, never looked, but, with his cutlass in his hand, plunged headlong down after Jack. The descent was about thirty yards, and almost perpendicular. Both of them had preserved their cutlasses in the fall.

Here was the stage, – on which two of the stoutest hearts, that were ever hooped with ribs, began their bloody struggle.

The little boy, who was ordered to keep back, out of harm's way, now reached the top of the precipice, and, during the fight, shot Jack in the belly.

Sam was crafty, and cooly took a roundabout way to get to the field of action. When he arrived at the spot where it began, Jack and Reeder had closed, and tumbled together down another precipice, on the side of the mountain, in which fall they both lost their weapons.

Sam descended after them, who also lost his cutlass, among the trees and bushes in getting down.

When he came to them, though without weapons, they were not idle; and, luckily for Reeder, Jack's wounds were deep and desperate, and he was in great agony.

Sam came up just time enough to save Reeder; for, Jack had caught him by the throat, with his giant's grasp. Reeder then was with his right hand almost cut off, and Jack streaming with blood from his shoulder and belly; both covered with gores and gashes.

In this state Sam was umpire; and decided the fate of the battle. He knocked Jack down with a piece of a rock.

When the lion fell, the two tigers got upon him, and beat his brains out with stones.

The little boy soon after found his way to them. He had a cutlass, with which they cut off Jack's head, and THREE-FINGERED HAND, and took them in triumph to Morant Bay.

There they put their trophies into a pail of rum; and, followed by a vast concourse of negroes, now no longer afraid of Jack's *Obi*, blowing their shells and horns, and firing guns in their rude method, they carried them to Kingston, and Spanish Town; and claimed the rewards offered by the King's Proclamation, and the House of Assembly.

Notes

1. Benjamin Moseley, "Three-fingered Jack", in *A Treatise on Sugar. With Miscellaneous Medical Observations*, 2nd ed. (London: G.G. and J. Robinson, 1800), 197–205.
2. Walter Earle, *Obi: or, The History of Three-Fingered Jack* (London: Earle and Hernet, 1800).
3. Srinivas Aravamudan, ed., *Obi: or, The History of Three-Fingered Jack* (Peterborough, ON: Broadview, 2005), 10–15.
4. Moseley's story of Jack is preceded by an account of "The science of Obi", 190–97; see Aravamudan, *Obi*, 162–64.
5. [Author's note:] He was slain on Saturday 27th of January, 1781.
6. This statement conflicts with newspaper reports and the official proclamation referred to in note 7 below.
7. The text of the second proclamation is printed in full as a footnote in *A Treatise on Sugar*. A reward of £300 was offered for "apprehending, or bringing in the head of that daring Rebel, called 'Three-fingered Jack' ". He is described as leading "a very desperate gang of Negro Slaves" which "hath for many months past, committed many robberies, and carried off many Negro and other Slaves . . . and hath also committed several murders". Smaller rewards were offered for the capture of any member of his gang.
8. The resolution is printed in another footnote. Dated 29 December 1780, it promised freedom to any slave who captured or killed the rebel, also a pardon and freedom to "any one of his accomplices" who would "kill the said Three-fingered Jack, and bring in his head, and hand wanting the fingers".

REPORT FROM A SELECT COMMITTEE OF THE HOUSE OF ASSEMBLY, APPOINTED TO INQUIRE INTO THE ORIGIN, CAUSES, AND PROGRESS OF THE LATE INSURRECTION (1818)

It is clear from this account of the rising in Barbados in 1816, popularly known as "Bussa's Rebellion", that the main concern of the Committee was to absolve plantation owners and the Barbadian legislature from blame, whether for maltreatment of the slaves or for other reasons. The underlying causes, it concluded, were rumours that had reached slaves in Barbados from England of the exertions of Wilberforce and his supporters "to ameliorate their condition, and ultimately effect their emancipation"; these, together with news of the introduction of the slave registry bill in 1815, had given rise among slaves to "the mistaken idea that the Registry Bill was actually their Manumission". The immediate cause of the insurrection was found to be the deferment of that hope until "the Slaves were led to attempt that by force which they had vainly expected as an original gift from England." Statements taken from white estate managers, overseers, doctors, officers at the courts martial and rectors of the parishes involved, and from a few "free People of Colour", are transcribed in an appendix. Although the Committee lamented the scarcity of direct evidence from insurgents themselves, owing to the "unavoidable destruction" of some of the leaders during the revolt and "the subsequent execution of others", confessions or depositions taken from prisoners were also transcribed.[2]

It appears to your Committee, that on the fourteenth of April eighteen six-
teen, an Insurrection commenced amongst the Negroes in the Parish of
St. Philip, which extended itself, during the course of that night and the
following days, into the adjoining Parishes of Christ Church, St. John, and
St. George. That the first check was put to the progress of the Insurgents on
the Monday forenoon, in the Parish of Christ Church; and that the
Insurrection was almost entirely suppressed by the night of the following
Tuesday.

That, during this period of anarchy and confusion, nearly the whole of
the four largest and most valuable Parishes exposed to the ravages of the
Insurgents – the canes upon one-fifth of the Estates of the Island burnt – the
dwelling-houses and buildings upon a great number broken open or
destroyed – the white Inhabitants (many of whom escaped with difficulty)
either compelled to seek their safety in flight, and leave their properties a
prey to these infuriated ravagers, or condemned to be the witnesses of their
destruction – and the loss of property to the amount of One Hundred and
Seventy Thousand Pounds, – were the immediate effects of an Insurrection,
which has deprived the Colony of nearly four hundred of its finest Slaves,
and in its ulterior consequences has brought an heavy expense upon its
Inhabitants, and given a rude shock to the whole system of British
Colonization in the West Indies.

[No further comments appear in the report on the actions of the
army and militia, or the executions and deportments which led to
the colony being "deprived" of large numbers of its finest slaves.]

Appendix

(A)   *The Examination of* DANIEL, *a Slave belonging to the Plantation called*
     "The River."

This Examinant saith, That he is a Carpenter on *The River* Plantation. That,
about three weeks before the Insurrection, he was in his house on the above
Estate, about six in the evening, when Cain Davis (a free coloured man)
called out, and enquired if he was in the house? whereupon he went out to

him in the broad road. That, when Examinant went out to him, he (Cain Davis) asked him if he had heard the good news? – upon which Examinant answered, that he had not. That Cain Davis then said, that the Negroes were all to be free – that the Queen and Mr. Wilberforce had sent out to have them all freed, but that the Inhabitants of the Island were against it; – that he had been at *Cox-hall*, and had seen it in the Newspapers; and that it was a great shame that they were not all freed, and that they must fight for it: that he (Cain Davis) was ready to do so with them, as he had some children who were slaves: and that he had a corn-stalk heap at his house, and that he would set it on fire as a signal to them to begin. Examinant further saith, that after this he returned into his house, and shortly after, in an adjoining house, he heard Sarjeant (another free coloured man) call to him; that presently Sarjeant came into his house, and told him he had seen Cain Davis that afternoon; that both of them had been at *Cox-hall*, and had been reading the Newspapers, by which they found that the Negroes were all to be free. Examinant further saith, that after this he heard nothing more on the subject; nor did he see Cain Davis, or Sarjeant, until Good Friday night, – when he saw them at a dance, at *The River*, where Busso (belonging to *Bayley's* Estate) also was. That Busso, Davis, and Sarjeant, conversed together aside, but Examinant had no conversation, or heard any thing that night respecting the circumstances above stated. Examinant further saith, that when he saw the fires on Easter night, he concluded that what Davis had told him was right. Examinant saith, that he was very well treated by those who had charge of the Estate: that he does not think the Insurrection was occasioned from ill-treatment to the slaves, but was owing to the reports which were about, that the negroes were to be freed; that he himself has always been kindly treated; and, particularly, had been suffered twice, for some weeks each time, to go to sea in Messrs. Wason & Cobham's schooner, for his health.

(B)   *The Examination of* KING WILTSHIRE, *a Slave belonging to the Plantation called* "Bayley's".

This Examinant saith, That just before Christmas, eighteen hundred and fifteen, there was a report that the negroes were to be freed, and that their freedom was to be given them through a black woman who was a Queen, for whom Mr. Wilberforce acted in England: that some free coloured men, namely, Cain Davis, Roach, and Sarjeant, had told him this. That Examinant had never heard of any other reason. That he does not think that the slaves rose on account of ill-treatment – of any want of food – or not having been well taken care of; but that he believes the opinion amongst the negroes (generally) was, that they were to be freed. – And Examinant further saith, That Cain Davis told him, that he had seen in the English Newspapers, that the negroes were to be manumitted through the means aforesaid, but that it appeared that the Gentlemen of this Island wished to withhold their Manumissions; and that therefore they must fight for it, if they did not have their freedom by Christmas.

(C)   *The Examination of* CUFFEE NED, *a Slave belonging to* "Three Houses" *Plantation.*

This Examinant saith, That long before Easter, there was an opinion generally entertained amongst the slaves, that they were to be set free through the means of people in England. That, previous to the Insurrection, he had heard several negroes say, they had heard it read in the Papers that they were to be free: that a slave by the name Davy, at *Palmer's*, was one whom he had heard say so. – That a man named Sampson (Mr. Brathwaite's butler) came home from town on the Saturday evening previous to the Insurrection, and said to the negroes, "Well, this day's Newspaper has done our business, – for the Packet has arrived, and brought our freedom."

This Examinant further saith, That he was told that the negroes had been freed in some of the Islands, and that they were to be freed in all the West Indies, and that in one they had fought for it and got it. And, upon being asked if he should recollect the name of the Island if he heard it? and having answered in the affirmative, several Islands were named; but when Saint Domingo was named, he said "that was the Island – he knew it by the name of *Mingo*." Further saith, that the negroes did not revolt from any ill-treatment or want of food; and that, before the report that the negroes had been freed in England, they were very quiet, and never thought of obtaining their freedom.

(D)   *The Confession of* ROBERT, *a Slave belonging to the Plantation called* "Simmons'":

Who saith, that some time the last year, he heard the negroes were all to be freed on New-year's Day. That Nanny Grig (a negro woman at *Simmons'*, who said she could read) was the first person who told the negroes at *Simmons'* so: and she said she had read it in the Newspapers, and that her Master was very uneasy at it: that she was always talking about it to the negroes, and told them that they were all damned fools to work, for that she would not, as freedom they were sure to get. That, about a fortnight after New-year's Day, she said the negroes were to be freed on Easter-Monday, and the only way to get it was to fight for it, otherwise they would not get it; and the way they were to do, was to set fire, as that was the way they did in Saint Domingo. Further saith, that Jackey, the Driver at *Simmons'*, said he would send to the other Drivers and Rangers,[3] and to the head Carters about, and to Bussoe (at *Bayley's*), to turn out on Easter Monday to give the Country a light, and let every body know what it was for: and that John (at *Simmons'*) was the person who carried the summons from Jackey: that Jackey was one of the head men of the Insurrection, and that he had heard him say that he was going to point out a good great house to live in, but he did not say which: that Jackey sent also to a free man in *The Thicket* (who could read and write), to let the negroes at *The Thicket* know, that they might give their assistance. That he does not recollect the man's name, but if he saw him, he should know him: that he lives about *The River* Estate, and was at *Simmons'*, with Jackey, two Sundays before Easter. – Further saith, that Mingo, at *Byde-Mill* (the Ranger), came to *Simmons'* on Sunday before Easter: that he saw him go to Jackey's house; and that, in passing the said Jackey's house, he heard Mingo say, that on Sunday night next they were to turn out and give the Country a light, and the Country would be as sure to him as the coat on his back. That he heard Jackey say, that Washington Francklin was to be Governor, and to live at *Pilgrim*. Jackey used to go very often (sometimes at night) to see Washington Francklin: that he has heard Jackey tell Will Nightingale (who was Jackey's brother-in-law, and belongs to Mrs. Nightingale), to go to Washington Francklin, and he would tell him what was to be done. That the reason he came to hear these things, was, because Jackey's children were fond of him, and he was in the habit of going to Jackey's house and playing with his children, when the conversations mentioned passed. – He further saith, that on Easter Day, Jackey (at *Simmons'*) told Mingo to go about and pick up all the men, and muster them up at his house, and he would tell them what to do. That Mingo accordingly mustered up the men, and gave all names, and told them they were to meet Judge Gittens' men below his garden. That in the evening, when the whip snapped, all *Simmons'* people came out to know what it snapped for; and after they came as far as the water-mill, Jackey told them what it was for. That Jackey, Mingo, and John Baynes, went towards Judge Gittens', and shortly afterwards two fields of canes in that direction were set on fire. – He further saith, that King William (of *Sunberry*) came to *Simmons'* Estate on Monday forenoon (with a red coat and gun) with a gang, and said, "I see nothing in the Manager's house – you, *Simmons'* people must have taken every thing out; if you had not, we would not trouble the buildings": and then gave orders to break up and burn; and gave orders to William Green, of *Congo Road*, to set fire to the trash heap. That Prince William, of *The Grove* (Mr. Hunt's), came also on Monday forenoon, on horseback, with the gang, with a sword in his hand, holding it upright over the horse's head, and gave orders to lick down the sick-house, and also to burn the field of canes above the sick-house; and rode about the yard, and ordered the mill to be put in the wind. That Toby, of *The Chapel*, came with a gun in his hand, and gave orders to shoot every one that did not join them, and marched about the yard with a gun on his shoulder. That Little Sambo, belonging to *The Adventure*, came with the gang to *Simmons'*, armed with a sword, and began to lick down the old mill door, in which they kept the provisions. That Jack, belonging to Mr. Doughty, had a sword and a long knife in his hands, and came up to him (Robert) and said, "I will chop you down if you do not join us." – That Thomas, from *Congo Road*, came with the gang of rebels on Monday forenoon, and was the first that began to chop at the boiling-house door, with a hatchet; and ordered Mingo (belonging to *Congo Road*) to take charge of a box of carpenters' tools which was in the boiling-house. That a man called Charles, belonging to *Sandford's*, was on horseback with the gang, and rode about the yard giving orders. That Thomas, belonging to Mr. Carter, came armed with a sword, and was the first to lick down the door of the sick-house.

(Q)   *The Examination of* JOSEPH GITTENS, Esq.

[Gittens was the manager of Padmore's plantation, in the parish of
St Philip. Estate managers and overseers were asked five set questions, the two main ones, questions 3 and 5, concerning the living
and working conditions of the slaves, and the testifier's opinion as
to the motives and causes of the insurrection. The striking similarities between their accounts of conditions arise because the managers were, in effect, simply claiming exact adherence to the rules
for housing, food, clothing, working hours and punishments laid
down in the Slave Laws.]

Ans. to Q. 3. – The slaves were in most respects as comfortably situated, and
in general as healthy, as most in the Island. They had not only as much food
as was fully sufficient to sustain their health and strength, but very often
could spare some to sell: – it consisted of grain and roots of different sorts,
molasses and rum (in proportion to their labour); with salt, and salted cod-
fish, or other salt provisions. For clothing, they had pennistone, osnaburgs,[4]
checks, caps, and handkerchiefs. – The period during which they were kept
at work, I consider, never exceeded nine hours in the twelve; and I was in the
frequent habit of giving them a day, or a half-day. They had as good and
warm houses as the negroes on most Estates; and, when sick, were sent to
the hospital, where the Plantation Apothecary attended them with every
care. When punishment was necessary, moderate chastisement, or solitary
confinement, were the measures I adopted for that purpose; – and I can
assert, without the fear of contradiction, that I never practised unnecessary
rigour or severity.

    Ans. to Q. 5. – Long before the Insurrection, it appeared to me that the
slaves were inclined to presume upon and to abuse the great indulgences
granted them by Proprietors and Overseers, – such as, permitting them to
have dances (frequently) on Saturday and Sunday evenings – easing their
labour by the use of every species of machinery which could have that effect
– suffering them to become comparatively rich, by rearing and selling poultry, sheep, goats, hogs, and their superfluous allowance of corn and roots, –
all of which induced them to assume airs of consequence, and put a value

on themselves unknown amongst slaves of former periods. Their minds being, as I conceive, thus prepared for any act of insubordination, towards the end of the year 1815, evil-disposed and designing persons got amongst them, and taught them to believe that the Registry Bill was an Act of the Government at home to set them free; that their freedom was, in contempt of the King's or Prince Regent's orders, withheld from them by their Owners; and that, therefore, the only way to obtain it was by force of arms. These motives and causes (as far as I am able to judge), I think, led to the Insurrection.

(S)   *The Examination of* JOSEPH CONNEL, *Esq.* [Connel was manager of The Thicket plantation, in the parish of St Philip.]

Ans. to Q. 3. – The slaves on the above Plantation appeared, at the time I entered on the business, and up to the time of the Insurrection, to be perfectly contented and happy. They had an ample meal dressed for them every day at noon, exclusive of 1½ pint of Guinea[5] or 2½ pints of Indian corn, or 4½ lbs. of yams or potatoes per day; – ginger tea was served to them every morning, at the time they were collected in the yard previous to going to work, which was about six o'clock; – one pound of salted or pickled fish, half a pint of salt, and one and a half pint of molasses per week; besides many extra indulgences, such as peas, plantains, &c.; – they also had, on Festivals, pork or beef, and sometimes flour. – For clothing, they had an annual allowance of pennistone, osnaburgs, hats, caps, and handkerchiefs. The children were clothed in proportion, agreeably to their size, and they all appeared, generally, clean and well dressed. Their hours of labour were from six o'clock in the morning until nine, when they had half an hour given them for breakfast-time; again from half-past nine until one, when they came home and received their dinner, with something to drink, and had one and a half hour's suspension from labour; and from half-past two until six in the evening, when they were dismissed to their houses. They also had, about once a month, and sometimes oftener, a day or half a day, as the business of the Plantation would allow. – When correction was necessary (which was very seldom), they were flogged with rods; and if the crime was of any magnitude, they were confined in a solitary room, until they were made sensible of their error.

(T)   *The Examination of* THOMAS STOUTE, *Esq.* [Stoute was manager
on Mapp's plantation, in the parish of St Philip.]

Ans. to Q. 5. – I conceive, as far as I am able to judge, that the Insurrection
was produced by the negroes (in the first instance) abusing those indulgences which, for many years past, Owners of Slaves in this Island had been
in the habit of granting them, such as having constant parties and dances on
Saturday and Sunday evenings (at which they were most gaily attired); their
food increased; whilst their labour was diminished; and their general condition considerably ameliorated, compared to what it was thirty or forty years
before. All this naturally, I conceive, tends to give them more exalted ideas
of their own value and consequence; and as they considered themselves
advancing more to his level, lessen that of the Master in their eyes: and it
may be that many attributed this alteration on the part of their Owners, to
motives of apprehension, rather than to a spontaneous and philanthropic
desire to better their condition, and make the burden of slavery sit on them
as light as possible. In this state of feeling, the Registry Bill which was introduced into the House of Commons, was pointed out to them by evil-
minded and mischievous persons, as a measure intended by the
Government at home to emancipate them. It was industriously reported to
them, that the King had purchased them for the purpose of emancipating
them, and that their Owners, in defiance of such authority, withheld their
freedom from them, and that they could only obtain it by force. Such appear
to me, to the best of my judgment, to be the causes, immediate and remote,
which led to the Rebellion.

(W)   *The Examination (upon Oath) of* LEWIS YOUNG, *of the Parish of St.
Philip, Practitioner of Physic and Surgery.*

[Young testified that he had "practised for thirty years, as an
Apothecary" in St Philip.]

The situation of the slaves, at the period of the Insurrection on the 14th of
April, 1816, was of such a nature, that many of the poor white inhabitants of
the Parish, as I know from ocular demonstration, and from their own
acknowledgments, would have rejoiced to have enjoyed only a part of their

comforts; and with regard to the care and attention which they previously received from their Owners and Overseers, according to my observations, it was dictated by principles of lenity and kindness; and the slaves, previous to a report of freedom which was spread amongst them in 1815, appeared happy in and content with their situations. – With respect to their treatment in the time of sickness, I invariably recommended every thing that was necessary, and always observed that my directions were duly complied with; and, in extreme illness, so anxious were the Owners and Overseers for their recovery, that white servants were employed to administer the medicines, and to see that the nurses did their duty: – in fact, the Overseers and Apothecaries, independent of their humane feelings towards their fellow-creatures, were obliged, from a regard to their own interest, to endeavour to prolong the lives of the slaves, and to keep them in health, because, if they did not, the Owners or their Representatives would have dismissed the Overseers and Apothecaries from their respective employments . . . .

As to the causes which produced the Insurrection, I am of opinion that it was partly owing to the increased wealth and means of information of the slaves, who, from their manual labour having been materially lessened within the last few years, by the employment of horned cattle, carts, and ploughs, to perform the most laborious parts of the business, and from the great efforts made by Owners and Overseers, not only to keep them in health, but to make them comfortable, – granting them many indulgences – suffering them to keep cattle, and some even horses – to have large dwelling-houses – great and frequent entertainments, with dancing, costly apparel, trinkets, &c. – had become more impatient of restraint; but principally to a mistaken notion that the Registry Bill, mentioned in 1815, contained their Manumissions, sent them by the King, but which were withheld from them by their Owners. I do most solemnly avow, that soon after I heard of the Registry Bill, I discovered dissatisfaction, and experienced great disobedience in my own slaves (who were ever before humble and obedient), and they caused me, from their ill-behaviour, to endeavour to remonstrate and point out to them the meaning of the Bill; but only one, out of twenty-four adults, appeared to believe what I was saying.

Notes

1. *The Report from a Select Committee of the House of Assembly, appointed to inquire into the origin, causes, and progress of the late insurrection* (Barbados: by order of the Legislature, 1818), 3–4; appendix, 26–55.

2. For an extended account of the rebellion, see Michael Craton, *Testing the Chains: Resistance to Slavery in the British West Indies* (Ithaca: Cornell University Press, 1982), 254–66.

3. *Rangers*: slaves with special responsibility for looking after boundaries and conducting business between estates.

4. *pennistone*: coarse woollen cloth; *osnaburgs*: trousers made of coarse linen.

5. *Guinea*: cornflour.

MATTHEW GREGORY LEWIS (1775–1818)

Journal of a West India Proprietor (1834)[1]

Three months after Lewis's arrival at his Cornwall estate in 1816, a conspiracy to rebel was discovered in the neighbouring parish of St Elizabeth, but the ringleaders were caught and the plot was foiled. Lewis's own estate was not involved in the conspiracy, but because of his relatively liberal views and lenient treatment of his slaves he found himself caught up in local rumours and suspicions.

March 15.[1]

On opening the Assize-court for the county of Cornwall on March 4, Mr. Stewart, the Custos of Trelawny, and Presiding Judge, said in his charge to the jury, he wished to direct their attention in a peculiar manner to the infringement of slave-laws in the island. . . . Many out of the country, and *some in it*, had thought proper to interfere with our system, and by their insidious practices and dangerous doctrines to call the peace of the island in question, and to promote disorder and confusion. . . . I read all this with the most perfect unconsciousness; when, lo, and behold! I have been assured from a variety of quarters, that all this was levelled at myself! It is I (it seems) who am "calling the peace;" who am "promoting disorder and confusion;" who am "infringing the established laws!" By "insidious practices"

is meant (as I am told) my over-indulgence to my negroes; and my endeavouring to obtain either redress or pardon for those belonging to other
estates, who occasionally appeal to me for protection: while "dangerous
doctrines" alludes to my being of opinion, that the evidence of negroes
ought at least to be *heard* against white persons. . . .

March 16 [referring to the adultery of a slave].[2]

It is only to be wished, that the negroes would content themselves with
these fashionable peccadilloes; but unluckily there are some palates among
them which require higher seasoned vices; . . . a plan has just been discovered in the adjoining parish of St. Elizabeth's, for giving themselves a grand
fête by murdering all the whites in the island. The focus of this meditated
insurrection was on Martin's Penn.

March 22.[3]

Mr. Plummer came over from St. James's today, and told me, that the "insidious practices and dangerous doctrines" in Mr. Stewart's speech were
intended for the Methodists, and that only the charge to the grand jury
respecting "additional vigilance" was in allusion to myself; but he added that
it was the report at Montego Bay, that, in consequence of my over-indulgence to my negroes, a song had been made at Cornwall, declaring that I
was come over to set them all free, and that this was now circulating
through the neighbouring parishes. If there be any such song (which I do
not believe), I certainly never heard it. However, my agent here says, that he
has reason to believe that my negroes really have spread the report that I
intend to set *them* free in a few years; and this merely out of vanity, in order
to give themselves and their master greater credit upon other estates. . . .

The two ringleaders of the proposed rebellion have been condemned at
Black River, the one to be hanged, the other to transportation. The plot was
discovered by the overseer of Lyndhurst Penn (a Frenchman from St.
Domingo) observing an uncommon concourse of stranger negroes to a
child's funeral, on which occasion a hog was roasted by the father. He stole

softly down to the feasting hut, and listened behind a hedge to the conversation of the supposed mourners; when he heard the whole conspiracy detailed. It appears that above two hundred and fifty had been sworn in regularly, all of them Africans; not a Creole was among them. But there was a *black* ascertained to have stolen over into the island from St. Domingo, and a *brown* Anabaptist missionary, both of whom had been very active in promoting the plot.[4] They had elected a King of the Eboes, who had two Captains under him; and their intention was to effect a complete massacre of all the whites on the island; for which laudable design His Majesty thought Christmas the very fittest season in the year, but his Captains were more impatient, and were for striking the blow immediately. The next morning information was given against them: one of the Captains escaped to the woods; but the other, and the King of the Eboes, were seized and brought to justice. On their trial they were perfectly cool and unconcerned, and did not even profess to deny the facts with which they were charged. Indeed, proofs were too strong to admit of denial; among others, a copy of the following song was found upon the King, which the overseer had heard him sing at the funeral feast, while the other negroes joined in the chorus: –

'Song of the King of the Eboes'[5] . . .

The Eboe King said, that he certainly had made use of this song, and what harm was there in his doing so? He had sung no songs but such as his brown priest had assured him were approved of by John the Baptist. "And who, then, was John the Baptist?" He did not very well know; only he had been told by his brown priest, that John the Baptist was a friend to the negroes, and had got his head in a pan!

March 26.[6]

Young Hill was told at the Bay this morning, that I make a part of the Eboe King's song! According to this report, "good King George and good Mr. Wilberforce" are stated to have "given me a paper" to set the negroes free (i.e. an order), but that the white people of Jamaica will not suffer me to show the paper, and I am now going home to say so.

1818. February 25.[7]

A negro, named Adam, has long been the terror of my whole estate. He was accused of being an Obeah-man, and persons notorious for the practice of Obeah had been found concealed from justice in his house, who were afterwards convicted and transported. He was strongly suspected of having poisoned more than twelve negroes, men and women; and having been displaced by my former trustee from being principal governor, in revenge he put poison in his water-jar. Luckily he was observed by one of the house servants, who impeached him, and prevented the intended mischief. For this offence he ought to have been given up to justice; but being brother of the trustee's mistress she found means to get him off, after undergoing a long confinement in the stocks. I found him, on my arrival,[8] living in a state of utter excommunication; I tried what reasoning with him could effect, reconciled him to his companions, treated him with marked kindness, and he promised solemnly to behave well during my absence. However, instead of attributing my lenity to a wish to reform him, his pride and confidence in his own talents and powers of deception made him attribute the indulgence shown him to his having obtained an influence over my mind. This he determined to employ to his own purposes upon my return; so he set about forming a conspiracy against Sully, the present chief governor, and boasted on various estates in the neighbourhood that on my arrival he would take care to get Sully broke, and himself substituted in his place. In the mean while he quarrelled and fought to the right and to the left; and on my arrival I found the whole estate in an uproar about Adam. No less than three charges of assault, with intent to kill, were preferred against him. In a fit of jealousy he had endeavoured to strangle Marlborough with the thong of a whip, and had nearly effected his purpose before he could be dragged away: he had knocked Nato down in some trifling dispute, and while the man was senseless had thrown him into the river to drown him; and having taken offence at a poor weak creature called Old Rachael, on meeting her by accident he struck her to the ground, beat her with a supple-jack, stamped upon her belly, and begged her to be assured of his intention (as he eloquently worded it) "to kick her guts out." The breeding mothers also accused him of having been the cause of the poisoning of a particular spring, from which they were in the habit of fetching water for their children, as Adam on that morning had been seen near the spring without having any business there, and he had been heard to caution his little daughter against drinking water from it that day, although he stoutly denied both circumstances. Into the bargain, my head blacksmith being perfectly well at five o'clock, was found by his son dead in his bed at eight; and it was known that he had lately had a dispute with Adam, who on that day had made it up with him, and had invited him to drink, although it was not certain that his offer had been accepted. He had, moreover, threatened the lives of many of the best negroes. Two of the cooks declared, that he had severally directed them to dress Sully's food apart, and had given them powders to mix with it. The first to whom he applied refused positively; the second he treated with liquor, and when she had drunk, he gave her the poison, with instructions how to use it. Being a timid creature, she did not dare to object, so threw away the powder privately, and pretended that it had been administered; but finding no effect produced by it, Adam gave her a second powder, at the same time bidding her remember the liquor which she had swallowed, and which he assured her would affect her own destruction through the force of Obeah, unless she prevented it by sacrificing his enemy in her stead. The poor creature still threw away the powder, but the strength of imagination brought upon her a serious malady, and it was not till after several weeks that she recovered from the effects of her fears. The terror thus produced was universal throughout the estate, and Sully and several other principal negroes requested me to remove them to my property in St. Thomas's, as their lives were not safe while breathing the same air with Adam. However, it appeared a more salutary measure to remove Adam himself; but all the poisoning charges either went no further than strong suspicion, or (any more than the assaults) were not liable by the laws of Jamaica to be punished, except by flogging or temporary imprisonment, which would only have returned him to the estate with increased resentment against those to whom he should ascribe his sufferings, however deserved. However, on searching his house, a musket with a plentiful accompaniment of powder and ball was found concealed, as also a considerable quantity of materials for the practice of Obeah: the possession of either of the above articles (if the musket is without the consent of the proprietor) authorises the magistrates to pronounce a sentence of transportation. In consequence of this discovery, Adam was immediately committed to gaol; a slave court was summoned, and today a sentence of transportation from the island was pronounced, after a trial of three hours . . . .

The Obeah ceremonies always commence with what is called, by the negroes, "the Myal dance." This is intended to remove any doubt of the chief Obeah-man's supernatural powers; and in the course of it, he undertakes to show his art by killing one of the persons present, whom he pitches upon for that purpose. He sprinkles various powders over the devoted victim, blows upon him, and dances round him, obliges him to drink a liquor prepared for the occasion, and finally the sorcerer and his assistants seize him and whirl him rapidly round and round till the man loses his senses, and falls on the ground to all appearances and the belief of the spectators a perfect corpse. The chief Myal-man then utters loud shrieks, rushes out of the house with wild and frantic gestures, and conceals himself in some neighbouring wood. At the end of two or three hours he returns with a large bundle of herbs, from some of which he squeezes the juice into the mouth of the dead person; with others he anoints his eyes and stains the tips of his fingers, accompanying the ceremony with a great variety of grotesque actions, and chanting all the while something between a song and a howl, while the assistants hand in hand dance slowly round them in a circle, stamping the ground loudly with their feet to keep time with his chant. A considerable time elapses before the desired effect is produced, but at length the corpse gradually recovers animation, rises from the ground perfectly recovered, and the Myal dance concludes. After this proof of his power, those who wish to be revenged upon their enemies apply to the sorcerer for some of the same powder, which produced apparent death upon their companion, and as they never employ the means used for his recovery, of course the powder once administered never fails to be lastingly fatal. It must be superfluous to mention that the Myal-man on this second occasion substitutes a poison for a narcotic. Now, among other suspicious articles found in Adam's hut, there was a string of beads of various sizes, shapes, and colours, arranged in a form peculiar to the performance of the Obeah-man in the Myal dance. Their use was so well known, that Adam on his trial did not even attempt to deny that they could serve for no purpose but the practice of Obeah; but he endeavoured to refute their being his own property, and with this view he began to narrate the means by which he had become possessed of them. He said that they belonged to Fox (a negro who was lately transported), from whom he had taken them at a Myal dance held on the estate of Dean's Valley; but as the assistants at one of these dances are by law condemned to death equally with the principal performer, the court had the humanity to interrupt his confession of having been present on such an occasion, and thus saved him from criminating himself so deeply as to render a capital punishment inevitable. I understand that he was quite unabashed and at his ease the whole time; upon hearing his sentence, he only said very coolly, "Well! I ca'n't help it!" turned himself round and walked out of court. That nothing might be wanting, this fellow had even a decided talent for hypocrisy. When on my arrival he gave me a letter filled with the grossest lies respecting the trustee, and every creditable negro on the estate, he took care to sign it by the name which he had lately received in baptism; and in his defence at the bar to prove his probity of character and purity of manners, he informed the court that for some time past he had been learning to read, for the sole purpose of learning the Lord's Prayer. The nick-name by which he was generally known among the negroes in this part of the country, was Buonaparte, and he always appeared to exult in the appellation. Once condemned, the marshal is bound under a heavy penalty to see him shipped from off the island before the expiration of six weeks, and probably he will be sent to Cuba. He is a fine-looking man between thirty and forty, square built and of great bodily strength, and his countenance equally expresses intelligence and malignity. The sum allowed for him is one hundred pounds currency, which is scarcely a third of his worth as a labourer, but which is the highest value which a jury is permitted to mention.

Notes

1. Lewis, *Journal*, 220–22.
2. Ibid., 224–25.
3. Ibid., 226–28.

4. The governor of Jamaica wrote to the secretary of state that evidence was
   given "that Nightly Meetings had been held on the property to which the two
   Slaves, who were brought to Trial, belonged. That the object of their Meeting
   was to impress the Slaves generally with a belief that Mr Wilberforce was to be
   their Deliverer, and that if the White Inhabitants did not make them free, they
   ought to make themselves free . . . . It further appeared in the Evidence that
   these two slaves have taught the others to believe that there was no necessity of
   being Christened by the Clergymen of the Parish, for that they had permission
   to baptize from a Negro Preacher belonging to Earl Balcarres, and the Negroes
   so baptized ever after paid a part of what they possessed to the head Preacher
   whom they call the Bishop." Quoted in Richard Hart, *Slaves Who Abolished
   Slavery: Blacks in Rebellion* (Kingston: University of the West Indies Press, 2002),
   226. Shirley Gordon contends, however, that "slaves, increasingly aware of anti-
   slavery legislation in Britain, used such an occasion as a funeral as an opportunity for discussion, the generation of optimism, and, on occasion, for specific
   plotting. This particular event is not convincing as a plot so much as an occasion for keeping up the spirits with dreams of freedom". Shirley C. Gordon,
   God Almighty Make Me Free: Christianity in Preemancipation Jamaica
   (Bloomington: Indiana University Press, 1996), 54.
5. See page 454.
6. Lewis, *Journal*, 232.
7. Ibid., 350–57.
8. That is, on Lewis's first visit to his Cornwall estate in 1816.

BERNARD M. SENIOR (FL. 1815–34)

Jamaica, as It Was, as It Is, and as It May Be (1835)[1]

The author states that he lived in Jamaica from 1815 to 1834 and was "personally present, in one of the most disturbed districts" during the 1831 uprising, and involved in the efforts to protect the whites and bring the rebellion to an end. He is listed in the *Jamaica Almanack* of 1822 as the owner of Salt-Spring estate, with three hundred slaves, and an officer in the St Elizabeth Regiment of the militia. The following excerpt from his narrative of the rebellion is valuable as a first-hand account of events in his own locality. Though he shows no sympathy for the rebels, he is at pains to record their viewpoint in an approximation to their own speech.

On the borders of St. Elizabeth, but just within the line of Manchester parish, is a penn property, called "New Forest," on which are about one hundred and fifty slaves. The proprietor being a major in the militia, was, of course, called to his duty the moment it was ascertained that an insurrection had broken out. This residence being about seventy miles from the place where the commencement of the burning was perceived, it will not be wondered at, that his wife, a lady of firm mind, experienced no particular fears or anxiety at being left at home as usual. On the next morning to that on which the people should have returned to work after the holidays, she was not more surprised than confounded at the following occurrence. While sitting on the sofa, with her needle-work before her on the table, as was her usual custom after breakfast, the head driver most unceremoniously walked into the room with a red jacket on, and a hat and feather on his head. As, however, it was the first day after that in which the Christmas holidays ought to have ceased, she fancied that another day had been granted to the people, and that the individual before her was merely come to show how well he looked in his merry making garb; she therefore accosted him thus, but probably with some trifling difference of words: – "Well, driver! I see you're a soldier to day!" "Oh! yes ma'am (at another time it would have been 'Missus,') we be all soldier now." "Then you don't turn out (that means, go to work) till to morrow, I suppose." "Oh yes, ma'am, we all turn out on every property all over de island." "I don't understand you, driver." "No ma'am, me tell you de plain trute." On this, he cooly seated himself on the sofa with his mistress, which act, of course, terribly alarmed her; but her natural strength of mind upheld her for the time, and she evinced no signs of fear. "Ma'am," he continued, "you no my missus now, we all free. Star come to de corner of de moon, just as Baptist parson tell we; Christmas come, same him say; buckra order we to work; same him tell we; we no for work, else we never get free; we 'blige to burn ebery ting, and take free. All we burning and ebery ting going on well, ma'am. Dem will soon be here, den we for burn dis house and all de works besides on all de properties. Me tink say, ma'am, you neber hearey what going on in St. James." "Why, driver, you astonish me, but it cannot be true; however, I shall soon know, for I expect your master every moment." "True, ma'am, all true," said the driver, "ebery estate in St. James' burnt down; and nigger fight buckra two, three time, some kill, great many shoot, ma'am. We sure to gain de day, but I come to see you again bye and bye." During this last speech, he had got up and gradually moved to the door, but when concluding the sentence, he gave a significant look and shake of the head, which, when combined with the familiarity of his demeanour throughout, gave the lady good reason to prognosticate evil. Her situation may easily be imagined. The only alternative was, a note to her husband; but innumerable difficulties arose as to the mode of conveyance, lest it should be intercepted. At length she fixed on one that fortunately succeeded, and her mind was soon relieved by a removal to a safe retreat. This, and such like facts, will convince the reader what were the ideas and intentions of the negroes, should they have succeeded in their diabolical career.

It was now ascertained that the rebels had made good their quarters at several places in the vicinity of their late defeat, and parties were sent out against those at Barneyside, Mackfield, Prospect, Barracks, and various other properties. Prisoners continued to be forwarded to Savannah-le-Mar [*sic*], Montego Bay, Black River, Lacovia, Y.S., and other places, for trial, and courts martial sat almost daily. Such as were absolutely taken under arms, with the rebels, required little to convict them; but it was astonishing to mark the ingenuity with which many of them set up a defence; and it was dreadful to witness the hardihood with which others would maintain the justice of their cause. One stout able fellow in particular, tried at Black River, charged with burning down a set of works, and killing a white man, by firing at him over a fence, pleaded Not guilty. The case proceeded, and every fact was indisputably proved by sufficient and competent evidence. The prisoner had also the benefit of the talents of Mr. B——n, the protector of slaves, who although perfectly confident of the man's guilt, used all his professional skill (as in duty alone bound) to avert his fate. Not satisfied with these, he claimed to be himself heard, and the prayer was at once granted by the court.

There appeared in his countenance and demeanour neither fear nor anxiety, but a perfect confidence in a favourable result, from the moment he commenced his oration till its conclusion, which was nearly to the following effect. "'Cause massa (meaning the presiding judge) and toder buckra gentlemen, (the court and jury,) so good to make me 'peak for myself, me will tell de whole plain trute, case all dem toder niger tell lie 'pon me, for make dem own case good. Oh! massa, dat boy Bill, him one big lie, me know him from small pick-ninny, him always vile boy, you no for believe him, massa. Him teal, him lie, him tief corn, him neber tend to him work, but all time run-away, and 'tay in de bush tiefing for we cocoa and nyam. Him catch we fowl, den go sell dem to buckra, long distance off. Hie!!! Gentlemen him too vile, him too much bad for true. Well, massa, me hearee say, dat parson B——ll, parson K——bb, and parson W——rne, and plenty ob dem at Baptist Chapel at Montego Bay, tell de niggers dem, dat Wilberforce and de King of England give we free long time, and massa gubna (the governor) have de free paper, but for we, buckra, no will make him give de paper to we, case dem want we always for dem slave for eba and eba. Saturday, for we nigger, day before Christmas, me tell Caesar, say – Caesar, you no Baptist!

Him say, Yes, me Baptist for true. Me say, den, you no hearee, for you parson
say we nigger for free aftah Christmas! Him say, Yes, and dem tell we dat if
buckra ax we for work we no for work, else we tay slave all we life aftah!
dem tell we, no harm to burn house, if buckra force we to work. Dem say,
we no for shed blood, but dem say, if buckra tied inside house, and house
burn, nigger no shed blood, fire burn him, but nigger know noting 'bout it,
fire do what him like. Caesar, you been to chapel last week; 'Yes me go and
hearee all;' What you hearee? 'Hie! you fool, for true!' him say, 'you no
sabay, soon Christmas come, daddy ruler Sharp[2] carry ebery body into bush,
and make fire burn sugar work and ebery ting, den dere Gardiner, Dove,
and plenty more carry on, till all de property in de island burn, den we kill
all de buckra-men, and take lady for we wife.'"

With considerable patience the court heard the prisoner thus far, and
then directed him to confine his narrative to what he considered might avert
his fate, but that he was not to take up the time of the court by stating conversations irrelevant to the case. He seemed as if recollecting himself, and
then proceeded. –

"Yes, massa, dat what me for do, tank massa, sar, just as me telling buckra,
dat what Caesar tell me, so me keep Christmas quite merry; and tink no
harm. Bym-bye me hearee say, dem burning all about Montego Bay, and
Susan tell me busha, (overseer) and book-keeper left de property, and gone to
keep guard, bym-bye, 'bout first cock-crow, me sleeping in me niggar house,
dem wake me and tell me say, me must come 'long and burn massa property;
me say No; dem say Yes, you for go wid we, or we for ded (kill) you. Captain
M'Cail give you orders, and you for come now; dem great many wid gun,
some hab sword and muschett, so dem force me hard out, and gib me one
fire-stick, and command me for fire busha house. Well, massa, me could no
help myself; dem people 'tranger to me, Massa, but when busha house take
fire, me see plenty property-people firing de works. So, massa, dem tell lie
'pon me, you see me neba burn de works!" {Here the prisoner evinced great
satisfaction from the idea that he had entirely done away with that charge in
the indictment, as some of the jurors found difficulty in suppressing their
laughter at the ingenuity thus exhibited.}[3] "Bym-bye dem courage me up,
Massa, and gib me rum, and tell me say, me for be captain, 'cause me capital
shot. Me no know dem name, gentlemen, but just after de day-light come

good, one dem call Quashie, hand me for him gun and tell me say, Now, captain, you see book-keeper do come, you for shoot him, else him ride back and tell soldier to come and take we. Me say, No, me no can do for book-keeper, him nebah trouble me, and him gib me fippence last week! Hie, him say, you frighten now, dam you, you no see dis pistol, Colonel Gardiner give me order for shoot you ded, if you no do for book-keeper, and him make you captain so soon you get buckra out of de way. Massa, me frighten him shoot me, him curse me so; den, massa, de liquor take me head, and me tand close to wall; but, massa, dey tell lie again 'pon me, dere *no fence day*. And, massa, Mr. Smit *no white man*, him fader white man, but him moder quadroon. So, massa, gentlemen buckra, you see it all lie, all heap o'lies dem tell; so please make me go back, and I'll tend to massa work."

The prisoner, on concluding this artful appeal, evinced great gratification, until informed that, had not the indictment been so fully and clearly proved against him by a host of witnesses, his elaborate defence could not in any way avail him, as he was charged with the crime of arson in its general acceptation, which included all burning, also with joining the rebels; and that although every fence was not a wall, yet every wall must certainly be deemed a fence: and further, that the law of the land recognized as white persons all born of such as the book-keeper's parents. On sentence of death being passed upon him, he totally lost his presence of mind, and was removed in that state.

Notes

1. Bernard M. Senior, *Jamaica, as It Was, as It Is, and as It May Be . . . Also an authentic narrative of the negro insurrection of 1831 . . . By a Retired Military Officer* (London: T. Hurst, 1835), 224–30.
2. Sam Sharpe, a Baptist deacon, was the leader of the 1831 uprising, sometimes known as the "Christmas Rebellion". He is now a national hero of Jamaica. His officers included Robert Gardner (given the rank of colonel) and Thomas Dove (captain). Sharpe gave himself up to the authorities in 1832, was tried and executed. For the most detailed modern account of the rebellion, see Hart, *Slaves Who Abolished Slavery*.
3. Brackets as in original text.

BRYAN EDWARDS (1743–1800)

"The Negro's Dying Speech" (1777)[1]

This poem was first published in the *Universal Magazine of Knowledge and Pleasure*. It was reprinted in Edwards's *Poems, written chiefly in the West Indies* (1792) under a new title, "Stanzas, Occasioned by the Death of Alico, An African Slave, Condemned for Rebellion, in Jamaica, 1760", but otherwise unaltered. Tacky's rebellion (see pages 316–18 above) took place when Edwards was only eighteen, but his empathy with the mutinous feelings of newly enslaved Africans remained constant. While deploring the violence that accompanied slave revolts, he also argued that their recurrence was a prime reason for reform of the conditions of slavery.[2]

The Negro's Dying Speech on his being executed for Rebellion in the Island of Jamaica

'Tis past: – ah! calm thy cares to rest!
    Firm and unmov'd am I: –
In Freedom's cause I bar'd my breast, –
    In Freedom's cause I die.

Ah stop! thou dost me fatal wrong: –   5
    Nature will yet rebel;
For I have lov'd thee very long,
    And lov'd thee very well.

To native skies and peaceful bow'rs
    I soon shall wing my way;   10
Where joy shall lead the circling hours,
    Unless too long thy stay.

O speed, fair sun! thy course divine;
    My Abala remove; –
There thy bright beams shall ever shine,   15
    And I for ever love!

On those blest shores – a slave no more!
    In peaceful ease I'll stray;
Or rouse to chace the mountain boar,
    As unconfin'd as day!   20

No Christian Tyrant there is known
    To mark his steps with blood,
Nor sable Mis'ry's piercing moan
    Resounds thro' ev'ry wood!

Yet have I heard the melting tongue,   25
    Have seen the falling tear;
Known the good heart by pity wrung,
    Ah! that such hearts are rare!

Now, Christian, glut thy ravish'd eyes
    – I reach the joyful hour;   30
Now bid the scorching flames arise,
    And these poor limbs devour:

But know, pale Tyrant, 'tis not thine
    Eternal war to wage;
The death thou giv'st shall but combine   35
    To mock thy baffled rage.

O Death, how welcome to th' opprest!
   Thy kind embrace I crave;
Thou bring'st to Mis'ry's bosom rest,
   And Freedom to the Slave!   40

Notes

1. Bryan Edwards, "The Negro's Dying Speech on his being executed for Rebellion in the Island of Jamaica", in *Universal Magazine of Knowledge and Pleasure* 61 (November 1777): 270–71.
2. See Alan Richardson, ed., *Slavery, Abolition and Emancipation: Writings in the British Romantic Period*, vol. 4, *Verse* (London: Pickering and Chatto, 1999), 25.

JOHN MARJORIBANKS (1759–96)

"Stanzas on the Execution of a Negro" (1792)[1]

Stanzas on the Execution of a Negro, at Spanish-town, Jamaica, August 1785

When Brutus struck the fatal steel
    Through the Imperial Caesar's breast,
The glorious deed, the patriot's zeal,
    Stood thro' the subject world confess'd.
Nor yet has time destroy'd the name,   5
    Impartial ages love to praise;
In story brightly shines his fame,
    Immortal as the poet's lays.
Yet Brutus stabb'd a gen'rous heart,
    In whose affections fast he grew;   10
To whom he ow'd a filial part,
    It was a parent Brutus slew.
He never felt the galling chain,
    The lash that lacerates the slave;
But favours (all conferr'd in vain)   15
    Were the sole fetters Caesar gave!

But see! poor Azubal in torments dies!
    At which my soul in agonies recoils!

See how he writhes! Ah hear his horrid cries!
    Whilst with slow cruelty the furnace broils!   20
Say, what was Azubal's atrocious crime,
    Compar'd to Brutus' celebrated deed?
(Candour regards no colour and no clime;
    And Freedom smiles as oft as tyrants bleed!)

No friendly bosom did he wound;   25
    No acts of kindness had he known;
Compell'd to till a foreign ground,
    For ever exil'd from his own!
Still agonising mem'ry drew
    The sweets that bless'd his Afric shore;   30
The days of slumb'ring ease he knew;
    The friends he must behold no more!
Indignant still recalls the day
    European ruffians first drew near;
When, vainly struggling, forc'd away   35
    From all that ever could be dear!
Beneath reluctant labour faint,
    Say what reward awaits his pains?
The whip's the solace of his plaint;
    And rest is granted but in chains!   40
Ideal loss of Liberty inspir'd
    The haughty Roman to destroy his friend;
But keener injuries the Negro fir'd
    To end a tyrant, and to kill a fiend.
Brutus still seems a parricide to me,   45
    And Reason gives reluctantly applause;
But to poor Azubal my praise is free,
    Who boldly perish'd in a juster cause.[2]

Notes

1. John Marjoribanks, "Stanzas on the Execution of a Negro, at Spanish-town, Jamaica, August 1785", from Marjoribanks, *Slavery*.
   [Author's note:] This unhappy man had run off the estate to which he belonged. Having been some time afterwards met by one of the book-keepers, who attempted to seize him, a struggle ensued, in which the white man was killed.

2. [Author's note:] The name of *Azubal* is fictitious; I wish I could add also that the circumstances are imaginary. But these verses were actually written a few days after the execution of a Negro, who was *roasted to death at a slow fire* on the race-course near Spanish-town, for the crime before mentioned. Of the many strong arguments which have been urged in favour of the abolition of the Slave-Trade, one of the most obvious and incontrovertible, is surely this: That the constant importation of savage and untamed spirits into the islands, not only subjects the white inhabitants to frequent alarm, danger, and sometimes death itself (to which they are seldom or never exposed from the Creole Negroes); but also affords the plea of necessity to punishments the most shocking to humanity, and highly disgraceful to the colonies of a civilized nation.

EDWARD RUSHTON (1756–1814)

West-Indian Eclogues (1787)[1]

Rushton asserts in the preface that during his residence in the West Indies he had personally witnessed the "barbarities" he describes in the eclogues. His prime motive for publishing them, he explains, was reformative: "if these Eclogues shall contribute, in their humble sphere, to prevent *excessive* punishments from being *unnecessarily* inflicted on that wretched race, to whom they relate, – the author of them will receive the highest gratification, of which his mind is capable". The text here is from the first edition. It was dedicated to Beilby Porteus, then bishop of Chester, "in gratitude for his discourse on the civilization, improvement, and conversion, of the negro-slaves in the British islands in the West-Indies, and for his continued patronage of every subsequent endeavour to obtain those salutary objects".[2] Rushton's eclogues are lavishly embellished with notes on climate, natural history and the treatment of slaves, but only those referring to slaves are reprinted here.

Eclogue the First

Scene – Jamaica. *Time* – Morning.

The Eastern clouds declare the coming day,
The din of reptiles slowly dies away;

The mountain tops just glimmer on the eye,
And from their bulky sides the breezes fly;
The Ocean's margin beats the varied strand,   5
Its hoarse deep murmurs reach the distant land.
The sons of Mis'ry, Britain's foulest stain,
Arise from friendly sleep to pining pain;
Arise, perchance, from dreams of Afric's soil,
To Slav'ry, hunger, cruelty, and toil: –   10
When slowly moving to their tasks assign'd,
Two sable friends thus eas'd their labouring mind.

                    JUMBA.
Oh say, Adoma, whence that heavy sigh?
Or is thy Yaro sick – or droops thy Boy?
Or say what other woe –

                    ADOMA.
                          These wounds behold.   15

                    JUMBA.
Alas! by them too plain thy griefs are told!
But whence, or why these stripes? My injur'd friend,
Declare how one so mild could thus offend.

                    ADOMA.
I'll tell thee, Jumba. – 'Twas but yesterday,
As in the field we toil'd our strength away,   20
My gentle Yaro with her hoe was nigh,
And on her back she³ bore my infant Boy.
The sultry heats had parch'd his little throat,
His head reclin'd I heard his wailing note.
The Mother, at his piteous cries distress'd,   25
Now paus'd from toil and gave the cheering breast.
But soon alas! the savage Driver⁴ came,
And with his cow-skin cut her tender frame;
Loudly he tax'd her laziness, – and then
He curs'd my boy, and plied the lash again!   30
– Jumba, I saw the deed, – I heard her grief!
Could I do less? – I flew to her relief;

I fell before him – sued, embrac'd his knee,
And bade his anger vent itself on me,
Spurn'd from his feet I dar'd to catch his hand,   35
Nor loos'd it, Jumba, at his dread command:
For, blind with rage, at one indignant blow
I thought to lay the pale-fac'd villian low!
But sudden stopp'd; for now the whites came round,
They seiz'd my arms, – my Yaro saw me bound!   40
Need I relate what follow'd?
                    JUMBA.
                         Barb'rous deed!
Oh! for the pow'r to make these tyrants bleed!
These, who in regions far remov'd from this,
Think, like ourselves, that liberty is bliss,
Yet in wing'd houses cross the dang'rous waves,   45
Led by base av'rice, to make others slaves: –
These, who extol the freedom they enjoy,
Yet would to others every good deny: –
These, who have torn us from our native shore
Which (dreadful thought) we must behold no more:–   50
These, who insult us through the weary day,
With taunts our tears, with mocks our griefs, repay:
Oh! for the pow'r to bring these monsters low,
And bid them feel the biting tooth of woe!
                    ADOMA.
Jumba, my deep resolves are fix'd! my friend,   55
This life, this slavish journey, soon shall end.
These fest'ring gashes loudly bid me die,
And by our sacred Gods I will comply.
Yes, Jumba, by our great *Fetish*[5] I swear,
This, worse than death, I cannot, will not, bear.   60
                    JUMBA.
What! tamely perish? No, Adoma, no –
Thy great revenge demands a glorious blow.
But dar'st thou bravely act in such a cause?

Friends may be found, – what say'st thou? – why this pause?
ADOMA.
Jumba, thou mov'st me much. – Thy looks are wild,   65
Thy gestures passionate –
JUMBA.
If to be mild
In such a cause were virtue, – on the ground
Jumba would crawl, and court the causeless wound.
– How oft, my friend, since first we trod these plains
Have trivial faults call'd forth the bitt'rest pains!   70
How oft our Tyrants, at each dext'rous lash
With joyous looks have view'd each bleeding gash;
How oft to these, with tortures still uncloy'd,
Have they the Eben's prickly branch[6] applied!
And shall we still endure the keenest pain,   75
And pay our butchers only with disdain?
Shall we, unmov'd, still bear their coward blows?
– No: – vengeance soon shall fasten on our foes,
Lend but thy succour. –
ADOMA.
Comfort to my soul
Thy words convey, and ev'ry fear controul.   80
Their last, base, cruel act so steels my heart,
That in thy bold resolves I'll bear a part.
JUMBA.
Enough: – Our glorious aims shall soon succeed,
And thou in turn shall see th' oppressors bleed.
Soon shall they fall, cut down like lofty Canes,   85
And (oh! the bliss) from us receive their pains.
Oh! 'twill be pleasant when we see them mourn,
See the fell cup to their own lip return,
View *their* pale faces prostrate on the ground,
Their meagre bodies gape with many a wound.   90
View with delight each agonizing grin,
When melted wax[7] is dropp'd upon *their* skin: –

Then bid them think –
ADOMA.

     Hark from yon plantain trees,
Methought a voice came floating on the breeze.
– Hark! – there again –
JUMBA.

      'Tis so: our tyrants come. –   95
At eve we'll meet again – mean time be dumb.

Eclogue the Second

Time – Evening.

The twinkling Orbs which pierce the gloom of night
Now shine with more than European light. . . .
The wearied Negroes to their sheds return,
Prepare their morsels, and their hardships mourn,
Talk o'er their former bliss, their present woes;   5
Then sink to earth, and seek a short repose.
– 'Twas now the sable friends, in pensive mood,
In a lone path their doleful theme renew'd.
ADOMA.

Jumba, those words sunk deep into my heart,
Which thou in friendship didst this morn impart.   10
Still at my toil my mind revolv'd them o'er,
But grew, the more I mus'd, dismay'd the more.
Oh! think on Pedro, gibbeted alive![8]
Think on his fate – six long days to survive! –
His frantic looks, – his agonizing pain, –   15
His tongue outstretch'd to catch the dropping rain;
His vain attempts to turn his head aside,
And gnaw the flesh which his own limbs supplied;
Think on his suff'rings, when th' inhuman crew,
T' increase his pangs, plac'd Plantains in his view,   20
And bade him eat –

JUMBA.

      If thus thy promise ends,
If thus thy dastard heart would aid thy friends,
Away, mean wretch, and view thy Yaro bleed,
And bow submissive to th' unmanly deed! –
Thou speak'st of Pedro. – He possess'd a soul,   25
Which nobly burst the shackles of controul.
He fell betray'd, but boldly met his death;
And curs'd his tyrants with his latest breath.
– But go, Adoma, since to live is sweet,
Go, like a dog, and lick the white man's feet;   30
Tell them that hunger, slav'ry, toil, and pain,
Thou wilt endure, nor ever once complain:
Tell them, though Jumba dares to plot their fall,
That thou art tame, and wilt submit to all,
Go poor submissive slave. – Go, meanly bend,   35
Court the pale butcher, and betray thy friend.

ADOMA.

How! – I betray my friend! – Oh, Jumba, cease;
Nor stab Adoma with such words as these,
Death frights me not; I wish revenge like thee;
But oh! I shudder at their cruelty.   40
I could undaunted, from the craggy steep
Plunge, and be swallow'd in the raging deep;
Fearless I could with manchineal,[9] or knife,
Or cord, or bullet, end this hated life.
But oh, my friend, like Pedro to expire,   45
Or feel the pangs of slow-consuming fire, –
These are most terrible! –

JUMBA.

      A ling'ring pain
Thou fear'st, and yet canst bear thy servile chain!
Canst bear incessant toil, and want of food,
Canst bear the Driver's lash to drink thy blood!   50
Say, doom'd to these, what now does life supply

But ling'ring pain, which must at length destroy?
– Yet go, poor timid wretch, go fawn and grieve:
And as those gashes heal, still more receive:
Go, and submit, like oxen to the wain; –   55
But never say thou fear'st a ling'ring pain.

       ADOMA.

Thy charge is just. But, friend, there still remain
Two ways to free us from this galling chain.
Since we can bid our various sorrows cease
By quitting life, or how, or when we please: 60
Or we can quickly fly these cruel whites
By seeking shelter on the mountains' heights,
Where wild hogs dwell, where lofty Cocoas grow,
And boiling streams of purest waters flow.
There we might live; for thou with skilful hand   65
Canst form the bow, and jav'lin, of our land.
There we might freely roam, in search of food,
Up the steep crag, or through the friendly wood,
There we might find –

       JUMBA.

              Alas! thou dost not know
The King of all those mountains is our foe;[10]   70
His subjects num'rous, and their chief employ
To hunt our race, when fled from slavery.
Lur'd by the hope of gain such arts are tried,
No rocks can cover us, no forests hide.
Against us ev'n the chatt'ring Birds combine,   75
And aid those hunters in their curs'd design:
For oft, through them,[11] the fugitives are caught,
And, strongly pinion'd, to their tyrants brought.
O'er vale, or mountain, thus where'er we go,
The suff'ring Negro surely finds a foe.   80

       ADOMA.

Ah, Jumba, worse, much worse our wretched state, . . .
Thus vex'd, thus harrass'd, than that fishes fate,

Which frequent we beheld when wafted o'er
The great rough waters from our native shore.
He, as the tyrants of the deep pursu'd, 85
Would quit the waves their swiftness to elude,
And skim in air; – when lo! a bird of prey
Bends his strong wing, and bears the wretch away!
No refuge, then, but death –

JUMBA.

What! tamely die!
No, vengeance first shall fall on tyranny! 90
We'll view these white men gasping in their gore; –
Then let me perish! Jumba asks no more.

ADOMA.

Oh! peace, – think where thou art; thy voice is high:
Quick drop the dang'rous theme. – My shed is nigh;
There my poor Yaro will our rice prepare; – 95
I pray thee come. –

JUMBA

Away, and take thy fare,
For me, I cannot eat, – haste to thy shed,
Farewell, be cautious, – think on what I've said.

Eclogue the Third

Time – Noon.

. . . Now oxen to the shore in pond'rous wains,
Drag the rich produce of the juicy canes.
Now wearied Negroes to their sheds repair,
Or spreading tree, to take their scanty fare:
Whose hour expir'd, the shell[12] is heard to blow, 5
And the sad tribe resume their daily woe.
'Twas now, beneath a Tam'rind's cool retreat,
Two sable friends thus mourn'd their wretched fate.

CONGO.

Oh Quamina! how roll'd the Suns away,

When thus upon our native soil we lay;   10

When we repos'd beneath the friendly shade,

And quaff'd our palmy wine, and round survey'd

Our native offspring sporting free as air,

Our num'rous wives the chearing feast prepare:

Saw plenty smile around our cane-built sheds,   15

Saw Yams shoot up, and Cocoas lift their heads.

– But now ah! sad reverse! our groans arise,

Forlorn and hopeless, far from all we prize:

Timid we tremble at our tyrants' frown,

And one vast load of mis'ry bends us down.   20

QUAMINA.

Yes, – those were times which we in vain may mourn,

Times which, my Congo, never will return!

Times, ere the scourge's hated sound was known,

Or hunger, toil, and stripes, had caus'd a groan.

Times, when with arrows arm'd, and trusty bow,   25

We oft repell'd each rude, invading, foe.

Times, when we chac'd the fierce-ey'd beasts of prey

Through tangled woods, which scarcely know the day:

When oft we saw, in spite of all his care,

The bulky Elephant within our snare.   30

CONGO.

Twelve moons are past, for still I mark them down,

Since the fell trading race attack'd our town,

Since we were seiz'd by that inhuman band,

Forc'd from our wives, our friends, and native land.

Twelve long, long moons they've been, and since that day   35

Oft have we groan'd beneath a cruel sway.

Oft has the taper'd scourge, where knots and wire

Are both combin'd to raise the torture higher,

Brought bloody pieces from each quiv'ring part,

Whilst tyrant whites have sworn 'twas dext'rous art.   40

QUAMINA.

Sharks seize them all! their love of torture grows,
And the whole Island echoes with our woes.
Didst thou know Jumba? – Some close, list'ning ear,
Heard him last eve denounce in tones severe,
Deep vengeance on these whites. In vain he fled: 45
This morn I saw him number'd with the dead!

CONGO.

A fate so sudden! – And yet why complain?
The white mans pleasure is the Negroes pain.

QUAMINA.

Didst thou e'er see, when hither first we came,
An ancient Slave, Angola was his name?   50
Whose vig'rous years upon these hills were spent,
In galling servitude, and discontent:
He late, too weak to bear the weighty toil,
Which all endure who till this hated soil,
Was sent, as one grown useless on th' estate,   55
Far to the town to watch his Master's gate,
Or to the house each morn the fuel bring,
Or bear cool water from the distant spring:
With many a toil, with many a labour more,
Although his aged head was silver'd o'er,   60
Although his body like a bow was bent,
And old, and weak, he totter'd as he went.

CONGO.

I knew him not,

QUAMINA.

      Often, each labour sped,
Has he with aching limbs attain'd his shed.
Attain'd the spot, dejected and forlorn,   65
Where he might rest his aged head 'till morn.
Where, wearied out, he op'd the friendly door,
And, entring, prostrate sunk upon the floor.
Feeble and faint some moons he toil'd away;

(For trifles toils become as men decay)   70
When late beneath the driver's lash he fell,
And scourg'd, and tortur'd, bade the world farewell.
                    CONGO.
But why the scourge? Wherefore such needless rage?
Is there no pity, then, for weak old age?
                    QUAMINA.
'Twas part of his employ, with empty pail,   75
To crawl for water to a neighb'ring vale:
And as he homeward bore the liquid load,
With trembling steps along the rugged road,
His wither'd limbs denied their wonted aid:
– The broken vessel his mishap betray'd.   80
This his offence: – for this, thrown on the ground,
His feeble limbs outstretch'd, and strongly bound,
His body bare, each nerve convuls'd with pain,
I saw and pitied him – but ah! in vain.
Quick fell the lash: his hoary head laid low,   85
His eyes confess'd unutterable woe.
He sued for mercy: the big tear apace,
Stole down the furrows of his aged face.
His direful groans (for such they were indeed!)
Mix'd with his words when e'er he strove to plead,   90
And form'd such moving eloquence, that none,
But flinty-hearted Christians could go on.
At length releas'd, they bore him to his shed:
Much he complain'd, and the next morn was dead.
                    CONGO.
And was this all? Was this th' atrocious deed?   95
Which doom'd this hoary sufferer to bleed?
May ev'ry curse attend this pallid race,
Of earth the bane, of manhood the disgrace.
May their dread Judge, who, they pretend to say,
Rules the whole world with undivided sway,   100
May he (if such he hath) display his pow'r,

Poison their days, appall their midnight hour,
Bid them to fear his wrathful, stern, controul,
Pour his whole cup of trembling on their soul,
'Till they, repentant, these foul deeds forego,[13]   105
And feel their hearts distress'd with others woe!

Eclogue the Fourth

Time – Midnight.

With dreadful darkness, now the Isle is crown'd
And the fierce northern tempest howl'd around.
Loud roars the surf; the rocks return the roar,
And liquid fire seems bursting on the shore.
Swift darts the light'ning in fantastic guise,   5
And bellowing thunder rolls along the skies.
Convuls'd, the big black clouds drop sheets of rain,
And uproar lords it, o'er the dark domain.
At this dread hour, deep in an orange grove,
The sad Loango mourn'd his absent love.   10
  "Three nights in this appointed gloom I've past,
No Quamva comes, – and this shall be my last,
Hoarse thunder, cease thy roar: – perchance she stays,
Appall'd by thee, thou light'ning's fiery blaze:
'Tis past the hour: – chill North, thy blasts restrain,   15
And thou, black firmament, hold up thy rain:
Let Quamva come, my wife, my sole delight,
Torn from my arms by that accursed white;[14]
That pale-fac'd villain, – he, who through the day
O'erlooks our toils, and rules with bloody sway;   20
By him, who proud of lordship o'er the field,
By daily tortures made my Quamva yield;
Him, who has stol'n my treasure from my arms,
And now perhaps, now riots on her charms!

Oh! 'tis too much: – Come dark revenge and death;   25
He bravely falls, who stops a tyrant's breath.
"Roar on, fierce tempests: – Spirits of the air
Who rule the storms, oh! grant my ardent pray'r.
Assemble all your winds, direct their flight,
And hurl destruction on each cruel White: –   30
Sweep canes, and Mills, and houses to the ground,
And scatter ruin, pain, and death around: –
Rouse all you blasting fires, that lurk on high,
And 'midst his pleasures, let the plund'rer die!
But spare my Quamva, who, with smother'd sighs,   35
The odious rape endures, but not enjoys,
Wishing the Tyrant's senses drown'd in sleep,
That she enraptur'd may her promise keep.
Oh! 'tis too much: – Come dark revenge, and death;
He bravely falls, who stops a tyrant's breath.   40
"Yet let me pause. 'Tis said that woman's mind,
Still changes like the Hurricane's fierce wind,
Ranging from man to man, as shifts the Bee,
Or long-bill'd Humming-bird, from tree to tree.
How if she like the White, his gaudy cloaths,   45
His downy bed for pleasure and repose;
His shrivel'd frame, his sickly pallid face;
And finds a transport in his weak embrace.
It may be so. – Oh! vengeance on her head,
It is, it is: – She likes the Driver's bed.   50
For this she stays. – Ye hidden scorpions creep,
And with your pois'nous bites invade their sleep;
Ye keen Centipedes, oh! crawl around,
Ye sharp-tooth'd Snakes, inflict your deadly wound.
Fool that I was to think her woman's soul,   55
The love of beads, and fin'ry could controul:
Or think that one so beauteous would endure,
My lowly bed, a mat upon the floor;
My Yam, or Plantain, water from the spring,

And the small bliss Loango's love could bring.   60
– No, 'tis too plain: – Come dark revenge, and death,
And steel my soul to stop a wanton's breath . . . .
Three long, long nights still absent! 'Tis too plain,
The white man pleases, and my hopes are vain.
Come then, revenge, and 'midst this horrid roar   65
My thirsty knife shall drink their streaming gore.
Come, swiftly come, and aid me to surprise
These guilty lovers acting o'er their joys;
Just then – great Afric's Gods! – to strike the blow!
Just then – what transports would the stroke bestow!   70
Just then – my brain's on fire! – Come, pointed blade,
And poor Loango's vengeance justly aid.[15]
Three, three must fall! for Oh! I'll not survive;
I dread the white man's gibbeting alive,
Their wiry tortures, and their ling'ring fires: –   75
These he escapes, who by the knife expires.
Come then, revenge! – The deed will soon be o'er,
And then Loango views his native shore;
Rides on the fleeting clouds through airy roads,
Nor stops 'till plac'd in Afric's bless'd abodes.   80
Come pointed blade; – the Tyrant's house is nigh: –
And now for vengeance, death, and liberty! – "
Then to the place, with frenzy fir'd, he fled,
And the next morn beheld the mangled dead! –

Notes

1. Edward Rushton, *West-Indian Eclogues* (London: W. Lowndes and J. Philips, 1787).

2. The "discourse" referred to was the bishop's *Sermon preached before the Incorporated Society for the Propagation of the Gospel in Foreign Parts* (London: J.F. and C. Rivingtons, 1784), in which slave owners generally were urged to emulate the humane treatment of slaves on the estates in Barbados belonging to the Society.

3. [Author's note:] Three, and sometimes four, weeks are allowed for the recovery of the female slaves after child-bed. They are then sent into the field, and toil in common with their fellow-slaves, the infant being either carried on the back of its mother, or placed on the ground near the spot she is directed to work.

4. [Author's note:] Though the Negro-drivers on this Island are in general black-men, yet sometimes a subordinate European is stationed on the field, in order to superintend the whole. Wishing to ingratiate himself with his superiors, and to gain the reputation of being active and vigilant, he daily, under the mask of what is termed *necessary discipline*, inflicts the severest punishments, for the most trifling offences. The cow-skin, which is in common use, is a durable whip, composed of the tapered slips of cow or buffalo-hide, twisted to a point, to which is added such a lash as the *tormentors* may think the best fitted for what they in a facetious tone have been heard to term, *cutting up the black-birds.*

5. [Author's note:] The *Fetish* or *Fetiche* is a name given by the negroes to their deities: some of whom are supposed (in Guinea) to preside over whole provinces, and others, of an inferior rank, over single families only. These supposed divinities are sometimes trees, the head of an ape, or bird, or any other object of a wild fancy; but they are held by the negroes in the highest veneration.

6. [Author's note:] When the body of the unhappy sufferer is cut into furrows by the operation of the lash, it is frequently scourged a second time with a branch of the Eben, strongly beset with sharp thorns. This greatly increases the torments of the sufferer; but it is said to let out the congeal'd blood, and to prevent a mortification. The last step of this process of cruelty, is to wash the mangled wretch with a kind of pickle; or to throw him headlong into the sea, the effect of the salt-water being supposed to be nearly equal to that of the pickle.

7. [Author's note:] When the bodies of the negroes are covered with blood, and their flesh torn to pieces with the driver's whip, beaten pepper, and salt, are frequently thrown on the wounds, and a large stick of sealing-wax dropped down, in flames, leisurely upon them.

8. [Author's note:] A punishment not uncommon in the West-Indies. Some of the miserable sufferers have been known to exist a week in this most dreadful situation. (See a most affecting account of one instance of this kind, in the Rev. Mr. Ramsay's Treatise).

9. *manchineal*: a highly poisonous tree, described as "the most destructive tree in the universe" in Luffman's *Brief Account of Antigua*, 71: "the fruit bears a near resemblance to the golden pippin, but incloses a stone, and is a most subtle poison; the sap drawn from its body and branches, is the most venomous of poisons; the dust that falls from its flowers is poison, and the very droppings from its beautiful leaves after rain are poison".

10. In a long note Rushton outlines the history of the Maroons of Jamaica from the defeat of the Spanish in 1655, through their conflicts with the British and down to the peace treaty of 1740 and the settlement of the Maroons as a free people in their own territory. He concludes, "The chief service expected from them was, and still is, – to bring back to the planters those wretches, whom hunger, or cruelty, forces to the mountains for shelter. They are allowed a premium for every fugitive they restore, and are remarkably vigilant in their employment."

11. [Author's note:] Certain birds, commonly called in Jamaica black-birds, frequent the inmost recesses of the woods; and at the sight of a human being, they begin a loud and continual clamour, which is heard at a considerable distance. Their noise serves as a guide to the mountain-hunters, who immediately penetrate into that part of the wood, and seize the fugitives.

12. [Author's note:] A large Conch shell is used in some plantations to summon the slaves to their labour. On others the call is made by a bell.

13. [Author's note:] Some few plantations on this island might be enumerated, where by kind and judicious treatment, the Africans have so far multiplied, as to render the purchase of new Negroes (as they are termed) altogether unnecessary. Might not this become general? – The same causes, if suffered to operate fully as they ought, would universally produce the same effects. Setting aside every motive of humanity, sound policy naturally dictates such proceedings as these. And a few, and those not expensive, encouragements held forth to this dejected race, would produce the desired effect: such as the allowance of more ease, and better food, to the Negroes, and a grant of particular privileges, nay even freedom, to those mothers who have brought up a

certain number of children. And the expence of such humane provisions, as well as the temporary abatement (if any should happen) in the exertions of any given number of slaves, would soon be amply repaid, even to the largest plantation, by the savings of the money usually expended in the annual purchase of fresh slaves, and by the great, and acknowledged, superiority of home-born Negroes to those imported from Africa.

[Rushton acknowledges that he is "indebted for many of these observations" to the sermon by Beilby Porteus referred to in the dedication.]

14. [Author's note:] This cruel practice of the white master, or driver, in forcing the wives of the Negroes to a compliance, cannot be too severely reprobated. It has produced the most fatal consequences in every part of the West Indies. One instance, which occurred in Jamaica, shall be particularly mentioned. In the first skirmishes which happened with the Spaniards, after the English obtained possession of the Island, those Spanish slaves, in general, who had deserted from their former masters, fought under the English banners with great courage. One slave, in particular, was observed, by Colonel D'Oyley, the then English governor, to have exerted himself with uncommon intrepidity, and to have killed several Spaniards in close engagement. On inquiry it was found that this Negro had loved a young female slave to distraction; that he had been married to her for some years before the English invaded the Island; and that a short time before that invasion the tyrant, his master, had barbarously torn her from him, and compelled her to submit to his rapacious will. The injured husband implored, and remonstrated: and he was answered – by the whip. The disturbances, consequent upon the English invasion, afforded him an opportunity of an interview with his beloved wife. He told her, in a few words, that he still loved her with too sincere a passion, not to be sensible of what he had lost; but as their former days of love, and purity, could never return, he would not live to see her another's, when she could not be his own; for that, however innocent she might be in intention, he never could take an adulteress into his arms. *"Thus, therefore"* (says he) *"I now exert the rights of a husband:"* – and plunged his poniard into her heart! He immediately fled to the English. And, in his first engagement with his former masters, having observed his cruel tyrant in the Spanish line, he flew to the place where he fought, and soon laid him, with several other Spaniards, at his feet. Colonel D'Oyley declared him free, on the field of battle; and accompanied the grant of his freedom with the gift of a small plantation, upon which he lived ever afterwards in quiet, but with a thoughtfulness, and melancholy, which he could never overcome. He survived to a very advanced term of life, dying in the year 1708. His son behaved with the utmost gallantry against the

French, in their invasion of Jamaica in A.D. 1695; and hazarded his life, on several occasions, against the mountain-Negroes, whilst they continued in rebellion.

15. [Author's note:] The desire of revenge is an impetuous, a ruling passion, in the minds of these African slaves. *'Being heathens not only in their hearts, but in their lives, and knowing no distinction between vice and virtue, they give themselves up freely to the grossest immoralities, without being even conscious they are doing wrong.'* (Bishop of Chester's Sermon, before quoted.) But were it necessary, many instances might be adduced to shew, that some negroes are capable of kind, nay even of heroic actions. The story of Quashi, related by Mr. Ramsay, is one signal proof of this assertion. Another can be given by the Author of these Eclogues; who was preserved from destruction by the humanity of a Negro slave. His deliverance, however, was purchased at a price which he must ever deplore. For, in saving his life, the brave, the generous, African lost his own!

[The full story as related to William Shepherd is given in his life of the author prefixed to *Poems and Other Writings*. On one of his voyages to the West Indies Rushton became friendly with a slave named Quamina and taught him to read. Quamina was in a boat taking Rushton back to his ship from the shore when it capsized, and heavy waves swept the sailors off the keel to which they were clinging. "In this extremity Rushton swam towards a small water cask, which he saw floating at a distance. Quamina had gained this point of safety before him; and when the generous negro saw that his friend was too much exhausted to reach the cask, he pushed it towards him – bade him good-bye – and sunk, to rise no more." For Ramsay's account of Quashi, see pages 104–6 above.]

Part 4.

On the Haitian Revolution

"A rebel Negro armed & on his guard", from John Gabriel Stedman, *Narrative of a Five Years' Expedition against the Revolted Negroes of Surinam in Guiana on the Wild Coast of South America from the years 1772 to 1777* (London: J. Johnson, and J. Edwards, 1796), 2: facing p. 88. Courtesy of the Trustees of the National Library of Scotland.

A PARTICULAR ACCOUNT OF . . . THE INSURRECTION OF THE NEGROES IN ST. DOMINGO (1792)[1]

This pamphlet was sponsored by the West India Committee in Britain as propaganda against the campaign for abolition of the slave trade. It reached a fourth edition within months of first publication and contributed substantially to the impact of the rebellion on the British public. "People here are all panic-struck with the transactions in St. Domingo, and the apprehensions or pretended apprehensions of the like in Jamaica and other of our islands", Wilberforce wrote.[2] The pamphlet was accepted as an authentic record of events, even by abolitionists, although they rejected its polemical message. It provoked combative responses from, among others, Thomas Clarkson,[3] and William Roscoe.[4] The text here is from the first edition, which uses the present tense for narrative purposes; later editions changed this to the past tense.

SIRS,

The General Assembly of the French part of St. Domingo has appointed us a deputation to address you. –

In that character, our first duty is to assure you of the inviolable attachment of this important part of the empire to the Mother-Country, before we describe to you the terrible events which are now working its destruction, and solicit the earliest and most effectual succour to save, if it yet be possible, its wretched remains.

Long have we foreseen the evils which afflict us, and which doubtless will end in our annihilation, if the national justice and power interpose not speedily for our relief.

We come to lay before you some particulars which yet will give but an imperfect idea of our disasters and of our situation.

The General Assembly of the French part of St. Domingo, after having been constituted at Leogane, had appointed to hold its sessions in the town of the Cape. The deputies were gradually assembling there for the purposes of their mission.

Several of them arriving on the 16th (August) at the district of Limbé, distant six leagues from the Cape, were there witnesses of the burning of a trash-house on Chabaud's plantation.

The incendiary was a negro-driver of Desgrieux's plantation. Armed with a cutlass, he fled; M. Chabaud sees, pursues, and overtakes him; they fight; the negro is wounded, taken, and put in irons.

Being interrogated, he deposes, "that all the drivers, coachmen, domestics, and confidential negroes, of the neighbouring plantations and adjacent districts, have formed a plot to set fire to the plantations and to murder all the whites." He marks out, as ring-leaders, several negroes of his master's plantation, four of Flaville's, (situated at Acul, three leagues from the Cape,) and the negro Paul, driver on Blin's plantation at Limbé.

The municipality of Limbé proceeds to M. Chabaud's; and, on putting the same questions, receives the like answers from the incendiary negro. The municipality presents the examination in form of a verbal process to the Northern Provincial Assembly; and, informing Flaville's attorney (or manager) of the names of the conspirators that are about him, advises his securing and lodging them in the prison of the Cape.

This man, of a mild and gentle disposition, inclined more to confidence than suspicion, assembles the negroes under his command, and, communicating the information he received from the municipality, tells them he cannot give credit to a plot so atrocious, and offers them his head if they desire it. With one voice they answer, that the deposition of Desgrieux's driver is a detestable calumny, and swear an inviolable attachment to their manager.

He had the weakness to believe them, and his credulity has been our ruin. The municipality of Limbé demands from M. Planteau, attorney of Blin's plantation, that they may examine the negro Paul. This slave, being interrogated, replies – "that the accusation brought against him is false and injurious; that, full of gratitude to his master, from whom he was daily experiencing acts of kindness, he would never be found concerned in plots that might be framed against the existence of the whites and against their property."

In return for this perfidious declaration, and under assurance from M. Planteau that Paul deserved credit, he was released.

In this state matters continued till the 21st, when the public force of Limbé, at the requisition of the municipality, proceeded to Desgrieux's plantation, to take into custody the negro cook, accused of being a ringleader: the negro flies; finds out the negro Paul of Blin's plantation, and, in conjunction with the other conspirators, they prepare fire and sword, destined for the completion of their horrible designs.

In the night, between the 22d and 23d, twelve negroes reach the sugar-house of Noé's plantation, at Acul, seize upon the apprentice refiner; drag him before the great house, where he expires under their wounds. His cries bring out the attorney of the estate, who is laid breathless on the ground by two musket balls. The wretches proceed to the apartment of the head refiner, and assassinate him in his bed. A young man, lying sick in a neighbouring chamber, they leave for dead under the blows of their cutlasses; yet he has strength to crawl to the next plantation, where he relates the horrors he has witnessed, and that the *surgeon* only was spared; an exception which was repeated in respect to the surgeons in general, of whose abilities the negroes had reckoned they might stand in need.

The plunderers proceed to Clement's plantation, and there kill the proprietor and the refiner.

Day begins to break and favours the junction of the ill-disposed, who spread over the plain with dreadful shouts, set fire to houses and canes, and massacre the inhabitants.

That same night the revolt had broken out on the three plantations of Galifet.[5] At one of which, the blacks, with arms in their hands, make way into the chamber of the refiner, with a design to assassinate him, but only wound him in the arm; favoured by the night, he escapes, and runs to the great house. The whites, who reside there, unite for their defence. M. Odeluc, a member of the General Assembly, and attorney for the concerns of Galifet, comes to the Cape, and gives information there of the insurrection of his negroes. Escorted by the patrol, he reaches the plantation, seizes the ring-leaders, and returns at their head to the town. Immediately he sets out again, with twenty men in arms, that he may restore tranquillity and maintain order. But the negroes are all united, and attack him. *Their standard was the body of a white child empaled upon a stake.*[6] M. Odeluc, addressing himself to his coachman, whom he perceived among the foremost, exclaims – "Wretch, I have treated thee ever with kindness, why dost thou seek my death?" "True," he replied, "but I *have promised* to massacre you:" and that instant a hundred weapons are upon him. The majority of the whites perished with him, particularly M. Averoult, also a member of the General Assembly.

At the very same time Flaville's gang (that which had so recently sworn fidelity to the attorney) is armed, revolts, enters the apartments of the whites, and murders five of them who reside on the plantation. The attorney's wife, on her knees, begs the life of her husband. The inexorable negroes assassinate the husband, and tell the wife that she and her daughters are reserved for their pleasures.

M. Robert, a carpenter, employed on the same plantation, is seized by the negroes, who bind him between two planks, and saw him deliberately in two.

A youth, aged sixteen, wounded in two places, escapes the fury of the cannibals, and it is from him we learn these facts. The sword then is exchanged for the torch; fire is set to the canes, and the buildings soon add to the conflagration; it is the appointed signal; revolt is the word; and, with the speed of lightning, it bursts out on the neighbouring plantations; wherever there are whites, there are so many victims slaughtered; men, women, the infant, and the aged, expire undistinguished under the knife of the assassins.

A colonist is murdered by the very negroe whom he had most distinguished by acts of kindness. His wife, stretched upon his body, is forced to satisfy the brutality of the murderer.

M. Cagnet, inhabitant of Acul, seeking to escape from these horrors, embarks for the Cape. His domestic negroe begs permission to attend him. Such a mark of attachment determines his master to leave him as a guard upon the plantation, that he may endeavour to preserve it. But M. Cagnet has hardly set foot on-board when he sees that slave, with a torch in his hand, setting fire to his property.

Expresses being sent to the Cape, armed citizens and troops of the line are dispatched thence; they proceed towards the strongest body of mutineers, and destroy a part of them; but, finding the number of revolters increasing in centuple proportion to their losses, and being unable to keep their ground, they retreat in expectation of a reinforcement, which arrived, but only in the night, headed by M. de Touzard, who took the command of the little army.

M. de Touzard, perceiving that the revolters were rallying on Latour's plantation, marched thither. Their number might be from three to four thousand. The moment the artillery was ready to play to disperse them, the negroes pretended to surrender. M. de Touzard advanced; many of them exclaimed, that they would return to their duty. He trusted to their repentance, and retired. Humanity and the interests of the colony enjoined his forbearance, but it was not long before he was undeceived; the negroes separated indeed, but only that they might recruit their numbers with all the neighbouring gangs. The army was returned into the town to take new steps for putting an end to the disorder. The revolters profited by this interval to fill up the measure of their depredations. Our communications with the adjacent districts became impeded. We were alarmed lest the disorder had reached them, and our fears were soon realized. We learnt, by means of persons escaped by sea, that Limbé, Plaisance, Port Margot, were a prey to like horrors, and every citizen, in detailing his misfortunes, discovered to us new crimes.

M. Potier, inhabitant of Port Margot, had taught his negro-driver[7] to read and write. He had given him his liberty, which the fellow enjoyed; he had bequeathed him 10,000 livres, which were soon to be paid to him; he had also given to this negro's mother a piece of land, on which she cultivated coffee. The monster seduces the gang of his benefactor and of his mother, burns and destroys their possessions, and obtains, for this action, a promotion to the generalcy.

At Great River, an inhabitant, M. Cardineau, had two natural sons of colour, to whom he had given their liberty, and who, in their childhood, had been the objects of his tenderest care. They accost him with a pistol at his breast, and demand his money. He consents; but no sooner have they obtained it than they stab him.

At Acul, M. Chauvet du Breuil, deputy to the General Assembly, is assassinated by a mulatto, aged sixteen, his natural son, to whom he destined his fortune, having manumitted him from his childhood.

At the Great Ravine of Limbé, a colonist, father of two young ladies, whites, is bound down by a savage ring-leader of a band, who ravishes the eldest in his presence, delivers the younger over to one of his satellites; their passion satisfied, they slaughter both the father and the daughters.

M. and Mad. Baillon, with their son-in-law and daughter, encouraged by their negroes, remain on their plantation; but the depredations of those, whom they have most trusted, warn them that it is time to fly. The nurse of Mad. Baillon, the younger, confesses to her there is not an instant to be lost, and offers to attend them. An old servant engages to conduct their steps. Luckily Mad. Baillon's nurse was wife of Paul Blin, one of the negro generals, and she obtained from him some provisions for [her] master's family. At her intreaty he even promised to provide, at a distant *barquadier*,[8] a canoe to carry the fugitives to the Cape. But how great their grief at seeing a little skiff, without a mast, or oars, or rowers! One of them tries to embark in it; the flimsy boat oversets, and his life, with difficulty, is saved. Again, they apply to Paul, and his wife reproaches him with breaking his promise. He replies, "that he only provided this as a preferable mode of death to that which the revolters had prepared for the unhappy family:" Terrified at this recital, despair gives them new strength; they set off on foot, and after performing a journey of five leagues only, in twenty-one days, every day encompassed with dangers, they arrive at Port Margot, whence they reach the Cape.

Mean time the flames gained ground on all sides. La Petite Anse, la Plaine du Nord, the district of Morin, Limonade, presented only heaps of ashes and of dead bodies.

Nothing, one would think, could deepen the horrors of this recital; and yet, Sirs, it is marked with features of a still more dreadful character, when we see that the slaves, which had been most kindly treated by their masters, were the soul of the Insurrection: it was *they* who betrayed and delivered their humane masters to the assassin's sword; it was *they* who seduced and stirred up to revolt the gangs disposed to fidelity. It was *they* who massacred whomsoever refused to become their accomplice. What a lesson for *the Amis des Noirs!*[9] what a heart-breaking discovery to the colonists themselves, to whom futurity could suggest nothing but motives of despair, if, in the midst of so many crimes, there had not yet been found slaves who gave proof of an invincible fidelity, and who made manifest their determination to detest the seduction of those who would, with promises of liberty, enveigle them to certain destruction. That liberty is theirs; but it is the gift of their masters, the reward of their attachment, and it has been ratified by the representatives of the colony, amidst the transports of universal gratitude.

Notes

1. *A Particular Account of the Commencement and Progress of the Insurrection of the Negroes in St. Domingo, which began in August last; Being a Translation of the Speech made to the National Assembly, The 3rd of November, 1791, by the Deputies from the General Assembly of the French part of St. Domingo* (London: J. Sewell, 1792).
2. See Geggus, *Slavery, War, and Revolution*, 124.
3. In *The True State of the Case, respecting the Insurrection at St. Domingo* (Ipswich, 1792).
4. See below, page 393.
5. [Translator's note:] At the Cape, it was a proverbial mode of expressing any man's happiness – 'Ma foi, il est heureux comme un negre de Galifet.' 'He is as happy as one of Galifet's negroes'.
6. This lurid detail does not appear in the descriptions of the attack on Gallifet given by other witnesses and may be a fiction, but "it was accepted as true by many readers, and often repeated as a symbol, and condemnation, of the insurrection"; Laurent Dubois, *Avengers of the New World: The Story of the Haitian Revolution* (Cambridge, MA: Belknap, 2004), 111.
7. [Translator's note:] The French word is *commandeur*, signifying, a negro trusted with the direction of a small party when at work.

8. *barquadier*: wharf; a Jamaican term, from Sp. embarcadero, probably gallicized by English settlers. Cassidy and Le Page, *Dictionary of Jamaican English*.

9. [Translator's note:] Or *friends of the blacks*, by which name is distinguished, in France, the party that have seconded the English project for abolishing the Slave-Trade. [The *Amis des Noirs*, however, went further than the British Society for the Abolition of the Slave Trade by calling for the total abolition of slavery.]

WILLIAM ROSCOE

An Inquiry into the Causes of the Insurrection (1792)[1]

Roscoe's authorship of this well-known pamphlet is attested by his
son Henry in his *Life of William Roscoe*.[2] It was published anonymously during the parliamentary debate on Wilberforce's bill for
abolition of the slave trade in response to *A Particular Account* (page
385 above) and to combat the exploitation of the St Domingo rebellion as propaganda for the anti-abolitionists. The pamphlet begins
with the excerpt given here.

After a contest of five years, between the Friends of Justice and the African
Slave-Dealers, the moral, physical, and political evils, of that disgraceful traf-
fick, have been fully developed and ascertained to the kingdom at large. The
conviction of truth has been followed by the glow of honest indignation,
and the voice of the people has called upon their Legislators, to wash away
the national stain. Contradicted in their bold assertions, and refuted in their
arguments, the abettors of this trade had almost withdrawn themselves
from a struggle in which their own weapons recoiled upon themselves: for it
may justly be remarked, that the most expeditious method of forming an
abhorrence of the Slave Trade, is to read the pieces written in its defence.

At this juncture, when nothing remained but for the Representatives of
the people to comply with the wishes of their Constituents, in pronouncing

the Abolition of this Trade, another, and it is to be hoped a last attempt is made by its advocates to influence the publick mind: – An insurrection of the Negroes has taken place in the Island of St. Domingo, and this circumstance is to be adduced as a proof of the dangerous consequences to arise from the proposed measure. – "Beware," say the Partizans of this Trade, "how you interfere with the concerns of your West Indian Islands – let the example of the French deter you from proceeding a step further in so dangerous a path." But let us be allowed to ask, How far the events that have taken place in St. Domingo apply to the question now before the British House of Commons? – Were these disturbances the consequences of an Abolition of the Trade by the French? – No – Even the eloquence of Mirabeau was in this instance ineffectual. Were they the result of any regulations made by the Assembly for the government or relief of the Slaves? No: for the decrees of the Assembly on the subject uniformly purport, "that all regulations on that head should originate with the Planters themselves." If those dreadful disorders are chargeable to the National Assembly, it is because they did *not* interfere: – because they left the black labourers in the islands at the mercy of their masters; and, after having declared that all mankind was born equal, sanctioned a decree that gave the lie to the first principles of their constitution.

Of the several pieces that have made their appearance on this subject, the address or remonstrance of "the Deputies of St. Domingo to the National Assembly of France,"[3] calls for particular notice. But before we proceed to an examination into the causes of the enormities it records, let us be permitted a few reflections on the awful scenes that the Island of St. Domingo has of late exhibited: the picture of these outrages forms indeed the most striking part of the narrative in question. The destruction of flourishing plantations; the burning of houses; the slaughter of the whites by secret treachery, or open revolt; the gross violations of female chastity; the dissolution of all the bonds of subordination, and all the attachments of society, contribute to fill the dreadful sketch.

Are these enormities to be lamented? they surely are. Can they excite our wonder? by no means. What is the state of the labouring negro? Is he not a being bound down by force? labouring under constant compulsion? driven to complete his task by the immediate discipline of the whip? – Are affection, lenity, and forbearance the result of oppression and abuse? When the native ferocity of Africa is sharpened by the keen sense of long continued injury, who shall set bounds to its revenge?

Again, how have the fierce dispositions of savage life been counteracted or improved by the example of their white superiors? Resistance is always justifiable where force is the substitute of right; nor is the commission of a civil crime possible in a state of slavery. Yet the punishments that have been devised in the French islands to repress crimes, that could only exist by the abuse of the Slave Holder, are such as nature revolts at. How often have these unfortunate beings beheld their fellows, beat, in famine and distraction, the bars of an iron cage, in which they were doomed to pass in inconceivable misery the last days of their existence? Is it not known, that in these wretched islands a human being has resigned his life in the torments of a slow-consuming fire? An unavenged instance of an act so awfully atrocious, marks out for perdition the country that could suffer it. When the oppressor thus enforces his authority, what must be the effects of the sufferer's resentment?

In the forcible violation of female chastity we trace the most detestable extreme of brutality, and, in the estimation of sensibility, the loss of life is preferable to its disgrace: but modesty is not confined to the capacity of a blush, nor sensibility to a particular form and feature. Let this account then be settled between the African Trader, or the imperious Planter, who compels to his embrace the unwilling object of his lust, and the exasperated Slave, who gratifies by this hateful act, not his sensuality, but his resentment.

But let us suppose, that the sense of shame is incompatible with a black complexion, and that the negro could witness without emotion the gross abuse of the object of his affection; let us suppose too, that the unnatural punishments before mentioned were forgotten, because they were rare; and that the daily discipline of the whip was unheeded, because it was so modified as seldom to be the immediate occasion of death. Yet the Negro had other examples before his eyes. A dissention had arisen amongst the Holders of the Slaves; those who had before united in oppressing them, were now at variance amongst themselves. They had proceeded to open violence; whilst the Slaves waited the event with silence, though not with indifference. One party obtained an early superiority; the leader of the weaker number was taken, and the Negroes were spectators of the death of Ogé, a man who partook of their colour, and who was broken alive upon the wheel.[4] Twenty-five of his followers shared the same fate. If the cold-blooded sons of Europe, educated in the habits of improved society, and affecting to feel the precepts of a mild and merciful religion, can thus forget themselves, and insult their own nature, ought they to wonder that the African should imitate the pattern, and if possible improve upon their example?

Notes

1. William Roscoe, *An Inquiry into the Causes of the Insurrection of the Negroes in the Island of St. Domingo* (London: J. Johnson, 1792).

2. Henry Roscoe, *Life of William Roscoe* (London: T. Cadell, 1833), 1:89.

3. [Author's note:] Translated into English, and published under the title of '*A Particular Account of the Commencement and Progress of the Insurrection of the Negroes in St. Domingo.*' It is scarcely necessary to observe, that its being printed (in France) *by order of the National Assembly*, gives it no additional authenticity; it being a measure always adopted in papers of this length, in order to afford the Members an opportunity of considering them. [See page 385 above.]

4. Vincent Ogé (1750–91), a free coloured man, was sent to France in 1789 to plead before the National Assembly for civil rights for the free coloureds of St Domingo and for emancipation of the slaves. His pleas were rejected and when, on his return to the island in 1790, the governor also refused to grant his petitions, Ogé raised a rebellion. It was defeated and he was convicted of treason and executed in the barbarous manner described by Roscoe.

Bryan Edwards (1743–1800)

An Historical Survey of the French Colony in the Island of St. Domingo (1797)[1]

Edwards accompanied the British naval force sent from Jamaica to St Domingo in 1791 to relieve the French colonists, arriving on 26 September, a month after the outbreak of the rebellion. His narrative is heavily indebted to *A Particular Account* (above, page 385), sometimes using identical phrasing. Edwards probably had access to the colonial deputies' report while he was still in Jamaica before returning to England in 1792, but the verbal parallels suggest that he may have been the actual translator. He also gathered material from witnesses on the island and from other French sources; in the preface he claims that, "having personally visited that unhappy country soon after the revolt of the negroes in 1791, and formed connexions there, which have supplied me with regular communications ever since, I possess a mass of evidence, and important documents". He sometimes adds details not found in *A Particular Account* and heightens the rhetoric, both for polemical purposes and for dramatic effect.

The qualified sympathy with slave rebellion which Edwards showed in earlier writings did not extend to the St Domingo revolution, which he presents as a gruesome demonstration of the incendiary effect of anti-slavery propaganda, and a warning to planters in the British West Indies. Edwards's *Historical Survey* was included in editions of his *History of the West Indies* from 1798 onwards, and was revised in 1800 to incorporate corrections and additions, but his account of the 1791 rebellion remained substantially unchanged. The text here is from the 1797 edition.

From Preface[2]

The rebellion of the negroes in St. Domingo, and the insurrection of the mulattoes . . . had one and the same origin. It was not the strong and irresistible impulse of human nature, groaning under oppression, that excited either of those classes to plunge their daggers into the bosoms of unoffending women and helpless infants. They were driven into those excesses – reluctantly driven – by the vile machinations of men calling themselves philosophers (the proselytes and imitators in France, of the Old Jewry associates in London[3]) whose pretences to philanthropy were as gross a mockery of human reason, as their conduct was an outrage on all the feelings of our nature, and the ties which hold society together!

It is indeed true, that negro-rebellions have heretofore arisen in this and other islands in the West Indies, to which no such exciting causes contributed: but it is equally certain that those rebellions always originated among the newly-imported negroes only; many of whom had probably lived in a state of freedom in Africa, and had been fraudulently, or forcibly, sold into slavery by their chiefs. That cases of this kind do sometimes occur in the slave trade, I dare not dispute, and I admit that revolt and insurrection are their natural consequence.

But, in St. Domingo, a very considerable part of the insurgents were – not Africans, but – Creoles, or natives. Some of the leaders were favoured domesticks among the white inhabitants, born and brought up in their families. A few of them had even received those advantages, the perversion of which, under their philosophical preceptors, served only to render them pre-eminent in mischief; for having been taught to read, they were led to imbibe, and enabled to promulgate, those principles and doctrines which led, and always will lead, to the subversion of all government and order.

Rebellion of the Negroes in the Northern Province, and Enormities committed by them.[4]

It was on the morning of the 23d of August, just before day, that a general alarm and consternation spread throughout the town of the Cape, from a report that all the negro slaves in the several neighbouring parishes had revolted, and were at that moment carrying death and desolation over the adjoining large and beautiful plain to the North-east. The governor, and most of the military officers on duty, assembled together; but the reports were so confused and contradictory, as to gain but little credit; when, as daylight began to break, the sudden and successive arrival, with ghastly countenances, of persons who had with difficulty escaped the massacre, and flown to the town for protection, brought a dreadful confirmation of the fatal tidings.

The rebellion first broke out on a plantation called Noé, in the parish of Acul, nine miles only from the city. Twelve or fourteen of the ringleaders, about the middle of the night, proceeded to the refinery, or sugar-house, and seized on a young man, the refiner's apprentice, dragged him to the front of the dwelling-house, and there hewed him into pieces with their cutlasses: his screams brought out the overseer, whom they instantly shot. The rebels now found their way to the apartment of the refiner, and massacred him in his bed. A young man lying sick in a neighbouring chamber, was left apparently dead of the wounds inflicted by their cutlasses; he had strength enough however to crawl to the next plantation, and relate the horrors he had witnessed. He reported, that all the whites of the estate which he had left were murdered, except only the surgeon, whom the rebels had compelled to accompany them, on the idea that they might stand in need of his professional competence. Alarmed by this intelligence, the persons to whom it was communicated immediately sought their safety in flight. What became of the poor youth I have never been informed.

The revolters (consisting now of all the slaves belonging to that plantation) proceeded to the house of a Mr. Clement, by whose negroes also they were immediately joined, and both he and his refiner were massacred. The murderer of Mr. Clement was his own postillion, a man to whom he had always shewn great kindness. The other white people on this estate contrived to make their escape.

At this juncture, the negroes on the plantation of M. Flaville, a few miles distant, likewise rose and murdered five white persons, one of whom (the *procureur* or attorney for the estate) had a wife and three daughters. These unfortunate women, while imploring for mercy of the savages on their knees, beheld their husband and father murdered before their faces. For themselves, they were devoted to a more horrid fate, and were carried away captives by the assassins.

The approach of day-light served only to discover sights of horror. It was now apparent that the negroes on all the estates in the plain acted in concert, and a general massacre of the whites took place in every quarter. On some few estates, indeed, the lives of the women were spared, but they were reserved only to gratify the brutal appetites of the ruffians; and it is shocking to relate, that many of them suffered violation on the dead bodies of their husbands and fathers!

In the town itself, the general belief for some time was, that the revolt was by no means an extensive, but a sudden and partial insurrection only. The largest sugar-plantation on the plain was that of Mons. Gallifet, situated about eight miles from the town, the negroes belonging to which had always been treated with such kindness and liberality, and possessed so many advantages, that it became a proverbial expression among the lower white people, in speaking of any man's good fortune to say *il est heureux comme un negre de Gallifet* (he is as happy as one of Gallifet's negroes). M. Odeluc, the attorney, or agent, for this plantation, was a member of the general assembly, and being fully persuaded that the negroes belonging to it would remain firm in their obedience, determined to repair thither to encourage them in opposing the insurgents; to which end, he desired the assistance of a few soldiers from the town-guard, which was granted him. He proceeded accordingly, but on approaching the estate, to his surprise and grief he found all the negroes in arms on the side of the rebels, and (horrid to tell!) *their standard was the body of a white infant, which they had recently impaled on a stake!*[5] M. Odeluc had advanced too far to retreat undiscovered, and both he, and a friend that accompanied him, with most of the soldiers, were killed without mercy. Two or three only of the patrole, escaped by flight; and conveyed the dreadful tidings to the inhabitants of the town.

By this time, all or most of the white persons that had been found on the several plantations, being massacred or forced to seek their safety in flight, the ruffians exchanged the sword for the torch. The buildings and cane-fields were every where set on fire; and the conflagrations, which were visible from the town, in a thousand different quarters, furnished a prospect more shocking, and reflections more dismal, than fancy can paint, or the powers of man describe . . . .

The inhabitants [of the town], being strengthened by a number of seamen from the ships, and brought into some degree of order and military subordination, were now desirous that a detachment should be sent to attack the strongest body of the revolters. Orders were given accordingly; and M. de Touzard, an officer who had distinguished himself in the service of the North Americans, took the command of a party of militia and troops of the line. With these he marched to the plantation of a M. Latour, and attacked a body of about four thousand of the rebel negroes. Many were destroyed, but to little purpose; for Touzard, finding the number of revolters to encrease in more than a centuple proportion to their losses, was at length obliged to retreat; and it cannot be doubted, that if the rebels had forthwith proceeded to the town, defenceless as it then was towards the plain, they might have fired it without difficulty, and destroyed all its inhabitants, or compelled them to fly to the shipping for refuge . . . .

To such of the different parishes as were open to communication either by land or by sea, notice of the revolt had been transmitted within a few hours after advice of it was received at the Cape; and the white inhabitants of many of those parishes had therefore found time to establish camps, and form a chain of posts, which for a short time seemed to prevent the rebellion spreading beyond the Northern province.[6] Two of those camps however, one at Grande Riviere, the other at Dondon, were attacked by the negroes (who were here openly joined by the mulattoes) and forced with great slaughter. At Dondon, the whites maintained the contest for seven hours; but were overpowered by the infinite disparity of numbers, and compelled to give way, with the loss of upwards of one hundred of their body. The survivors took refuge in the Spanish territory.

These two districts therefore; the whole of the rich and extensive plain of the Cape, together with the contiguous mountains, were now wholly abandoned to the ravages of the enemy; and the cruelties which they exercised, uncontrouled, on such of the miserable whites as fell into their hands, cannot be remembered without horror, nor reported in terms strong enough to convey a proper idea of their atrocity.

They seized Mr. Blen, an officer of the police, and having nailed him alive to one of the gates of his plantation, chopped off his limbs, one by one, with an axe.

A poor man named Robert, a carpenter by trade, endeavouring to conceal himself from the notice of the rebels, was discovered in his hiding-place; and the savages declared *that he should die in the way of his occupation:* accordingly they bound him between two boards, and deliberately sawed him asunder.

M. Cardineau, a planter of Grande Riviere, had two natural sons by a black woman. He had manumitted them in their infancy, and bred them up with great tenderness. They both joined in the revolt; and when their father endeavoured to divert them from their purpose, by soothing language and pecuniary offers, they took his money, and then stabbed him to the heart.

All the white, and even the mulatto children whose fathers had not joined in the revolt, were murdered without exception, frequently before the eyes, or clinging to the bosoms, of their mothers. Young women of all ranks were first violated by a whole troop of barbarians, and then generally put to death. Some of them were indeed reserved for the further gratification of the lust of the savages, and others had their eyes scooped out with a knife.

In the parish of Limbé, at a place called the Great Ravine, a venerable planter, the father of two beautiful young ladies, was tied down by a savage ringleader of a band, who ravished the eldest daughter in his presence, and delivered over the youngest to one of his followers: their passion being satisfied, they slaughtered both the father and the daughters.

Amidst these scenes of horror, one instance however occurs of such fidelity and attachment in a negro, as is equally unexpected and affecting. Mons. and Madame Baillon, their daughter and son-in-law, and two white servants, residing on a mountain plantation about thirty miles from Cape François, were apprized of the revolt by one of their own slaves, who was himself in the conspiracy, but promised, if possible, to save the lives of his master and his family. Having no immediate means of providing for their escape, he conducted them into an adjacent wood; after which he went and

joined the revolters. The following night, he found an opportunity of bringing them provisions from the rebel camp. The second night he returned
again, with a further supply of provisions; but declared that it would be out
of his power to give them any further assistance. After this, they saw nothing of the negro for three days; but at the end of that time he came again;
and directed the family how to make their way to a river which led to Port
Margot, assuring them they would find a canoe on a part of the river which
he described. They followed his directions, found the canoe, and got safely
into it; but were overset by the rapidity of the current, and after a narrow
escape, thought it best to return to their retreat in the mountains. The
negro, anxious for their safety, again found them out, and directed them to a
broader part of the river, where he assured them he had provided a boat; but
said it was the last effort he could make to save them. They went accordingly, but not finding the boat, gave themselves up for lost, when the faithful
negro again appeared like their guardian angel. He brought with him
pigeons, poultry and bread; and conducted the family, by slow marches in
the night, along the banks of the river, until they were within sight of the
wharf at Port Margot; when telling them they were entirely out of danger,
he took his leave for ever, and went to join the rebels. The family were in the
woods nineteen nights[7] . . . .

To detail the various conflicts, skirmishes, massacres, and scenes of
slaughter, which this exterminating war produced, were to offer a disgusting
and frightful picture; – wherein we should behold cruelties unexampled in
the annals of mankind; human blood poured forth in torrents; the earth
blackened with ashes, and the air tainted with pestilence. It was computed
that, within two months after the revolt first began, upwards of two thousand white persons, of all conditions and ages, had been massacred; – that
one hundred and eighty sugar plantations, and about nine hundred coffee,
cotton, and indigo settlements had been destroyed (the buildings thereon
being consumed by fire), and one thousand two hundred christian families
reduced from opulence, to such a state of misery as to depend altogether for
their clothing and sustenance on publick and private charity. Of the insurgents, it was reckoned that upwards of ten thousand had perished by the
sword or by famine; and some hundreds by the hands of the executioner; –
many of them, I grieve to say, under the torture of the wheel; – a system of

revenge and retaliation, which no enormities of savage life could justify or excuse.[8]

Notes

1. Bryan Edwards, *An Historical Survey of the French Colony in the Island of St. Domingo* (London: John Stockdale, 1797).
2. Dated London, December 1796.
3. The reference, as Edwards explains in chapter 7, is to "the British association for the abolition of the slave trade, which held its meetings in the Old Jewry in London; and the society called *Les Amis des Noirs* in Paris"; cf. *A Particular Account*, page 392n9, above. For discussion of modern theories about the origins of the revolt, see Geggus, *Slavery, War, and Revolution*.
4. From chapter 6.
5. See *A Particular Account*, page 391n6, above.
6. [Author's note:] It is believed that a general insurrection was to have taken place throughout the colony on the 25th of August (St. Louis's day); but that the impatience and impetuosity of some negroes on the plain, induced them to commence their operations two days before the time.
7. [Author's note, 1801 edition:] This account was communicated by Madame Baillon herself to a friend of the author, who was with him at St. Domingo, and who spoke French like a native: from that same friend I received it the same day, and immediately committed the particulars to writing.
8. [Author's note:] Two of these unhappy men suffered in this manner under the window of the author's lodging's, and in his presence, at Cape François, on Thursday the 28th of September 1791. They were broken on two pieces of timber placed crosswise. One of them expired on receiving the third stroke on his stomach, each of his legs and arms having been first broken in two places; the first three blows he bore without a groan. The other had a harder fate. When the executioner, after breaking his legs and arms, lifted up the instrument to give the finishing stroke on the breast, and which (by putting the criminal out of his pain) is called *le coup de grace*, the mob, with the ferociousness of cannibals, called out *arretez!* (stop) and compelled him to leave his work unfinished. In that condition, the miserable wretch, with his broken limbs doubled up, was put on a cart-wheel, which was placed horizontally, one end of the axle-tree being driven into the earth. He seemed perfectly sensible, but uttered not a groan. At the end of forty minutes, some English

seamen, who were spectators of the tragedy, strangled him in mercy. As to all
the French spectators (many of them persons of fashion, who beheld the scene
from the windows of their upper apartments), it grieves me to say that they
looked on with the most perfect composure and *sang froid*. Some of the ladies,
as I was told, even ridiculed, with a great deal of unseemly mirth,
the sympathy manifested by the English at the sufferings of the wretched
criminals.

"Life and Character of Toussaint L'Ouverture" (1805)[1]

Rainsford, an Irishman, served as an officer in the British Army in the American War of Independence and in the Netherlands, before going to the West Indies in the 1790s. He retired about 1803 with the rank of captain. *An Historical Account of the Black Empire of Hayti*, from which this extract is taken, is a much enlarged version of Rainsford's *Memoir of Transactions that took place in St. Domingo in the Spring of 1802*. In the latter work he described his personal encounter with Toussaint in 1798 and related how Toussaint had ordered his release when he was afterwards captured by rebel soldiers and condemned to death as a spy. He gives the sources of his description of Toussaint here as oral tradition, "MS. account", *Memoires du General Toussaint* and, surprisingly, Dubroca's denigratory *Vie de Toussaint-Louverture* (1802).

Toussaint L'Ouverture was born a slave in the year 1745, on the estate of Count de Noé, at a small distance from Cape François, in the northern province of St. Domingo, a spot since remarkable as the very source of revolution, and site of a camp, (that of Breda,) from whence its native general has issued mandates more powerful than those of any monarch on the earth.

While tending his master's flocks, the genius of Toussaint began to

expand itself, by an attention towards objects beyond the reach of his com-
prehension; and without any other opportunity than was equally possessed
by those around him, who remained nearly in impenetrable ignorance, he
learnt to read, write, and use figures. Encouraged by the progress he rapidly
made in these arts, and fired with the prospect of higher attainments, he
employed himself assiduously in the further cultivation of his talents. His
acquirements, as is oftentimes the case, under such circumstances, excited
the admiration of his fellow slaves, and fortunately attracted the attention of
the attorney, or manager of the estate, M. Bayou de Libertas. This gentleman, with a discrimination honorable to his judgment, withdrew Toussaint
from the labor of the fields, to his own house, and began the amelioration of
his fortune, by appointing him his postilion, an enviable situation among
slaves, for its profit, and comparative respectability.

This instance of patronage by M. Bayou, impressed itself strongly on the
susceptible mind of Toussaint. True genius and elevated sentiments are
inseparable; the recollection of the most trivial action, kindly bestowed in
obscurity, or under the pressure of adverse circumstances, warms the heart
of sensibility, even in the hour of popular favor, more than the proudest
honors. This truth was exemplified by the subsequent gratitude of
Toussaint towards his master. He continued to deserve and receive promotion, progressively, to offices of considerable confidence . . . .

At the age of twenty-five Toussaint attached himself to a female of similar character to his own, and their union cemented by marriage, which does
not appear to have been violated, conferred respectability on their offspring.
Still he continued a slave; nor did the goodness of M. Bayou, although it
extended to render him as happy as the state of servitude would admit, ever
contemplate the manumission of one who was to become a benefactor to
him and his family.

In the comforts of a situation possessing a degree of opulence, Toussaint
found leisure to extend the advantages of his early acquisitions, and by the
acquaintance of some priests, who possessed little more of the character
than the name, acquired the knowledge of new sources of information, and
a relish for books of a superior order than first attracted his attention; the
author of whom he became the most speedily enamoured, was the Abbé
Raynal, on whose history and speculations in philosophy and politics he was

intent for weeks together, and never quitted, but with an intention to return, with renewed and additional pleasure[2] . . . .

Continuing on the estate on which he was born, when the deliberations preceding the actual rebellion of the slaves, were taking place upon the plantation of Noé, the opinion of him who was always regarded with esteem and admiration was solicited. His sanction was of importance, as he had a number of slaves under his command, and a general influence over his fellow negroes. Among the leaders of this terrible revolt were several of his friends, who he had deemed worthy to make his associates for mutual intelligence; yet, from whatever cause is not ascertained, he forbore in the first instance to join in the contest of liberty. It is probable that his manly heart revolted from cruelties attendant on the first burst of revenge in slaves about to retaliate their wrongs and sufferings on their owners. He saw that the innocent would suffer with the guilty; and that the effects of revolution regarded future, more than present justice . . . .

There were ties which connected Toussaint more strongly than the consideration of temporary circumstances. These were, gratitude for the benefits received from his master, and generosity to those who were about to fall, – not merely beneath the stroke of the assassin, for that relief from their sufferings was not to be allowed to all, but likewise the change of situations of luxury and splendour, to an exile of danger, contempt, and poverty, with all the miseries such a reverse can acumulate.

Toussaint prepared for the emigration of M. Bayou de Libertas, as if he had only removed for his pleasure, to the American continent. He found means to embark produce that should form a useful provision for the future; procured his escape with his family, and contrived every plan for his convenience: nor did his care end here, for after M. Bayou's establishment in safety at Baltimore, in Maryland, he availed himself of every opportunity to supply any conceived deficiency, and, as he rose in circumstances, to render those of his *protégé* more qualified to his situation, and equal to that warm remembrance of the services he owed him, which would never expire.

Having provided for the safety of his master in the first instance, Toussaint no longer resisted the temptations to join the army of his country, which had (at this period) assumed a regular form. He attached himself to the corps under the command of a courageous black chief, named Biassou, and was appointed next in command to him. Though possessed of striking abilities, the disposition of this general rendered him unfit for the situation which he held; his cruelty caused him to be deprived of a power which he abused. No one was found equally calculated, to supply his place, with the new officer, Toussaint; therefore, quitting for ever a subordinate situation, he was appointed to the command of a division.

If during this early period of his life, the black general had shone conspicuously, through every disadvantage, with the brightest talents and the milder virtues, he now rose superior to all around him, with the qualities and rank of an exalted chief. Every part of his conduct was marked by judgment and benevolence. By the blacks, who had raised him to the dignity he enjoyed, he was beloved with enthusiasm; and, by the public characters of other nations, with whom he had occasion to communicate, he was regarded with every mark of respect and esteem. General Laveaux called him "the negro, the Spartacus, foretold by Raynal, whose destiny it *was* to avenge the wrongs committed on his race:" and the Spanish Marquis d'Hermona declared, in the hyperbole of admiration, that "if the Supreme had descended on earth, he could not inhabit a heart more apparently good, than that of Toussaint L'Ouverture" . . . .

It probably may be expected that something should be mentioned of the general character of Toussaint; and, if there was any object predominant in the wishes of the writer during his sojourn at the Cape, it was – to ascertain the traits of peculiarity in that individual, – to judge of the views, and of the motives that actuated him. The result of his observations was in every respect favorable to this truly great man. Casual acts of justice and benignity may mark the reign of anarchy itself, and complacency sometimes smooth the brow of the most brutal tyrant; but when the man, possessed for a considerable period, of unlimited power, (of whose good actions no venal journalist was the herald, but, to transcribe his errors a thousand competitors were ready) has never been charged with its abuse; but, on the contrary, has preserved one line of conduct, founded by sound sense and acute discernment on the most honorable basis, leaning only to actions of magnanimity and goodness; he has passed the strongest test to which he can be submitted; who, with the frailties of human nature, and without the adventitious aids of those born to rule, held one of the highest situations in society.

His government does not appear to have been sullied by the influence of any ruling passion; if a thirst of power had prompted him alone, he would have soon ceased to be a leader of insurgents; had avarice swayed him, he, like many others, could have retired early in the contest, with immense riches, to the neighbouring continent; or had a sanguinary revenge occupied his mind, he would not so often have offered those pathetic appeals to the understanding, which were the sport of his colleagues, on crimes which the governors of nations long *civilized* would have sentenced to torture! His principles, when becoming an actor in the revolution of his country, were as pure and legitimate, as those which actuated the great founders of liberty in any former age or clime.

Notes

1. Marcus Rainsford, "Life and Character of Toussaint L'Ouverture", in *An Historical Account of the Black Empire of Hayti: comprehending a view of the principal transactions in the revolution of Saint Domingo* (London: James Cundee; C. Chapple, 1805).
2. G.T.F. Raynal's *Histoire philosophique et politique des établissements et du commerce des Européens dans les deux Indes* (1770), an influential anti-slavery work, first appeared in English translation in 1776 and was frequently reprinted up until 1806. Rainsford, 244n, adds a list of other books which were "conspicuous in the library of Toussaint", principally military memoirs from Herodotus and Caesar to Marshal Saxe.

WILLIAM WORDSWORTH (1770–1850)

"To Toussaint L'Ouverture" (1802)[1]

This famous sonnet was first published in February 1803 but was written in August 1802 during Toussaint's imprisonment, when Wordsworth was himself in France. The driving force behind the resistance of Toussaint's black army to the French expeditionary force was the belief that, in spite of his proclamation to the contrary, Napoleon's intention was to reimpose slavery in the French colonies. There is no evidence, however, that Wordsworth was following events in St Domingo closely. The Toussaint of his poem, as "Chieftain" of an independent republic, symbolizes rather the timeless struggle of the human spirit against tyrannic forces.

Toussaint, the most unhappy Man of Men!
Whether the all-cheering sun be free to shed
His beams around thee, or thou rest thy head
Pillowed in some dark dungeon's noisome den,[2]
O miserable Chieftain! where and when
Wilt thou find patience? Yet die not; do thou
Wear rather in thy bonds a cheerful brow:
Though fallen Thyself, never to rise again,
Live, and take comfort. Thou hast left behind

Powers that will work for thee; air, earth, and skies;

There's not a breathing of the common wind

That will forget thee; thou hast great allies;

Thy friends are exultations, agonies,

And love, and Man's unconquerable mind.

Notes

1. William Wordsworth, "To Toussaint L'Ouverture", *Morning Post* (2 February 1803).
2. Lines 2–4 were changed in Wordsworth's *Poems* (1807) to
    Whether the whistling Rustic tend his plough
    Within thy hearing, or thy head be now
    Pillowed in some deep dungeon's earless den.

EDWARD RUSHTON (1756–1814)

"Toussaint to his Troops" (1806)[1]

The poem clearly refers to the period between January and April 1802, when Toussaint was leading his army of liberated slaves against the French expeditionary force sent by Napoleon Bonaparte and commanded by General Leclerc. Although Bonaparte had issued a proclamation that slavery would not be reimposed in St Domingo, Toussaint distrusted his pledge. There was scepticism among some abolitionists also: writing early in 1802, James Stephen argued that "the true though unavowed purpose of the French government in this expedition, is to restore the old system of Negro slavery in St. Domingo, and in the other colonies where it has been subverted".[2] Rushton's poem was first published in his *Poems*, 1806.

Whether forced from burning shores,
Where the tawny lion roars;
Whether doom'd, with stripes and chains,
Here to dress your native plains;
Men of noble bearing, say,   5
Shall we crouch to Gallia's sway;
Shall we wield again the hoe,
Taste again the cup of woe;
Or shall we rouse, and, with the lightning's force,
Blast the relentless foe, and desolate his course?   10

When the world's eternal Sire
Placed on high yon glorious fire,
Were the splendid beams design'd
For a part of human kind?
No! ye sable warriors, no!   15
All that live partake the glow:
Thus, on man, the impartial God
Light, and wind, and rains bestow'd;
And widely thus were pour'd his dearest rights,
And he who slights the gift – the Almighty donor slights.   20

Now with canvass white as foam,
See the vaunted legions come,
Nerved by freedom, once they rose
And o'erwhelm'd a world of foes:
Now by freedom nerved no more,   25
Lo! the miscreants seek our shore;
Yes, the French, who waste their breath,
Chaunting liberty or death,
Sweep the blue waves at usurpation's word,
And bring, oh, fiends accursed! oppression or the sword.   30

Men, whose famish'd sides have felt
Strokes by dastard drivers dealt;
Men, whose sorrowing souls have borne
Wrong and outrage, toil and scorn;
Men, whose wives the pallid brood   35
Have, by torturing arts subdu'd;
Friends of Toussaint! warriors brave!
Call to mind the mangled slave!
And, oh! remember, should your foes succeed,
That not yourselves alone, but all you love, must bleed!   40

Fathers! shall the tiny race,
Objects of your fond embrace,
They who 'neath the tamarind tree,
Oft have gaily climb'd your knee,
Fathers, shall those prattlers share,   45
Pangs that slaves are doom'd to bear?
Shall their mirth and lisping tones
Be exchanged for shrieks and groans?
And shall those arms that round your necks have twined,
Be to the twisted thong and endless toil consign'd!   50

Towering spirits! ye who broke
Slavery's agonizing yoke;
Ye, who like the whirlwind rush'd,
And your foes to atoms crush'd;
Ye, who from Domingo's strand,   55
Swept the daring British band;
Ye, oh warriors! ye, who know
Freedom's bliss and slavery's woe,
Say! shall we bow to Bonaparte's train,
Or with unshaken nerves yon murderous whites disdain?   60

From those eyes that round me roll,
Wildly flash the indignant soul;
On those rugged brows I see,
Stern unyielding liberty.
Yes! your daring aspects show,   65
France shall soon repent the blow;
Soon shall famish'd sharks be fed;
Vultures soon shall tear the dead;
Oh glorious hour! now, now, yon fiends defy,
Assert great nature's cause, live free, or bravely die.   70

Notes

1. Edward Rushton, "Toussaint to his Troops", in *Poems and Other Writings by the late Edward Rushton* (1824).
2. James Stephen, *The Crisis of the Sugar Colonies; or, an enquiry into the objects and probable effects of the French expedition to the West Indies* (London: J. Hatchard, 1802).

MATTHEW JAMES CHAPMAN (1796–1865)

Barbadoes, and Other Poems (1833)[1]

Chapman was born in Barbados but educated in England; he qualified as a doctor before returning to the West Indies. He claims in
the preface that his descriptions of "the state of society" in
Barbados adhered strictly to "literal truth", but also indicates that
his main purpose is to oppose the emancipation campaign (then in
its final stages). His anti-emancipationist argument is reinforced by
lengthy notes, which are not reproduced in full here. Part I
describes the contented lives of slaves and the patriarchal care of
the masters, concluding in the verse given here.

Our island-slaves once loved their father-friend,
Content with his their happiness to blend;
And still would love him; – but from England goes
A moving narrative of negro-woes;
Of brands and tortures, only known by name –
Of lawless power and slavery's damning shame.
The senseless zealot arms the negro's hand,
And bids him whirl the torch and bear the brand;
Leave all the peaceful joys he knows behind;
Cast love and mercy to the babbling wind;

Baptise himself in fire, and through a sea
Of blood and battle wade to liberty!
Hence comes the plot, the agony of strife,
The toil of treason, and the waste of life;
The sound of battle, rushing through the trees;
The hurried tramp of frantic savages!
The slave, infuriate, pants for Freedom's smiles,
And Hayti's fate attends our Eden-isles.[2]

Part II. Insurrection. St. Domingo.

[The extract below is sandwiched between further descriptions of
happy slave life and warnings of the danger of "immediate emancipation".]

Blood-stained Rebellion shews her frightful head;[3]
On pour the insurgents, by fierce passions led;
Baptised in blood and fire, they urge their way,
Spread their wild flames, and curse the lingering day.
Hope bids them rule their rulers, and embrace
The blooming daughters of a fairer race.
Scarce does the wind outstrip their maddened speed;
Lust their incentive, Liberty their meed.[4]
   Down comes the gushing light of dewy morn;
Dread day! when thousands wish themselves unborn.
For a short space rebellion seems to thrive;
Onward they swarm, like wasps that storm a hive.
The fires still rage; the rich plantations burn;
Dismay rains terrors from her brazen urn;
Riot and rapine hang on murder's car,
And all the horrors of a servile war.
Rebellion has not prospered; still our isle
Sees with delight her train of virgins smile;
And the fond wife forgets her late alarms,
And slumbers peaceful in her husband's arms.

  Far other fate, far other end was thine,
Hispaniola![5] fruit nor fruitful vine
Was spared in mercy; the unconscious child
In vain put forth his little arms and smiled;
The nurse dashed down the infant from her breast,
And o'er its mangled limbs her joy expressed.
The hapless consort saw his slaves deflower
The lovely blossom of his nuptial bower;
The husband of an hour beheld his bride,
His virgin spouse, in beauty's early pride –
The long expected of his heart and bed –
Insulted, naked, violated, dead!
No plea for mercy would the savage hear;
The virgin's shriek, the old man's speechless tear,
The scream of childhood, and the well-known face
Of kindness, failed to move the ruthless race.
  What wildering shrieks mid smouldering ruins rise!
What screams of terror, and what anguished cries!
The groans of pain, the curses of despair,
Madness and riot, rend the troubled air.
The delicate of women saved to be
A rude barbarian's wanton; and the free
Bound to the wheel, or sawn, – like planks in twain,
Tortured and bruised and flayed and piecemeal slain!
Few, few escaped; the rest are dead to fame –
Remembered not – or with a blighted name.
Thus fell the good, the lovely, and the brave!
Such are the tender mercies of the slave!

Notes

1. Matthew James Chapman, *Barbadoes, and Other Poems* (London: James Fraser, 1833), 41–42, 78–79.
2. *our Eden-isles*: the British West Indies, probably referring here to the 1831 rebellion in Jamaica.
3. This passage, referring to the short-lived rebellion of 1816 in Barbados, follows lengthy descriptions of the contented lives of the slaves.
4. [Author's note:] It is well known that one of the chief motives of the negroes to rebellion is a desire to appropriate the white women. Their idea of liberty is to take possession of the property of their masters, and to get slaves to work for them. The jealousies among them, and the efforts of some to reduce others to the condition of being their bondsmen, will not better their lot: the great mass of the negroes of St. Domingo, it is known, are in a state of abject slavery; their condition under the French was much happier.
5. [Author's note:] The reader is referred to Mr. Bryan Edwards's *History of St. Domingo* for an account of the horrors of a servile war.

Part 5.

Songs

"View of the Estate Alkmaar" and "Representation of a Tent Boat or
Plantation Barge", from John Gabriel Stedman, *Narrative of a Five Years'
Expedition against the Revolted Negroes of Surinam in Guiana on the Wild
Coast of South America from the years 1772 to 1777* (London: J. Johnson, and
J. Edwards, 1796), 1: facing p. 93. Courtesy of the Trustees of the National
Library of Scotland.

A. Songs of the Enslaved

Most songs of the enslaved survive, often only as fragments, through quotation or transcriptions in printed works by white West Indian residents or visitors during the pre-emancipation period. "Quaco Sam" (page 448 below) is a rare example of a song which survived into the twentieth century through oral tradition. Unlike the impersonations of slave songs by white writers, those composed by the enslaved seldom self-consciously "represent" the conditions of slavery as such; nevertheless they provide telling evidence of their culture and consciousness. As Kamau Brathwaite points out, many songs "carried on the West African tradition of ridicule"; some merely laughed at Europeans, but very often the ridicule was turned against the masters.[1] The degree to which the longer songs or "ballads" were edited by the writers who recorded them is virtually impossible to determine.

Note

1. Edward Kamau Brathwaite, *The Folk Culture of the Slaves in Jamaica* (London: New Beacon, 1981), 20.

IMPROMPTU SONGS

Robert Renny, a Scotsman who lived in Jamaica from 1799 to 1802, observed that "the songs of the Negroes are commonly *impromptu*; and there are amongst them individuals, who resemble the *improvisatori*, or extempore bards of Italy".[1] James Phillippo, a Baptist missionary resident in Jamaica from 1823 to 1842, elaborates:

> On estates, or in particular districts, there were usually found one or more males or females, who, resembling the improvisatori or extempore bards of Italy and ancient Britons, composed lines and sung them on festive occasions. These ballads had usually a ludicrous reference to white people, and were generally suggested by some recent occurrence.[2]

Renny describes the song he hears on his first day in Jamaica as follows:

> As soon as the vessel in which the author was passenger arrived near to Port Royal in Jamaica, a canoe, containing three or four black females, came to the side of the ship, for the purpose of selling oranges, and other fruits. When about to depart, they gazed at the passengers, whose number seemed to surprise them; and as soon as the canoe pushed off, one of them sung the following words, while the others joined in the chorus, clapping their hands regularly while it lasted.

> New-come buckra,
>   He get sick,
> He take fever,
>   He be die;

He be die.
New come, &c.

The song, as far as we could hear, contained nothing else, and they continued singing it, in the manner just mentioned, as long as they were within hearing.[3] The following was, in the year 1799, frequently sung in the streets of Kingston

One, two, tree,
   All de same;
Black, white, brown,
   All de same,
   All de same.
One, two, &c.[4]

"One, Two, Tree" was still being sung in Jamaica in the 1820s and 1830s.[5]

Another song from pre-emancipation Jamaica, in which the mocking fatalism of "New-Come Buckra" is extended to all ranks and races, is recorded by Phillippo:

Sangaree[6] kill de captain,
O dear, he must die;
New rum kill de sailor,
O dear, he must die;
Hard work kill de neger,
O dear, he must die.
La, la, la, la, &c.[7]

An impromptu chorus was heard in Jamaica in 1817–21 by Thomas Cooper, who quotes it in a footnote to his account of methods used by overseers in beating slaves: "It is well known that the Negroes will make a song out of any thing. On one occasion, I listened to a party of old women, boys, and girls, singing the following in our kitchen: *O massa! O massa! on Monday morning they lay me down, And give me thirty-nine on my bare rump. O massa! O massa!*".

Another extempore snatch of song is quoted in *Transatlantic Sketches* by Captain J.E. Alexander, who as a young army officer journeyed widely in the West Indies in 1831–32. In Tobago he noted:

On Saturday night a negro wench balancing an empty bottle on her
head, and rattling a calabash filled with small pebbles, advances with a
dancing step to the manager [of a plantation], and sings,

Ax de bottle what he da want,
Massa full him, massa full him.[8]

Matthew Lewis's *Journal of a West India Proprietor* contains several examples of impromptu singing by slaves. In 1816, anxious about reports of "a
rebellious song issuing from Cornwall" (see above, page 347), he

listened more attentively to the negro chaunts; but they seem, as far as
I can make out, to relate entirely to their own private situation, and to
have nothing to do with the negro state in general. Their favourite,
"We varry well off," [see page 222] is still screamed about the estate by
the children; but among the grown people its nose has been put out of
joint by the following stanzas, which were explained to me this morning. For several days past they had been dinned into my ears so incessantly, that at length I became quite curious to know their import,
which I learned from Phillis, who is the family minstrel.

The song is headed "Negro Song at Cornwall"; the explanations in paren-
theses are supplied by Lewis:

Hey-ho-day! me no care a dammee! (i.e. a damn)
Me acquire a house, (i.e. I have a solid foundation to build on)
Since massa come see we – oh!

Hey-ho-day! neger now quite eerie, (i.e. hearty)
For once me see massa – hey-ho-day!
When massa go, me no care a dammee,
For how them usy we – hey-ho-day![9]

Orlando Patterson notes that Lewis is mistaken in thinking that the songs
"have nothing to do with the negro state in general", pointing out that in
this song, even while praising a kind master, "the slaves could not resist
referring to the brutality of the overseer which was their usual lot" when
the master was absent.[10] The defiant insouciance so characteristic of these
spontaneous utterances is itself a form of resistance to white authority, a
refusal to be cowed, even by physical assault. A vivid illustration occurs in

Marly when some women, unfairly flogged by an overzealous overseer, retaliate by singing their usual chorus of "I Don't Care a Damn, Oh!" (see page 256). The ironical nature of such statements is encapsulated in the Jamaican proverb "When man say him no min', den him min' ."[11]

Lewis explains the following as "the song of a wife whose husband had been Obeahed by another woman, in consequence of his rejecting her advances". He glosses *cutacoo* as "a basket made of matting":

> Me take my cutacoo,
> and follow him to Lucea,
> and all for love of my bonny man-O
> My bonny man come home, come home!
> Doctor no do you good.
> When neger fall into neger hands,
> Buckra doctor no do him good more.
> Come home, my gold ring, come home![12]

One song plays a key part in a so-called "Nancy-story" story related by Lewis, about a cruelly treated little girl, Sarah Winyan, and her miraculous escape from a wicked aunt:

> Ho-day, poor me, O!
> Poor me, Sarah Winyan, O!
> They call me neger, neger!
> They call me Sarah Winyan, O![13]

The discomfiture of white people was a regular source of derision to the enslaved, but the narrator of Marly claims that their mockery was sometimes tempered with sympathy. When a relatively humane overseer was dismissed, "although they seemed vexed for the sake of their old Busha, at his being ordered away from what had long been his home, it furnished them with materials for a song, and during the afternoon the gangs kept singing: 'Massa turn poor buckra away oh! / But massa can't turn poor neger away oh!' "

The narrator explains that "in the estimation of the generality of the negroes, nothing is so bad as being turned off the property on which they were born and which is their home." Thus, "when a white man is removed, the negroes feel and pity his desolate condition, and think themselves happy in comparison".[14]

"Take Him to the Gulley" is an extreme example of the custom of turning hardship into song. It is referred to in several sources from 1790 onwards, but the longest version is in Lewis's *Journal* of 29 January 1818, in which he quotes, as the refrain of "a popular negro song",

> "Take him to the Gulley! Take him to the Gulley!
> But bringee back the frock and board." –
> "Oh! massa, massa! me no deadee yet!" –
> "Take him to the Gulley! Take him to the Gulley!
> Carry him along!"

The song commemorates a notorious atrocity of the previous century, as Lewis explains.

> This alludes to a transaction which took place some thirty years ago, on an estate in this neighbourhood called Spring-Garden; the owner of which (I think the name was Bedward) is quoted as the cruellest proprietor that ever disgraced Jamaica. It was his constant practice, whenever a sick negro was pronounced incurable, to order the poor wretch to be carried to a solitary vale upon his estate, called the Gulley, where he was thrown down, and abandoned to his fate; which fate was generally to be half devoured by the john-crows, before death had put an end to his sufferings. By this proceeding the avaricious owner avoided the expence of maintaining the slave during his last illness; and in order that he might be as little a loser as possible, he always enjoined the negro bearers of the dying man to strip him naked before leaving the Gulley, and not to forget to bring back his frock and the board on which he had been carried down. One poor creature, while in the act of being removed, screamed out most piteously "that he was not dead yet;" and implored not to be left to perish in the Gulley in a manner so horrible. His cries had no effect upon his master, but operated so forcibly on the less marble hearts of his fellow-slaves, that in the night some of them removed him back to the negro village privately, and nursed him there with so much care, that he recovered, and left the estate unquestioned and undiscovered. Unluckily, one day the master was passing through Kingston, when, on turning the corner of a street

suddenly, he found himself face to face with the negro, whom he had supposed long ago to have been picked to the bones in the Gulley of Spring-Garden. He immediately seized him, claimed him as his slave, and ordered his attendants to convey him to his house; but the fellow's cries attracted a crowd round them, before he could be dragged away. He related his melancholy story, and the singular manner in which he had recovered his life and liberty; and the public indignation was so forcibly excited by the shocking tale, that Mr. Bedward was glad to save himself from being torn to pieces by a precipitate retreat from Kingston, and never ventured to advance his claim to the negro a second time.[15]

A fictionalized account of this infamous practice appeared in Dallas's *Short Journey to the West Indies* (1790).[16] See also "The Poor Negro Beggar's Petition and Complaint", pages 145 to 147 above, and Stewart's *Account of Jamaica*, page 206 above. A version of the song was still current in Jamaica in 1906 as "Carry Him Along".[17]

Notes

1. Robert Renny, *An History of Jamaica* (London: J. Cawthorn, 1807), 168.
2. James Phillippo, *Jamaica: Its Past and Present State* (London: John Snow, 1843), 189.
3. Cf. *Sketches and Recollections*, 26: "When walking round the Cathedral [in Bridgetown, Barbados], the party were *comforted* by blacky's remark: 'Ah! look dem Buckra, in a church-yard; dem get fever in de hot sun – dem soon come in a church-yard – dem go dead!' "
4. Renny, *History of Jamaica*, 241.
5. Phillippo, *Jamaica*, 190.
6. John Stewart, in *Account*, 198–99, comments at length on the heavy drinking habits of white settlers in Jamaica, though he believed such "riotous debauches" were becoming less common in 1808: "these horrid and wanton excesses sent more wretched men to their graves, than either the insalubrity of the climate, or the unavoidable diseases of the country". He explains *sangaree* as "Madeira wine diluted with water, and sweetened".
7. Phillippo, *Jamaica*, 189n.

8. J.E. Alexander, *Transatlantic Sketches: comprising visits to the most interesting scenes in North and South America, and the West Indies* (London: R. Bentley, 1833), 1:191–92.

9. Lewis, *Journal*, 233.

10. Orlando Patterson, *The Sociology of Slavery: An Analysis of the Origins, Development and Structure of Negro Slave Society* (London: MacGibbon and Kee, 1967), 256.

11. Recorded by Charles Rampini in *Letters from Jamaica* (Edinburgh: Edmonston and Douglas, 1873), appendix.

12. Lewis, *Journal*, 253.

13. Ibid., 292.

14. *Marly*, 145–46.

15. Lewis, *Journal*, 322–24.

16. Dallas, *Short Journey*, 2:106–8.

17. Walter Jekyll, *Jamaican Song and Story* (1907), quoted in D'Costa and Lalla, *Voices in Exile*, 28–30.

Work Songs

Songs sung by field slaves during their work must have been plentiful, but very few identifiable as such survive. The first three songs below are plantation songs; the rest are boat songs.

"Guinea Corn", a well-known song in Jamaica in the eighteenth century and later, was printed in the *Columbian Magazine*.[1] Guinea corn, the name of several varieties of grain, was a staple crop in the Caribbean: it was ground into flour and used in various other ways.

> Guinea Corn, I long to see you
> Guinea Corn, I long to plant you
> Guinea Corn, I long to mould you
> Guinea Corn, I long to weed you
> Guinea Corn, I long to hoe you
> Guinea Corn, I long to top you
> Guinea Corn, I long to cut you
> Guinea Corn, I long to dry you
> Guinea Corn, I long to beat you
> Guinea Corn, I long to trash you
> Guinea Corn, I long to parch you
> Guinea Corn, I long to grind you
> Guinea Corn, I long to turn you
> Guinea Corn, I long to eat you.

"The climax of the song came with the word *eat*, when 'as though satiated with the food, or tired with the process for producing it', the singers bestowed 'an hearty curse on the grain, asking where it came from'."[2]

The next song appears in J.B. Moreton's *West India Customs and Manners* (1793). Moreton lived in Jamaica for several years during the 1780s, first as a book-keeper on different plantations, later as a clerk or merchant in Kingston. He is unusual among white West Indians of his time for his open condemnation of slavery and the slave trade. In a section describing the character and conduct of enslaved Africans he explains:

> When working, though at the hardest labour, they are commonly singing; and though their songs have neither rhime nor measure, yet many are witty and pathetic. I have often laughed heartily, and have been as often struck with deep melancholly at their songs: – for instance, when singing of the Overseer's barbarity to them:
>
> Tink dere is a God in a top,[3]
> No use me ill, Obissha!
> Me no horse, me no mare, me no mule,
> No use me ill, Obissha![4]

Moreton continues:

> *Or, thus:*
> If me want for go in a Ebo,[5]
> Me can't go there!
> Since dem tief me from a Guinea,
> Me can't go there!
>
> If me want for go in a Congo,
> Me can't go there!
> Since dem tief me from my tatta,[6]
> Me can't go there!
>
> If me want for go in a Kingston,
> Me can't go there!
> Since massa go in a England,
> Me can't go there![7,8]

John Stedman, in his *Narrative of a Five Years' Expedition*, records a snatch of song typical of those sung by "the barge rowers or boat negroes" of Suriname. He describes their practice as "not unlike that of a *clerk* performing to the congregation, one person constantly pronouncing a sentence extempore, which he next hums or whistles, and then all the others repeat the same in chorus; another sentence is then spoken, and the chorus is a second time renewed, &c." The words in italics are Stedman's paraphrase of the local Creole.

> one bus adiosi-o da so
> *One buss[9] good-by o 'tis so*
> adiosso me dego
> *good-by girl I must go*
> me loby fo fighty me man o
> *I love for to fight like a man o*
> Amimba me dego na boosy o da so
> *Amimba I go to the woods o 'tis so*
> adiosso me dego.
> *good-by girl, I must go.*[10]

Thomas Staunton St Clair, who also spent some time in the Guianas as a young army officer (1805–8), gives a vivid account of a long river journey in *A Residence in the West Indies and America*:

> As the sun increased in power the labour of our boatmen became more fatiguing. Colonel Nicholson and I breakfasted in the boat, and he ordered his servant, Ogilvie, to give the boatmen something to eat and a glass of rum each. After this refreshment, the bowman commenced with a verse of his own composition, which was repeated by the whole crew, and they made us laugh heartily at some of their Negro poetry, which was meant as a panegyric on the governor and myself. The heat of the day was overpowering, and every now and then one of these men, who were built like Hercules, would spring from the boat dripping with perspiration, and rising from the water immediately place himself again on his bench and pull with renewed vigour. These Negroes, in rowing, never stop from the moment they set out till the company is landed at the place of destination, and continue, even against the tide, tugging, sometimes night and day, for twenty-four hours together, all the time singing in chorus the most absurd verses composed by themselves, to keep up their spirits.[11]

A longer fragment, from a boat-song heard by Trelawney Wentworth while travelling in the West Indies in 1830–32, is recorded in his *West India*

Sketch Book. He describes being rowed across from Tortola to St Thomas in the Virgin Islands by a crew of oarsmen.

> For some distance they had pulled at an easy rate and in silence, as if made unconscious of the work they were engaged in, by the absorbing interest of the passing scenes, but at length they were roused to activity by the word of preparation for a song having been passed among them, and the negro pulling the oar nearest to us, began a singular prelude which sounded between a grunt and a groan, like a paviour's accompaniment to his labour, or the exordium of a quaker, when "the spirit" begins to move. He became more energetic with each succeeding stroke of the oar, which produced a corresponding ardour, and greater precision in pulling among the other rowers, and when this was effected, another negro, whose countenance bore the stamp of much covert humour and sagacity, and who appeared to be a sort of *improvisatore* among them, commenced a lively strain which accorded exactly in time with the motion of pulling, each line of the song accompanying the impetus given to the boat, and the whole crew joining in chorus in the intervals between every stroke of the oars. The subject matter of the song was as discursive and lengthy as Chevy Chase; and it showed an aptitude at invention on the part of the leader, as well as a tolerable acquaintance with the weak side of human nature, on the score of flattery: a small portion of it will suffice. The words in italics form the chorus.

> Hurra, my jolly boys,
>   *Fine time o' day.*
> We pull for San Thamas boys,
>   *Fine time o' day.*
> San Thamas hab de fine girl,
>   *Fine time o' day.*
> Nancy Gibbs and Betsy Braid,
>   *Fine time o' day.*
> Massa cum fra London town,
>   *Fine time o' day.*
> Massa is a hansome man,
>   *Fine time o' day.*

Massa is a dandy-man,
  Fine time o' day.
Him hab de dollar, plenty too,
  Fine time o' day.
Massa lub a pretty girl,
  Fine time o' day.
Him lub 'em much, him lub 'em true,
  Fine time o' day.
Him hunt 'em round de guaba bush,
  Fine time o' day.
Him catch 'em in de cane piece,
  Fine time o' day, &c.[12]

A boat-song heard by Captain J.E. Alexander in Essequibo and recorded in his *Transatlantic Sketches* (1833) is clearly a local variant of the traditional English sea-shanty "So Early in the Morning". Recalling a journey by canoe on Tappacooma Lake, Alexander says the "negroes merrily plied the paddles, and we brushed past the overhanging trees to their favourite song of 'Velly well, yankee, velly well oh!'"

De bottley oh! de bottley oh!
De neger like de bottley oh!
Right early in de marning, de neger like de bottley oh!
A bottle o' rum, loaf a bread,
Make the neger dandy oh!
Right early in de marning, de neger like de bottley oh![13]

Henry Murray recorded a "Stevedore's song" sung at a fisherman's funeral wake in Jamaica in the 1840s). The reference to Bonaparte suggests that it dates from the pre-emancipation period. It also appears to be a variant of an English folk song "Bony Was a Warrior":

Bony was a good boy,
Sing hal le ho!
Bony was a good boy,
Sing hal le ho!

O! poor Bony, boy,
Sing hal le ho!
O! poor Bony, boy,
Sing hal le ho!

Bony mek de Dubs [doubloons] fly,
Sing hal le ho!
Bony mek de Guineas fly,
Sing hal le ho, &c.[14]

Notes

1. Published in Kingston, Jamaica; vol. 2 (May 1797): 766–67.
2. Quoted from the *Columbian Magazine* in Brathwaite, *Folk Culture*, 18.
3. *in a top*: in the sky. Ashanti religion and Christianity both popularly conceived of the deity as dwelling in the sky. For the conception of God as a kind of super-overseer, the ultimate or only guarantor of justice in the slave system, cf. Equiano: a slave, robbed of his property by a white man, asks "'what me must do? I can't go to any body to be righted;' then, said the poor man, looking up above, 'I must look up to God Mighty in the top for right' " (page 125 above).
4. J.B. Moreton, *West India Customs and Manners*, new ed. (London: J. Parsons; W. Richardson; H. Gardner; and J. Walter, 1793), 152–53.
5. *Ebo* and *Congo* are footnoted by Moreton as "Countries in Africa".
6. *tatta*: father.
7. Permission was normally required for slaves to leave their estate, but was liable to be withheld for disciplinary or other reasons, especially, as evidently here, in the absence of the plantation owner.
8. Moreton, *West India Customs*, 153.
9. *buss*: kiss.
10. Stedman, *Narrative*, 2:258–59.
11. Thomas Staunton St Clair, *A Residence in the West Indies and America: with a narrative of the expedition to the Island of Walcheren* (London: R. Bentley, 1834), 2:152–53
12. Trelawney Wentworth, *The West India Sketch Book* (London: Whittaker and Co., 1834), 1:240–42.
13. Alexander, *Transatlantic Sketches*, 1:131.
14. Henry Murray, *Manners and Customs of the Country, A Generation Ago: Tom Kittle's Wake* (Kingston: R. Jordon, 1869), 28.

Dancing Songs

Singing was an essential part of the dances performed on Saturday nights or festive occasions in Jamaica. J.B. Moreton quotes two examples of songs he heard at Saturday dances, explaining how hundreds of slaves would gather and

> dance and sing till morning; nay, sometimes they continue their balls without intermission till Monday-morning . . . . When dancing, they form themselves into a circular position, adjoining some of their huts, and continue all in motion, singing so loud, that of a calm night they may be heard at about two miles distance – thus:
>
> Hipsaw! my deaa! you no do like a-me!
> You no jig like a-me! you no twist like a-ame!
> Hipsaw! my deaa! You no shake like a-me!
> You no wind like a-me! Go, yondaa!
> Hipsaw! my deaa! You no jig like a-me!
> You no work him like a-me! you no sweet him like a-me![1]
>
> *Or, thus:*
> Tajo, tajo, tajo! tajo my mackey massa![2]
> O! laud, O! tajo, tajo, tajo!
> You work him, mackey massa!
> You sweet me, mackey massa!
> A little more, my mackey massa!
>
> Tajo, tajo, tajo! tajo my mackey massa!
> O! laud, O! tajo, tajo, tajo!
> I'll please my mackey massa!
> I'll jig to mackey massa!
> I'll sweet my mackey massa!"[3]

It is evident from Moreton's description of the manner of dancing that these songs have a sexual meaning:

> The droll capers, and wanton gestures and attitudes – the languishing glances and grimaces, so consequential and serious, of those flat-nosed damsels, timed to admiration by their jetty beau partners, are truly curious: It is very amazing to think with what agility they twist and move their joints: – I sometimes imagined they were on springs or hinges, from the hips downwards; whoever is most active and expert at wriggling, is reputed the best dancer. You will find amongst them many beautiful young creatures; so that you cannot possibly look on unmoved: they have too many alluring tricks to seduce and lead men astray.[4]

Carolyn Cooper offers a more nuanced reading of these songs; the second, she says, represents "role-playing as a strategy for survival". The woman alternately flatters and entices her master, aware that, in the unequal power play between them, her function is "to feed the ego of Mackey Massa by proclaiming his sexual skill", while his is "to continue to favour her by allowing her to keep the work".[5]

Topical events were quickly incorporated into songs, as the following two fragments show. The chorus of a song in praise of the Duke of Wellington was heard by Matthew Lewis at the "John-Canoe" (Jonkonnu) celebrations at Black River on 1 January 1816, six months after the battle of Waterloo:

> Come, rise up, our gentry,
> And hear about Waterloo;
> Ladies, take your spy-glass,
> And attend to what we do;
> For one and one makes two,
> But one alone must be,
> Then singee, singee Waterloo,
> None so brave as he![6]

The following "Song sung by the Set-Girls" is quoted in the text accompanying Isaac Mendez Belisario's vivid series of lithographs, *Sketches of Character . . . of the Negro Population in the Island of Jamaica* (1837). The final line suggests that the song may have been composed before emancipation, although the apprenticeship system which was in force from 1834 to 1838 was virtually slavery by another name. Belisario, the first known Jamaican-born artist, is renowned for his picturesque portrayals of the Jonkonnu masquerades. He describes the songs contemptuously as being "chanted at the top of their voice, with an accompaniment of instruments, for the most part out of tune, and played by musicians, *rather* carelessly dressed". He remarks on the "incongruities" in this particular text: "a love-sick *fair-one*, absolutely enamoured of a soldier she has *never seen*, and in conclusion, presuming the King is in love with her." It certainly appears garbled, probably in the process of oral transmission; it perhaps referred originally to news of the replacement of one regiment – to which the soldier with the "bonny Scotch plaid" belonged – by another. Belisario supplies only one stanza, but there must have been others.

> There is a Regiment of the 64th, we expect from home,
> From London to Scotland away they must go,
> There was one among them, that I really love well,
> With his bonny Scotch plaid, and his bayonet so shining,
> Now pray my noble King, if you really love me well,
> Disband us from slavery, and set us at large.
> CHORUS. – La la la, la la la.[7]

Notes

1. Moreton, *West India Customs*, 156–57.
2. *tajo*: an exclamation of unknown etymology; *mackey*: good, fine; a phrase showing submission and respect. Cassidy and Le Page, *Dictionary of Jamaican English*.
3. Moreton, *West India Customs*, 157.
4. Ibid., 157–58. Paul Gilroy notes that in modern black American ghetto speech "the word work can mean dancing, labour, sexual activity or any nuanced combination of all three". *"There Ain't No Black in the Union Jack": The Cultural Politics of Race and Nation* (London: Hutchinson, 1992), 203.

5. Cooper, *Noises in the Blood*, 29–30.

6. Lewis, *Journal*, 57.

7. Isaac Mendez Belisario, *Sketches of Character, in Illustration of the Habits, Occupation, and Costume of the Negro Population in the Island of Jamaica*, part 1 (Kingston: n.p., 1837), no page numbers.

BALLADS: COMMENT AND SATIRE

"At their merry meetings, they have songs and ballads, adapted to such occasions, in which they give a full scope to a talent for ridicule, of which they are possessed in an uncommon degree; and in which, they amuse themselves, not only at the expense of the awkward *new-come* Negro, or *buckra*, but also at the follies and foibles of their masters and mistresses."[1] The following song from Moreton's *West India Customs and Manners* is prefaced thus:

> Some masters and overseers, of jealous, pimping dispositions, flog, and otherwise ill treat their black wenches, when they chance to get black children. I have been often diverted, and laughed heartily, when a raw, infatuated gaukey, or a doating, debilitated debauchee has been disappointed, after all his endearing fondness and amorous exertions, with his soft, slobber-chop bundle, to get a black, instead of an olive babe. I shall annex the song of a young woman who was in this predicament: – it is in the negroe dialect, and is no less true than curious".[2]

> *AIR. What care I for Mam or Dad.*[3]

> Altho' a slave me is born and bred,
>   My skin is black, not yellow:[4]
> I often sold my maidenhead
>   To many a handsome fellow.

> My massa keep me once, for true,
>   And gave me clothes, wid busses:
> Fine muslin coats, wid bitty,[5] too,
>   To gain my sweet embraces.

When pickininny him come black,
    My massa starve and fum[6] me;
He tear the coat from off my back,
    And naked him did strip me.

Him turn me out into the field,
    Wid hoe, the ground to clear-o;
Me take pickininny on my back,
    And work him te-me weary.

Him, Obissha, him de come one night,
    And give me gown and busses;
Him get one pickininny, white!
    Almost as white as missess.

Then missess fum me wid long switch,
    And say him da for massa;[7]
My massa curse her, "lying bitch!"
    And tell her, "buss my rassa!"[8]

Me fum'd when me no condescend;
    Me fum'd too if me do it;
Me no have no one for 'tand my friend,
    So me am forc'd to do it.

Me know no law, me know no sin,
    Me is just what ebba them make me;
This is the way dem bring me in;
    So God nor devil take me![9]

Moreton continues: "The virtue and chastity, as well as the lives and properties of the women, are at the command of the masters and overseers; they are perpetually exposed to the prostitution of them and their friends: it is pity that there is not some law to protect them from abuses so tyrannic, cruel and abominable."[10] Analysing this text, Carolyn Cooper demonstrates how the voice of the speaker is modulated to create a complex subjectivity, encompassing both pathos and defiance. At one level the song exposes "the tragic condition of the exploited black woman", who has no choice but to prostitute herself to the whites. But she is not merely a victim; her utterance proclaims a strong, individualized self, indicated by the qualifier *"Altho'* a slave me is born and bred", asserting her "refusal to be commodified by anybody but herself".[11]

A fragment of this song is quoted by Michael Scott in his semi-autobiographical novel *Tom Cringle's Log*. Scott lived in Jamaica from 1806 to 1822, as manager of a plantation and later as a merchant's clerk in Kingston. The narrator describes awaking early one morning to hear "a female, in a small suppressed voice" singing a "snatch of a vulgar Port Royal ditty, which I scarcely forgive myself for introducing here to polite society":

> Young hofficer come home at night,
> Him gave me ring and kisses;
> Nine months, one picaninny white,
> Him white almost like missis.
> But missis fum my back wid switch,
> Him say de shild for massa;
> But massa say him ———.

At this point the singer "broke off suddenly, as if disturbed by the approach of someone".[12]

Michael Scott heard the next piece sung to the tune of "Guinea Corn" by one of the performers at a "John Canoe" masquerade at Christmas-time in Kingston. The performer appeared "clothed in an entire bullock's hide, horns, tail, and the other particulars",[13] carrying John Canoe "perched on his shoulders, like a monkey on a dancing bear". After capering about with this load "as if it had been a feather", the dancer shook off John Canoe and sang the following, accompanying himself on a fiddle:

> Massa Buccra lob for see
> Bullock caper like monkee –
> Dance, and shump, and poke him toe,
> Like one humane person – just so. –
>
> But Massa Buccra have white love,
> Soft and silken like one dove.
> To brown girl – him barely shivel –
> To black girl – oh, Lord, de Devil!

But when him once two tree year here,
Him tink white lady wery great boder;
De coloured peoples, never fear,
Ah, him lob him de morest nor any oder.

But top – one time bad fever catch him,
Colour'd peoples kindly watch him –
In sick-room, nurse voice like music –
From him hand taste sweet de physic.

So alway come – in two tree year,
And so wid you massa – never fear;
Brown girl for cook – for wife – for nurse;
Buccra lady – poo – no wort a curse.[14]

As Carolyn Cooper points out, the mockery here is double-layered. The song charts the rake's progress of Massa from virtuous "white love" to brown girl, and ultimately (it is implied) to black "Devil". At the same time, "in its nativist account of Massa's prurient love of the near-human bullock capering like a monkee, [it] turns the masquerade into a metaphor of transgressive sexuality".[15]

"The Runaway", so titled by Lewis in his *Journal*, was recorded without further comment while he was staying at his Cornwall estate in Jamaica in January 1816.

Peter, Peter was a black boy;
    Peter, him pull foot one day:
Buckra girl, him[16] Peter's joy;
    Lilly white girl entice him away.
Fye, Miss Sally, fye on you!
Poor Blacky Peter why undo?
Oh! Peter, Peter was a bad boy;
Peter was a runaway.

Peter, him Massa thief – Oh! fye!
    Missy Sally, him say him do so.
Him money spent, Sally bid him bye,
    And from Peter away him go;
Fye, Missy Sally, fye on you!

Poor Blacky Peter what him do?
Oh! Peter, Peter was a sad boy;
Peter was a runaway!

Peter him go to him Massa back;
    There him humbly own him crime:
'Massa, forgib one poor young Black!
    Oh! Massa, good Massa, forgib dis time!' –
Then in come him Missy, so fine, so gay,
And to him Peter thus him say:
'Oh! Missy, good Missy, you for me pray!
Beg Massa forgib poor runaway!'

'Missy, you cheeks so red, so white;
    Missy you eyes like diamond shine!
Missy, you Massa's sole delight,
    And Lilly Sally, him was mine!
Him say – "Come, Peter, mid me go!" –
Could me refuse him? Could me say "no?" –
Poor Peter – "no" him could no say!
So Peter, Peter ran away!" –

Him Missy him pray; him Massa so kind
    Was moved by him prayer, and to Peter him say:
'Well, boy, for this once I forgive you! – but mind!
    With the buckra girls you no more go away!
Though fair without, they're foul within;
Their heart is black, though white their skin.
Then Peter, Peter, with me stay;
Peter no more run away!'[17]

"The Runaway" has a complex scenario, as one of the "cunning strategies" employed by enslaved men and women in negotiation with their masters,[18] and as a neat inversion of traditional gender and race roles. Peter's story is that he was driven to run away by being seduced by white Sally, then made to rob his master, and at last abandoned by Sally. Thus in the first stanza the white woman is presented as seductress of a black male, roles traditionally assigned to black women and white males respectively. By another twist, white Sally is persuaded by Peter's sexual flattery to plead with his master for his pardon. Finally, drawing on traditional black/white symbolism, the last stanza reverses a trope often used by Christian apologists, whereby Africans are deemed to have innocent ("white") souls beneath their black skins.

Cynric Williams heard the following song during his tour through Jamaica in 1823. Travelling along the coast between Port Morant and Port Antonio, he came to a river where he saw a group of black girls:

> at least a score, some washing clothes, some washing themselves, flouncing about like nereids. At my approach, those who were on the shore dashed into the water as if they had been wild ducks, and dived away like so many coots. When they were, according to their own notions, far enough from our masculine gaze, they emerged one by one, popping up their black heads, and shewing their ivory mouths as they laughed and made fun of me. I asked them if they were slaves. "Yes, yes," every one a slave. Not a mark, thought I, on these inky damsels – not a scratch: they were as sleek as moles. "Are you Christians?" "Yes, all Christen, all baptize, all hab new name" – "My name," cried one of them, "Alexandrina! my moder call me Wowski."[19] Another had renounced the title of Juno, to take the name of Deborah, and Proserpine had been transubstantiated to Magdalene. This Magdalene entertained me with a song.

> Hi! de Buckra, hi!
> You sabby wha for he da cross de sea,
> Wid him long white face and him twinkling yeye;
> He lub, make lub, as he preach to we,
> He fall on his knees, but he pray for me,
> Hi! de Buckra, hi!

> Hi! de Buckra, hi!
> Mass W—— F——e[20] da come ober de sea,
> Wid him roguish heart and him tender look;
> And while he palaver and preach him book,
> At the negro girl he'll winkie him yeye.
> Hi! de Buckra, hi!

There was a great deal more of this to the same tune, and much to the same purpose; however, I contented myself with taking down two stanzas of the ci-devant Proserpine's song, which she repeated several times for me, with some occasional differences; and as I was curious to know who had composed so many elegant verses, she had no hesitation in telling me that it was the butler of M——, on the other side of Port Antonio, who had been six or seven years in England, and was a 'collar (scholar, I presume). When he was in Scotland, continued the ex-queen of Tartarus, an old lady sent for him, and offered to make him *educate* for a missionary; to which he readily consented, and his master gave him his freedom on condition of the old lady's finding him another slave in his place on his return to Jamaica; because the missionary would otherwise still be a slave there. Mungo was sent to a Methodist school, and for three years cudgelled his brains with the Old and New Testament, besides learning a library of tracts &c.; but, at the end of the three years, he told the old lady that "negroes were good and bad, and the bible good and bad; that the missionaries preach one wife, and David and Solomon had seven hundred. That the negroes know all the good the bible said. 'Indeed!' said the old lady. 'and what is that?' 'Why, if they do good, they shall go to heaven; and if they do bad, they must go to hell.' So the old lady gave him *free* again to lib with him Massa, and he is butler as he was before. But (said Magdalen) he make song and tell stories, and preach like de missionaries, for fun, and tell how dey make love to black and brown girls".[21]

Williams clearly enjoyed the story, with its mockery of well-meaning attempts to turn Mungo into a Christian missionary to preach to his fellow Africans. In his own narrative, Williams firmly supports Jamaican planters in their opposition to the campaign for emancipation led by Wilberforce and others, and dismisses allegations of the cruel treatment of slaves as anti-slavery propaganda; hence his comment on the unscarred bodies of the black girls. He misses no opportunity to jibe at anti-slavery politicians in Britain, representing them as hypocritical, ill-informed and covertly racist. Whether he recognizes that he too, as a white visitor, is implicated in the girl's satire is unclear.[22]

"Quaco Sam" was first recorded in the twentieth century from oral sources and survives in variant forms, but it goes back to the eighteenth century. Barbara Lalla points out that the song is unusual in being "relatively long, well-preserved, varied in subject and therefore in language, and clearly associated with a specific historical and cultural context"; one stanza appears on pottery dating from around 1738.[23] The text used here is from the version printed by Lalla, which was obtained in Trelawny and passed on to the Jamaican historian and folklorist H.P. Jacobs. On internal evidence this version dates from 1812–23. It was sung to the tune of a song titled "The White Cockade".

> Howdy, Cousin Cubba,[24] me yerry lilly[25] news,
> Me yerry-seh yu buy one new pair a shoes,
> Me yerry-seh yu buy one dandy hat.
> Come tell mi, cousin Cubba, wha yu pay fi dat?
>   Wid me ring ding ding an a pam pam pam,
>   Mi nebba see a man lak-a Quaco Sam.
> Wedda rain or-a breeze or-a storm or-a sun,
> Mi nebba see a man lak-a Quaco Sam.
>
> Me yerry-seh one dance deh a Berry Hill,
> Unco Jack play de fiddly an wan hag fi kill.[26]
> Come tell mi, cousin Cubba, how ebry ting 'tan,
> Mek mi ax[27] Sista Susan, mek mi call Sista Ann.
>   Wid me ring ding ding, &c.
>
> Mi hab mi Regan gown, mi hab mi gin'am[28] cloak,
> Swalla-hankychi tie mi head, massa-tenky[29] tie mi troat.
> Da warra mo me wanty?[30] Mi hab mi junka pan[31]
> Fi goh a Berry Hill fi goh-see Quaco Sam.
>   Wid me ring ding ding, &c.
>
> Laud! How mi wi dance when mi yerry fiddly-an drum!
> Mi no tink pon backra wo'k, mi no ca' fe fum-fum![32]
> Mi wi dance di shay-shay, mi wi dance di Catchreel,[33]
> Mi wi dance till ebry craps[34] a mi foot-battam peel.
>   Wid me ring ding ding, &c.

Monday mawning Driba[35] Harry, when di cock da crow,
Tek him cudjo[36] a him han, knock 'im whip a Busha do.
Wi mi hoe a mi shoulda, wi mi bill da mi back,
Mi da mash putta-putta,[37] mi da tink pan Unco Jack.
    Wid me ring ding ding, &c.

Mi tek mi row a cane-piece side; di naygar-dem all da run,
An ebryone come behin' mi, him ketch di fum-fum.
Wi mi hoe da mi shoulda, chackolata da mi pan,
Mi da wo'k, mi da nyam,[38] mi da tink pan Quaco Sam.
    Wid me ring ding ding, &c.[39]

"If You Go to Nancy Clark", a song from Barbados, has a grim personal application. It was heard in Bridgetown in 1806 by Thomas St Clair, a Scottish army officer. In *A Residence in the West Indies* (1834) he explains that it was composed by "the Negroes of this island", in allusion to an incident involving "a black woman of considerable celebrity" who kept an inn at which the author stayed.

> These verses, on my landing, were howled about by every Negro in the place, and, on inquiry, I found them to have originated in the conduct of Nancy Clark towards a young girl of colour; she having, in a fit of jealousy, taken an opportunity of throwing in her face some aquafortis to destroy her beauty, which she succeeded in doing almost completely. Susy Austin, another woman of colour, kept the other inn, and, perhaps, might have bribed the poet for the second stanza.
>
> If you go to Nancy Clark,
> She will take you in the dark;
> When she get you in the dark
> She will give you aquafortis.
>
> If you go to Susy Austin,
> She will take you in the parlour;
> When she take you in the parlour,
> She will give you wine and water.[40]

The last song in this section is included only because it was reportedly sung by slaves, although it was almost certainly written by a white man. It is quoted by F.W.N. Bayley in his *Four Years' Residence in the West Indies* (1830), ostensibly to demonstrate the musical talents of blacks in the Leeward Islands:

> they have generally a good ear for music, they sing or whistle with wonderful correctness any tune they may have heard, they dance in excellent time, and are altogether very intelligent persons in anything connected with music. I remember when Mr. Thomas Haynes Bagby's [sic] song of
>> I'd be a butterfly, born in a bower
>> Where roses, and lilies, and violets meet, &c.

first came to Grenada. It had not been a week in the island before every black scamp in Georgetown was singing the air to the following parody.

> Me be a nigger boy, born in de hovel,
>> What plantain da shade from de sun wha da shine
> Me learn to dig wid de spade and de shovel,
>> Me learn to hoe up de cane in a line.
> Me drink my rum, in de calabash oval,
>> Me neber sigh for de brandy and wine;
> Me be a nigger boy, born in de hovel,
>> What plantain da shade from de sun wha da shine.
>> Me be a nigger boy,
>> Me be a nigger boy,
> When me live happy, wha for me repine?

> Me neber run from my massa' plantation.
>> Wha for me run? me no want for get lick;
> He gib me house, and me no pay taxation,
>> Food when me famish, and nurse when me sick.
> Willy-force nigger, he belly da empty,
>> He hab de freedom, dat no good for me:
> My massa good man, he gib me plenty,
>> Me no lobe Willy-force[41] better dan he.
>> Me be a nigger boy,
>> Me be a nigger boy,
> Me happy fellow, den why me want free?[42]

Bayley, a songwriter himself, is the likeliest author of this piece. The original ballad, "I'd Be a Butterfly", by Thomas Haynes Bayly (no relation to Bayley), was popular in Britain in the late 1820s. It proclaims the superiority of a brief, carefree existence to the troubled lives of the privileged:

> I'd never languish for wealth or for power,
> I'd never sigh to see slaves at my feet,
> . . . Those who have wealth must be watchful and wary,
> Power, alas! nought but misery brings.

The adaptability of such sentiments for pro-slavery propaganda is obvious.[43] Bayley devotes two chapters of *Four Years' Residence in the West Indies* to the subject of slavery and the "Question of Emancipation", in which he wheels out the standard anti-emancipation argument that "the slaves are totally free from the cares, the troubles, the poverty, and even the labor and anxieties of the British poor".[44] He later wrote a tract, *The Condition of the West India Slave*, in about 1833, contrasting their easy lives with the hardships suffered by children working in English factories.

Notes

1. Renny, *History of Jamaica*, 169. Renny appears to be distinguishing here between mockery of white men generally, as in "New-come Buckra" above, and mockery of white masters and mistresses in particular.
2. Moreton, *West India Customs*, 153–54.
3. "What Care I for Mam or Dad" was presumably a British popular song of the day, but I have failed to trace it.
4. The contrast is between incoming African slaves and those, like herself, born into slavery, many of whom were light-coloured as the outcome of sexual encounters of the kind the poem describes. Contemporaneous writings show that in "the inverted hierarchies of her deformed society the black woman is often the desired object"; Cooper, *Noises in the Blood*, 23.
5. *bitty*: money; a *bit* was a small Jamaican coin, worth a few pence.
6. *fum*: flog.
7. That is, he or she is the master's child (*him* in Jamaican Creole is masculine or feminine, subject or object).
8. *buss my rassa*: kiss my arse.

9. Moreton, *West India Customs*, 154–55.

10. Ibid., 155.

11. Cooper, *Noises in the Blood*, 19–36.

12. Michael Scott, *Tom Cringle's Log* (Edinburgh: William Blackwood and Sons, 1833), 1:258.

13. See Long's description from *History of Jamaica*, page 81 above.

14. Scott, *Tom Cringle*, 1:348–50. For a fuller account, see D'Costa and Lalla, *Voices in Exile*, 53–55.

15. Cooper, *Noises in the Blood*, 23–24.

16. [Lewis's note:] The negroes never distinguish between 'him' and 'her' in their conversation.

17. Lewis, *Journal*, 120–21.

18. Cooper, *Noises in the Blood*, 32–33.

19. Wowski is the name of a black servant in George Colman's stage hit *Inkle and Yarico: An Opera* (1787).

20. That is, Wilberforce. He never visited Jamaica in person and was not a preacher, but his well-known Christian principles made him readily assimilable into British missionary typology.

21. Cynric R. Williams, *A Tour through the Island of Jamaica, from the Western to the Eastern End, in the year 1823*, 2nd ed. (London: Thomas Hurst, Edward Chance and Co., 1827), 296–99.

22. For opposition among slaves to the teaching of missionaries, see Mary Turner, *Slaves and Missionaries: The Disintegration of Jamaican Slave Society* (Kingston: The Press, University of the West Indies, 1998), 74ff.

23. Barbara Lalla, "Quaco Sam: A Relic of Archaic Jamaican Speech", *Jamaica Journal*, no. 45 (1981): 20–29.

24. *Cubba* (*Cuba* in other texts): like Quaco, an African day name.

25. *yerry lilly*: hear a little.

26. "Unco Jack fe play de fiddle, one hog fe kill" in other texts.

27. *ax*: ask.

28. *Regan*: Regent (i.e., Regency); *gin'am*: gingham.

29. *swalla-hankychi*: neck-scarf; *massa-tenky*: gift from master.

30. *Da warra mo me wanty?*: What more do I want?

31. *junka*: short, chunky; *pan*: probably a mistake ("fan" in other texts).

32. *ca' fe fum-fum*: care about beatings.

33. *shay-shay*: a vigorous dance, probably of African origin (Cassidy and Le Page, *Dictionary of Jamaican English*); Lalla, however, suggests it derives from *sashay*, a figure in the quadrille. *Catchreel* is also problematic; variants in other texts are *cotch* (Scotch) reel and *Cod reel* (quadrille). The Scotch reel was already

popular in Jamaica by this time, and although the quadrille did not reach England until 1814, it might well have been introduced to Jamaica earlier from America; Lalla, "Quaco Sam", 26–27.

34. *craps*: scrap.
35. *Driba*: Driver.
36. *cudjo*: cudgel.
37. *mash putta-putta*: tread down the mud.
38. *nyam*: eat.
39. Lalla, "Quaco Sam", 21–22.
40. St Clair, *Residence in the West Indies*, 1:373–74.
41. [Bayley's note:] Africans who have served their apprenticeship during a certain period, and are now free, are called by the slaves 'Willy-force niggers,' meaning Wilberforce's negroes.
42. F.W.N. Bayley, *Four Years' Residence in the West Indies: during the years 1826, 7, 8, and 9*, 3rd ed. (London: W. Kidd, 1833), 438–39.
43. Cf. "Bonja Song", page 491 below.
44. Bayley, *Four Years' Residence*, 369.

Songs of Rebellion

Wilberforce assumed heroic status as champion of freedom when news of the success of his Slave Registry Bill of 1815 reached the West Indies. Rumours spread among the slaves that the purpose of the bill was to emancipate them but that the white planters were wilfully refusing to grant them their freedom.[1] An "African joke" in Jamaica ran as follows: "'Wilberforce,' said a negro on one occasion, in the midst of a group of his companions – 'Wilberforce – dat good name for true; him good buckra; him want fo make we free; and if him can't get we free no oder way him *will by force.*'"[2]

The title "Song of the King of the Eboes" was attached by Lewis to the following song, which he heard in Jamaica in March 1816:

> Oh me good friend, Mr. Wilberforce, make we free!
> God Almighty thank ye! God Almighty thank ye!
>   God Almighty make we free!
> Buckra in this country no make we free:
> What Negro for to do? What Negro for to do?
>   Take force by force! Take force by force!
>   *Chorus*
>   To be sure! To be sure! To be sure![3]

Traces of a similar song appear in reports of the rebellion in Barbados in April 1816. John C. Clarke relates that it was alleged in Parliament "that the slaves were taught a song by the *Baptist missionaries* which concluded with a chorus, 'We will be free – we will be free, / Wilberforce for ever!'" The claim was investigated and found to be false, among other reasons because there were "*no* Baptist missionaries . . . in the Island of Barbadoes to do good or evil".[4]

Another revolutionary song was heard by Mrs Carmichael in Trinidad in 1725–26.

> Soon after coming to Laurel-Hill, and subsequently to the meditated insurrection in Trinidad, I heard some of the negroes singing, as I thought, rather a singular song. I asked J. to sing it for me; he hesitated, and said, "Misses, it no good song." Why do you sing it then? "'Cause misses, it a funny song, and me no mean bad by it." At last I prevailed upon J. not only to sing the song (which turned out to be an insurrectionary song), but to explain it . . . .

> Fire in da mountain,
> Nobody for out him,
> Take me daddy's bo tick
> And make a monkey out him.
>   *Chorus.*
>   Poor John! nobody for out him, &c.

> Go to de king's goal,
> You'll find a doubloon dey;
> Go to de king's goal,
> You'll find a doubloon dey.
>   *Chorus.*
>   Poor John! nobody for out him, &c.

The explanation of this song is, that when the bad negroes wanted to do evil, they made for a sign a fire on the hill-sides, to burn down the canes. There is nobody up there, to put out the fire; but as a sort of satire, the song goes on to say, "take me daddy's bo tick," (daddy is a mere term of civility), take some one's dandy stick, and tell the monkeys to help put out the fire among the canes for John; (meaning John Bull).[5] The chorus means, that poor John has nobody to put out the fire in the canes for him. Then when the canes are burning, go to the goal [gaol], and seize the money. The tune to which this is sung, is said to be negro music; it is on a minor key, and singularly resembles an incorrect edition of an old Scotch tune, the name of which I do not recollect.[6]

According to E.L. Joseph, the first scholarly historian of Trinidad, there was "an intention, or supposed intention, of the negroes of Trinidad to revolt" at the beginning of the year 1819. "The alarmists, I suspect, got up this monstrous plot with great care, and after all it turned out a failure; not a single negro was hanged, or even flogged on the occasion. A similar alarm took place in 1823, with precisely the same result".[7] Bridget Brereton, the modern historian of Trinidad, comments that "it was very much an alleged plot only, supposed to be the result of unrest caused by discussion of the amelioration measures; i.e. it may have been invented to show how dangerous all such discussion was."[8] The song itself survived. It was recorded long afterwards by a white man born in 1867, who remembered in old age "the ditty which we children used to sing when we saw a bush fire on the hills.

> Fire in de Mountain
> Nobody dey to out um
> Take Daddy Booshum stick
> And make monkey out um."[9]

The writer explains that Daddy Booshum was a mythical figure used by nannies to scare children; he supposedly lived in the hills behind the governor's house and stole children, who were taken up to the hills, from which they never returned.

The following song in Haitian Creole dates from the successful struggle by former slaves of Saint-Domingue (Haiti) to defeat the French expeditionary force sent by Bonaparte in 1802. In spite of proclamations to the contrary, it was widely believed by the blacks that Bonaparte intended to restore slavery. The song was recorded (along with his translation into standard French) by J.B. Lemonnier-Delafosse, an army officer who was present in Le Cap during the siege of the city by the black rebels in 1802–3.

> Grenadiers, à l'assaut!
> ça qui mouri zaffaire à yo,
> gn'y a point papa
> gn'y a pas maman!
> Grenadiers, à l'assaut!
> ça qui mouri zaffaire à yo![10]

Although Lemonnier-Delafosse was an emphatic upholder of the slave system, he nevertheless recalled with awe the extraordinary courage and resolution of the ex-slaves. His description of their conduct is quoted here as translated by C.L.R. James in *The Black Jacobins* (1938):

> But what men these blacks are! How they fight and how they die! One has to make war against them to know their reckless courage in braving danger when they can no longer have recourse to stratagem. I have seen a solid column, torn by grape-shot from four pieces of cannon, advance without making a retrograde step. The more they fell, the greater seemed to be the courage of the rest. They advanced singing, for the Negro sings everywhere, makes songs on everything. Their song was a song of brave men and went as follows:
>
> > To the attack, grenadier,
> > Who gets killed, that's his affair.
> > > Forget your ma,
> > > Forget your pa,
> > To the attack, grenadier,
> > Who gets killed, that's his affair.
>
> This song was worth all our republican songs. Three times these brave men, arms in hand, advanced without firing a shot, and each time repulsed, only retired after leaving the ground strewed with three-quarters of their troop. One must have seen this bravery to have any conception of it. Those songs shouted into the sky in unison by 2,000 voices, to which the cannon formed the bass, produced a thrilling effect. French courage alone could resist it. Indeed large ditches, an excellent artillery, perfect soldiers gave us a great advantage. But for many a day that massed square which marched singing to its death, lighted by a magnificent sun, remained in my thoughts, and even today after more than 40 years, this majestic and glorious spectacle still lives as vividly in my imagination as in the moments when I saw it.[11]

CONTRARY VOICES

Notes

1. See Lewis, *Journal*, page 348 above.
2. Phillippo, *Jamaica*, 202.
3. Lewis, *Journal*, 228.
4. John C. Clarke, *Memorials of Baptist Missionaries* (London: Yates and Alexander, 1869), 73.
5. This sounds far-fetched; it seems more likely that "make a monkey out him" has the usual colloquial sense of "make a fool of him" (i.e., "John", perhaps shorthand for any white English planter); see Richard Allsopp, ed., *Dictionary of Caribbean English Usage* (Oxford: Oxford University Press, 1996), s.v. "John Bull".
6. Carmichael, *Domestic Manners*, 2:301–2.
7. E.L. Joseph, *History of Trinidad* (Port of Spain: n.p., 1838), 254.
8. Private communication.
9. Percy Fraser, "47 Years a Public Servant" (manuscript, Trinidad, 1937–48), 313; quoted by permission of Bridget Brereton, editor of a forthcoming edition.
10. J.B. Lemonnier-Delafosse, *Seconde campagne de Saint-Domingue* (Le Havre: n.p., 1846), 85–86.
11. C.L.R. James, *The Black Jacobins: Toussaint-L'Ouverture and the San Domingo Revolution* (London: Secker and Warburg, 1938), 304.

Funeral Songs and Chants

Although singing was an indispensable part of African burial rites, regrettably few examples survive from the pre-emancipation era. The following chant from Jamaica was recorded by Michael Scott, who gives a detailed description of the whole nocturnal "wake" at which it was performed during his residence on the island, from 1806 to 1822.[1] The chorus was sung by a circle of "about twenty women, all in their best clothes, sitting on the ground and swaying their bodies to and fro", accompanied by a group of four drummers, with a fifth man sounding a conch shell at intervals. The chant was sung by one of three men who "kept circling round the outer verge of the circle of women, naked all to their waist cloths, spinning about and about with their hands above their heads":

> "I say, broder, you can't go yet."
>   THEN THE CHORUS OF FEMALE VOICES.
> "When da morning star rise, den we put you in a hole."
>   CHORUS AGAIN.
> "Den you go in a Africa, you see Fetish dere."
>   CHORUS.
> "You shall nyam goat dere, wid all your family."
>   CHORUS.
> "Buccra can't come dere; say, dam rascal, why you no work?
>   CHORUS.
> "Buccra can't catch Duppy,[2] no, no."
>   CHORUS.[3]

R.R. Madden, in *A Twelvemonth's Residence in the West Indies*, records a gloomier chant from Jamaica, heard at a funeral in St Andrews in 1834. He explains that formerly a slave burial was "as joyous a solemnity as an Irish wake", but that "the negroes are no longer permitted to bury their dead by torchlight; to dance over their departed friends, and to frighten the isle from its propriety with their barbarous music".[4]

> On proceeding to the negro grounds, I heard a lugubrious concert of many African and Creole voices strike up, as I approached the hut of the deceased negro . . . . I stopped at a little distance to endeavour to catch the words, but I was not sufficiently acquainted with nigger tongue to make out more than a few words here and there of the chaunt they were giving, somewhat in the fashion of a recitativo. There were no African allusions to Fetish divinities, but an abundance of scriptural paraphrases, strangely applied to their ideas of the happiness of a future state, and the deserts of the dead woman . . . .
>
> > Gar Amighty see this very wicked world –
> > Him say, 'Sister, come away,
> > What for you no come to me?'
> > Sister say, 'O Gar Amighty,
> > Too much glad to come away!'
> > When one die, him sickness over;
> > Him leave all trouble in dis sinful world;
> > Him no nyam, no clothes, no sleep,
> > Him much too glad to come away.
>
> The last line was a chorus that was frequently repeated. I do not say these were the exact words, but they are very near the sense, and only a very small part of the chaunt in which they were repeated.[5]

The following song, from the burial rites for a black fisherman was recorded by Henry G. Murray, a brown Jamaican, in *Manners and Customs of the Country, A Generation Ago: Tom Kittle's Wake*.[6] It probably dates from the 1840s but is included here as a continuation of pre-emancipation traditions of funeral singing. Tom Kittle himself was a former slave, as many of the celebrants at his wake must have been also. This was sung at Tom's grave, "one man giving the song, the others joining in the refrain". Murray explains that the second stanza reflects "the African belief in disembodied spirits" and "their power to harm the living" (by returning after death as ghosts): hence the exhortation to Tom to *tan da dutty*, "stay in the earth".

> O! Tom, boy, gone before o! eh!
> O! Tom, boy, gone before o!
> If we dead or lib, o!
> We mammy want we, o!
>
> O! Tom, boy, tan da dutty, O!
> O! Tom, boy, tan da dutty, O! eh!
> Tom, boy, O tan where you da, O!
> If we dead or lib, O!
> We mammy want we, O![7]

A second song heard by Murray on the same occasion was sung during the wake itself. It concerned a notorious fisherman, John Joe, whose name, according to Murray, "survives in more ballads than one".

> Me len him my canoe,
>   Him broke my paddle,
> John Joe widdle waddle.
>
> Me len him my fish pot,
>   Him tief my net,
> John Joe, &c.
>
> Me len him my harpoon,
>   Him tief my line,
> John Joe, &c.
>
> John Joe no hab
>   None hat pon him head,
> John Joe, &c.
>
> John Joe no hab
>   No shut [shirt] pon him back,
> John Joe, &c.
>
> Ef I catch John Joe
>   I wi broke him neck,
> John Joe, &c.[8]

Notes

1. For the full version see Abrahams and Szwed, *After Africa*, 168–71; D'Costa and Lalla, *Voices in Exile*, 48–51.
2. [Scott's note:] Duppy, *Ghost*.
3. Scott, *Tom Cringle*, 1:204–5.
4. Madden, *Twelvemonth's Residence*, 1:183–84.
5. Ibid., 1:187–88.
6. Murray's full account of the burial and wake is printed in D'Costa and Lalla, *Voices in Exile*, 88–111.
7. Murray, *Manners and Customs*, 15.
8. Ibid., 17–18.

B. *Samuel Augustus Mathews (fl. 1760–1822)*

"Negro Songs" (1793)

A few imitation "negro songs" by Samuel Augustus Mathews, a white West Indian, were published in his book *The Lying Hero* in 1793. This work, "a fairly standard defence of slavery",[1] was written as a rejoinder to Moreton's attacks on the slave system and West Indian creole society in *Manners and Customs in the West India Islands*. It is of unusual interest for its reproduction of Kittitian Creole in prose and verse texts, and for its illustration of the life of a white tradesman in West Indian slave society. Mathews was born in St Kitts and spent most of his life on the island working as a master carpenter. Victoria Borg O'Flaherty writes that his "favourite haunts were the taverns and especially the market places frequented by slaves whose language he readily learnt", and that when visiting other islands he liked to go among the slaves disguised as one of them. He claimed that his "command of 'negro language' was so good that the slaves would not believe that he was really a 'bocra' [white] man".[2] Although his imitations were written to amuse white audiences in the West Indies, they appear to be based on the *kinds* of song which might be heard on the streets or plantations. It is possible that one or more of Mathews' songs was actually sung by the enslaved themselves.[3]

Only one copy of *The Lying Hero* is known to exist, but the songs survive in other sources also. They have been meticulously collated and edited by Philip Baker and his colleagues in *St Kitts and the Atlantic Creoles: The Texts of Samuel Augustus Mathews in Perspective*, from which the examples below are taken.[4] The free translations, from the same source, are by Philip Baker.

Buddy Quow

Melancholy song with expression and without drum

Vos motter Buddy Quow?
Aw bree Obeshay bong you,
You tan no sauby how
Daw bocra mon go wrong you, buddy Quow?

Chaw, tan way, lem me lone,
No so trouble begin now,
Aw goo mine tik von tone,
So knock you rotten shin now, bruk you bone.

No heart bun, morrogoo,
Es granny ungry do you;
Aw hab sum bobrocoo,
Aw bring dem, aw kumfoo you, morrogoo.

No ungry no so dry,
Foot true now no mo yerry;
Mek wataw foo me yie
Aw cry so tay aw weary vipe me yie.

Dat time Quasheba tell,
Ee go bring von pickney fimme,
Aw nawngaw so, aw sell
Daw hog me momy gim me, berry well.

Von kote aw buy um new,
Von rapper aw bin bring kum,
Von new honkisser too,
Aw neber bin go tink um nawsy, true.

Ven unco Quaco say
De pickney he bin kum mon,
Aw nawngaw morer tay
Me haut bin nock pum, pum, mon, true Gran Jay.

Gor mighty day law bup,
See how Quasheba do me,
Daw bocra mon ee lub,
Ee bring mulatto foo me, Gor na bub.

Ee yie, ee nose, ee mouth,
Me bin goo mine foo hitum,
Tan ebry mossel bout,
Like Obeshay bin pit him out he mout.

Translation
What's the matter, Buddy Quow?
I think the overseer must have hit you.
You don't seem to know how
the white man is going to wrong you, Buddy Quow.

Hey! Back off! Leave me alone!
Otherwise trouble will start now.
I've a good mind to take a stone
to knock your rotten shin now, and break your bones.

Don't get angry, pal.
If you're really hungry,
I've got some corn dumplings [?]
I'll go and get them for you, pal.

It's not hunger or thirst that troubles me.
Just listen to what I have to say.
It brings tears to my eyes.
I weep so much that I'm tired of wiping my eyes.

When Quasheba told me
she was going to have my child,
I was so proud. I sold
the pig that my mother gave me, for a good price.

I bought her a new coat.
I bought her a wrapper.
And a new handkerchief as well.
I never would have thought she'd behave so badly.

When Uncle Quaco said
"the child has been born, man"
I felt so proud that
my heart went boom, boom, man, really loud.

God Almighty in Heaven.
See how Quasheba has treated me!
It was the white man she loved
so she bore a mulatto child. God in Heaven!

Its eyes! Its nose! Its mouth!
I felt like hitting it.
I was trembling with rage.[5]
It was as if the overseer had spat it out of his mouth!

Sabina[6]

Historical song composed for the banjea

Shatterday nite au bin daw my house man,
Bin daw my house man, shed down so softly,
Tank long Sabina, mit mommy Cumba,
Mit unco Quaco, eh ha ha ha.

Me haut bin so grad now, hungry foo true now,
Shunting foo yeat day, herrin and fish man,
Pot bin daw bile, bile um so sweet man,
Set down so softly no tink pon notin,
Massa daw caw me Massa daw caw me,
Kum yaw Kibenna, wha you daw do da, eh ha ha ha.

Kum yaw me boy, go charry de paper foo Missy Tonsy
Go law Baksar, cookly my boy go,
Bring kum de haunsar, eh ha ha ha.

Wha me muss do now, hungry daw kill me,
Massa go sen me, run law Baksar man,
Paw bin so furer, yaw me da go now,
Yar me da run now, eh ha ha ha.

Foot wha aw yeat now, no ge you some man,
Yaw me da run now, no bin run furer man,
Meet Missy Tonsy, bin pon von hoss mon,
Gee um de paper, tay me, me boy
You run law you Masser, tay um to-morrow
Bring kum de haunsar, eh ha ha ha ha.

Me haut bin so grad now, hungry da kin me,
Yaw me da run now, yaw me da kum now,

Kum law me house man, house bin so dark now,
Chan see you han man, chan see you nose man,
Chan see you yie man, eh ha ha ha ha.

Caw pon Sabina, caw mommy Cumba,
Caw unco Quaco, no yerry notin, eh ha ha ha.

Wha me muss do now, go law me house man,
Sabina da sleep day, caun um, aw caun um,
Push um, aw shub um, shub um, aw push um,
Ee won gim me haunser, eh ha ha ha ha.

Wha me muss do now, hungry da kin me,
Tink say poo cretur, bex long ee Massa,
Dat time ee sen me, run naw Backsar man,
Paw bin so furer too. wha me muss do now,
Look foo de naunnom dat time aw fine um,
So me da set down, yam me da set down,
Naunnom so sweet now, dat time ee sweet me,
Set down so softly, no tink pon notin.
Aw yerry von sunting, sunting dau walk man,
Da walk law me house, man, tink say da jumbie,
Me haut bin so fraid now, jumbie go kin me,
Jumbie go yeat me, eh ha ha ha ha.

Dat time aw fraid so, trow down de naunnam,
Run pon de bed man, caw pon Sabina,
Mek um budge up man, dat time ee budge up,
Tay um, Sabina, sunting da walk yaw,
You no sauby wha he, eh ha ha ha ha.

Sabina bin tay me, bree say da jumbie,
Dat time ee tay me, me haut bin so fraid now,
Look foo de bamboa, kibber me head man,
Kibber me face man, kibber me yie man,

Dat time aw fraid so, jumbie da walk now,
Aw yerry ee foot man, yerry ee shoe man,
Since aw bin bawn man, aw nebber bin yerry,
Jumbie bin hab on shoe pon ee foot man,
Dat time aw yerry, aw caw pon Sabina,
Aw tay um, Sabina, wha binness jumbie
Da law me house man, aw no owe um notin.

Aw look foo me tick now, dat time aw fine um,
Lick way pon jumbie, yaw me da lick way,
Jumbie da bawl man, jumbie da run man,
Since aw bin bawn man, aw nebber bin yerry
Jumbie bin bawl so, yaw ee da run now,
Run close de doa man, opin ee doa man,
Yaw ee da run now, yaw ee da bawl now,
Aw hit um, aw tump um, dat time ee run so,
Jumbie he fall man, me haut ee so grad now,
Aw hit um, aw tump um tay aw bin weary.

Dat time aw wearyo, aw meet unco Quaco,
Ee begin to tay me, ee tay me,
You sauby who you dau bong day,
Aw tay um aw sauby, you no see dau jumbie,
Who sa dau jumbie, debbil dau jumbie,
You no see dau Massa.

Translation
On Saturday night I was in my house, man.
I was in my house, man, sitting down so comfortably.
I talked with Sabina; met Mommy Cumba;
met Uncle Quaco. Eh ha ha ha!

My heart was so happy and I was really hungry.
There was something to eat there – herring and fish, man.
The pot was boiling man, boiling so sweetly, man.

I was sitting so comfortably, not thinking about anything.
My master was calling me; my master was calling me.
"Come here, Kibenna! What are you doing there?" Eh ha ha ha!
"Come here, my boy. Take this paper to Mr Thompson.
Go down to Basseterre, quickly my boy, go!
Bring back the reply." Eh ha ha ha!

What should I do then? Hunger was killing me.
But master was sending me down to Basseterre, man.
The path was so far; yeah, I was going then.
Yeah, I was running then. Eh ha ha ha!

"The food that I eat now – I won't give you any, man."[7]
Yeah, I was running then, but I didn't run far, man.
I met Mr Thompson, he was on a horse, man,
I gave him the paper. He said to me: "My boy,
You run to your master, tell him that, tomorrow,
He'll get the answer." Eh ha ha ha ha!

My heart was so happy then, but I was dying of hunger.
Yeah, I was running then; yeah, I was coming home then.
I came back to my house, man; the house was so dark then.
You couldn't see your hand, man; couldn't see your nose, man;
You couldn't see your eyes, man. Eh ha ha ha ha!

I called at Sabina's house. I called out "Mommy Cumba!"
I called out "Uncle Quaco!" I heard no reply. Eh ha ha ha!

What could I do then? I went back to my house, man.
Sabina was sleeping there. I called her. I called her.
I pushed her. I shoved her. I pushed her. I shoved her.
She wouldn't answer me. Eh ha ha ha ha!

What should I do then? Hunger was killing me.
I thought: I'm a poor creature, angry with his master[8]

when he sent me to run down to Basseterre, man.
And the path was so far. What could I do then?
Look for some food. Then I found it.
So then I sat down; yeah, I was sitting down.
The food was so tasty. It really pleased me.
I was sitting down comfortably, not thinking about anything.
Then I heard something, something walking, man.
Walking in my house, man. I thought that it was Jumby.[9]
My heart was so afraid, now. Jumby was going to kill me.
Jumby was going to eat me. Eh ha ha ha!

As I was frightened, I threw the food down.
I ran to the bed, man, and called out "Sabina".
I made her move over; when she moved over,
I said to her, "Sabina, something is walking here.
Don't you know what it is?" Eh ha ha ha ha!

Sabina told me she thought that it was Jumby.
As soon as she told me that, my heart was so afraid.
I looked for the bed-cover. I covered my head, man.
I covered my face, man. I covered my eyes, man.
I was so afraid then. Jumby was coming.
I heard his footsteps, man. I heard his shoes, man.
Since the day I was born, man, I have never heard
Of Jumby wearing shoes on his feet, man.
When I heard that sound, I called out "Sabina".
I said to her, "Sabina, what business can Jumby
be having in my house, man. I don't owe him anything."

I looked for my stick. As soon as I found it,
I hit out at Jumby; yeah, I was beating him up.
Jumby was bawling, man; Jumby was running, man.
Since the day I was born, man, I have never heard
Jumby bawl like that. Yeah, he was running now.
Running close to the door, man; opening the door, man.

Yeah, he was running; yeah, he was bawling.
I hit him. I thumped him. As he ran off,
Jumby fell, man. My heart was so happy then.
I hit him, I thumped him, until I was tired.

When I was really tired, I met Uncle Quaco.
He began to speak to me; he said to me:
"Do you know who you were beating up there?"
I told him: "I know. Didn't you see it was Jumby?"
"Who says it was Jumby? – The heck it was Jumby!
Didn't you see that it was the Master?"

[A distorted and much abbreviated version of the following song,
described as "a genuine St Kitts negro song, by Sam Matthews",
was found in 1846 in St Vincent by Charles Day.[10] What Day meant
by "genuine negro song" is unclear; he may have thought Mathews
simply *transcribed* the song.]

My deary hunney

Shatteray nite aw cung la taun,
  Chaun fine my deary hunney,
Run roun de lemmon tree
  Chaun fine &c.
Aw look behine da guaba bush,
  Chaun fine &c .
Aw wash my pot, aw wash um clean,
  Chaun fine &c.
Aw put in pease, aw put in poke,
  Chaun fine &c.
Aw boil my pot, aw boil um sweet,
  Chaun fine &c.

Aw sweep my house, aw sweep um clean,
    Chaun fine &c.
Aw clean me nife, aw clean um shine,
    Chaun fine &c.
Aw mek my bed, aw mek um soff,
    Chaun fine &c.
Aw mek um up, aw shek um up,
    Chaun fine &c.

Translation
Saturday night I came to town,
I couldn't find my sweetheart.
I ran around the lemon tree, . . .
I looked behind the guava bush, . . .
I washed my pot, I washed it clean, . . .
I put in peas, I put in pork, . . .
I boiled my pot, I boiled it sweet, . . .
I swept my house, I swept it clean, . . .
I cleaned my knife, I made it shine, . . .
I made my bed, I made it soft, . . .
I made it up, I shook it up, . . .

[Trelawney Wentworth quotes "My Deary Hunney" as an example
of "a song, or rather a *chorus*, which the negroes sing" during crop-
time on St Kitts, "kept up, perhaps, by a few of them working
together, whilst the others at the same time sing some popular
English tune, recently imported".[11] He presumably copied the
words from Mathews, since his text is almost identical, but the fact
that he gives the tune as well suggests that he actually heard it being
sung.]

Notes

1. Bridget Brereton, "The Historical Context of Moreton's (1790) Attack on Slavery and Mathews", in Baker and Bruyn, *St Kitts*, 60.

2. Victoria Borg O'Flaherty quoting Mathews in "Samuel Augustus Mathews: His Life and Times", in Baker and Bruyn, *St Kitts*, 54.

3. See Baker and Winer, "Separating", in Baker and Bruyn, *St Kitts*, 116–17.

4. Baker and Bruyn, *St Kitts*, 8–47. For textual variants, notes and comments, see this edition.

5. [Translator's note:] A conjectural translation: lit. 'stand every muscle [*or* morsel] about'.

6. Another song about sexual betrayal by a white man. The speaker is sent on an errand by his master; it is supposed to occupy him for a long time, but on the way he meets the person he was going to see, and so returns earlier than expected.

7. [Translator's note:] These words seem to be addressed to Kibenna by some unidentified person.

8. [Translator's note:] Translation uncertain: Kibenna might be reflecting on why Sabina was asleep, i.e. that *she* was angry with the master for sending Kibenna to Basseterre.

9. *Jumby*: an evil spirit.

10. Charles W. Day, *Five Years' Residence in the West Indies* (London: Colburn and Co., 1852), 2:121–22; Philip Baker, Adrienne Bruyn, Neville Shrimpton and Lise Winer, "The Texts of Samuel Augustus Mathews", in Baker and Bruyn, *St Kitts*, 18.

11. From Wentworth, *West India Sketch Book*, 2:65.

C. Impersonations

WILLIAM COWPER (1731–1800)

"The Negro's Complaint" (1788)[1]

Cowper was a staunch opponent of slavery and the slave trade. He first aired his anti-slavery views in a verse satire, *Charity* (1782), and returned to the subject after the Quakers' petition to Parliament in 1783 for abolition of the slave trade, in his most famous work, *The Task* (1785). "The Negro's Complaint" was probably the most popular of many street ballads composed by British songwriters in support of the abolition campaign. It was first printed in a pamphlet which was circulated throughout England by the Committee for the Abolition of the Slave Trade.

The Negro's Complaint

To the tune "Hosier's Ghost" or
As near Porto Bello lying[2]

Forc'd from home and all its pleasures,
　　Afric's coast I left forlorn,
To encrease a stranger's treasures,

O'er the raging billow borne;
Men from England bought and sold me,   5
   Pay'd my price in paltry gold,
But though slave they have enroll'd me
   Minds are never to be sold.
Still in thought as free as ever
   What are England's rights, I ask,   10
Me from my delights to sever,
   Me to torture, me to task?
Fleecy locks and black complexion
   Cannot forfeit nature's claim;
Skins may differ, but affection   15
   Dwells in white and black the same.

Why did all-creating Nature
   Make the plant for which we toil?
Sighs must fan it, tears must water,
   Sweat of ours must dress the soil.   20
Think, ye masters iron-hearted
   Lolling at your jovial boards,
Think how many backs have smarted
   For the sweets your cane affords.

Is there, as ye sometimes tell us,   25
   Is there one who reigns on high?
Has he bid you buy and sell us
   Speaking from his throne the sky?
Ask him if your knotted scourges,
   Matches,[3] blood-extorting screws   30
Are the means which duty urges
   Agents of his will to use?

Hark – He answers. Wild tornadoes
   Strewing yonder sea with wrecks,
Wasting towns, plantations, meadows,   35

Are the voice with which he speaks.[4]
He foreseeing what vexations
   Afric's sons should undergo,
Fix'd their tyrant's habitations
   Where his whirlwinds answer – No.   40

By our blood in Afric wasted
   'Ere our necks received the chain,
By the mis'ries that we tasted
   Crossing in your barks the main,
By our suff'rings since ye brought us   45
   To the man-degrading mart,[5]
All-sustain'd with patience taught us
   Only by a broken heart –

Deem our nation brutes no longer
   'Till some reason ye shall find   50
Worthier of regard and stronger
   Than the colour of our kind.
Slaves of gold! Whose sordid dealings
   Tarnish all your boasted pow'rs
Prove that you have human feelings,   55
   'Ere you proudly question ours!

Notes

1. John D. Baird and Charles Ryskamp, eds., *The Poems of William Cowper* (Oxford: Clarendon Press, 1995), 3:13–14; typography standardized.
2. The tune has West Indian connections: "Admiral Hosier's Ghost", by Richard Glover, was an attack on Walpole's government; set in the context of Admiral Vernon's siege of Porto Bello (1739), it recalled the death from fever of Admiral Hosier and more than four thousand other sailors while blockading ports in the West Indies in an earlier campaign, 1726–27.
3. *matches*: meaning uncertain; "fetters" in some versions.
4. Cf. *The Task*, book 2, lines 53ff, where natural disasters are similarly seen as an expression of divine wrath against the evils of slavery (with footnote "Alluding to the late calamities in Jamaica"); Baird and Ryskamp, *Poems*, 2:139–40. Devastating hurricanes in Jamaica in 1780, 1781 and 1783 were reported in English newspapers.
5. *man-degrading mart*: slave market.

John Collins (1742–1808)
"The Desponding Negro" (1792)[1]

This poem, described as a "favourite new song", was first published in London as a broadsheet with musical accompaniment, and reprinted in *Scripscrapologia*, a collection of Collins's light verse, in 1804 (the text used here). Collins, an actor and playwright, had no known connection with the West Indies or the abolitionist campaign; his poem typifies the use of the slave trade as a popular topic for pathetic and sentimental verse. The propaganda value of "The Desponding Negro" was recognized, however, by Robert Wedderburn, who printed it in his journal *The Axe Laid to the Root*, at the end of an "Address to the Slaves of Jamaica" instructing them how to govern themselves when they attain their freedom: "Teach your children these lines, let them be sung on the Sabbath day, in remembrance of your former sufferings."[2]

On Afric's wide plains where the lion now roaring,
When freedom stalks forth the vast desert exploring,
I was dragg'd from my hut and enchain'd as a slave,
In a dark floating dungeon upon the salt wave.
    CHORUS
Spare a half-penny, spare a half-penny,
O spare a half-penny to a poor Negro boy.

5

Toss'd on the wide main, I all wildly despairing
Burst my chains, rush'd on deck with my eye balls wide glaring,
When the light'ning's dread blast, struck the inlets of day,
And its glorious bright beam sent for ever away.   10
    Spare, etc.

The despoiler of man his prospect thus losing
Of gain by my sale, not a blind bargain chusing,
As my value compar'd with my keeping was light,
Had me dash'd overboard in the dead of the night.
    Spare, etc.

And but for a bark, to Britannia's coast bound then,   15
All my cares by that plunge in the deep had been drown'd then,
But by moonlight deferr'd [I] was dash'd from the wave,
And reluctantly robb'd of a watery grave.
    Spare, etc.

How disastrous my fate, freedom's ground though I tread now,
Torn from home, wife and children, I wander for bread now,   20
While seas roll between us which ne'er can be cross'd,
And hope's distant glimmering in darkness is lost.
    Spare, etc.

But of minds foul and fair, when the judge and the ponderer,
Shall restore light and rest to the blind and the wanderer,
The European's deep dye may out-rival the foe,   25
And the soul of an Ethiop prove whiter than snow.
    Spare, etc.

Notes

1. John Collins, "The Desponding Negro", in *Scripscrapologia: or, Collins's Doggerel Dish of All Sorts* (Birmingham: n.p., 1804).
2. *The Axe Laid to Root*, vol. 2 (1817), quoted in McCalman, *Horrors of Slavery*, 90.

JOHN WOLCOT ["PETER PINDAR"] (1738–1819)

"Azid, or the Song of the Captive Negro"[1]

Wolcot spent over three years in Jamaica as physician to the Governor, Sir William Trelawney, and later as physician-general to the army (1768–72). The song below was first published in *Scots Magazine*, the text used here. It was reprinted without significant alterations in *The Works of Peter Pindar, Esq.* (1812), 4: 97–98.

Azid, or the Song of the Captive Negro

Poor Mora eye be wet wid tear,
 And heart like lead sink down wid wo;
She seem her mournful friends to hear,
 And see der eye like fountain flow.
No more she give me song so gay,   5
But sigh, "Adieu, dear Domahay."[2]

No more for deck her head and hair,
 Me look in stream bright gold to find;
Nor seek de field for flow'r so fair,
 Wid garland Mora hair to bind.   10

"Far off de stream!" I weeping say,
"Far off de fields of Domahay."

But why do Azid live a slave,
  And see a slave his Mora dear?
Come, let we seek at once de grave –   15
  No chain, no tyrant den we fear.
Ah me! I hear a spirit say,
"Come, Azid, come to Domahay."

Den gold I find for thee once more,
  For thee to fields for flow'r depart;   20
To please de idol I adore,
  And give wid gold and flow'r my heart.
Den let we die and haste away,
And live in groves of Domahay.

Notes

1. "Peter Pindar" [John Wolcot], "Azid, or the Song of the Captive Negro", *Scots
    Magazine*, no. 57 (August 1795): 517–18.
2. *Domahay*: Dahomey.

WILLIAM SHEPHERD (1768–1847)

"The Negro Incantation" (1797)[1]

Shepherd, a Unitarian minister, was a younger member of the Liverpool abolitionist group to which William Roscoe and Edward Rushton belonged. He wrote a life of Rushton as an introduction to his edition of Rushton's *Poems and Other Writings*, published in London in 1824. "The Negro Incantation" first appeared in the *Monthly Magazine* in July 1797 and was reprinted in *The Poetical Register* in 1803. Although the "Argument" refers specifically to the 1760 rebellion in Jamaica, the 1791 rebellion in Saint-Domingue and the Maroon War of 1795–96 in Jamaica would have given the poem topical resonance for readers in 1797.

ARGUMENT.

In the year 1760, a very formidable insurrection of the Jamaica Negroes took place. – This was instigated by the professors of a species of incantation, known among the blacks by the name of Obi. The Obi, says Mr. Edwards, is usually composed of a farrago of materials, viz. blood, feathers, parrots' beaks, dogs' teeth, alligators' teeth, broken bottles, grave-dirt, rum, and egg-shells. By the proper mixture and application of these materials, the Negroes imagine they can effectuate the destruction of their enemies. The

account of the above-mentioned circumstances, contained in Edwards's
History of the West Indies, gave birth to the following Ode:

Hail! ye sacred horrors hail!
Which brooding o'er this lonely vale,
Swell the heart, impearl the eye,
And raise the rapt soul to the sky.
Hail! spirits of the swarthy dead,   5
Who, flitting thro' the dreary shade,
To rouse your sons to vengeance fell,
Nightly raise the troublous yell!
Hail! Minister of Ill, whose iron pow'r
   Pervades resistless earth, and sea, and air,   10
Shed all thy influence on this solemn hour,
   When we with magic rites the white man's doom prepare.

Thus Congo spake, "what time the moon,
Riding in her highest noon!"[2]
Now beam'd upon the sable crowd,   15
Now vanish'd in the thickening cloud.
'Twas silence all – with frantic look,
His spells the hoary wizard took:
Bending o'er the quivering flame,
Convulsion shook his giant frame.   20
Close and more close the shuddering captives throng,
   With breath repress'd, and straining eye, they wait –
When midst the plantains bursts the awful song,
   The words of mystic might, that seal their tyrants' fate.

Haste! the magic shreds prepare –   25
Thus the white man's corpse we tear.
Lo! feathers from the raven's plume,
That croaks our proud Oppressor's doom.
Now to aid the potent spell,
Crush we next the brittle shell –   30

Fearful omen to the foe,
  Look! the blanched bones we throw.
From mouldering graves we stole this hallow'd earth,
  Which, mix'd with blood, winds up the mystic charm;
Wide yawns the grave for all of northern birth,   35
  And soon shall smoke with blood each sable warrior's arm.

Hark! the pealing thunders roll,
  Grateful to the troubled soul.
See! the gleamy lightnings play,
  To point you to your destin'd prey.   40
Hence! with silent foot and slow,
  And sudden strike the deadly blow:
Your foes, the palmy shade beneath,
  Lie lock'd in sleep – their sleep is death!
Go! let the memory of the smarting thong   45
  Outplead the pity that would prompt to save:
Go! let the Oppressor's contumelious wrong,
  Twice nerve the hero's arm, and make the coward brave.

Notes

1. William Shepherd, "The Negro Incantation", *The Poetical Register, and repository for fugitive poetry* (1803).
2. Quotation adapted from Milton, *Il Penseroso: The Poems of John Milton*, ed. John Carey and Alistair Fowler (London: Longmans, 1968), 67–68: "To behold the wandering moon, / Riding near her highest noon".

Eaglesfield Smith (ca. 1770–1838)

"The Sorrows of Yamba" (1795)[1]

Smith, a little known Scottish poet of radical political views, has been rescued from obscurity by Alan Richardson.[2] This poem was first published in the hugely popular series *Cheap Repository Tracts* (no. 17) by Hannah More, who added substantial extra material to give the poem an evangelical message. After line 72 her text interposes fifteen stanzas recounting a meeting on the seashore between Yamba and an English missionary, who converts her to Christianity, and it ends with Yamba's hope that her husband will similarly be converted by "Some dear Missionary good" so that they may be reunited in heaven. Two years later Smith published his own version in the *Universal Magazine* under the initials "E.S.J.", the text used here. Smith had no first-hand knowledge of the West Indies, but the wide circulation of the poem ensured that it fed into British perceptions of the meaning of colonial slavery.

Come, kind death, and give me rest,
 Yamba hath no friend but thee;
Thou canst ease my throbbing breast,
 Thou canst set a pris'ner free.

In St. Lucia's distant isle,   5
    Still with Afric's love I burn;
Parted many a thousand mile,
    Never, never to return.

Down my cheek the tears are dripping,
    Broken is my heart with grief,   10
Mangled is my flesh with whipping,
    Come, kind death, and give relief.

Born on Afric's golden coast,
    Once I was as blest as you;
Parents tender I cou'd boast,   15
    Husband dear and children too.

Whity man! he come from far,
    Sailing o'er the briny flood;
Who, with help of British tar,
    Buys up human flesh and blood.   20

With my baby at my breast,
    (Other two were sleeping by)
In my hut I sat at rest,
    With no thought of danger nigh.

From the bush at even tide,   25
    Rush'd the fierce man-stealing crew;
Seiz'd the baby by my side,
    Seiz'd the wretched Yamba too.

Then, for cursed thirst of gold,[3]
    Strait they bore me to the sea;   30
Cramm'd me down a slave ship's hold,
    Where were hundreds stow'd like me.

Naked on the platform lying,
    Now we cross the tumbling wave;
Shrieking, sick'ning, fainting, dying!   35
    Deed of shame for Britons brave!

At the savage captain's beck,
    Now like brutes they make us prance,
Smack the whip about the deck,
    And in scorn they bid us dance.   40

In groaning there I pass'd the night,
    And did roll my aching head;
At the break of morning light,
    My poor child was cold and dead.

Happy, happy, there she lies!   45
    Thou shalt feel the lash no more,
Thus full many a negro dies,
    Ere he reach the destin'd shore.

Drove like cattle to a fair,
    See they sell them young and old;   50
Child from mother too they tear,
    All for cursed thirst of gold.

I was sold to master hard,
    Some have masters kind and good;
And again my back was scarr'd;   55
    Bad and stinted was my food.

Poor and wounded, faint and sick,
    All expos'd to burning sky;
Master makes me grass to pick,
    And I now am near to die.   60

What! and if to death he send me,
    Savage murder tho' it be;
British Law will ne'er befriend me,
    They protect not slaves like me.

Mourning thus my friendless state,   65
    Ne'er may I forget the day,
That in dusk of even late,
    Far from home I dar'd to stray.

Dar'd, alas! with impious haste,
    Toward the roaring sea to fly;   70
Death itself I long'd to taste,
    Long'd to cast me in and die.

But tho' death this hour I find,
    Still with Afric's love I burn;
Where I left a spouse behind,   75
    Still to Afric's land I turn.

And when Yamba sinks in death,
    This her latest pray'r may be;
While she yields her parting breath,
    O! may Afric's land be free.   80

Thus where Yamba's native home,
    Humble hut of rushes stood,
Her happy sons again may roam,
    And Britons seek not for their blood.

Ye that boast to rule the waves,   85
    Bid no slave ship sail the sea:
Ye that never will be slaves,
    Bid poor Afric's land be free.

Notes

1. Eaglesfield Smith, "The Sorrows of Yamba", *Universal Magazine* no. 51 (July 1797), 43–44.
2. See Alan Richardson, " 'The Sorrows of Yamba,' by Eaglesfield Smith and Hannah More: Authorship, Ideology, and the Fractures of Antislavery Discourse", in *Romanticism on the Net*, ed. M. Eberle-Sinatra, http://www.ron.umontreal.ca, 28 November 2002.
3. [Author's note:] Auri sacra fames. VIRG. [From *Aeneid*, 3.57.]

C.F.D.

"Bonja Song" (ca. 1802)[1]

This popular song was first published in London as a music sheet signed "C.F.D." (the text used here), and was frequently reprinted in song collections in the early nineteenth century. The signature probably stands for Charlotte Dallas (d. 1793), sister of Robert Charles Dallas (see page 128), who lived with her family in Jamaica during her childhood. The song was printed, with the signature "Charlotte", in R.C. Dallas's own *Adrastus . . . and other poems* (published in London in 1823), in a section of poems by various authors inserted "for the satisfaction of preserving them". Dallas explains that the melody was "with very little variation, such as was caught by ear from some of the negroes. The writer of the words took down the notes and added the harmony." The text was mistakenly attributed to R.C. Dallas himself by Alexander Barclay, who quotes it in full to illustrate his contention that slaves in Jamaica were well treated and, having never known freedom, were happy in bondage.[2]

What are the joys of white man here?
   What are his pleasures say?
Me want no joys no ills me fear,
   But on my Bonja[3] play.
Me sing all day,[4] me sleep all night,   5

Me hab no care my heart is light.
Me tink not what to-morrow bring,
   Me happy, so me sing.

But White man's joys are not like mine,
   'Dho he look smart and gay: 10
He great, he proud, he haughty, fine,
   While I my Bonja play.
He sleep all day, he wake all night,
He full of care, his heart no light,   15
He great deal want, he little get,
   He sorry, so he fret.

Me envy not dhe White man dhen,
   Me poor, but me is gay;
Me glad at heart, me happy when   20
   Me on my Bonja play.
Me sing all day, me sleep all night,
Me hab no care, my heart is light;
Me tink not what to-morrow bring,
   Me happy, so me sing.   25

Notes

1. C.F.D., "Bonja Song" (London, n.p., ca. 1802).
2. Alexander Barclay, *A Practical View of the Present State of Slavery in the West Indies* (London: Smith, Elder, and Co., 1826), 212–13n.
3. [R.C. Dallas's note:] The Bonja is a kind of guitar – it is made of a gourd, with a piece of dried skin or parchment, to which are fixed a finger board and catgut strings.
4. [R.C. Dallas's note:]'I sing all day' may be charged with exaggeration by those who would substitute, 'I work all day;' but the fact is that the negroes are a singing race. And they not only sing at their feasts and their dances, but at their work. There is scarcely an occurrence that attracts particular attention which they will not turn into a song.

MATTHEW GREGORY LEWIS (1775–1818)
"Yarra" (1816)[1]

> Lewis notes in his journal for 1 April 1816: "At eight this morning we weighed anchor on our return to England." The song follows immediately afterwards.

Yarra

Poor Yarra comes to bid farewell,
   But Yarra's lips can never say it!
Her swimming eyes – her bosom's swell –
   The debts she owes you, these must pay it,
She ne'er can speak, though tears can start,   5
   Her grief, that fate so soon removes you;
But One there is, who reads the heart,
   And well He knows how Yarra loves you!

See, massa, see this sable boy!
   When chill disease had nipp'd his flower,   10
You came and spoke the word of joy,
   And poured the juice of healing power.
To visit far Jamaica's shore
   Had no kind angel deign'd to move you,

These laughing eyes had laugh'd no more,   15
    Nor Yarra lived to thank and love you.
Then grieve not, massa, that to view
    Our isle you left your British pleasures:
One tear, which falls in grateful dew,
    Is worth the best of Britain's treasures.   20
And sure, the thought will bring relief,
    What e'er your fate, wherever rove you,
Your wealth's not given by pain and grief,
    But hands that know, and hearts that love you.

May He, who bade you cross the wave,   25
    Through care for Afric's sons and daughters;
When round your bark the billows rave,
    In safety guide you through the waters!
By all you love with smiles be met;
    Through life each good man's tongue approve you: 30
And though far distant, don't forget,
    While Yarra lives, she'll live to love you!

Note

1.   Lewis, *Journal*, 242–43.

AMELIA OPIE (1769–1853)
"The Black Man's Lament" (1826)[1]

In the 1790s Opie joined the radical dissenting circle in London which included William Godwin and Mary Wollstonecraft, and became successful as a novelist and poet. Her knowledge of the West Indies was largely derived from Bryan Edwards's *History, Civil and Commercial, of the West Indies*, published in 1793. In 1802 she published *The Negro Boy's Tale*, an abolitionist poem for children in chapbook form, which had some success in spite of (or perhaps because of) its clumsy attempt to simulate Jamaican Creole. Opie later joined the Society of Friends and became a prominent figure in the anti-slavery movement. *The Black Man's Lament*, another anti-slavery chapbook aimed at young readers and illustrated with woodcuts, was particularly popular. Although obviously propagandist in intent, it was also esteemed for its educational value as a representation of the working practices of slaves on plantations.

Come, listen to my plaintive ditty,
   Ye tender hearts, and children dear!
And, should it move your souls to pity,
   Oh! try to *end* the griefs you hear.

There is a *beauteous plant*,[2] that grows   5
    In western India's sultry clime,
Which makes, alas! the Black man's woes,
    And also makes the White man's crime.

For know, its tall gold stems contain
    A sweet rich juice, which White men prize;   10
And that they may this *sugar* gain,
    The Negro toils, and bleeds, and *dies*.

But, Negro slave! *thyself* shall tell,
    Of past and present wrongs the story;
And would all British hearts could feel,   15
    To *end* those wrongs were *Britain's glory.*

    Negro speaks.

First to our own dear Negro land,
    His ships the cruel White man sends;
And there contrived, by armed band,
    To tear us from our homes and friends;   20

From parents, brethren's fond embrace;
    From tender wife, and child to tear;
Then in a darksome ship to place,
    Pack'd close, like bales of cotton there.

Oh! happy those, who, in that hour,   25
    Die from their prison's putrid breath!
Since they escape from White man's pow'r,
    From toils and stripes, and lingering death!

For what awaited us on shore,
    Soon as the ship had reach'd the strand,   30

Unloading its degraded store
    Of freemen, forc'd from Negro land?

See! eager White men come around,
    To choose and claim us for their slaves;
And make us envy those who found   35
    In the dark ship their early graves.

They bid black men and women stand
    In lines, the drivers in the rear:
Poor Negroes hold a *hoe* in hand,
    But they the wicked cart-whip bear.   40

Then we, in gangs, like beasts in droves,
    Swift to the cane-fields driven are;
There first our toil the weeds removes,
    And next we holes for plants prepare.

But woe to all, both old and young,   45
    Women and men, or strong or weak,
Worn out or fresh, those gangs among,
    That dare the toilsome line to break!

As holes must all *at once* be made,
    Together we must work or stop;   50
Therefore, the whip our strength must aid,
    And lash us when we pause or drop!

When we have dug sufficient space,
    The bright-eye top[3] of many a cane,
Lengthways, we in the trenches place,   55
    And *then* we trenches dig again.

We cover next the plants with mould;
    And e'en, ere fifteen days come round,

We can the slender sprouts behold,
   Just shooting greenly from the ground.   60

The weeds about them clear'd away,
   Then mould again by hand we throw;
And, at no very distant day,
   Here Negroes plough, and there they hoe.

But when the crops are ripen'd quite,   65
   'Tis then begin our saddest pains;
For then we toil both day and night,
   Though fever burns within our veins.

When 18 months complete their growth,
   Then the tall canes rich juices fill;   70
And we, to bring their liquor forth,
   Convey them to the bruising-mill.

That mill, our labour, every hour,
   Must with fresh loads of canes supply;
And if we faint, the cart-whip's power,   75
   Gives force which *nature's* powers *deny*.

Our task is next to catch the juice
   In leaden bed, soon as it flows;
And instant, lest it spoil for use,
   It into boiling vessels goes.   80

Nor one alone: four vessels more
   Receive and clear the sugar-tide.
Six coolers next receive the store;
   Long vessels, shallow, wooden, *wide*.

While cooling, it begins to grain,   85
   Or form in crystals white and clear;

Then we remove the whole again,
    And to the *curing-house* we bear.

Molasses there is drain'd away;
    The liquor is through hogsheads pour'd;   90
The scum falls through, the crystals stay;
    The casks are clos'd, and soon on board.

The ships to English country go,
    And bear the hardly-gotten treasure.
Oh! that good Englishmen could know   95
    How Negroes suffer for their pleasure!

Five months, we, every week, alas!
    Save when we eat, to work are driven:
Six days, three nights; then, to each class,
    Just twenty hours of rest are given.   100

But when the Sabbath-eve comes round,
    That eve which White men sacred keep,
Again we at our toil are found,
    And six days more we work and weep

"But, Negro slave, some men must toil.   105
    The English peasant works all day;
Turns up, and sows, and ploughs the soil.
    Thou wouldst not, sure, have Negroes play?"

Ah! no. But Englishmen can work
    Whene'er they like, and stop for breath;   110
No driver dares, like any Turk,
    Flog peasants on almost to death.

"Who dares an English peasant flog,
    Or buy, or sell, or steal away?

Who sheds his blood? treats him like dog,   115
   Or fetters him like beasts of prey?

"He has a cottage, he a wife;
   If child he has, that child is free.
I am depriv'd of married life,
   And my poor child were *slave* like *me*.   120

"Unlike his home, ours is a shed
   Of pine-tree trunks, unsquar'd, ill-clos'd;
Blanket we have, but not a bed,
   Whene'er to short, chill sleep dispos'd.

"Our clothing's ragged. All our food   125
   Is rice, dried fish, and Indian meal.
Hard, scanty fare! Oh would I could
   Make White men Negroes' miseries feel!"

"But could you not, your huts around,
   Raise plants for food, and poultry rear?   130
You might, if willing, till your ground,
   And then some wants would disappear."

"Work for ourselves and others too?
   When all our master's work is o'er,
How could we bear our own to do?   135
   Poor, weary slaves, hot, scourg'd, and sore!

"Sometimes, 'tis true, when Sabbath-bell
   Calls White man to the house of pray'r,
And makes poor blacks more sadly feel
   'Tis thought *slaves* have no *business* there: 140

"Then Negroes try the earth to till,
   And raise their food on Sabbath-day;
But Envy's pangs poor Negroes fill,
   That we must *work* while others *pray*.

"Then, where have we *one* legal right?   145
    White men may blind, whip, torture slave.
But oh! if we but strike one White,
    Who can poor Negro help or save?

"There are, I'm told, upon some isles,
    Masters who gentle deign to be;   150
And there, perhaps, the Negro *smiles*,
    But *smiling* Negroes *few* can see.

"Well, I must learn to bear my pain;
    And, lately I am grown more calm;
For Christian men come o'er the main,   155
    To pour in Negro souls a balm.

"They tell us there is one above
    Who died to save both bond and free;
And who, with eyes of equal love,
    Beholds White man, and *humble me*.   160

"They tell me if, with patient heart,
    I bear my wrongs from day to day,
I shall, at death, to realms depart,
    Where God wipes every tear away!

"Yet still, at times, with fear I shrink;   165
    For, when with sense of injury prest,
I burn with rage! and *then* I think
    I ne'er can *gain* that place of rest."

He ceas'd; for here his tears would flow,
    And ne'er resum'd his tale of *ruth*.   170
Alas! it rends my heart to know
    He only told a *tale of truth*.

Notes

1. Amelia Opie, *The Black Man's Lament; or, How to Make Sugar* (London: Harvey and Darton, 1826).
2. A long quotation describing the sugar plant, from William Beckford's *Descriptive Account of the Island of Jamaica* (London: T. and J. Egerton, 1790), is given in a footnote.
3. [Author's note:] The top shoots are *full of eyes*, or *gems*, as they are called.

APPENDIX

Authors and Texts Classified by Location

Barbados
Matthew James Chapman
Henry Evans Holder
Richard Ligon
George Pinckard
Report from a Select Committee of the House of Assembly
John Singleton
Richard Steele
Edward Thompson
John Augustine Waller

Grenada
Gordon Turnbull

The Guianas
Aphra Behn
C.S. ("Negro Slavery")
George Pinckard
John Stedman
George Warren

Jamaica
"Account of the Christmas Racket among the Negroes in Jamaica"
"Account of Obi"
William Beckford
Thomas Cooper
R.C. Dallas
Bryan Edwards
Philip Freneau
M.H. ("The Poor Negro Beggar's Petition and Complaint")
William Knibb
Jamaica, a Poem

Charles Leslie
Matthew Gregory Lewis
Edward Long
R.R. Madden
Marly; or, A Planter's Life in Jamaica
John Marjoribanks
A. McL. ("Lady Liberty")
Benjamin Moseley
"The Pleasures of Jamaica"
Edward Rushton
Bernard Martin Senior
Hans Sloane
John Stewart
Robert Wedderburn

Leeward Islands (Antigua, Dominica, Montserrat, St Kitts, Nevis, Virgin Islands)

Joseph Addison
Thomas Atwood
Olaudah Equiano
"The Field Negroe"
James Grainger
Samuel Augustus Matthew
Mary Prince
James Ramsay
John Singleton
Sketches and Recollections of the West Indies
Edward Thompson

Trinidad and St Vincent

"The African and Creole Slave Contrasted"
Mrs Carmichael
Ashton Warner

Bibliography

Primary Sources

Alexander, J.E. *Transatlantic Sketches: comprising visits to the most interesting scenes in North and South America, and the West Indies*. 2 vols. London: R. Bentley, 1833.

Atwood, Thomas. *The History of the Island of Dominica*. London: J. Johnson, 1791.

Bayley, F.W.N. *Four Years' Residence in the West Indies: during the years 1826, 7, 8, and 9*, 3rd ed. London: W. Kidd, 1833.

Beckford, William. *Remarks upon the Situation of Negroes in Jamaica, impartially made from local experience of nearly thirteen years in that island*. London: T. and J. Egerton, 1788.

Behn, Aphra. *Oroonoko: or, The Royal Slave. A True History*. London: Will. Canning, 1688.

Belisario, Isaac Mendez. *Sketches of Character, in Illustration of the Habits, Occupation, and Costume of the Negro Population in the Island of Jamaica*. Kingston: n.p., 1837–38.

Carmichael, Mrs [Alison]. *Domestic Manners and Social Condition of the White, Coloured and Negro Population of the West Indies*. 2 vols. London: Whittaker, Treacher, and Co., 1833.

Chapman, Matthew James. *Barbadoes, and Other Poems*. London: James Fraser, 1833.

Collins, John. *Scripscrapologia: or, Collins's Doggerel Dish of All Sorts*. Birmingham: n.p., 1804.

Cooper, Thomas. *Facts illustrative of the condition of the Negro slaves in Jamaica*. London: J. Hatchard and Son, 1824.

Cowper, William. *The Poems of William Cowper*, edited by John D. Baird and Charles Ryskamp. 3 vols. Oxford: Clarendon Press, 1995.

Dallas, R.C. *The History of the Maroons, from their origin to the establishment of their chief tribe at Sierra Leone*. 2 vols. London: T.N. Longman and O. Rees, 1803.

———. *A Short Journey in the West Indies, in which are interspersed, curious anecdotes and characters*. 2 vols. London: n.p., 1790.

Edwards, Bryan. *An Historical Survey of the French Colony in the Island of St. Domingo*. London: John Stockdale, 1797.

————. *History, Civil and Commercial of the British West Indies*. 3 vols. London: John Stockdale, 1793.

————. *Poems, written chiefly in the West Indies*. Kingston: n.p., 1792.

Equiano, Olaudah. *The Interesting Narrative of the Life of Olaudah Equiano, or Gustavus Vassa, The African. Written by Himself*. London: n.p., 1789.

Freneau, Philip. *Poems written between the years 1768 & 1794*. Monmouth, NJ: n.p., 1795.

Grainger, James. *The Sugar-Cane: A Poem in Four Books, with Notes*. London: R. and J. Dodsley, 1764.

Holder, H.E. *Fragments of a Poem, intended to have been written in consequence of reading Major Marjoribanks's Slavery*. Bath: R. Cruttwell, 1792.

Jamaica: A Poem, In Three Parts. Written in that Island, in the Year MDCCLXXVI. To which is annexed, A Poetical Epistle from the Author in that Island to a Friend in England. London: William Nicoll, 1777.

Lalla, Barbara. "Quaco Sam: A Relic of Archaic Jamaican Speech". *Jamaica Journal* 45 (1981): 20–29.

Lemonnier-Delafosse, J.B. *Seconde Campagne de Saint-Domingue*. Le Havre: n.p., 1846.

Leslie, Charles. *A New History of Jamaica, from the earliest accounts, to the taking of Porto Bello by Vice-Admiral Vernon. In Thirteen Letters from a Gentleman to his Friend*. London: J. Hodges, 1740.

Lewis, Matthew Gregory. *Journal of a West India Proprietor, kept during a residence in the island of Jamaica*. London: John Murray, 1834.

Ligon, Richard. *A True and Exact History of the Island of Barbados*. London: P. Parker and T. Guy, 1657.

Long, Edward. *The History of Jamaica*. 3 vols. London: T. Lowndes, 1774.

Luffman, John, *A Brief Account of the Island of Antigua, together with the customs and manners of its inhabitants, as well white as black: as also an accurate statement of the food, cloathing, labor, and punishment, of slaves. In Letters to a Friend. Written in the Years 1786, 1787, 1788*. London: T. Cadell, 1789.

Madden, R.R. *A Twelvemonth's Residence in the West Indies, during the transition from slavery to apprenticeship*. 2 vols. London: James Cochrane and Co., 1835.

Marjoribanks, John. *Slavery: An Essay in Verse . . . Humbly inscribed to Planters, Merchants, And others concerned in the Management or Sale of Negro Slaves*. Edinburgh: J. Robertson, 1792.

Marly; or, A Planter's Life in Jamaica. Glasgow: Richard Griffin and Co., 1828.

Mathews, Samuel Augustus. *St Kitts and the Atlantic Creoles: The Texts of Samuel Augustus Mathews in Perspective*, edited by Philip Baker and Adrienne Bruyn. London: University of Westminster Press, 1999.

Moreton, J.B. *West India Customs and Manners*. London: J. Parsons; W. Richardson; H. Gardner; and J. Walter, 1793.

Moseley, Benjamin. *A Treatise on Sugar. With Miscellaneous Medical Observations*. London: G.G. and J. Robinson, 1799.

Murray, Henry. *Manners and Customs of the Country, A Generation Ago: Tom Kittle's Wake*. Kingston: R. Jordon, 1869.

Opie, Amelia. *The Black Man's Lament*. London: Harvey and Darton, 1826.

A Particular Account of the Commencement and Progress of the Insurrection of the Negroes in St. Domingo, which began in August last; Being a Translation of the Speech made to the National Assembly, The 3rd of November, 1791, by the Deputies from the General Assembly of the French part of St. Domingo. London: J. Sewell, 1792.

Phillippo, James. *Jamaica: its Past and Present State*. London: John Snow, 1843.

Pinckard, George. *Notes on the West Indies: during the expedition under the command of the late General Sir Ralph Abercromby*. 3 vols. London: Longman, Hurst, Rees, and Orme, 1806.

Poems, on Subjects Arising in England, and the West Indies. By a Native of the West Indies. London: R. Faulder, 1783.

Prince, Mary. *The History of Mary Prince, a West Indian Slave, Related by Herself*. London: F. Westley and A.H. Davis, 1831.

Rainsford, Marcus. *An Historical Account of the Black Empire of Hayti: comprehending a view of the principal transactions in the revolution of Saint Domingo*. London: James Cundee; C. Chapple, 1805.

Ramsay, James. *An Essay on the Treatment and Conversion of African Slaves in the British Slave Colonies*. London: James Phillips, 1784.

Rawson, Mary Anne, ed. *The Bow in the Cloud; or, The Negro's Memorial. A collection of original contributions, in prose and verse, illustrative of the evils of slavery, and commemorative of its abolition in the British colonies*. London: Jackson and Walford, 1834.

Renny, Robert. *An History of Jamaica with Observations on the Climate* . . . London: J. Cawthorn, 1807.

The Report from a Select Committee of the House of Assembly, appointed to inquire into the origin, causes, and progress of the late insurrection. Barbados: by order of the Legislature. London: T. Cadell and W. Davies, 1818.

Roscoe, William. *An Inquiry into the Causes of the Insurrection of the Negroes in the Island of St. Domingo*. London: J. Johnson, 1792.

Rushton, Edward. *Poems and Other Writings by the late Edward Rushton*, edited by William Shepherd. London: Effingham Wilson, 1824.

———. *West-Indian Eclogues*. London: W. Lowndes and J. Philips, 1787.

St Clair, Thomas Staunton, *A Residence in the West Indies and America: with a narrative of the expedition to the Island of Walcheren*. 2 vols. London: R. Bentley, 1834.

Scott, Michael. *Tom Cringle's Log*. 2 vols. Edinburgh: William Blackwood and Sons, 1833.

Senior, Bernard M. *Jamaica, as It Was, as It Is, and as It May Be*. London: T. Hurst, 1835.

Singleton, John. *A General Description of the West-Indian Islands, . . . from Barbados to Saint Croix. Attempted in Blank Verse*. Barbados: n.p., 1767.

Sketches and Recollections of the West Indies. By a Resident. London: Smith, Elder, and Co., 1828.

Sloane, Hans, *A Voyage to the Islands Madera, Barbados, Nieves, S. Christophers and Jamaica*. 2 vols. London: n.p., 1707–25.

A Speech made by a Black of Guardaloupe, at the Funeral of a Fellow-Negro. In *A Letter from a Merchant at Jamaica to a Member of Parliament in London, touching the African Trade*. London: A. Baldwin, 1709.

Stedman, John Gabriel. *Narrative of a Five Years Expedition against the Revolted Negroes of Surinam in Guiana on the Wild Coast of South America from the years 1772 to 1777*. 2 vols. London: J. Johnson, and J. Edwards, 1796.

Stewart, John. *An Account of Jamaica, and its Inhabitants. By a Gentleman, long resident in the West Indies*. London: Longman, Hurst, Rees, and Orme, 1808.

Thompson, Edward. *Sailor's Letters. Written to Select Friends in England, During his Voyages and Travels in Europe, Asia, Africa, and America. From the year 1754 to 1759*. 2 vols. London: T. Becket, P.A. De Hondt, W. Flexney, and J. Moran, 1766.

Turnbull, Gordon. *An Apology for Negro Slavery: or the West-Indian planters vindicated from the charge of inhumanity*, 2nd ed. London: Stuart and Stevenson, 1786.

Waller, John Augustine. *A Voyage in the West Indies*. London: Sir R. Phillips and Co., 1820.

Warner, Ashton. *Negro Slavery Described by a Negro: being the narrative of Ashton Warner, a native of St. Vincent's*. London: Samuel Maunder, 1831.

Warren, George. *An Impartial Description of Surinam, upon the continent of Guiana in America*. London: Nathaniel Brooke, 1667.

Wedderburn, Robert. *The Horrors of Slavery; exemplified in the Life and History of the Rev. Robert Wedderburn*, edited by Iain McCalman. Edinburgh: Edinburgh University Press, 1991.

Wentworth, Trelawney. *The West India Sketch Book*. 2 vols. London: Whittaker and Co., 1834.

Williams, Cynric R. *A Tour through the Island of Jamaica, from the Western to the Eastern End, in the year 1823*, 2nd ed. London: Thomas Hurst, Edward Chance and Co., 1827.

Wolcot, John. *The Works of Peter Pindar, Esq.* 5 vols. London: J. Walker, G. Wilkie and J. Robinson: and G. Goulding and Co., 1812.

Secondary Sources

Abrahams, Roger D., and John F. Szwed, eds. *After Africa: Extracts from British Travel Accounts and Journals of the Seventeenth, Eighteenth and Nineteenth Centuries Concerning the Slaves, Their Manners, and Customs in the British West Indies.* New Haven: Yale University Press, 1983.

Adair, James Makittrick. *Unanswerable Arguments against the Abolition of the Slave Trade.* London: J.P. Bateman, 1790.

Allsopp, Richard, ed. *Dictionary of Caribbean English Usage.* Oxford: Oxford University Press, 1996.

An Answer to the Reverend James Ramsay's Essay . . . By some Gentlemen of St. Christopher. Basseterre, St Kitts: n.p., 1784.

Aravamudan, Srinivas, ed. *Obi: or, The History of Three-Fingered Jack.* Peterborough, ON: Broadview, 2005.

Ashcroft, Michael. "Robert Charles Dallas". *Jamaica Journal* 44 (1980): 94–101.

Baker, Philip, and Adrienne Bruyn, eds. *St Kitts and the Atlantic Creoles: The Texts of Samuel Augustus Mathews in Perspective.* London: University of Westminster Press, 1999.

Baker, Philip, and Lise Winer. "Separating the Wheat from the Chaff: How Far Can We Rely on Old Pidgin and Creole Texts?" In *St Kitts and the Atlantic Creoles: The Texts of Samuel Augustus Mathews in Perspective*, edited by Philip Baker and Adrienne Bruyn, 103–22. London: University of Westminster Press, 1999.

Baker, Philip, Adrienne Bruyn, Neville Shrimpton, and Lise Winer. "The Texts of Samuel Augustus Mathews". In *St Kitts and the Atlantic Creoles: The Texts of Samuel Augustus Mathews in Perspective*, edited by Philip Baker and Adrienne Bruyn, 45–47. London: University of Westminster Press, 1999.

Barclay, Alexander. *A Practical View of the Present State of Slavery in the West Indies.* London: Smith, Elder, and Co., 1826.

Basker, James G., ed. *Amazing Grace: An Anthology of Poems about Slavery 1660–1810.* New Haven: Yale University Press, 2002.

Bond, Donald F., ed. *The Spectator.* 5 vols. Oxford: Clarendon Press, 1965.

Brathwaite, Edward Kamau. *The Folk Culture of the Slaves in Jamaica.* London: New Beacon, 1981.

———. *Roots.* Ann Arbor: University of Michigan Press, 1993.

Brereton, Bridget. "The Historical Context of Moreton's (1790) Attack on Slavery and Mathews' (1793) Response". In *St Kitts and the Atlantic Creoles: The Texts of Samuel Augustus Mathews in Perspective,* edited by Philip Baker and Adrienne Bruyn, 59–62. London: University of Westminster Press, 1999.

———. *A History of Modern Trinidad 1783–1962.* Kingston: Heinemann, 1981.

Burnard, Trevor. *Mastery, Tyranny, and Desire: Thomas Thistlewood and His Slaves in the Anglo-Jamaican World.* Chapel Hill: University of North Carolina Press, 2004.

Burnett, Paula. *The Penguin Book of Caribbean Verse in English.* London: Penguin, 1986.

Carretta, Vincent. *Equiano the African: Biography of a Self-made Man.* Atlanta: University of Georgia Press, 2005.

Carretta, Vincent, and Philip Gould, eds. *Genius in Bondage: Literature of the Early Black Atlantic.* Lexington: University Press of Kentucky, 2001.

Cassidy, F.G., and R.B. Le Page, eds. *Dictionary of Jamaican English,* 2nd ed. Kingston: University of the West Indies Press, 2002.

Clarke, John C. *Memorials of Baptist Missionaries.* London: Yates and Alexander, 1869.

Cooper, Carolyn. *Noises in the Blood: Orality, Gender and the "Vulgar" Body of Jamaican Popular Culture.* London: Macmillan Education, 1993.

Craton, Michael. *Testing the Chains: Resistance to Slavery in the British West Indies.* Ithaca: Cornell University Press, 1982.

Davis, David Brion. *The Problem of Slavery in Western Culture.* Ithaca: Cornell University Press, 1966.

Day, Charles W. *Five Years' Residence in the West Indies.* 2 vols. London: Colburn and Co., 1852.

D'Costa, Jean, and Barbara Lalla, eds. *Voices in Exile: Jamaican Texts of the Eighteenth and Nineteenth Centuries.* Tuscaloosa: University of Alabama Press, 1989.

Dirks, Robert. *The Black Saturnalia: Conflict and Its Ritual Expression on British West Indian Slave Plantations.* Gainesville: University of Florida Press, 1987.

Dubois, Laurent. *Avengers of the New World: The Story of the Haitian Revolution.* Cambridge, MA: Belknap, 2004.

Felsenstein, Frank, ed. *English Trader, Indian Maid: Representing Gender, Race, and Slavery in the New World.* Baltimore: Johns Hopkins University Press, 1999.

Ferguson, Moira, ed. *The History of Mary Prince: A West Indian Slave.* Ann Arbor: University of Michigan Press, 1987.

———. *Subject to Others: British Women Writers and Colonial Slavery, 1670–1834.* New York: Routledge, Chapman and Hall, Inc., 1992.

Fraser, Lionel Mordaunt. *History of Trinidad.* 2 vols. Port of Spain: Government Printing Office, 1891, 1896.

Geggus, David. "British Opinion and the Emergence of Haiti, 1791–1805". In *Slavery and British Society 1776–1846*, edited by James Walvin, 123–49. London: Macmillan, 1982.

———. "Haiti and the Abolitionists: Opinion, Propaganda and International Politics in Britain and France, 1804–1838". In *Abolition and Its Aftermath: The Historical Context, 1790–1916*, edited by David Richardson, 115–40. London: F. Cass, 1985.

———. *Slavery, War, and Revolution: The British Occupation of Saint Domingue 1793–1798*. Oxford: Oxford University Press, 1982.

Gilmore, John. *The Poetics of Empire: A Study of James Grainger's* The Sugar Cane. London: Athlone Press, 2000.

Gilroy, Paul. *The Black Atlantic: modernity and double consciousness*. London: Verso, 1993.

Gordon, Shirley C. *God Almighty Make Me Free: Christianity in Preemancipation Jamaica*. Bloomington: Indiana University Press, 1996.

Goveia, Elsa V. *Slave Society in the British Leeward Islands at the End of the Eighteenth Century*. New Haven: Yale University Press, 1965.

Greene, Jack P. "'A Plain and Natural Right to Life and Liberty': An Early Natural Rights Attack on the Excesses of the Slave System in Colonial British America". *William and Mary Quarterly*, 3rd ser., 57 (2000): 793–808.

Hart, Richard. *Slaves Who Abolished Slavery: Blacks in Rebellion*. Kingston: University of the West Indies Press, 2002.

Heiland, Donna. "The *Unheimlich* and the Making of Home: Matthew Lewis's *Journal of a West India Proprietor*". In *Monstrous Dreams of Reason: Body, Self, and Other in the Enlightenment*, edited by Laura J. Rosenthal and Mita Choudhury, 170–188. Lewisburg, PA: Bucknell University Press, 2002.

Higman, B.W. *Slave Populations of the British Caribbean, 1807–1834*. Baltimore: Johns Hopkins University Press, 1984.

Hill, Errol. *The Jamaican Stage 1655–1900: Profile of a Colonial Theatre*. Amherst: University of Massachusetts Press, 1992.

James, C.L.R. *The Black Jacobins: Toussaint-L'Ouverture and the San Domingo Revolution*. London: Secker and Warburg, 1938.

Joseph, E.L. *History of Trinidad*. Port of Spain: n.p., 1838.

Krise, Thomas W., ed. *Caribbeana: An Anthology of English Literature of the West Indies 1657–1777*. Chicago: Chicago University Press, 1999.

Lambert, David. "Deadening, Voyeuristic and Reiterative? Problems of Representation in Caribbean Research". In *Beyond the Blood, the Beach and the Banana: New Perspectives in Caribbean Studies*, edited by Sandra Courtman. Kingston: Ian Randle, 2004

McCalman, Iain, ed. *The Horrors of Slavery and Other Writings by Robert Wedderburn*. Edinburgh: Edinburgh University Press, 1991.

Macaulay, Zachary, ed. *Negro Slavery; or, A view of some of the more prominent features of that society, as it exists in the United States of America and in the colonies of the West Indies, especially in Jamaica*. London: Hatchard and Son, and J. and A. Arch, 1823.

O'Flaherty, Victoria Borg. "Samuel Augustus Mathews: His Life and Times". In *St Kitts and the Atlantic Creoles: The Texts of Samuel Augustus Mathews in Perspective*, edited by Philip Baker and Adrienne Bruyn, 49–58. London: University of Westminster Press, 1999.

Patterson, Orlando. *The Sociology of Slavery: An Analysis of the Origins, Development and Structure of Negro Slave Society in Jamaica*. London: MacGibbon and Kee, 1967.

Porteus, Beilby. *Sermon preached before the Incorporated Society for the Propagation of the Gospel in Foreign Parts*. London: J.F. and C. Rivingtons, 1784.

Price, Richard, and Sally Price, eds. *Stedman's Surinam: Life in an Eighteenth-Century Slave Society*. Baltimore: Johns Hopkins University Press, 1992.

Ragatz, Lowell Joseph. *Guide for the Study of British Caribbean History 1763–1834*. Washington, DC: United States Government Printing Office, 1932.

Rampini, Charles J.G. *Letters from Jamaica*. Edinburgh: Edmoston and Douglas, 1973.

Richardson, Alan, ed. *Slavery, Abolition and Emancipation: Writings in the British Romantic Period*. Vol. 4, *Verse*. London: Pickering and Chatto, 1999.

Roscoe, Henry. *Life of William Roscoe*. 2 vols. London: T. Cadell, 1833.

Sandiford, Keith A. *The Cultural Politics of Sugar*. Cambridge: Cambridge University Press, 2000.

Senior, Olive. *Encyclopedia of Jamaican Heritage*. Kingston: Twin Guinep, 2003.

Sheller, Mimi. *Democracy after Slavery: Black Publics and Peasant Radicalism in Haiti and Jamaica*. Basingstoke: Macmillan Education, 2000

Stephen, James. *The Crisis of the Sugar Colonies; or, an enquiry into the objects and probable effects of the French expedition to the West Indies*. London: J. Hatchard, 1802.

Sypher, Wylie. *Guinea's Captive Kings: British Anti-Slavery Literature of the Eighteenth Century*. Chapel Hill: University of North Carolina Press, 1942.

Tobin, James. *Cursory Remarks upon the Reverend Mr. Ramsay's Essay*. London: G. and T. Wilkie, 1785.

Turner, Mary. *Slaves and Missionaries: The Disintegration of Jamaican Slave Society*. Kingston: The Press, University of the West Indies, 1998.

Walvin, James. *England, Slaves and Freedom, 1776–1838*. Basingstoke: Macmillan, 1986.

Ward, J.L. *British West Indian Slavery, 1750–1834: The Process of Amelioration*. Oxford: Oxford University Press, 1988.

Whitlock, Gillian. "Volatile Subjects: *The History of Mary Prince*". In *Genius in Bondage: Literature of the Early Black Atlantic*, edited by Vincent Carretta and Philip Gould, 72–86. Lexington: University Press of Kentucky, 2001.

Williamson, John. *Medical and Miscellaneous Observations, relative to the West India Islands*. 2 vols. Edinburgh: n.p., 1817.

Williamson, Karina, ed. *Marly; or, A Planter's Life in Jamaica*. Oxford: Macmillan Education, 2005.

Wood, Marcus, ed. *The Poetry of Slavery: An Anglo-American Anthology 1764–1865*. Oxford: Oxford University Press, 2003.

Wright, Richardson. *Revels in Jamaica 1682–1838*. New York: Dodd, Mead and Company, 1937.

INDEX